D0107494

3

GIGANT

BY HIROYA OKU

SEVEN SEAS ENTERTAINMENT PRESENTS

GIGANT™

story and art by **HIROYA OKU** **VOLUME 3**

TRANSLATION
Christine Dashiell

ADAPTATION
Jamal Joseph Jr.

LETTERING
Ray Steeves

INTERIOR LAYOUT
Christa Miesner

ORIGINAL COVER DESIGN
Yohei Sometani

COVER DESIGN
Nicky Lim

PROOFREADER
Kurestin Armada

EDITOR
J.P. Sullivan

PREPRESS TECHNICIAN
Rhiannon Rasmussen-Silverstein

MANAGING EDITOR
Julie Davis

ASSOCIATE PUBLISHER
Adam Arnold

PUBLISHER
Jason DeAngelis

GIGANT VOLUME 3
by Hiroya OKU

Original Japanese edition published by SHOGAKUKAN.
English translation rights in the United States of America, Canada, and the United Kingdom arranged with SHOGAKUKAN through Tuttle-Mori Agency, Inc.

Seven Seas press and purchase enquiries can be sent to Marketing Manager Lianne Sentar at press@gomanga.com. Information regarding the distribution and purchase of digital editions is available from Digital Manager CK Russell at digital@gomanga.com.

ISBN: 978-1-64505-755-0

Printed in Canada

First Printing: October 2020

10 9 8 7 6 5 4 3 2 1

FOLLOW US ONLINE: ***www.sevenseasentertainment.com***

READING DIRECTIONS

This book reads from ***right to left***, Japanese style. If this is your first time reading manga, you start reading from the top right panel on each page and take it from there. If you get lost, just follow the numbered diagram here. It may seem backwards at first, but you'll get the hang of it! Have fun!!

1
2
3
4
5
6
7
8
9

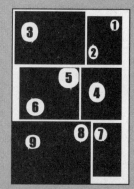

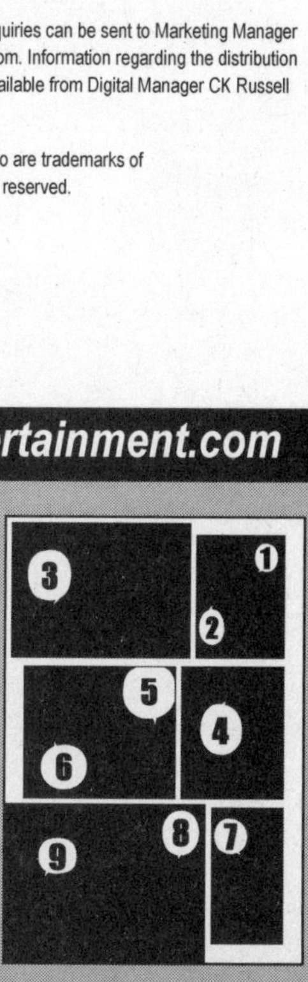

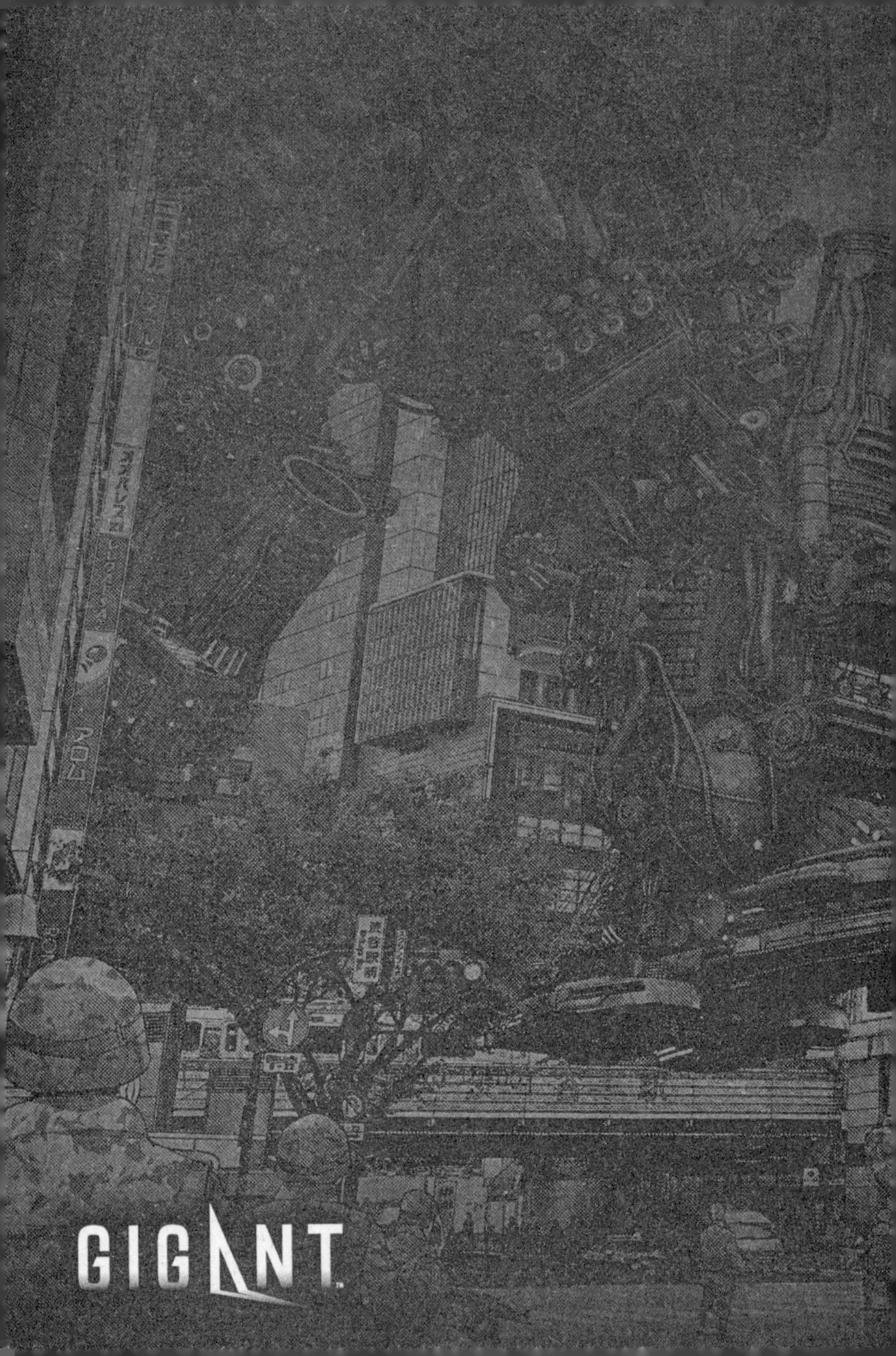
GIGANT

THE NEXT CHAPTER...

"GIGANT" CHAPTER THREE : END TO BE CONTINUED _

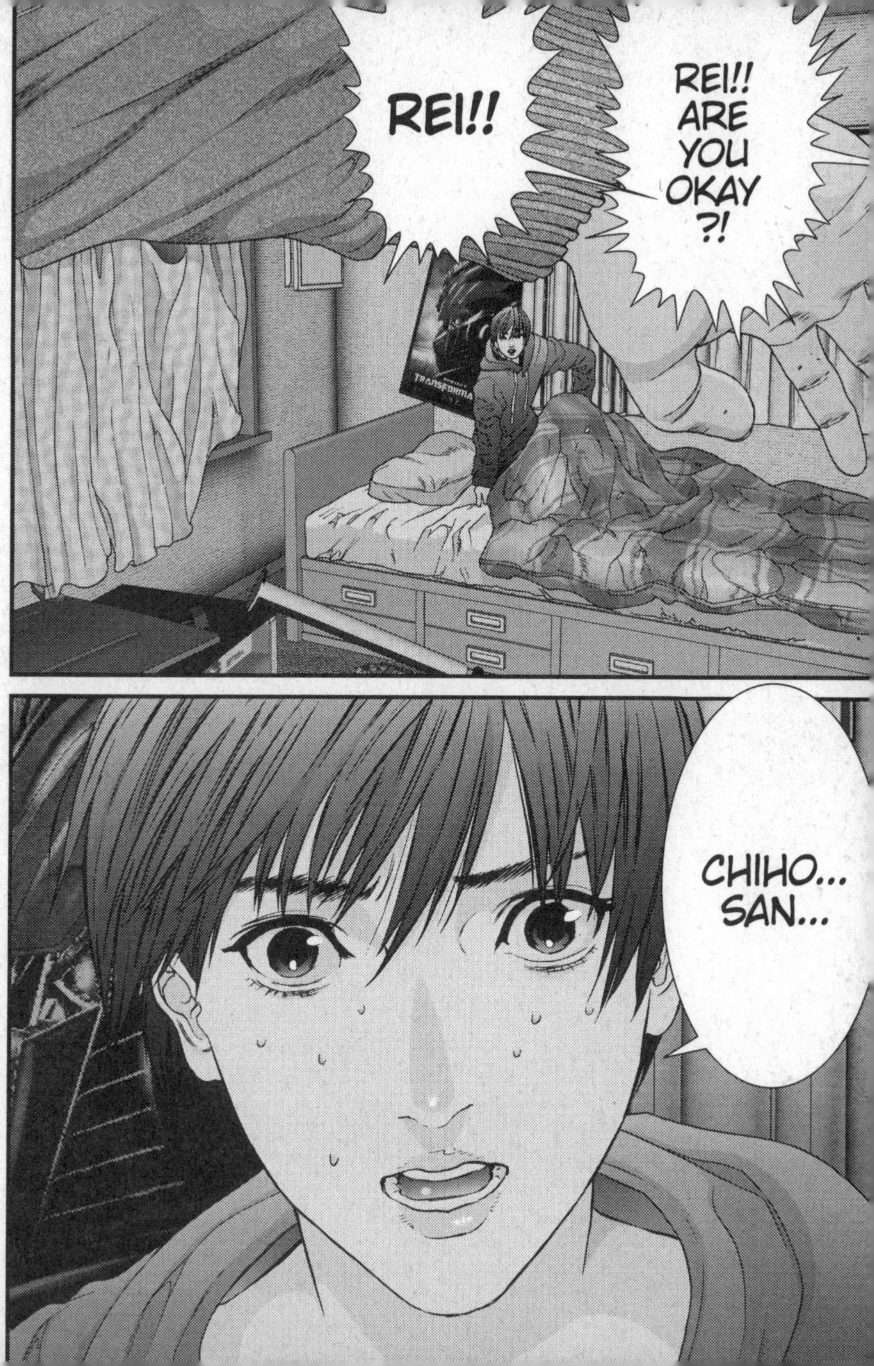
REI!! ARE YOU OKAY ?!
REI!!
CHIHO... SAN...

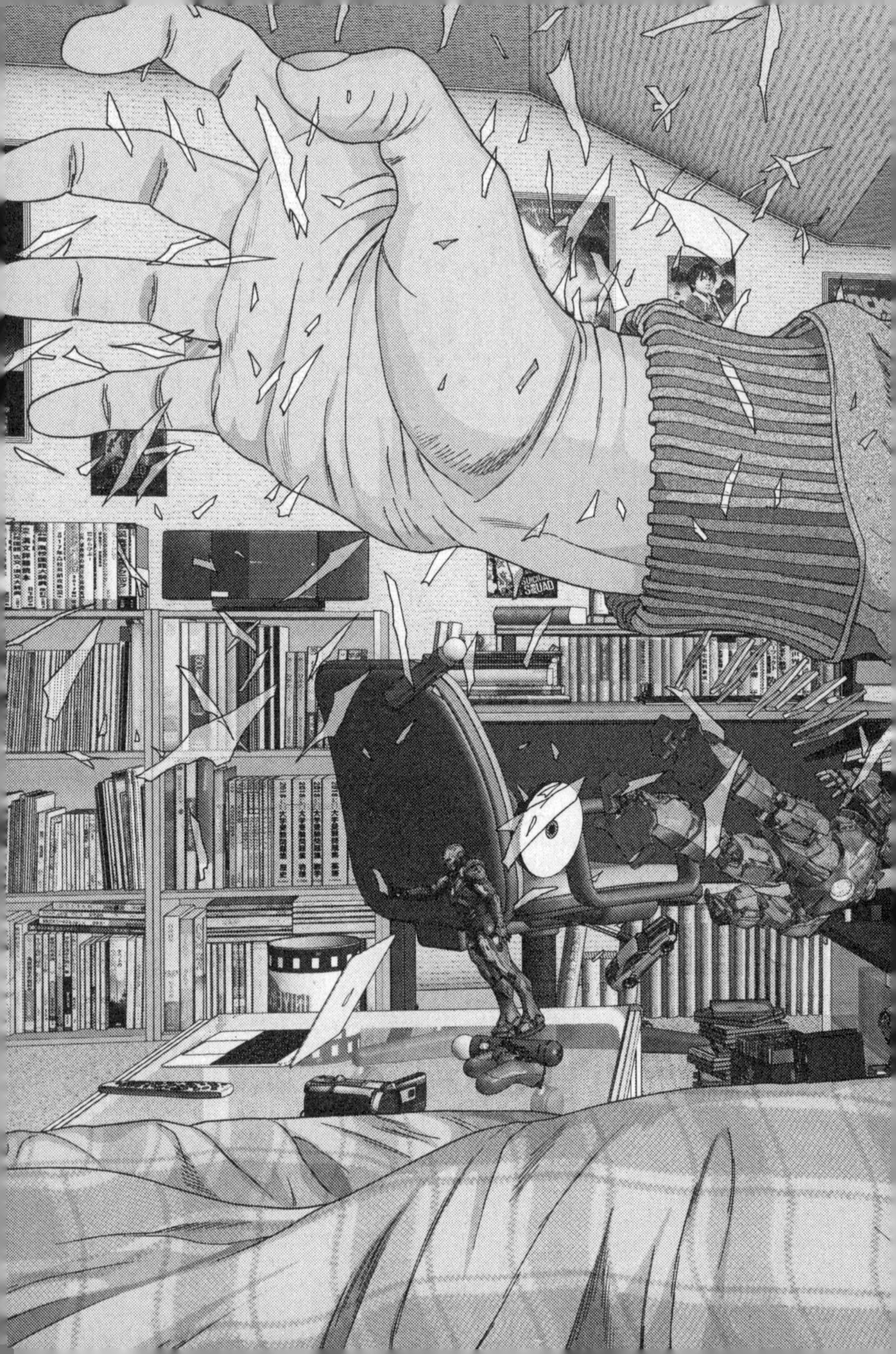
SUICIDE SQUAD

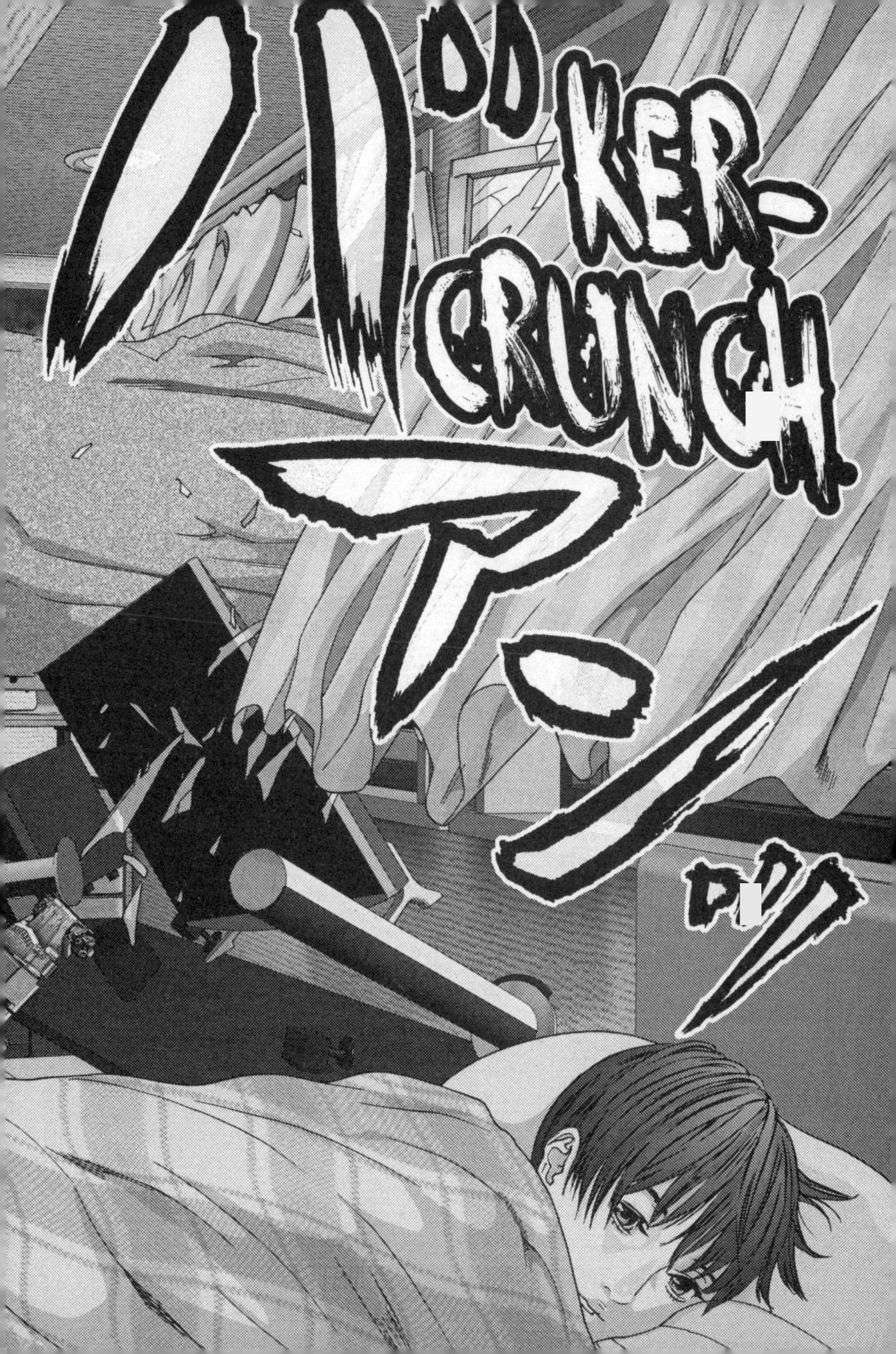
KER-CRUNCH

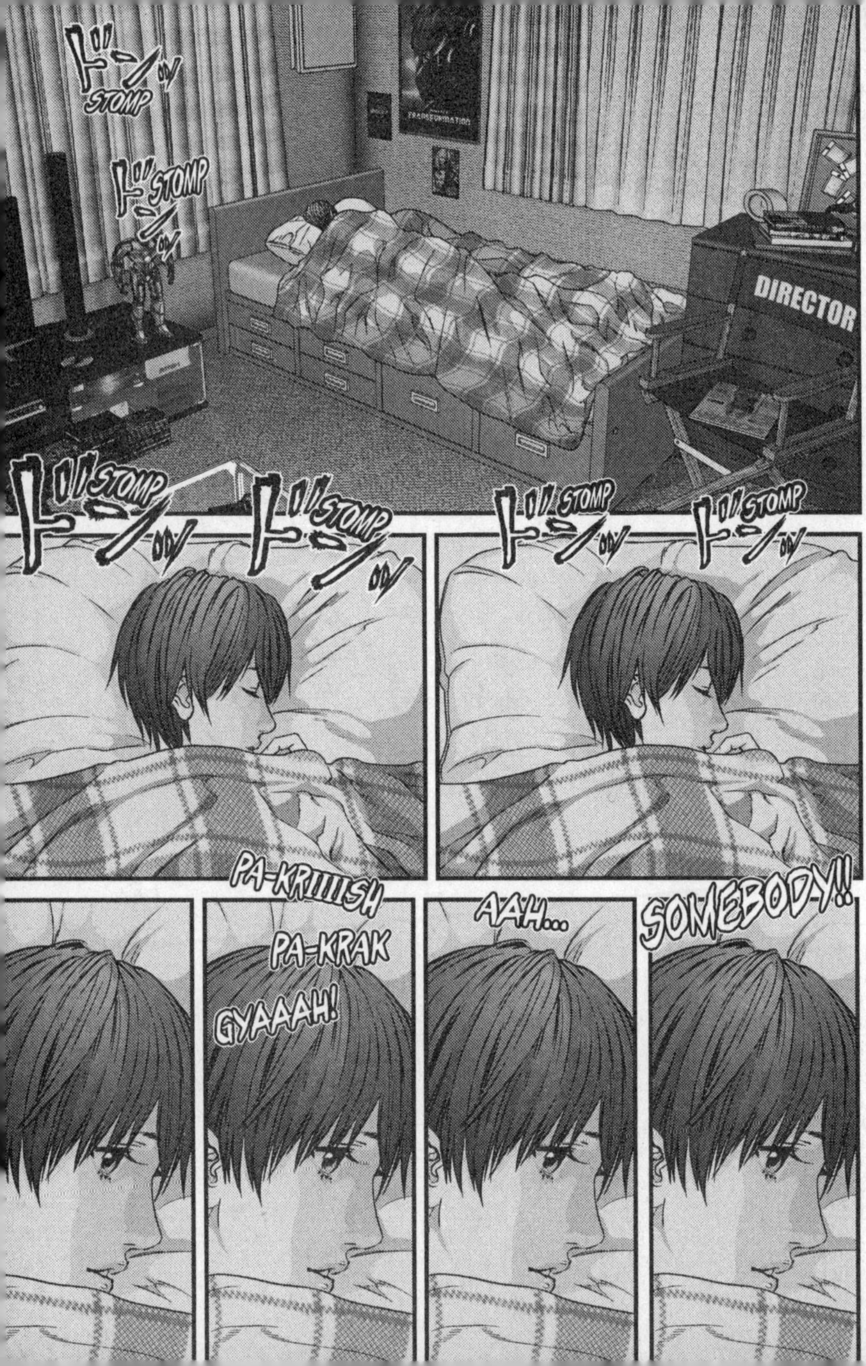

DIRECTOR
STOMP
STOMP
STOMP
STOMP
STOMP
STOMP
SOMEBODY!!
AAH...
PA-KRIIIIISH
PA-KRAK
GYAAAH!

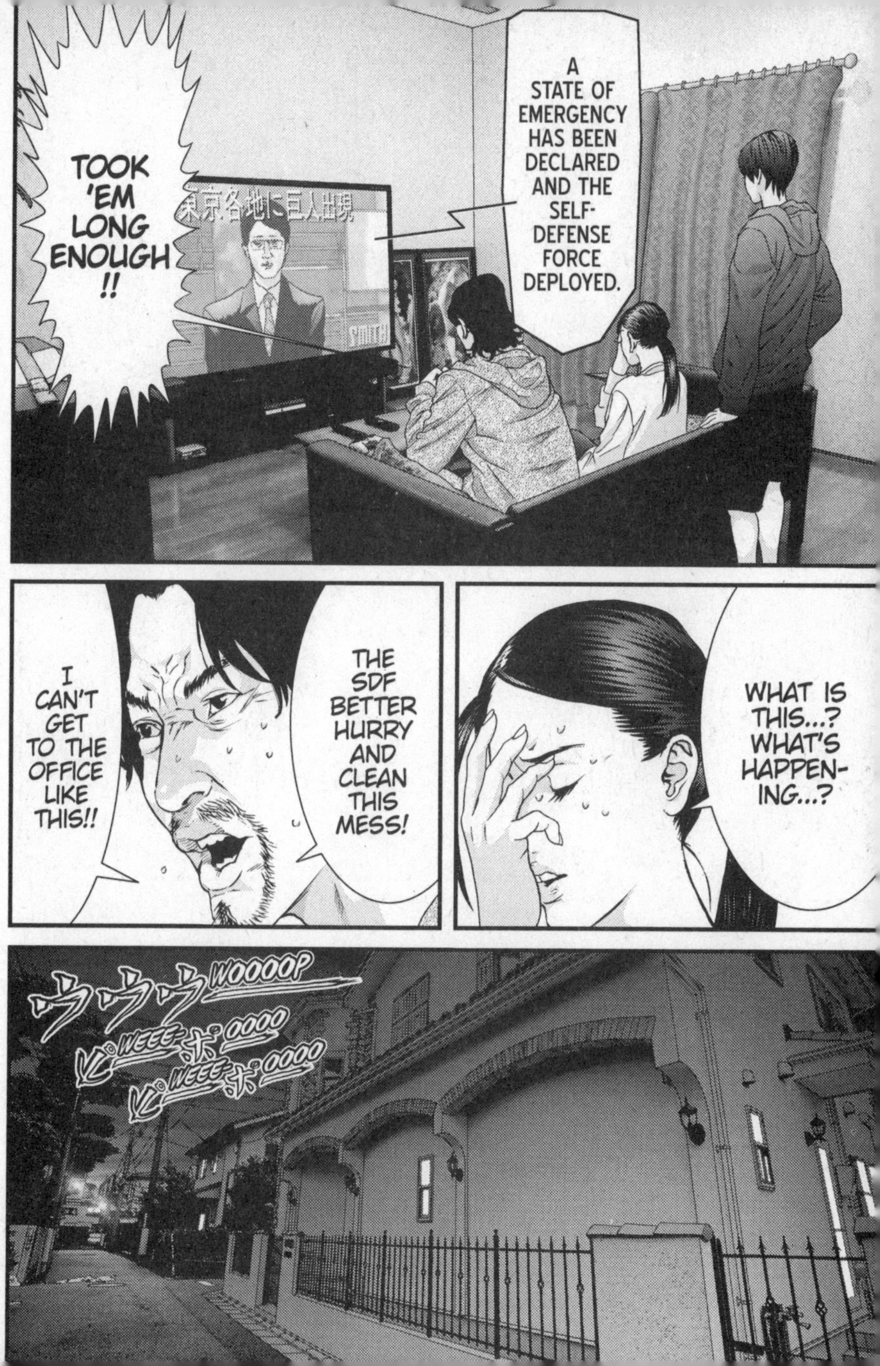

東京各地に巨人出現
A STATE OF EMERGENCY HAS BEEN DECLARED AND THE SELF-DEFENSE FORCE DEPLOYED.
TOOK 'EM LONG ENOUGH!!
WHAT IS THIS...? WHAT'S HAPPENING...?
THE SDF BETTER HURRY AND CLEAN THIS MESS!
I CAN'T GET TO THE OFFICE LIKE THIS!!
ウウウ WOOOOP
WEEEE ポ OOOO
WEEEE ポ OOOO

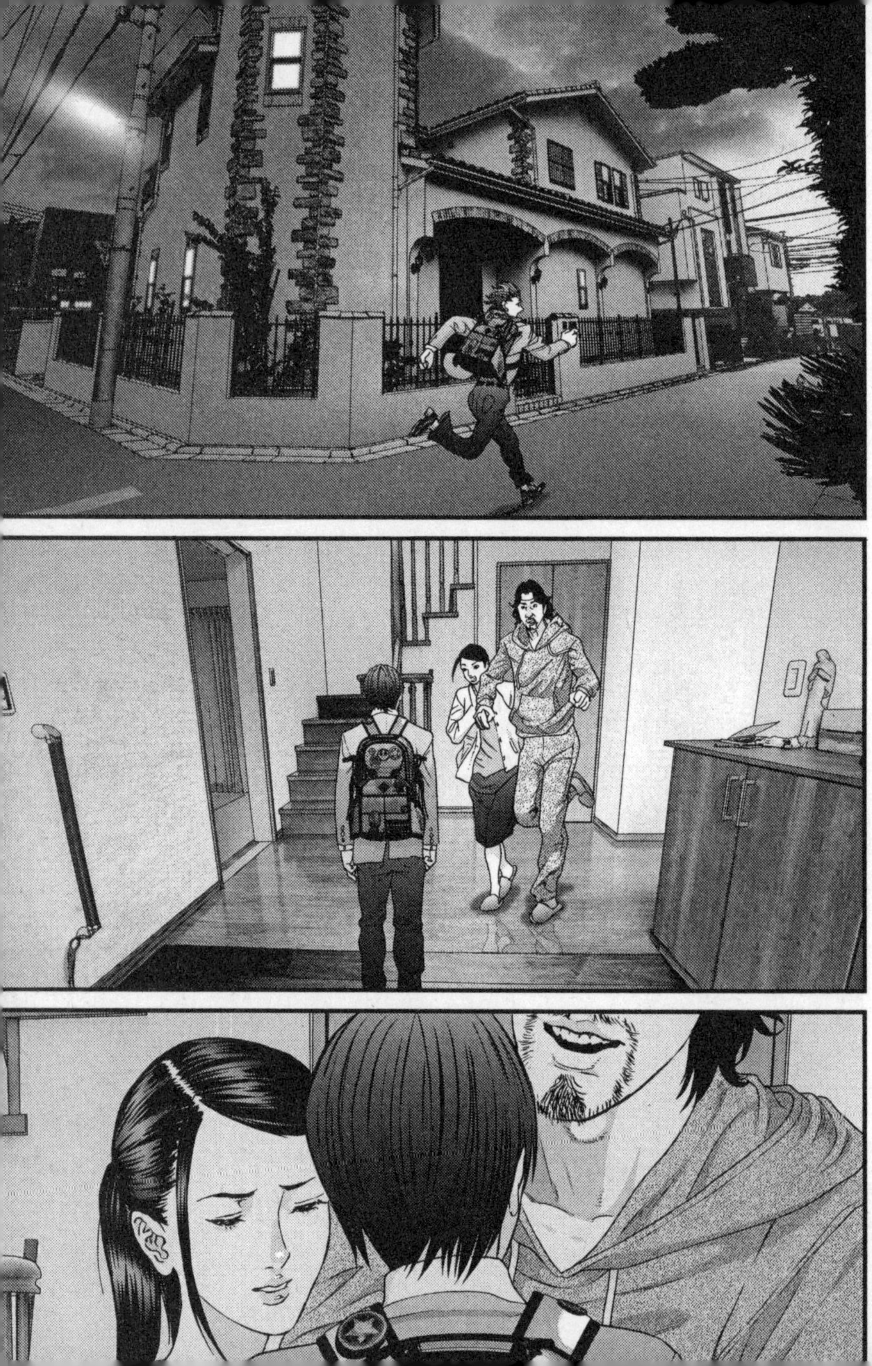

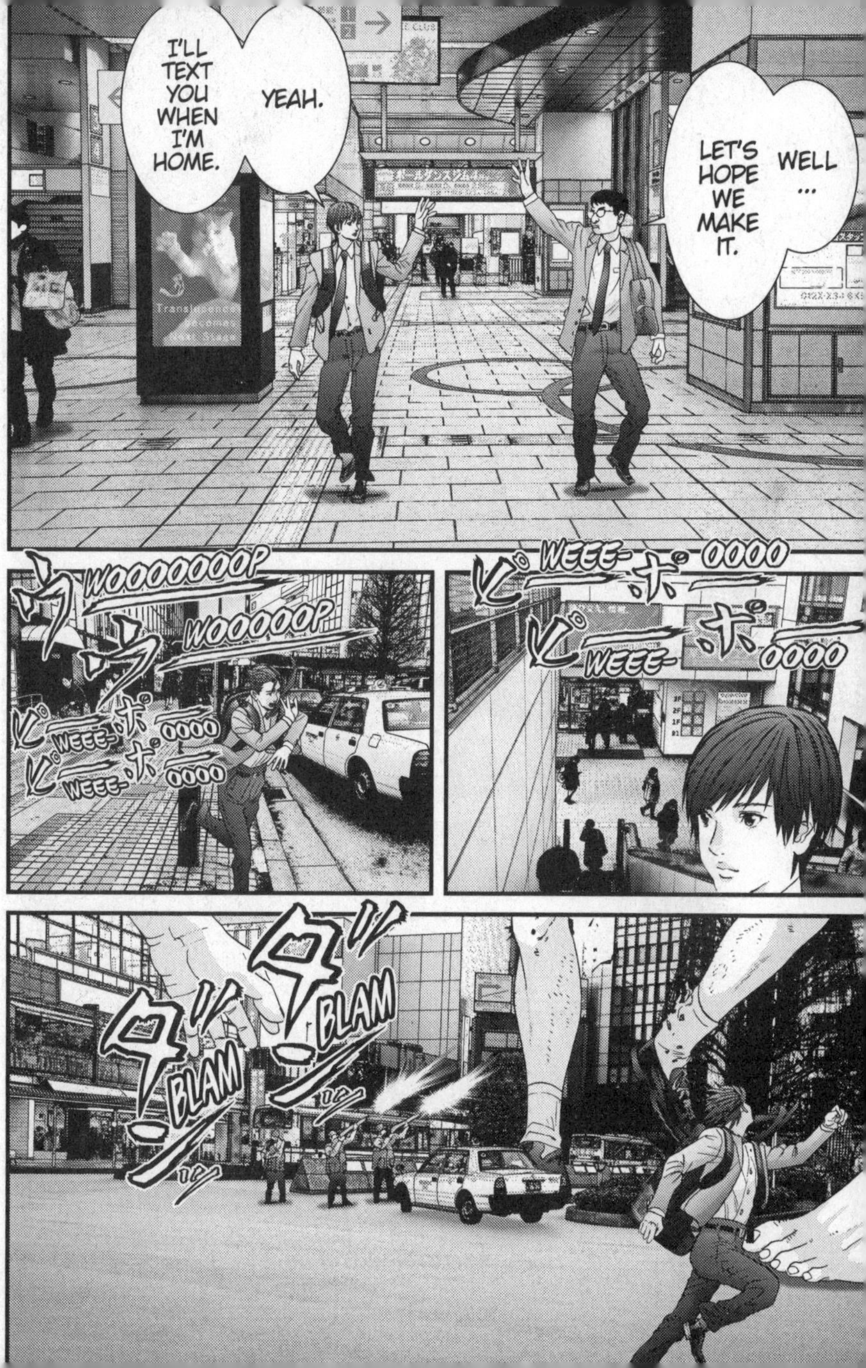
WELL ...
LET'S HOPE WE MAKE IT.
YEAH.
I'LL TEXT YOU WHEN I'M HOME.
WEEE-OOOO
WEEE-OOOO
WOOOOOOOP
WOOOOOP
WEEE-OOOO
WEEE-OOOO
BLAM
BLAM

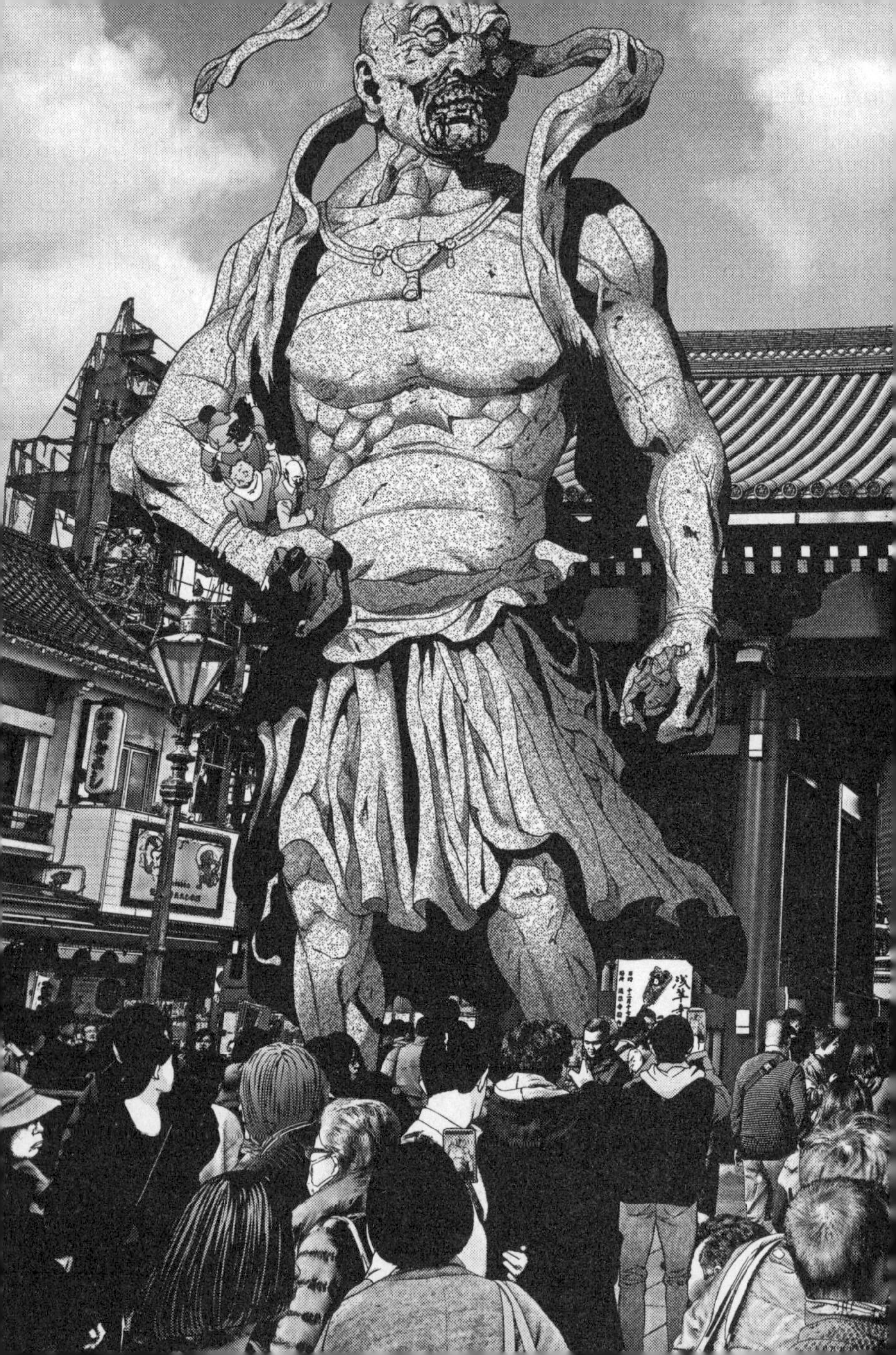

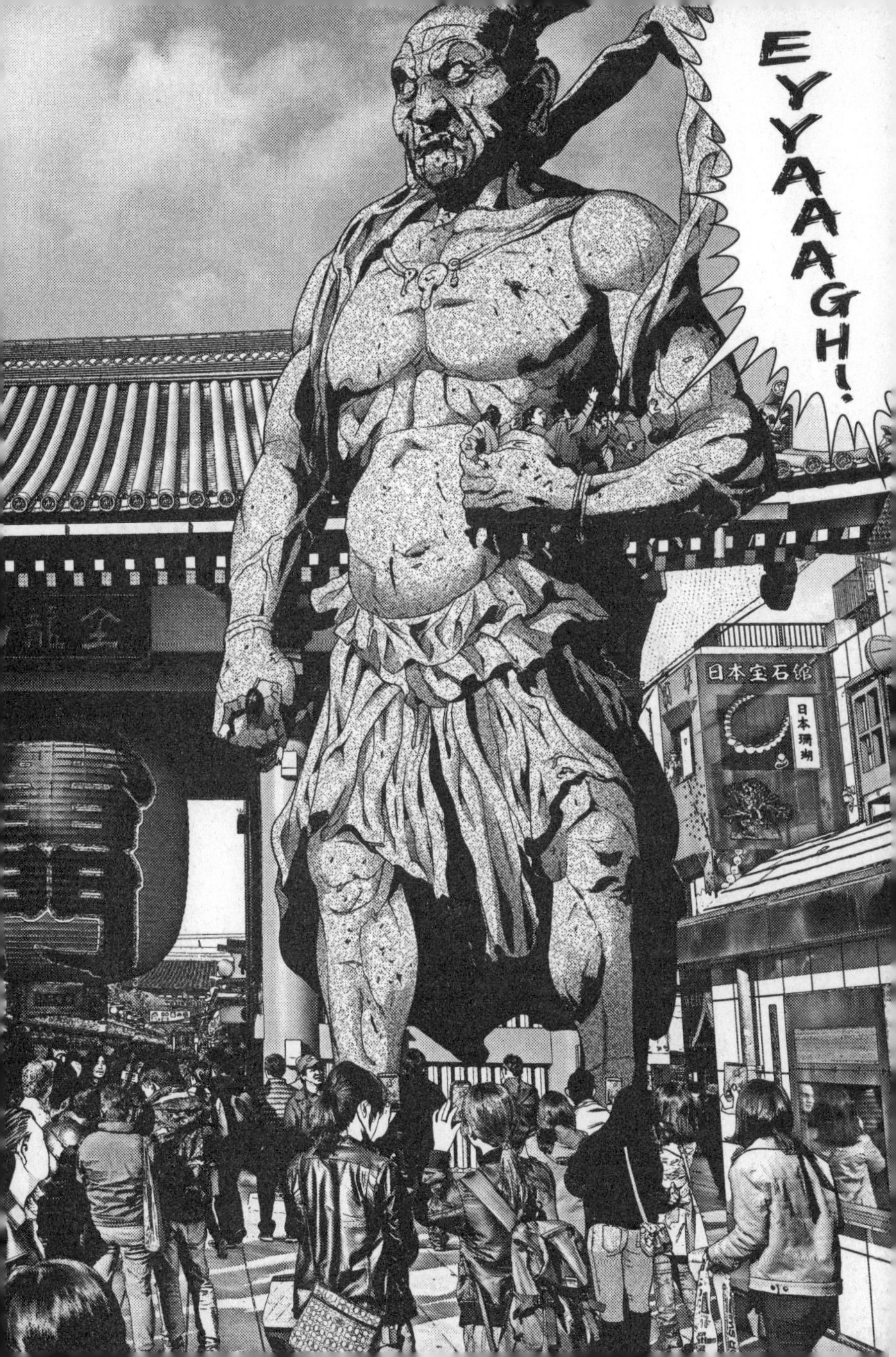
EYYAAAGH!
日本宝石館
日本珊瑚

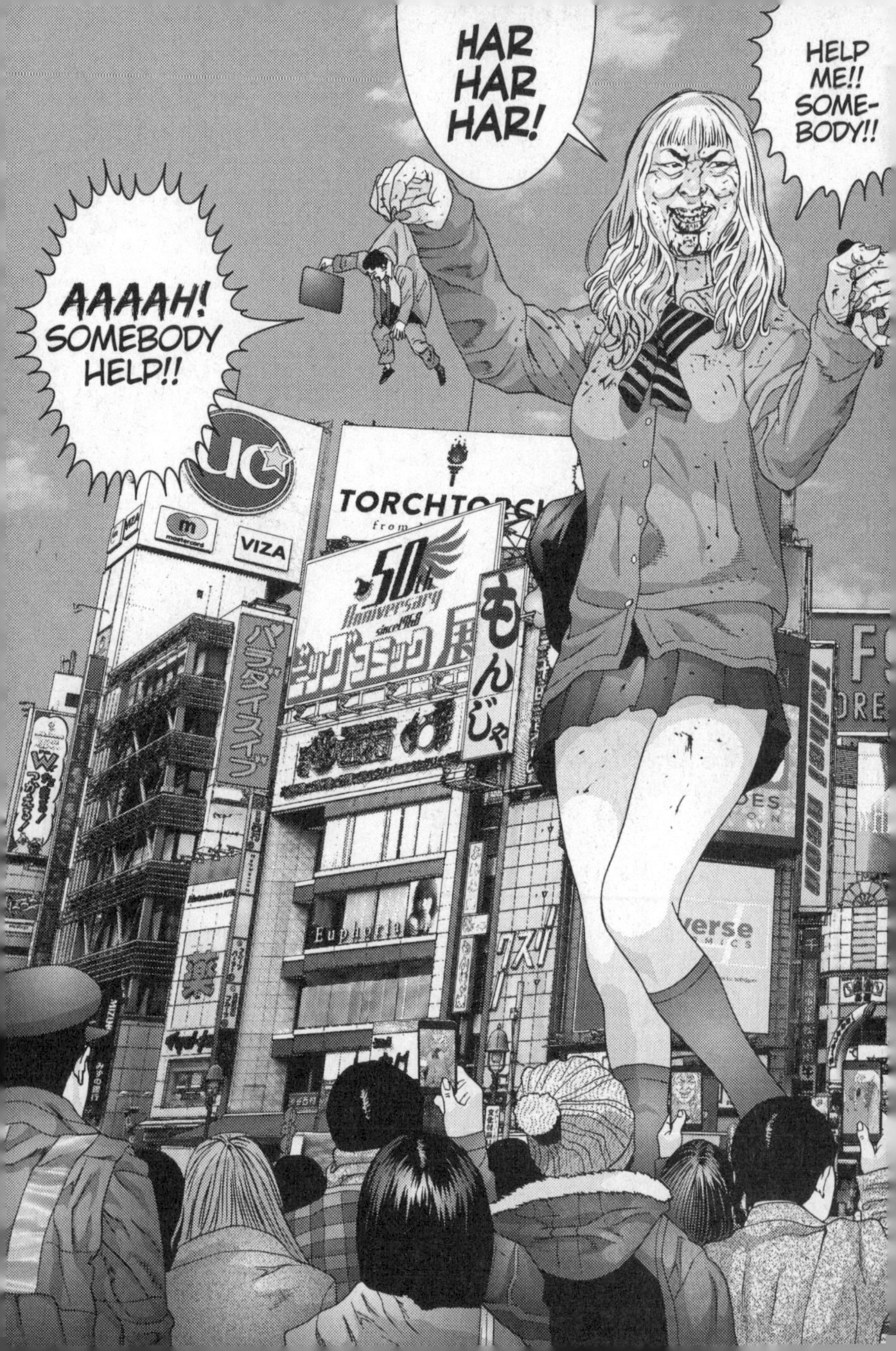
HELP ME!! SOME-BODY!!
HAR HAR HAR!
AAAAH! SOMEBODY HELP!!
VIZA
もんじゃ
パラダイスイブ

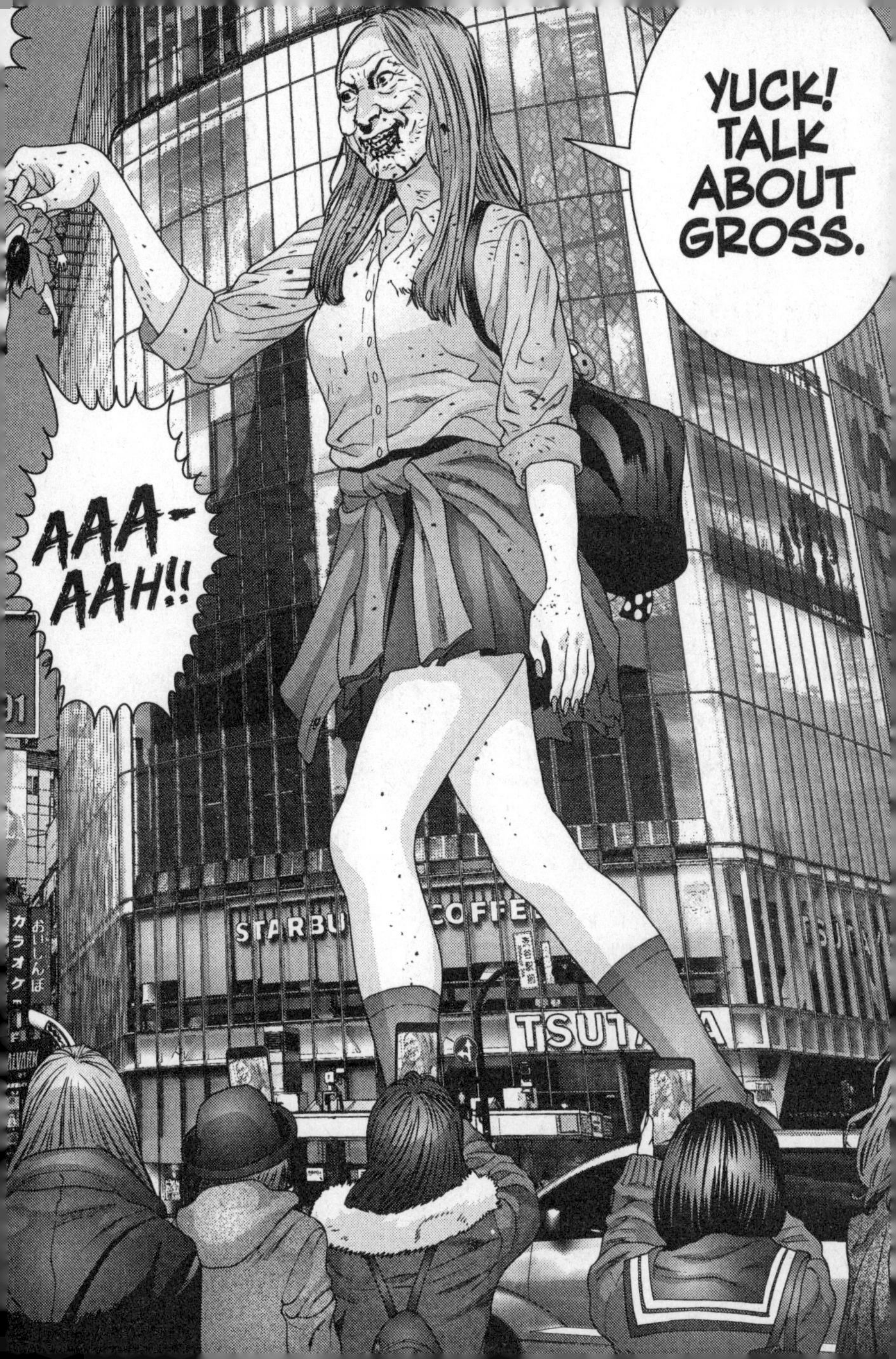
YUCK! TALK ABOUT GROSS.
AAA-AAAH!!

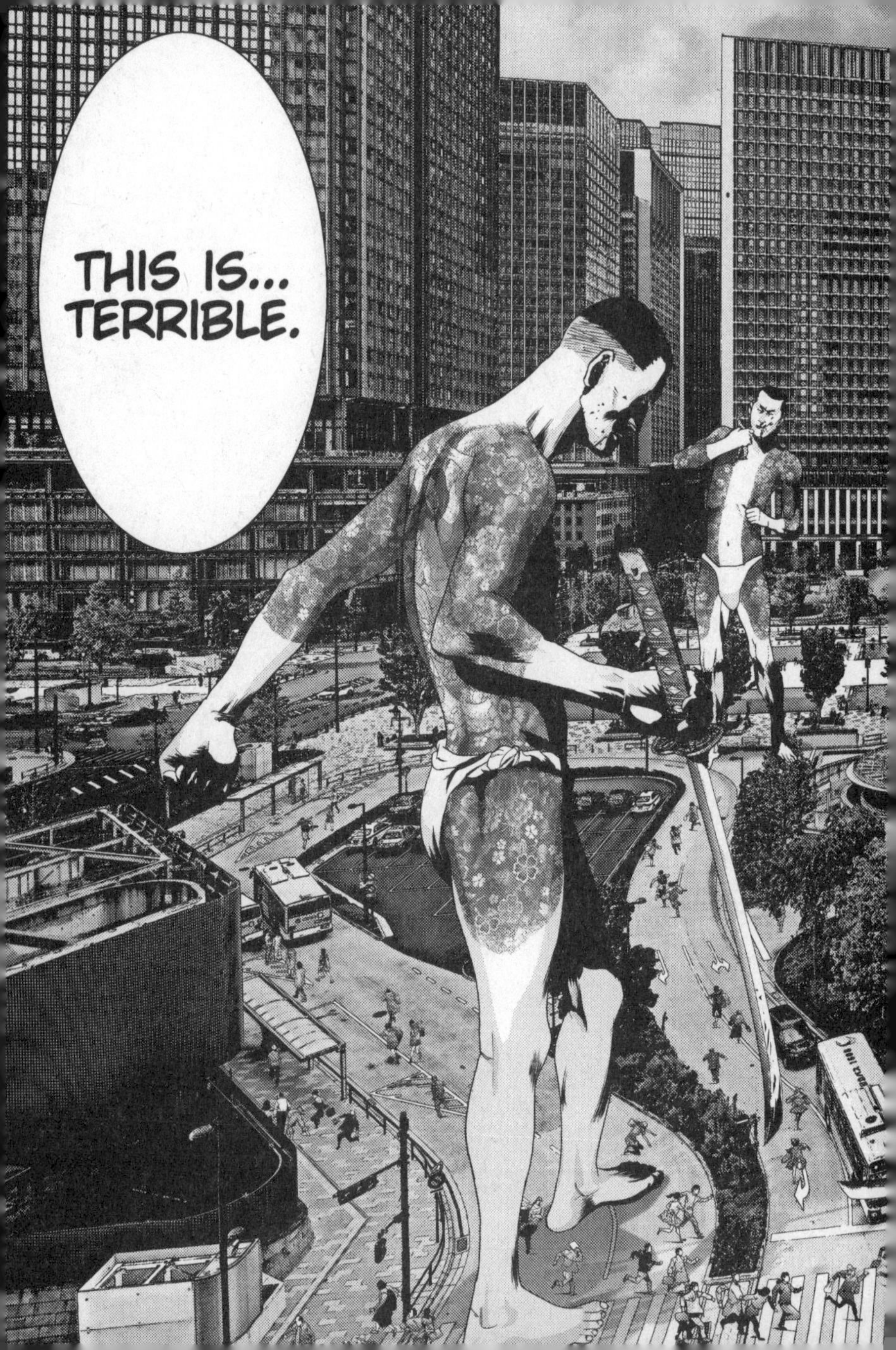
THIS IS... TERRIBLE.

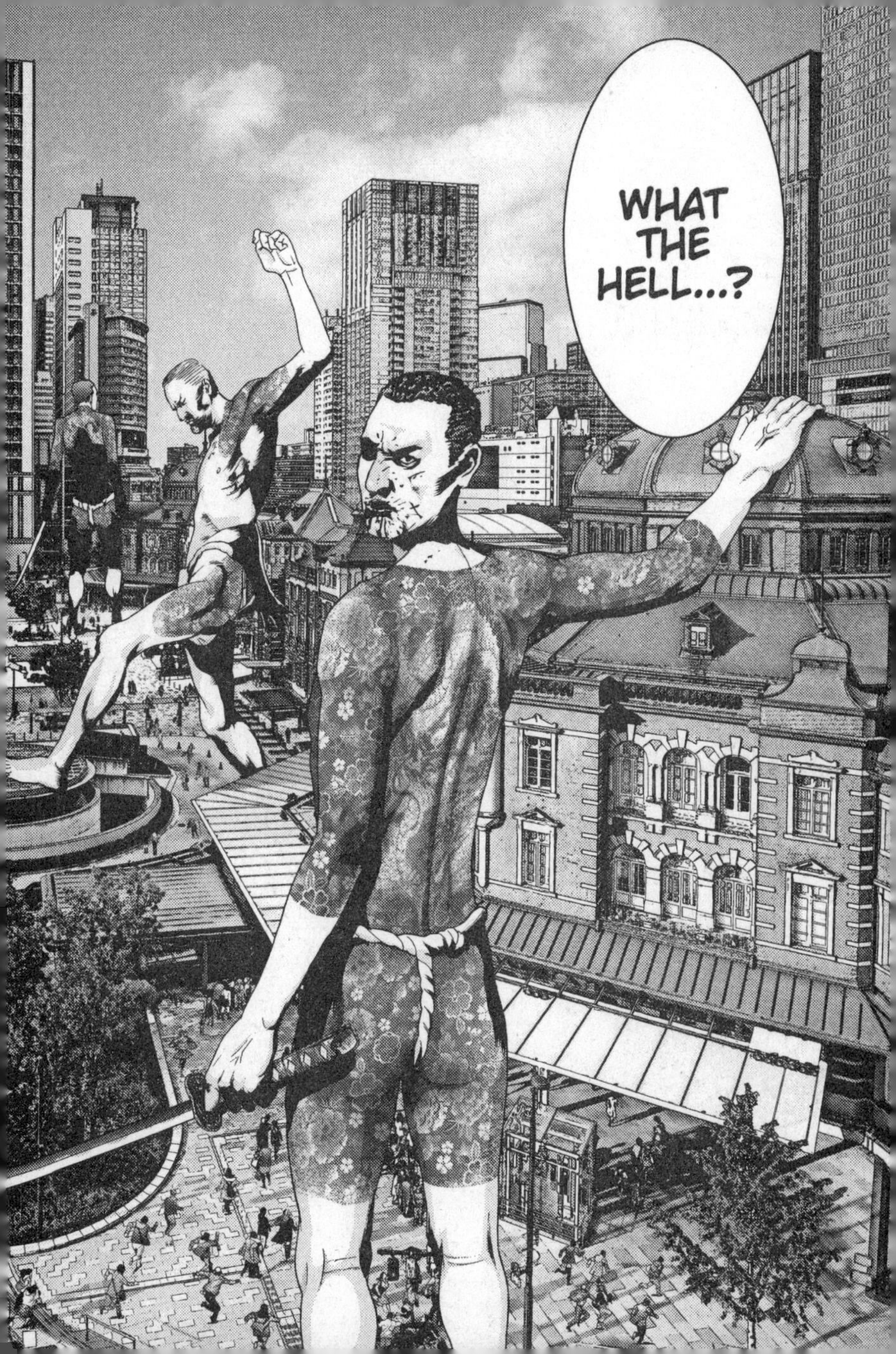
WHAT THE HELL...?

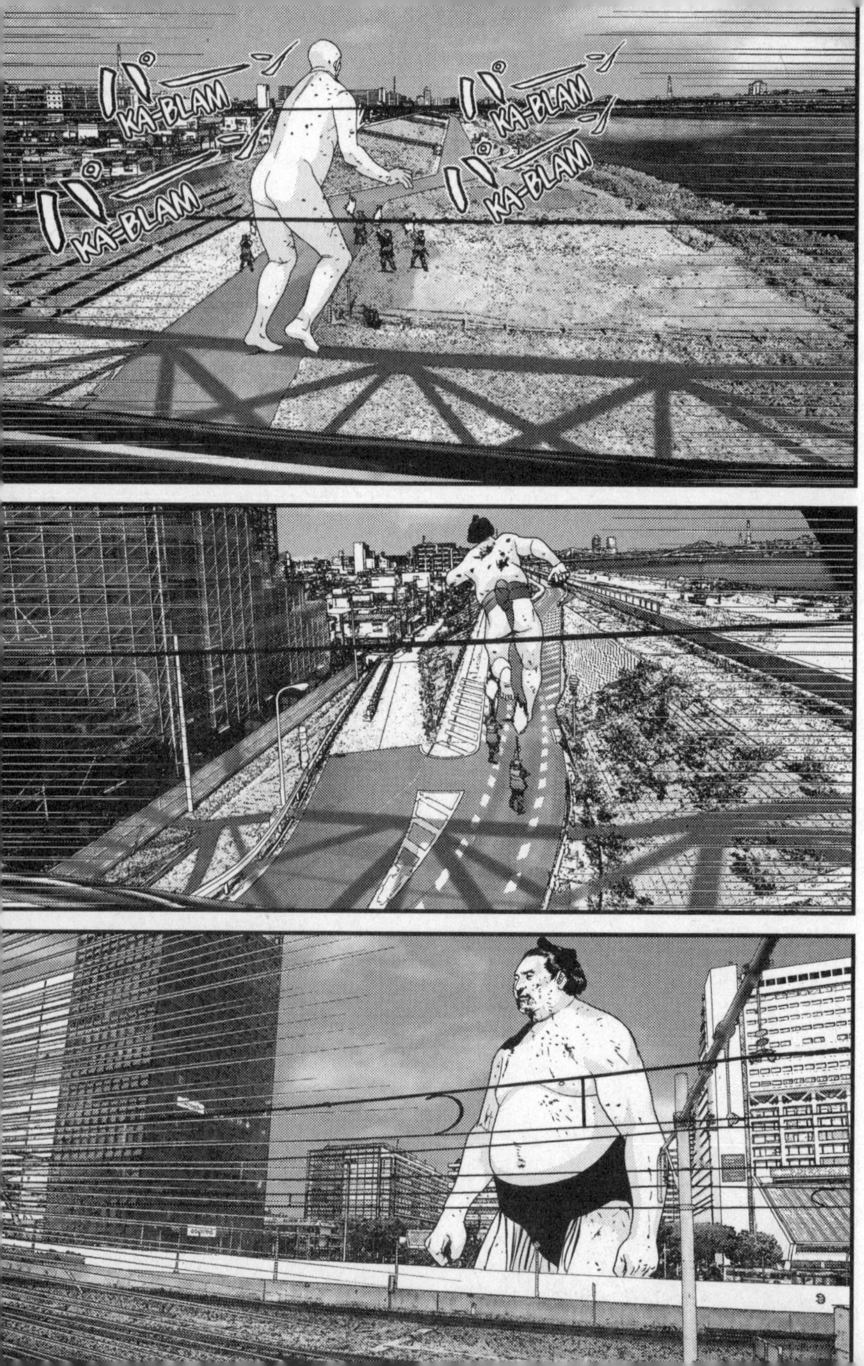
パ KA-BLAM
パ KA-BLAM
パ KA-BLAM
パ KA-BLAM

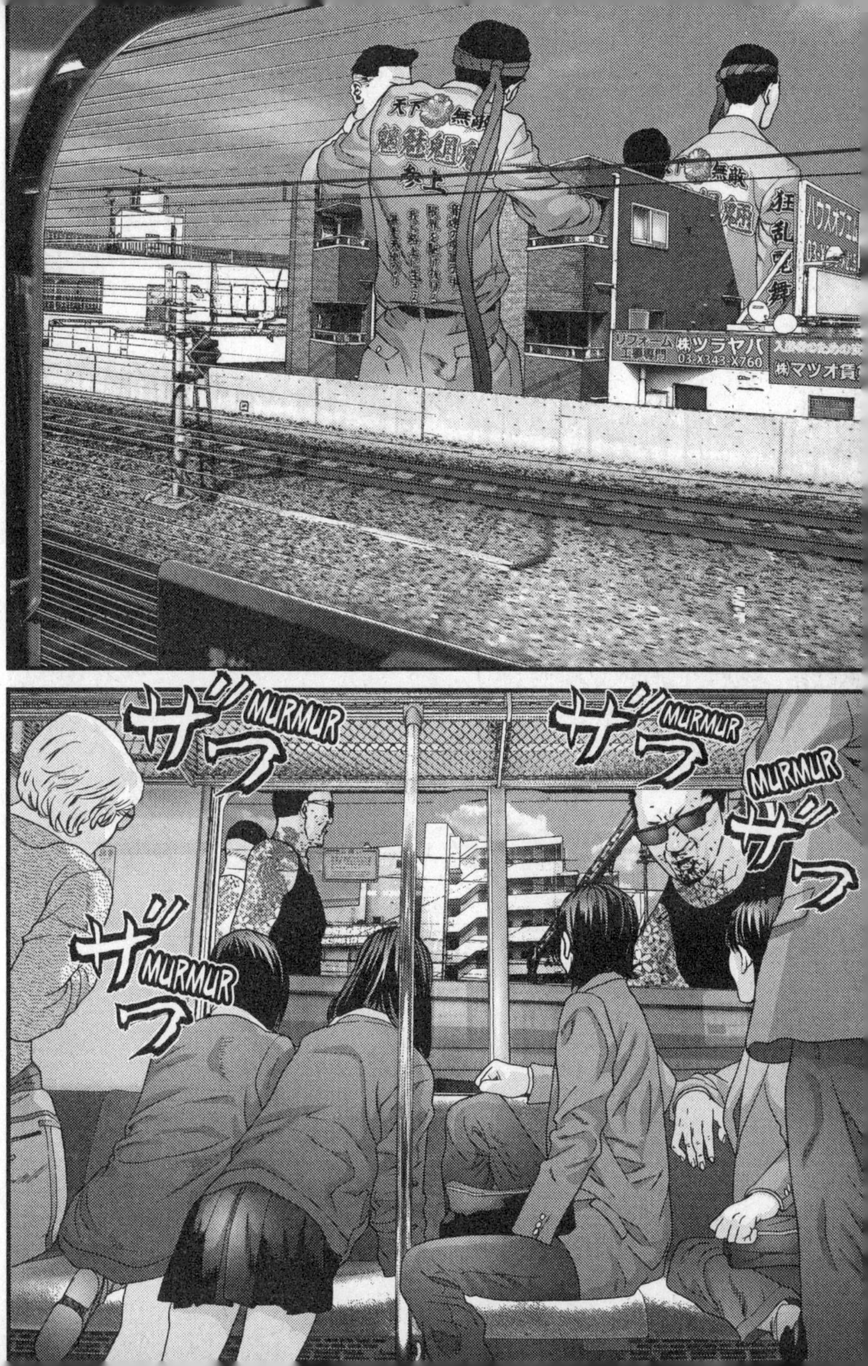
天下無敵
参上
天下無敵
リフォーム 工事専門
株ツラヤバ
03-X343-X760
株マツオ貸
ザワ MURMUR
ザワ MURMUR
ザワ MURMUR
ザワ MURMUR

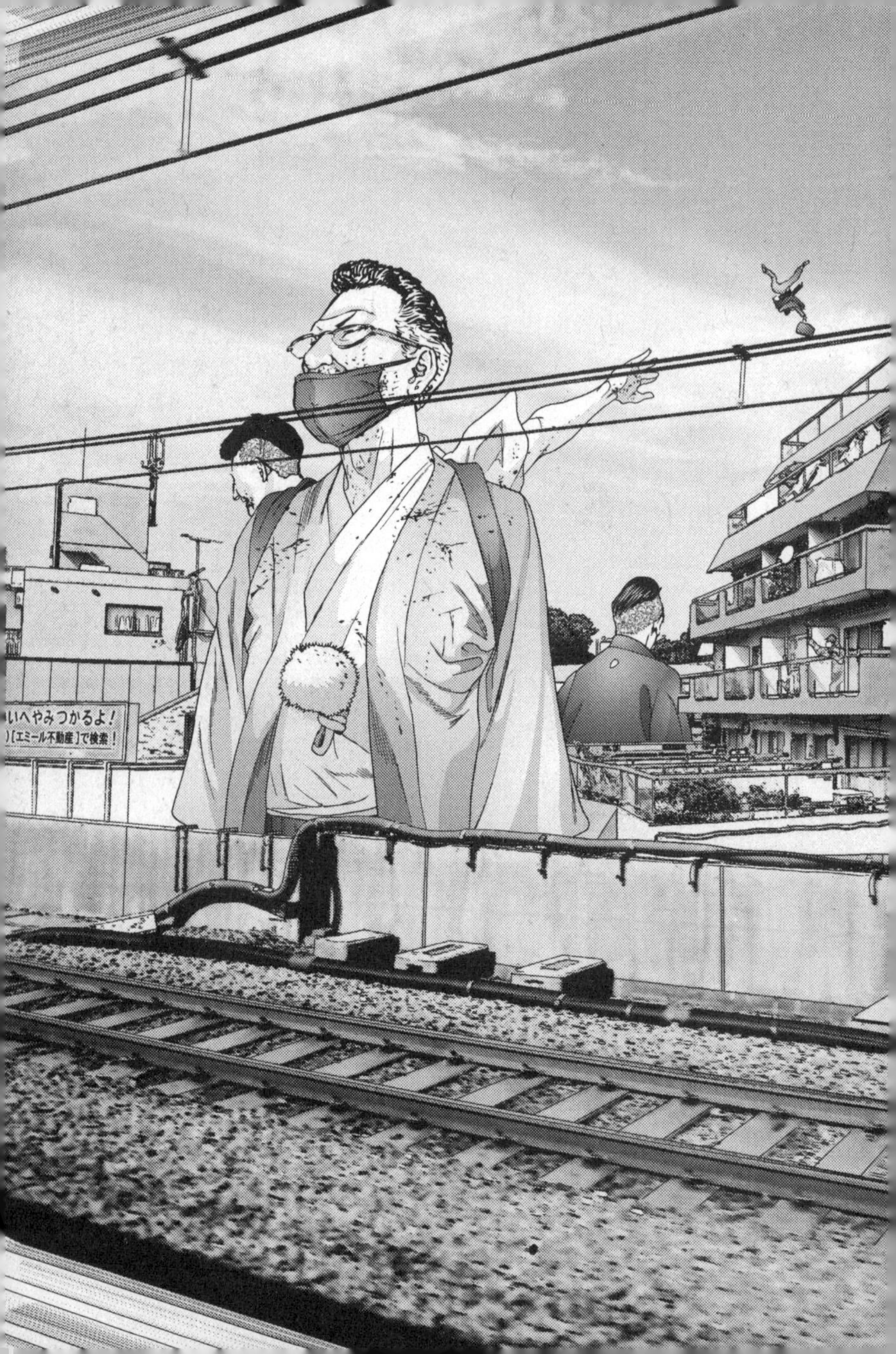
いへやみつかるよ！
[エミール不動産]で検索！

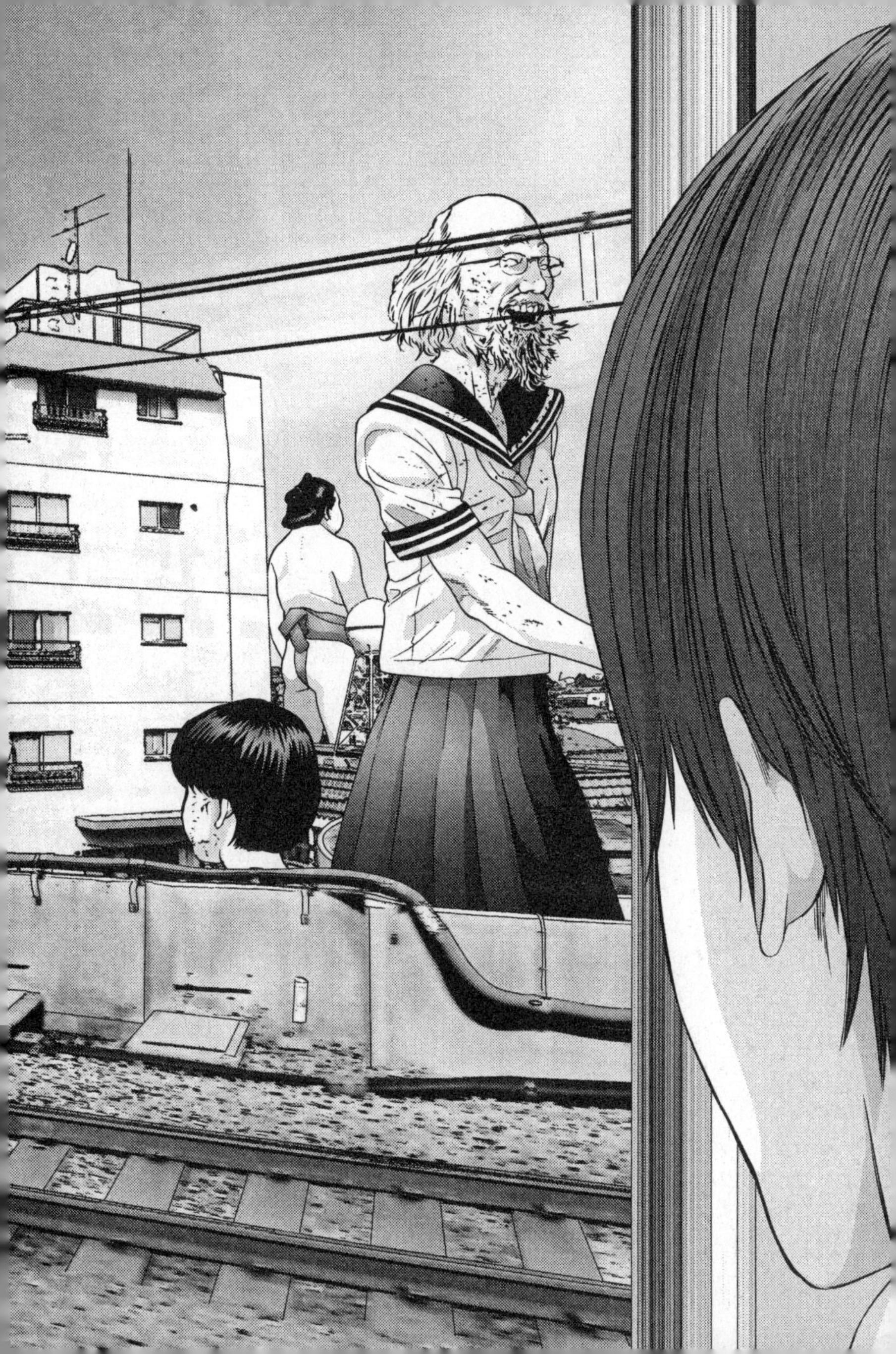

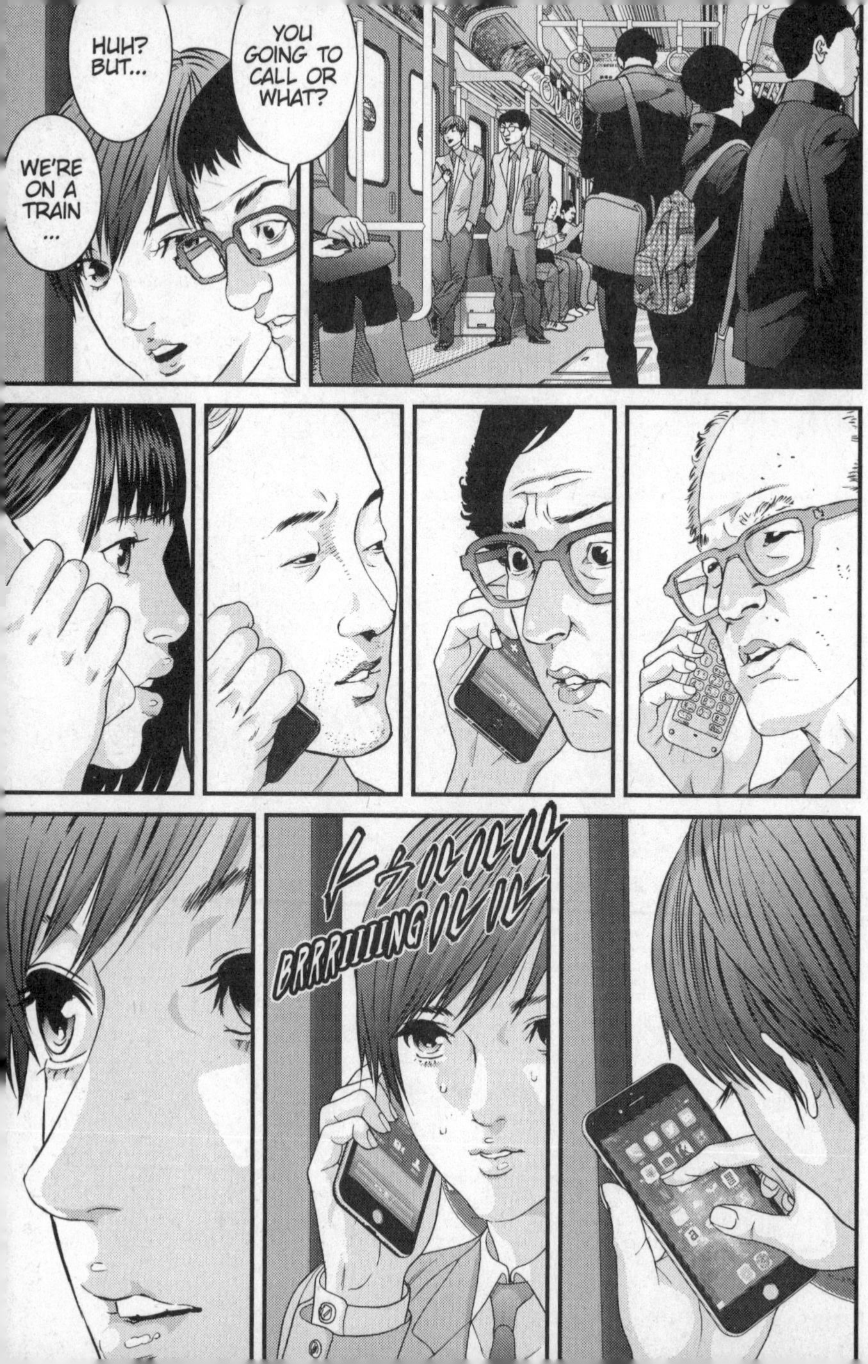
YOU GOING TO CALL OR WHAT?
HUH? BUT...
WE'RE ON A TRAIN ...
BRRRIIIING

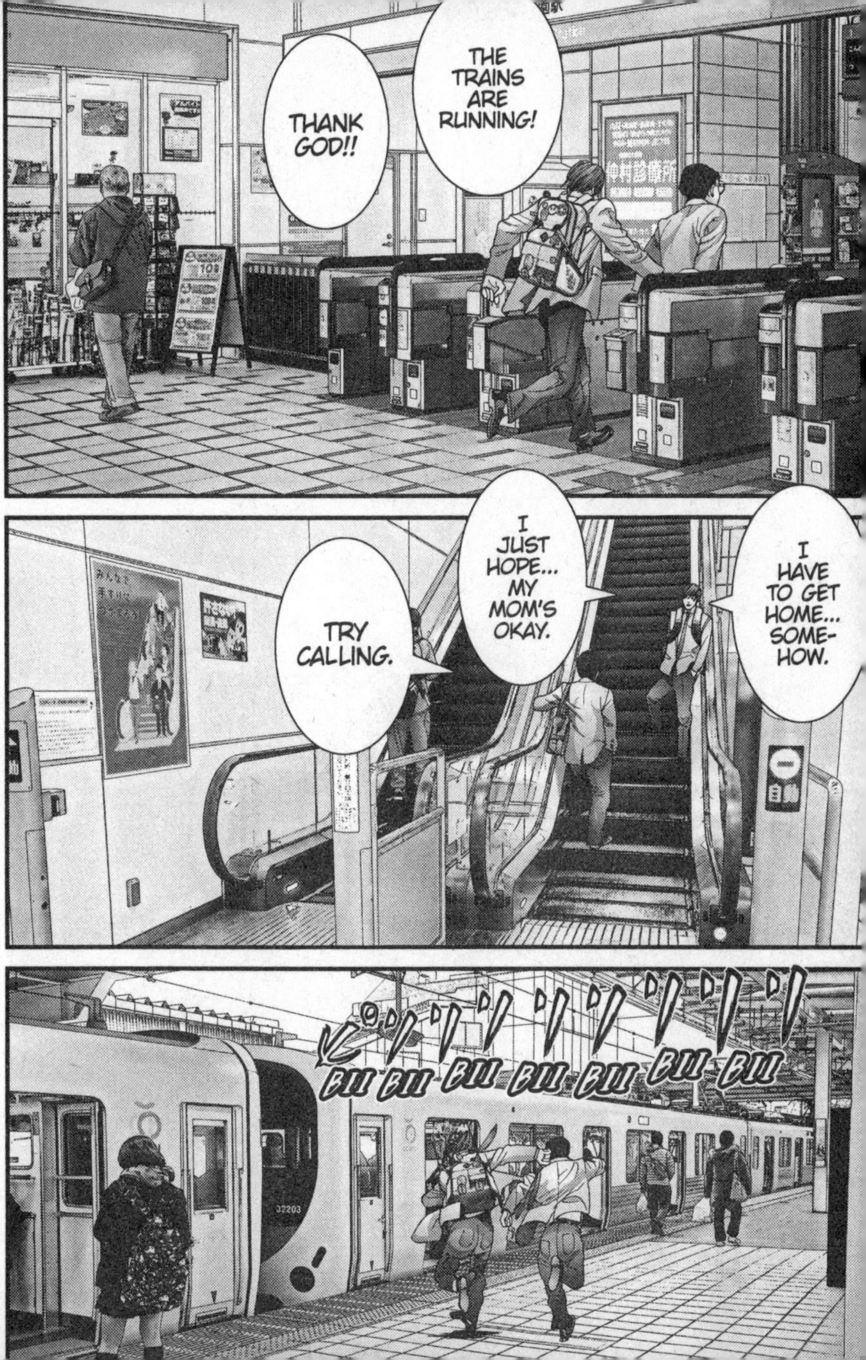
THE TRAINS ARE RUNNING!
THANK GOD!!
I HAVE TO GET HOME... SOME-HOW.
I JUST HOPE... MY MOM'S OKAY.
TRY CALLING.
BII BII BII BII BII BII BII

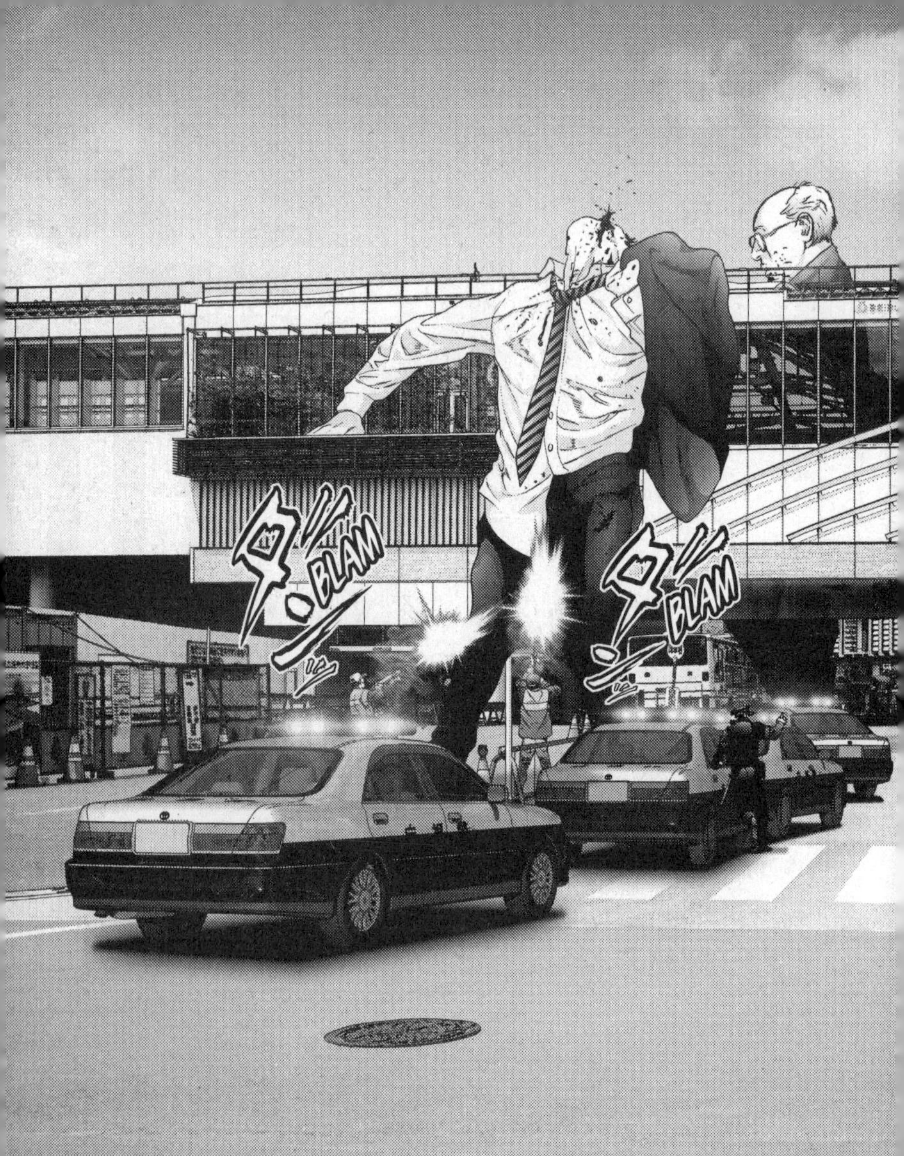
BLAM
BLAM

EPISODE 28: ROAD HOME

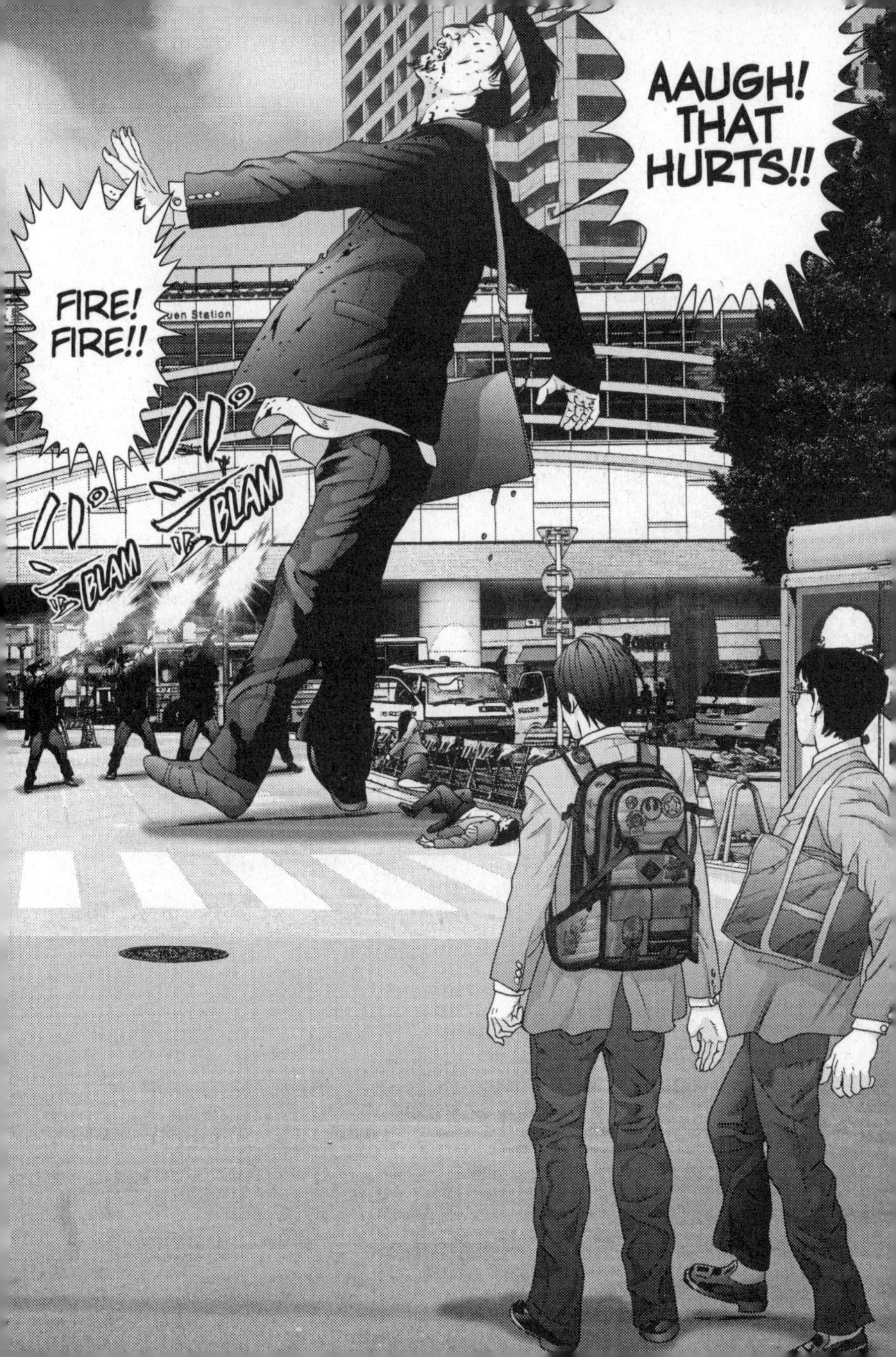
AAUGH! THAT HURTS!!
FIRE! FIRE!!
BLAM
BLAM

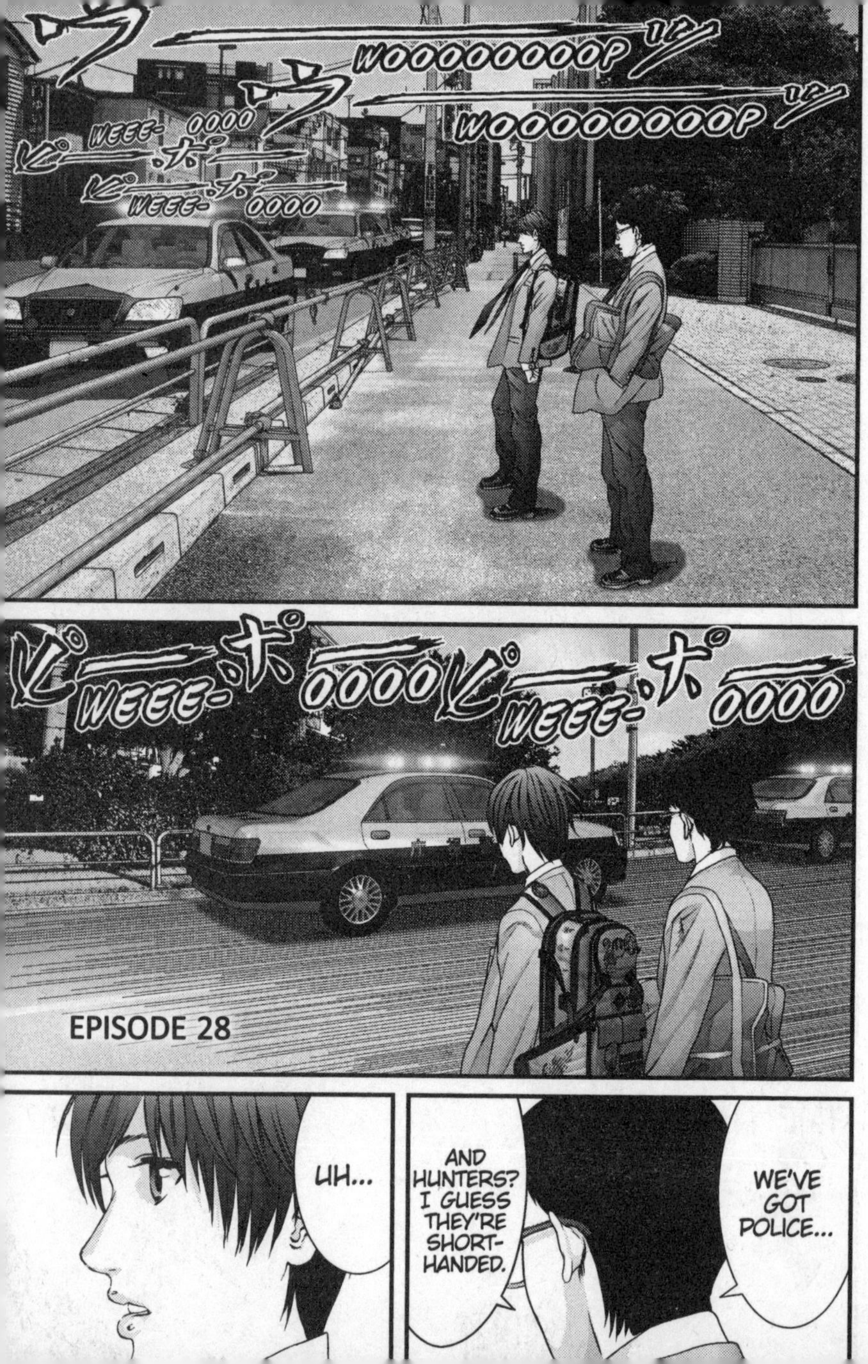
WOOOOOOOOP
WOOOOOOOOOP
WEEE- OOOO
WEEE- OOOO
WEEE- OOOO
WEEE- OOOO
EPISODE 28
WE'VE GOT POLICE...
AND HUNTERS? I GUESS THEY'RE SHORT-HANDED.
UH...

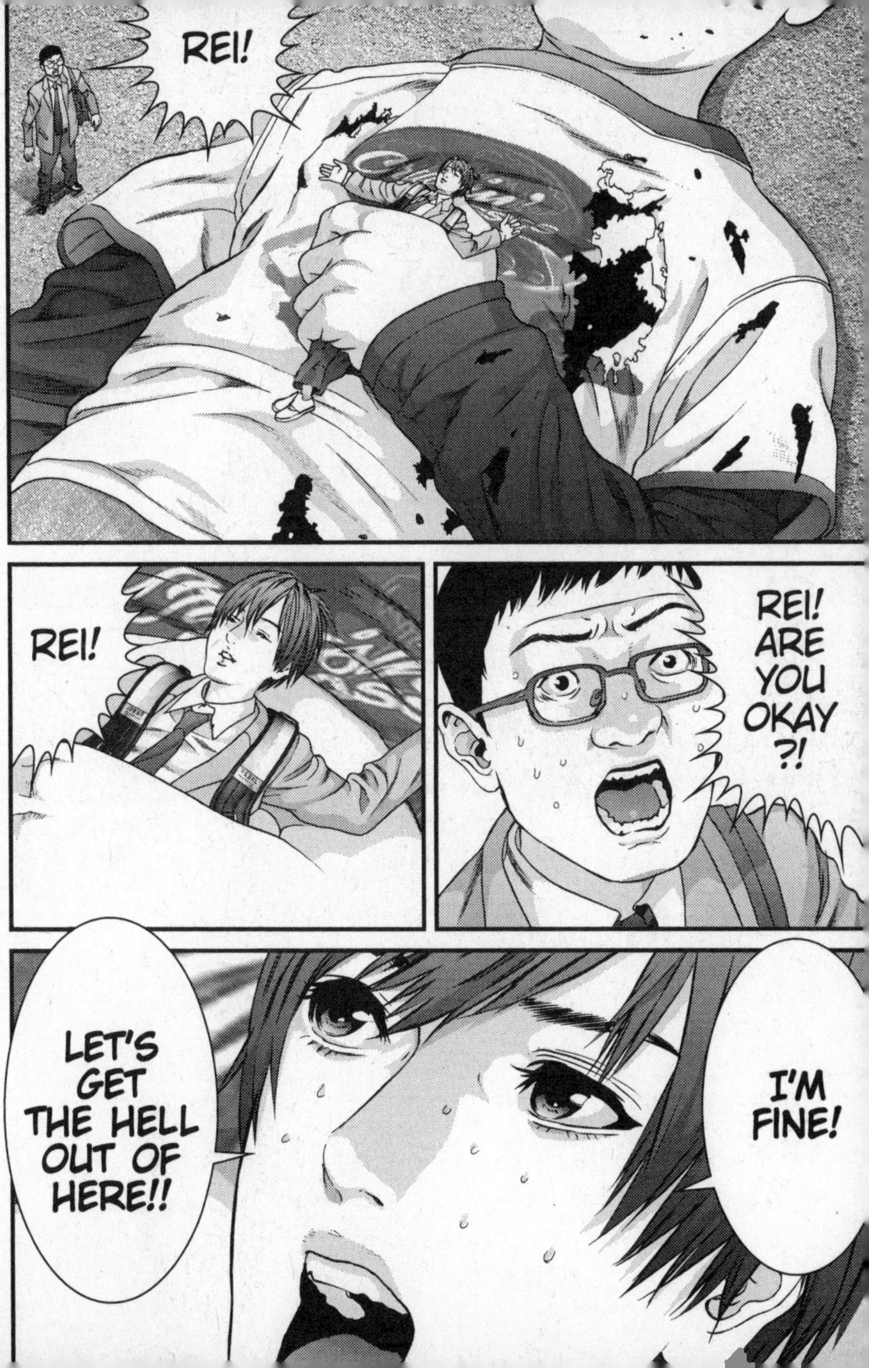
REI!
REI! ARE YOU OKAY?!
REI!
I'M FINE!
LET'S GET THE HELL OUT OF HERE!!

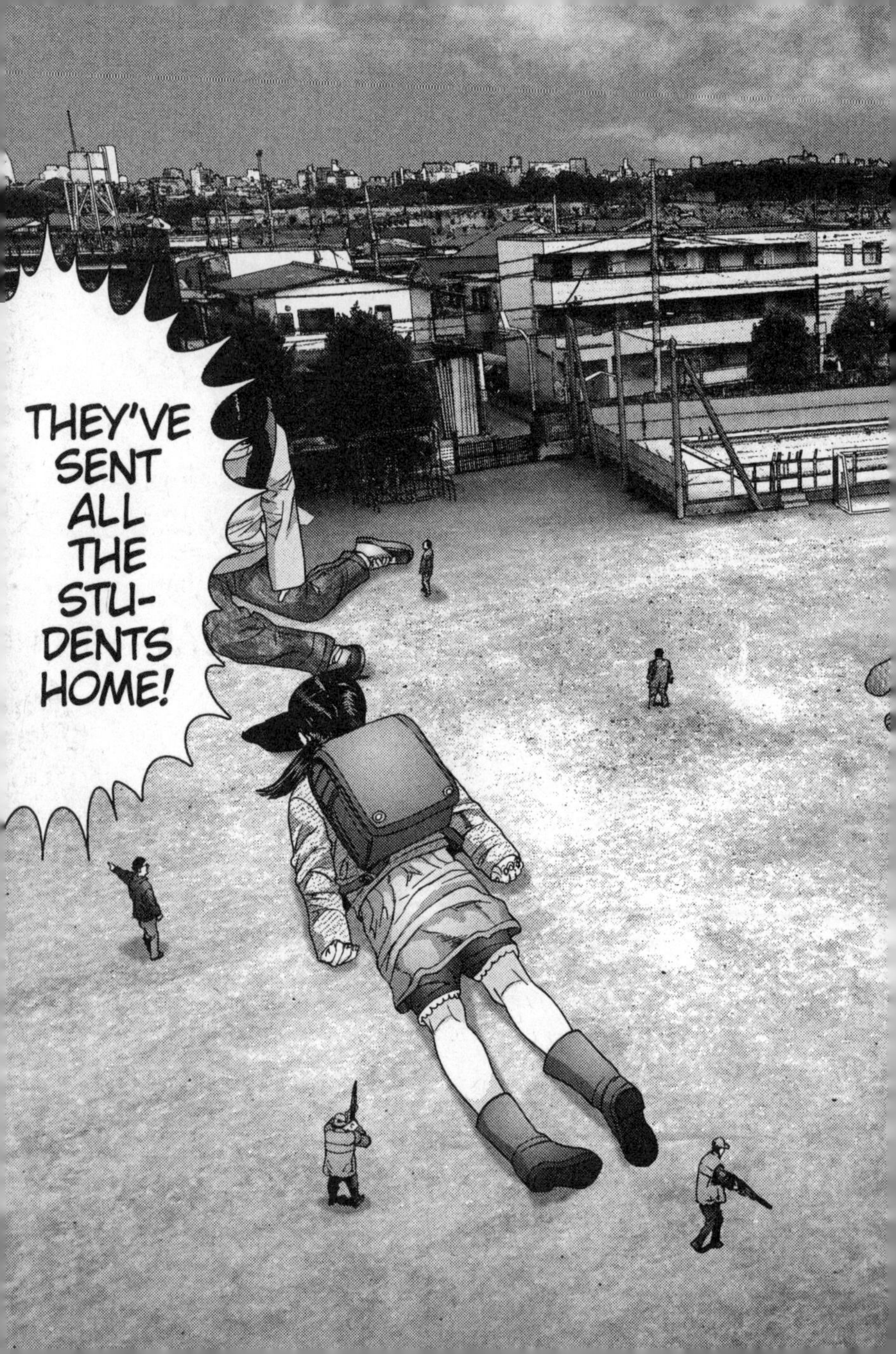
THEY'VE SENT ALL THE STU-DENTS HOME!

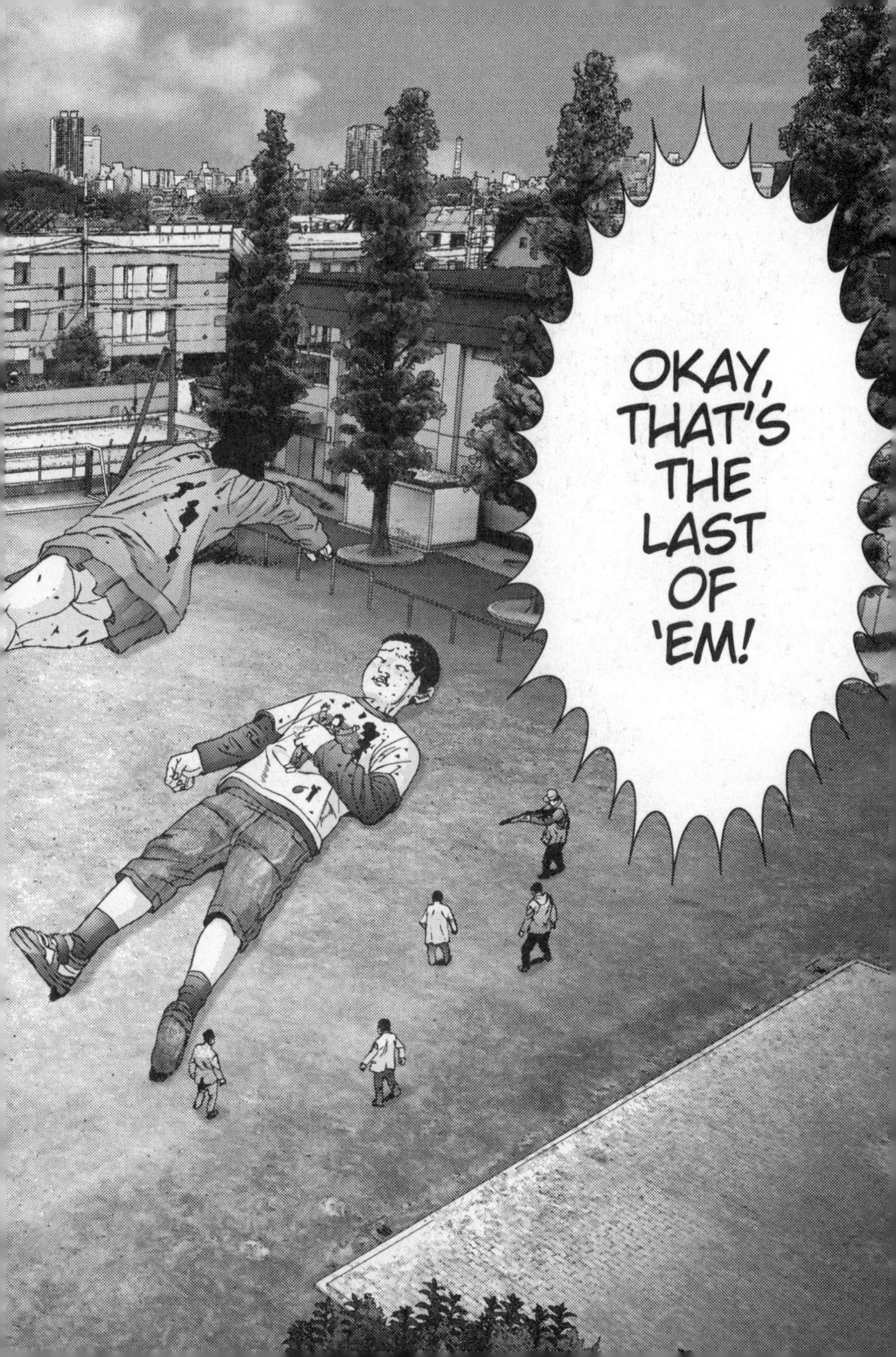
OKAY, THAT'S THE LAST OF 'EM!

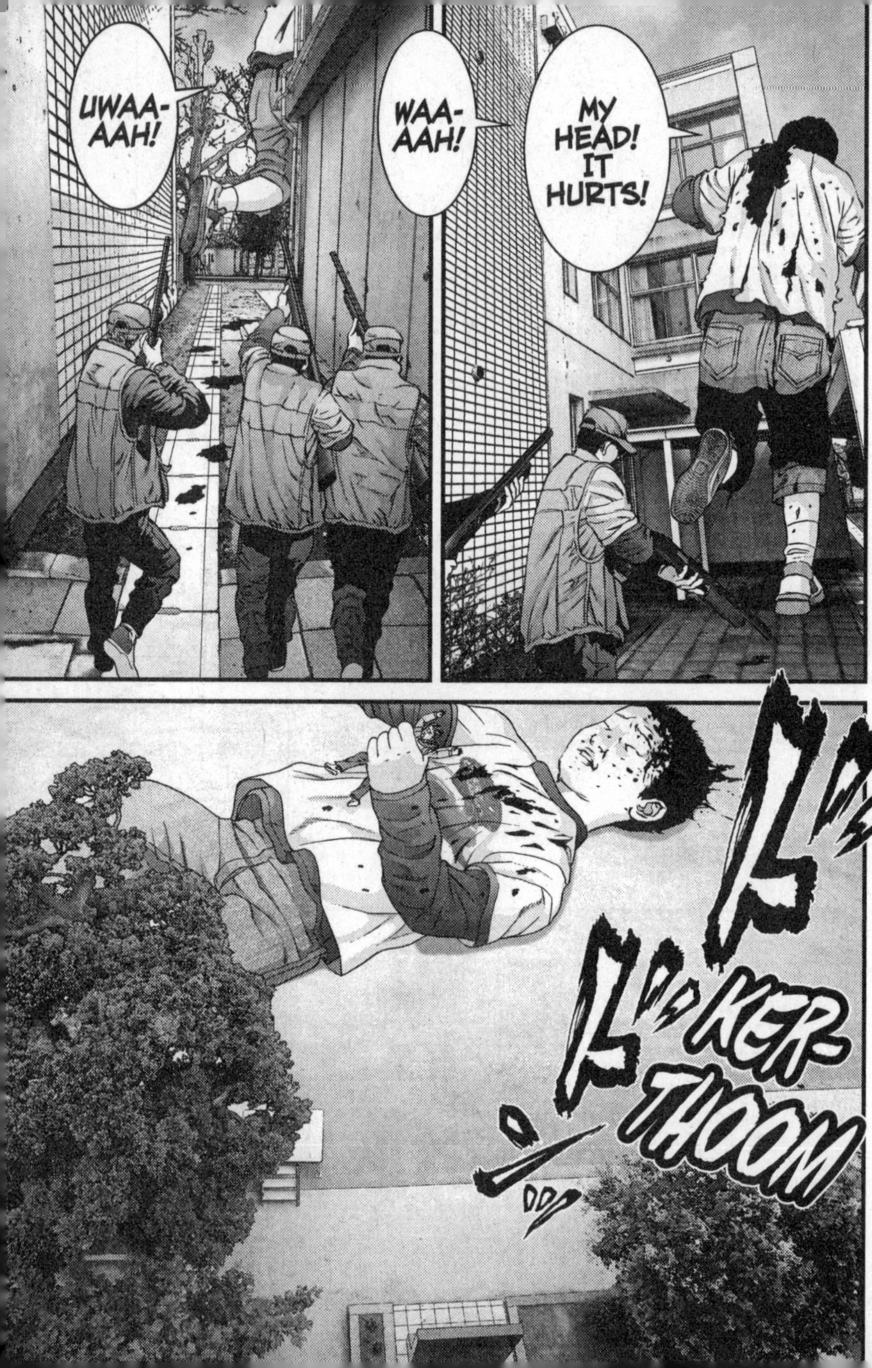
MY HEAD! IT HURTS!
WAA-AAH!
UWAA-AAH!
KER-THOOM

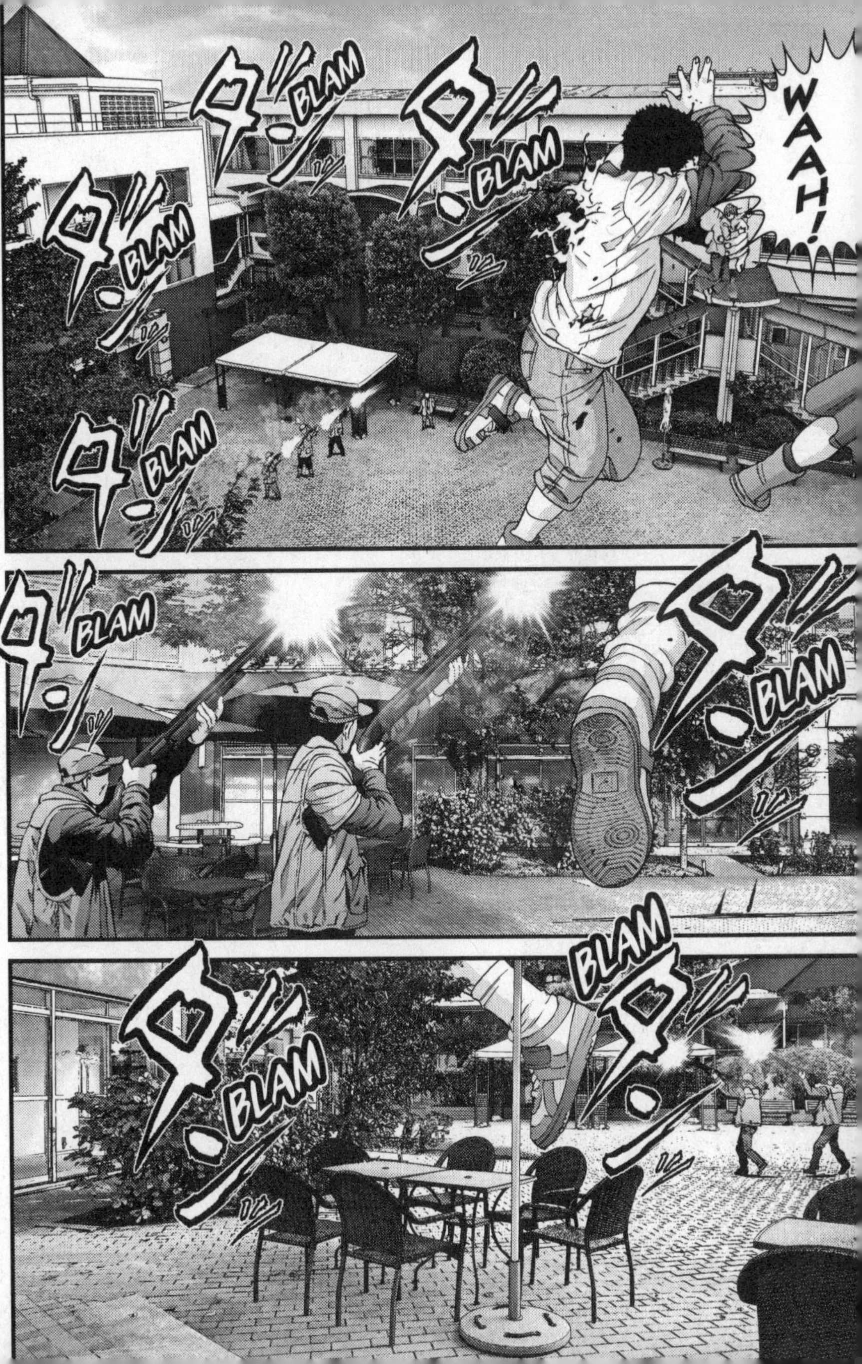
WAAH!
BLAM
BLAM
BLAM
BLAM
BLAM
BLAM
BLAM
BLAM

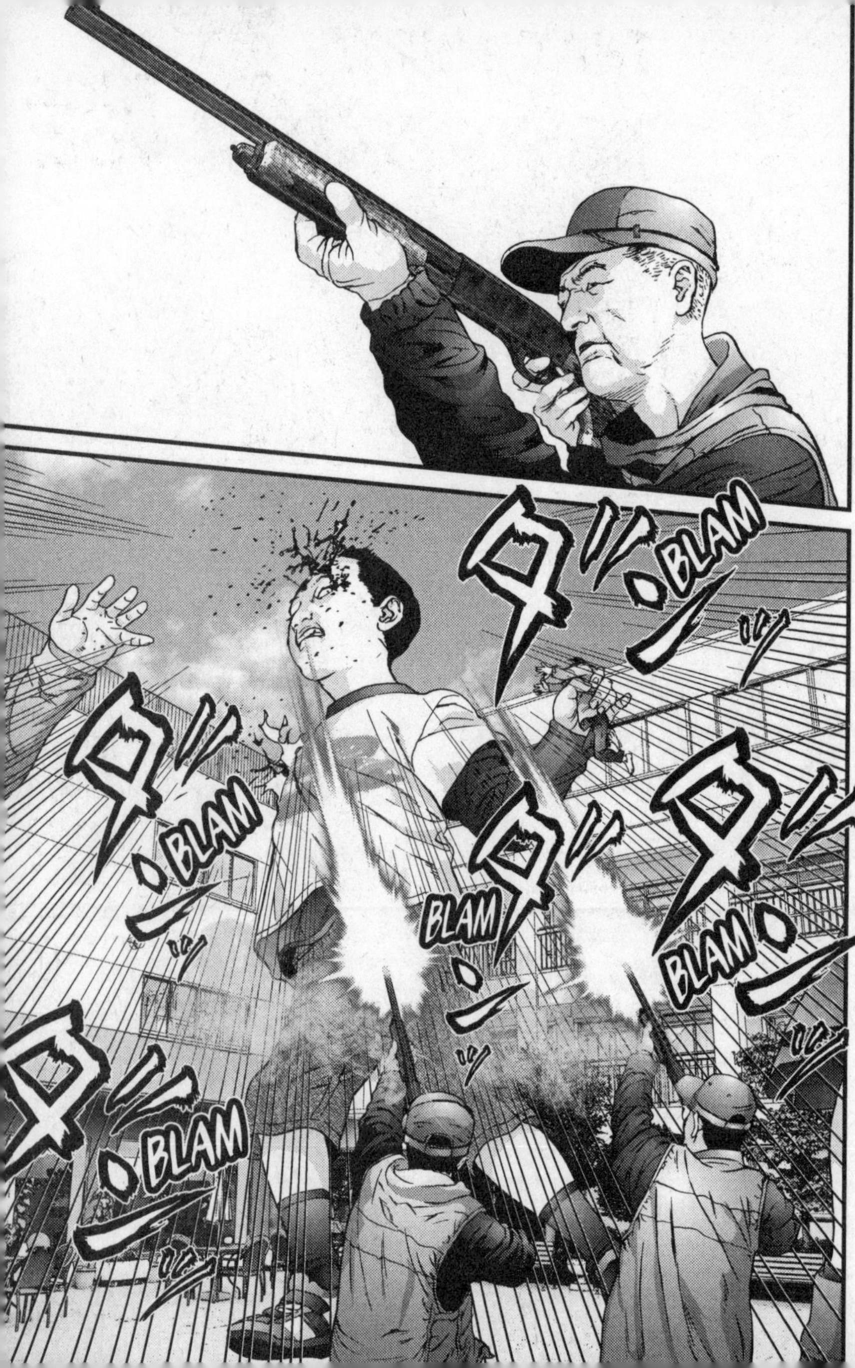
BLAM
BLAM
BLAM
BLAM
BLAM

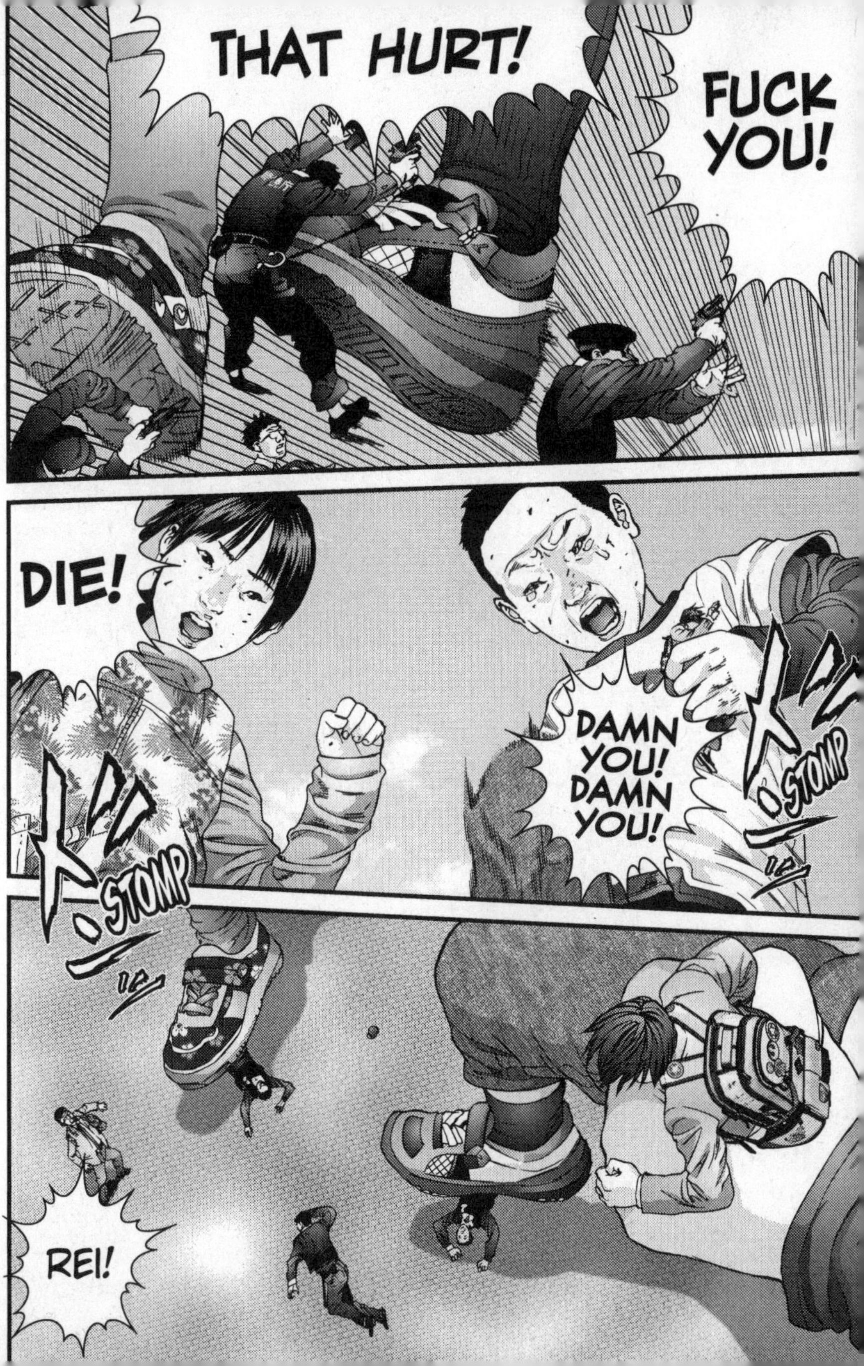
THAT HURT!
FUCK YOU!
DAMN YOU! DAMN YOU!
STOMP
DIE!
STOMP
REI!

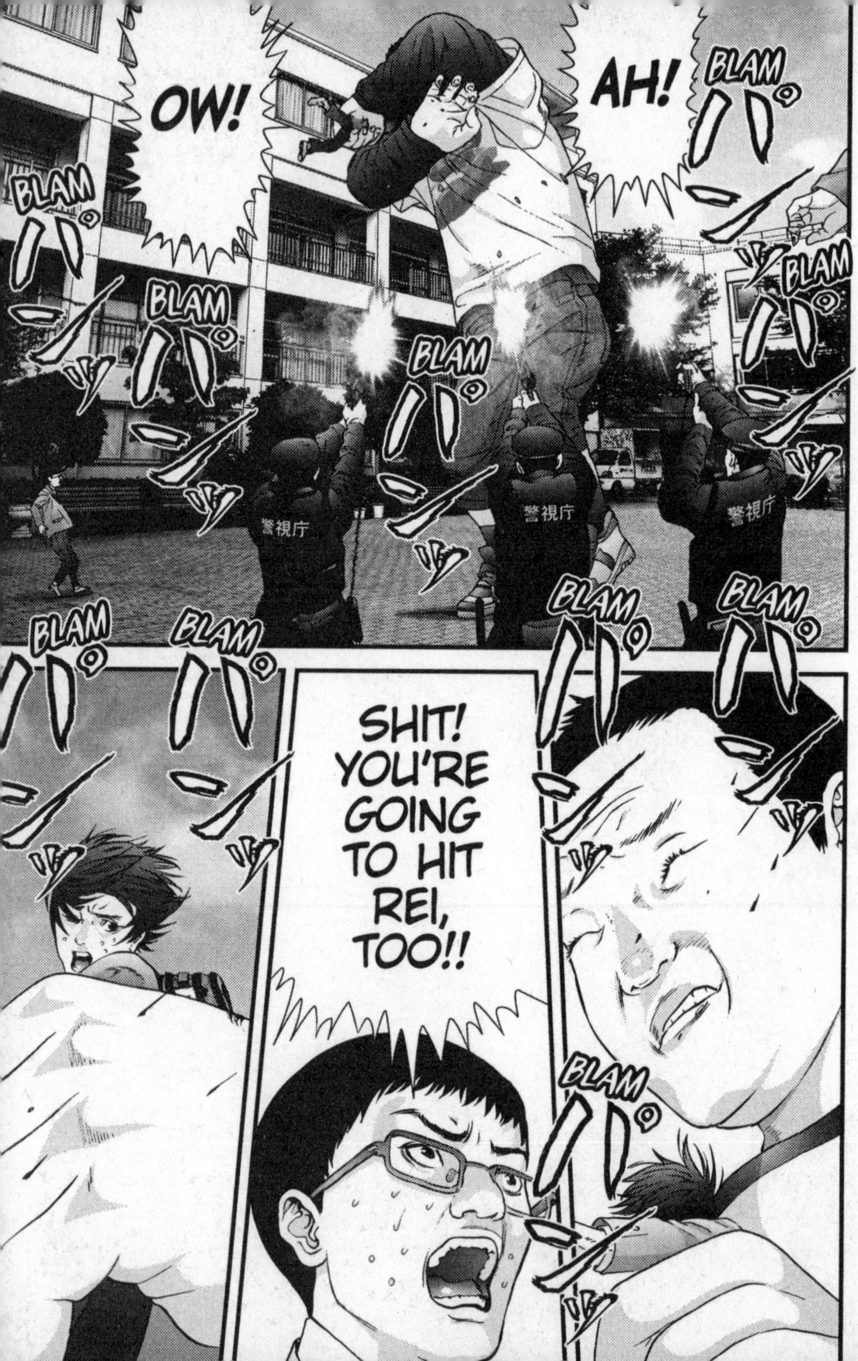
BLAM
AH!
OW!
BLAM
BLAM
BLAM
BLAM
警視庁
警視庁
警視庁
BLAM
BLAM
BLAM
SHIT! YOU'RE GOING TO HIT REI, TOO!!
BLAM
BLAM

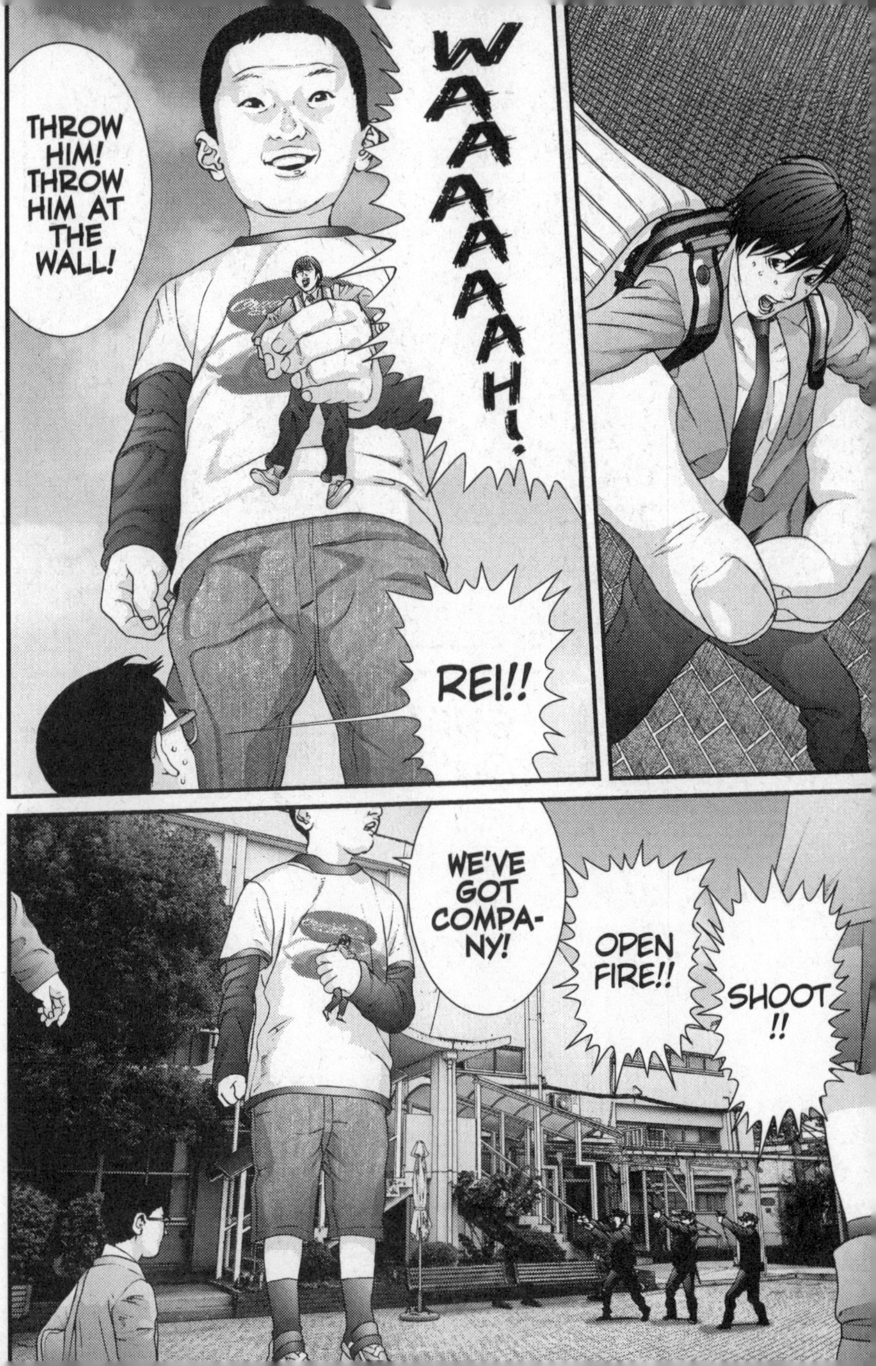
WAAAAAAH!
THROW HIM! THROW HIM AT THE WALL!
REI!!
SHOOT !!
OPEN FIRE!!
WE'VE GOT COMPA-NY!

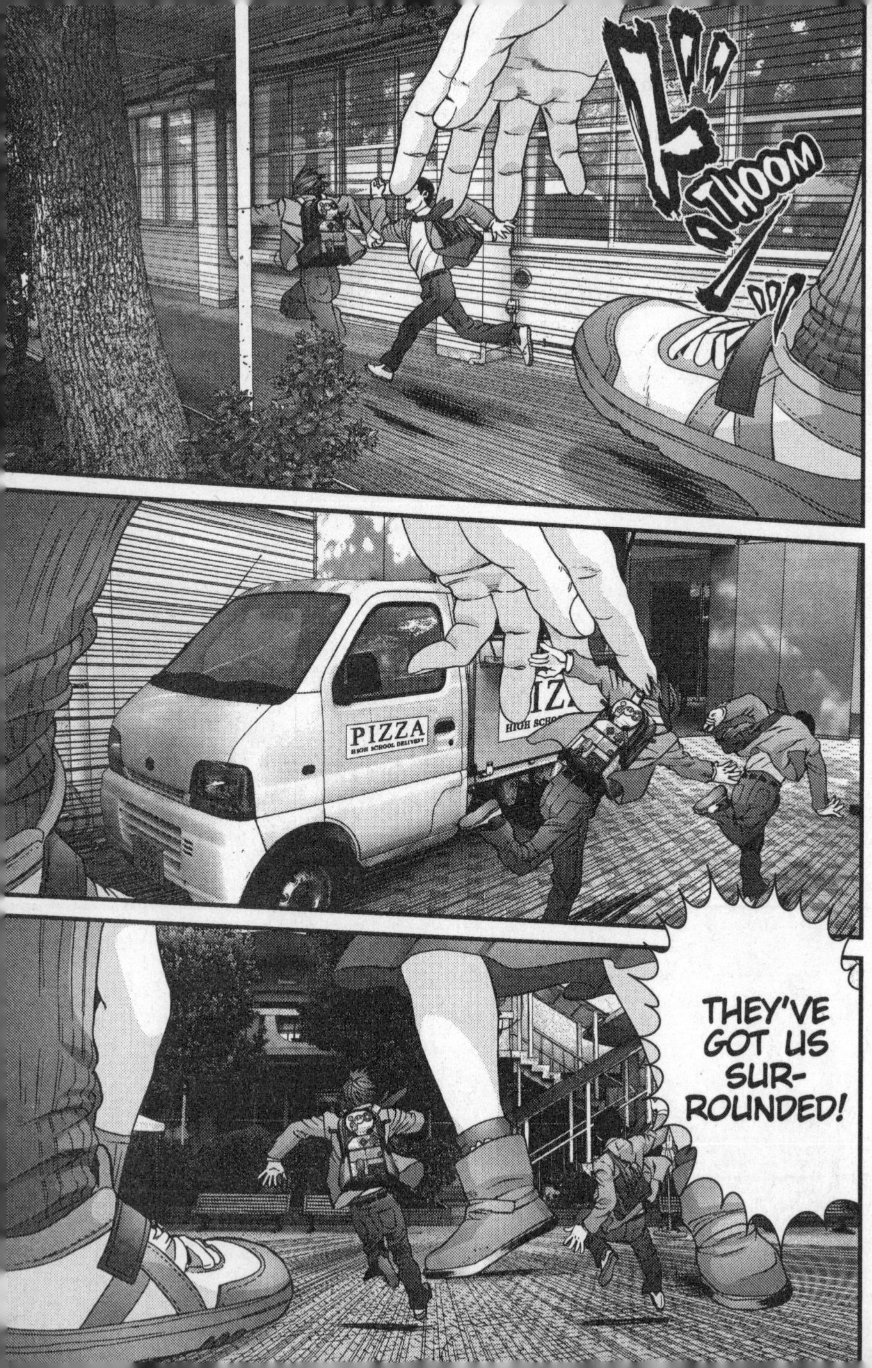
THOOM
PIZZA
HIGH SCHOOL DELIVERY
THEY'VE GOT US SUR-ROUNDED!

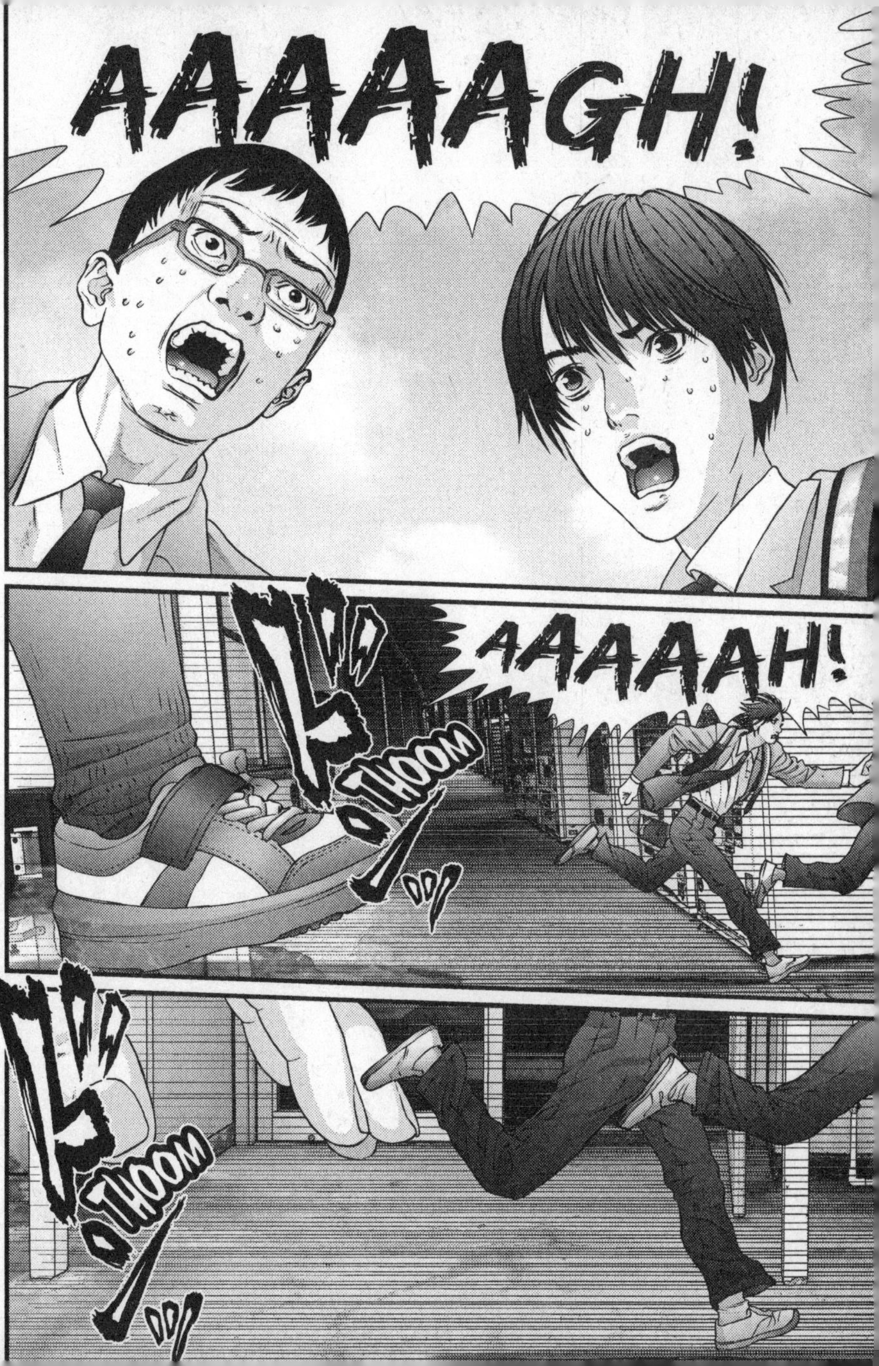
AAAAAGH!
AAAAAH!
THOOM
THOOM

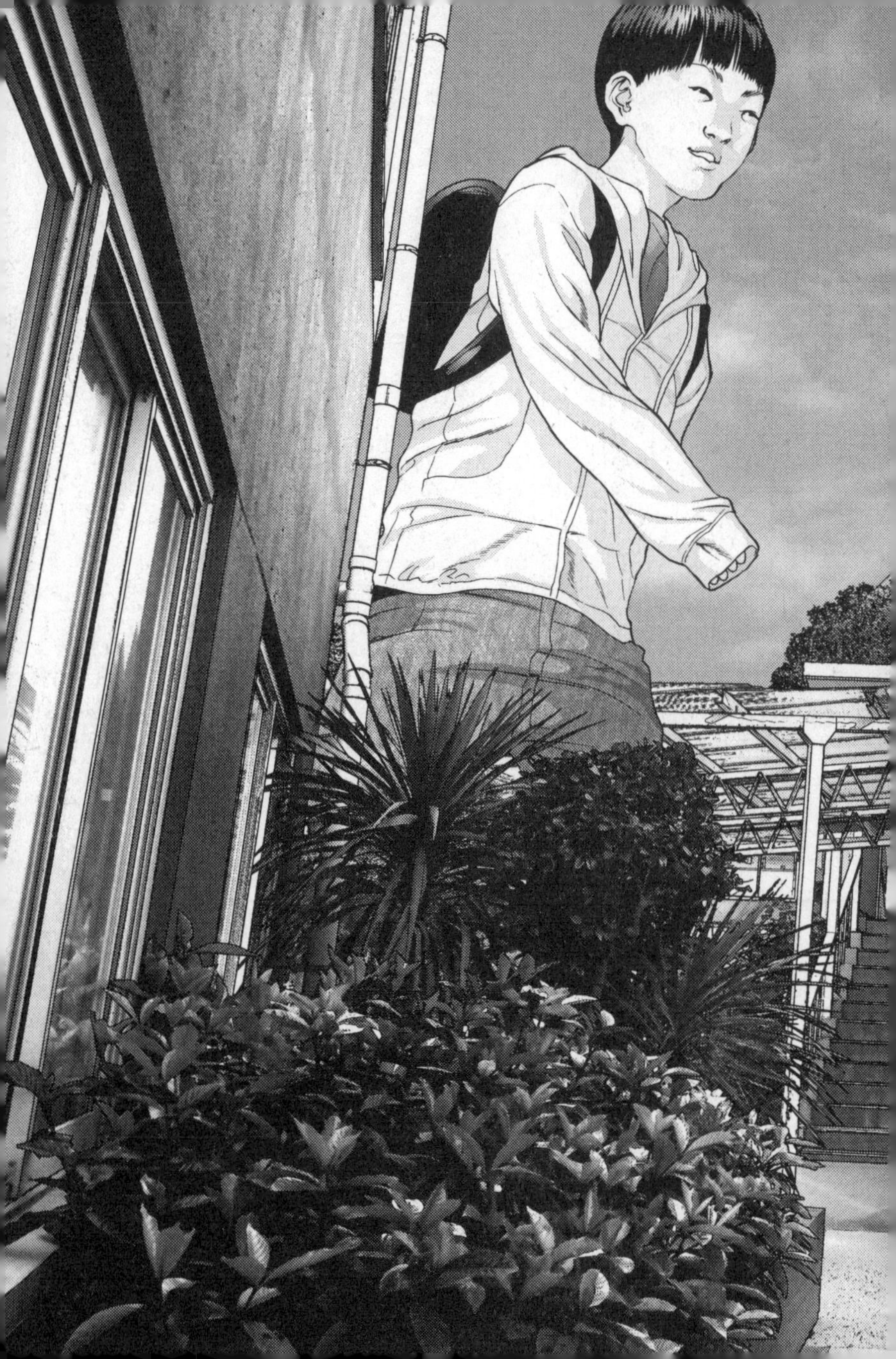

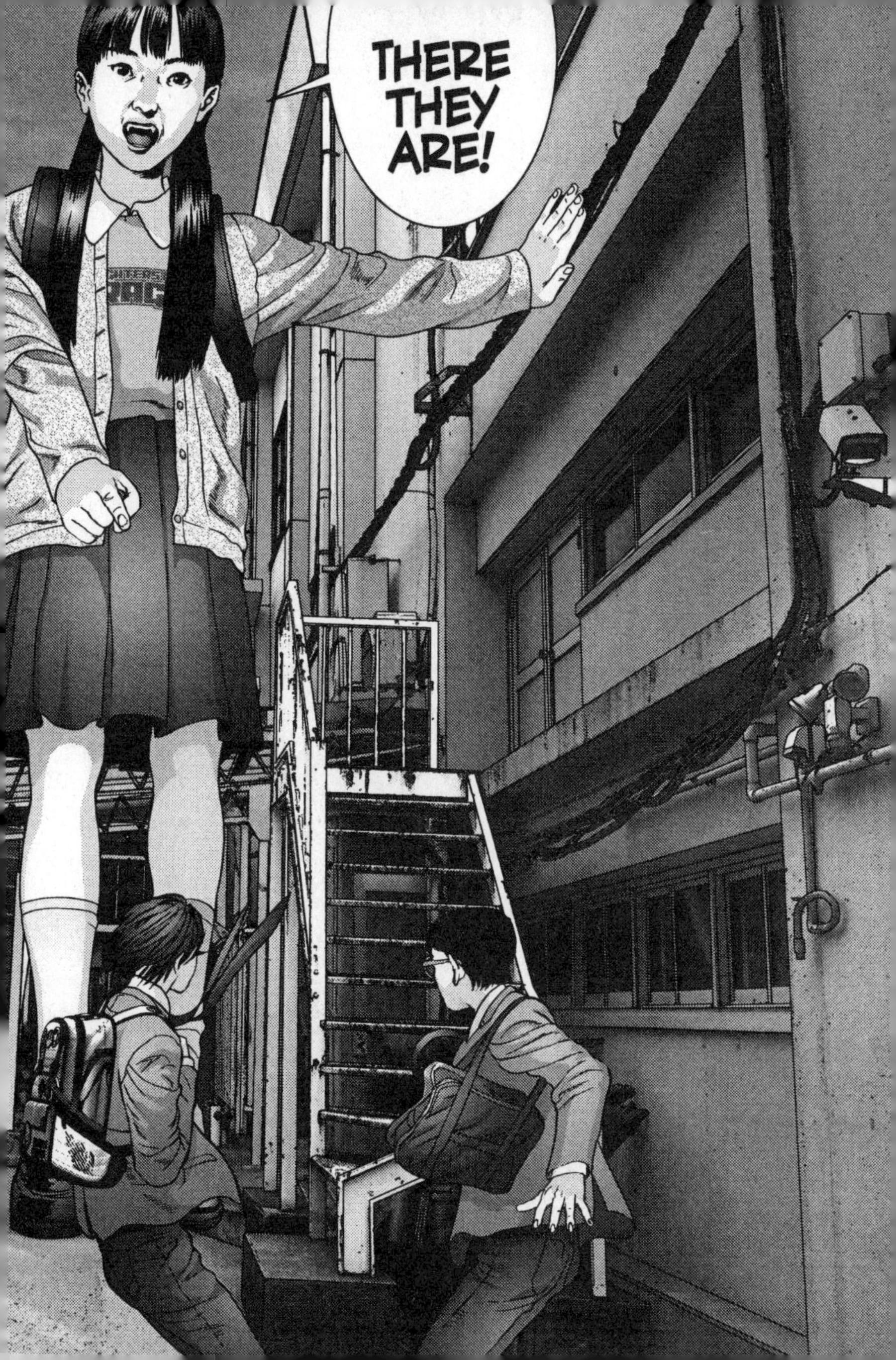
THERE THEY ARE!

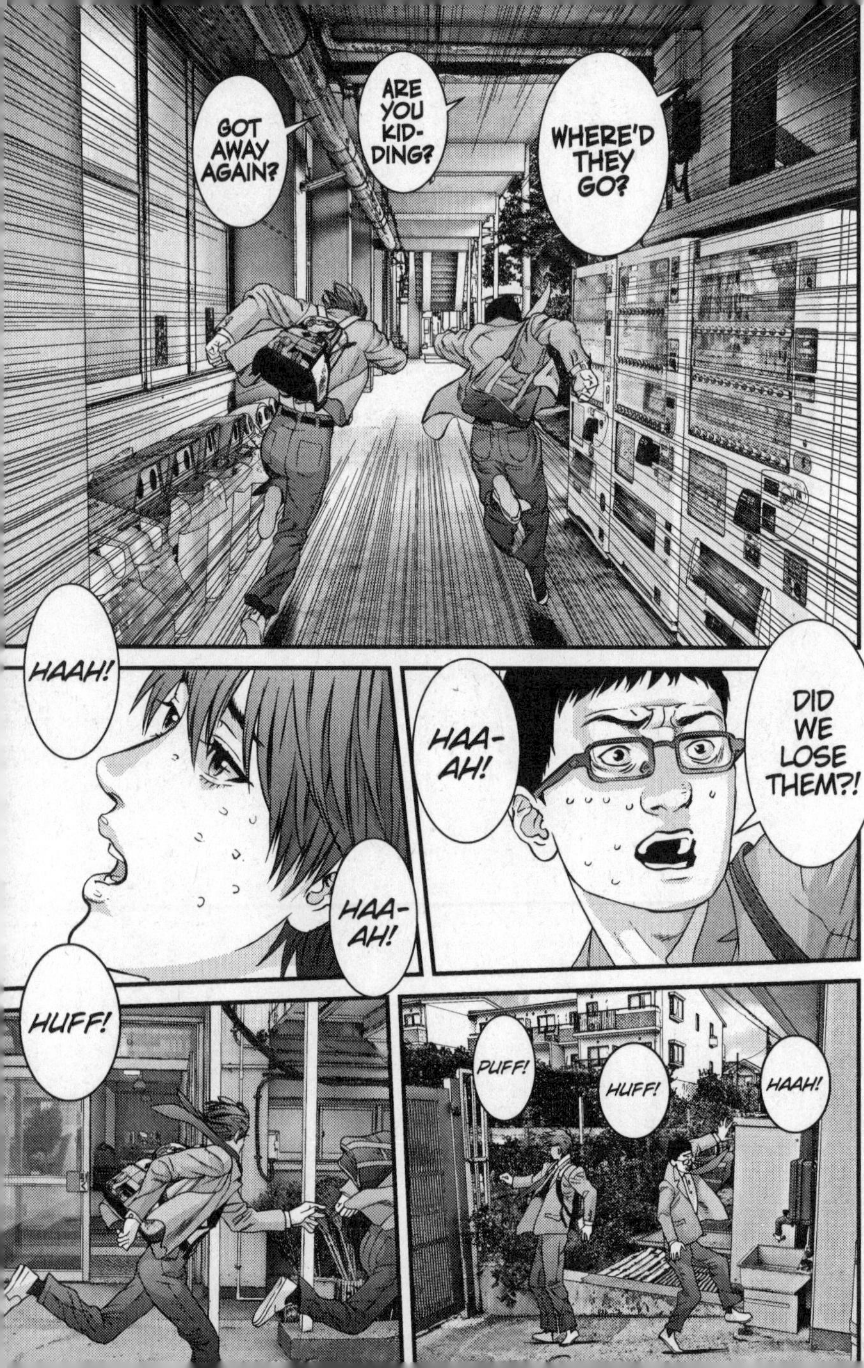
WHERE'D THEY GO?
ARE YOU KID-DING?
GOT AWAY AGAIN?
DID WE LOSE THEM?!
HAA-AH!
HAAH!
HAA-AH!
HAAH!
HUFF!
PUFF!
HUFF!

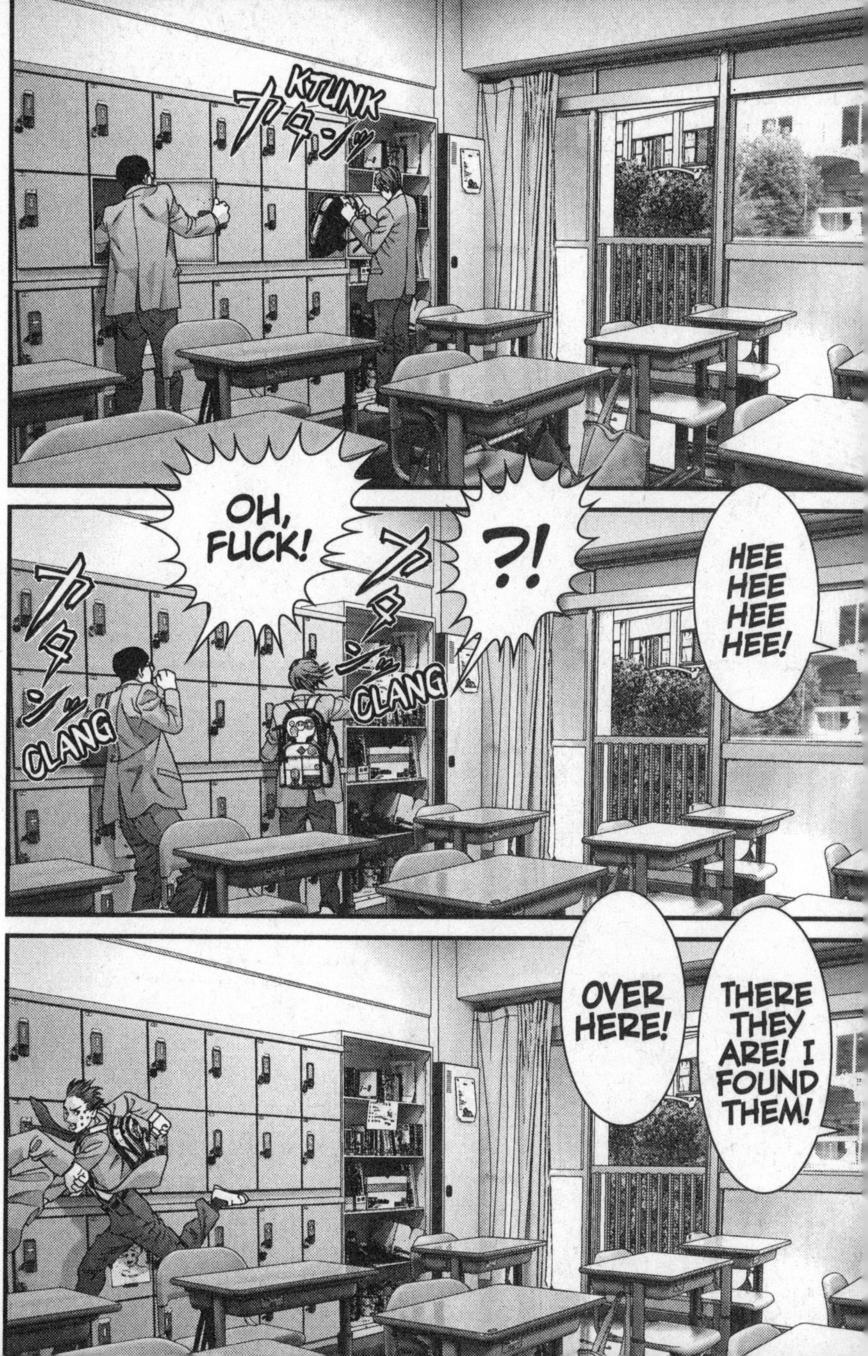
KTUNK
カタンッ
HEE HEE HEE HEE!
?!
OH, FUCK!
カタンッ
CLANG
カタンッ
CLANG
THERE THEY ARE! I FOUND THEM!
OVER HERE!

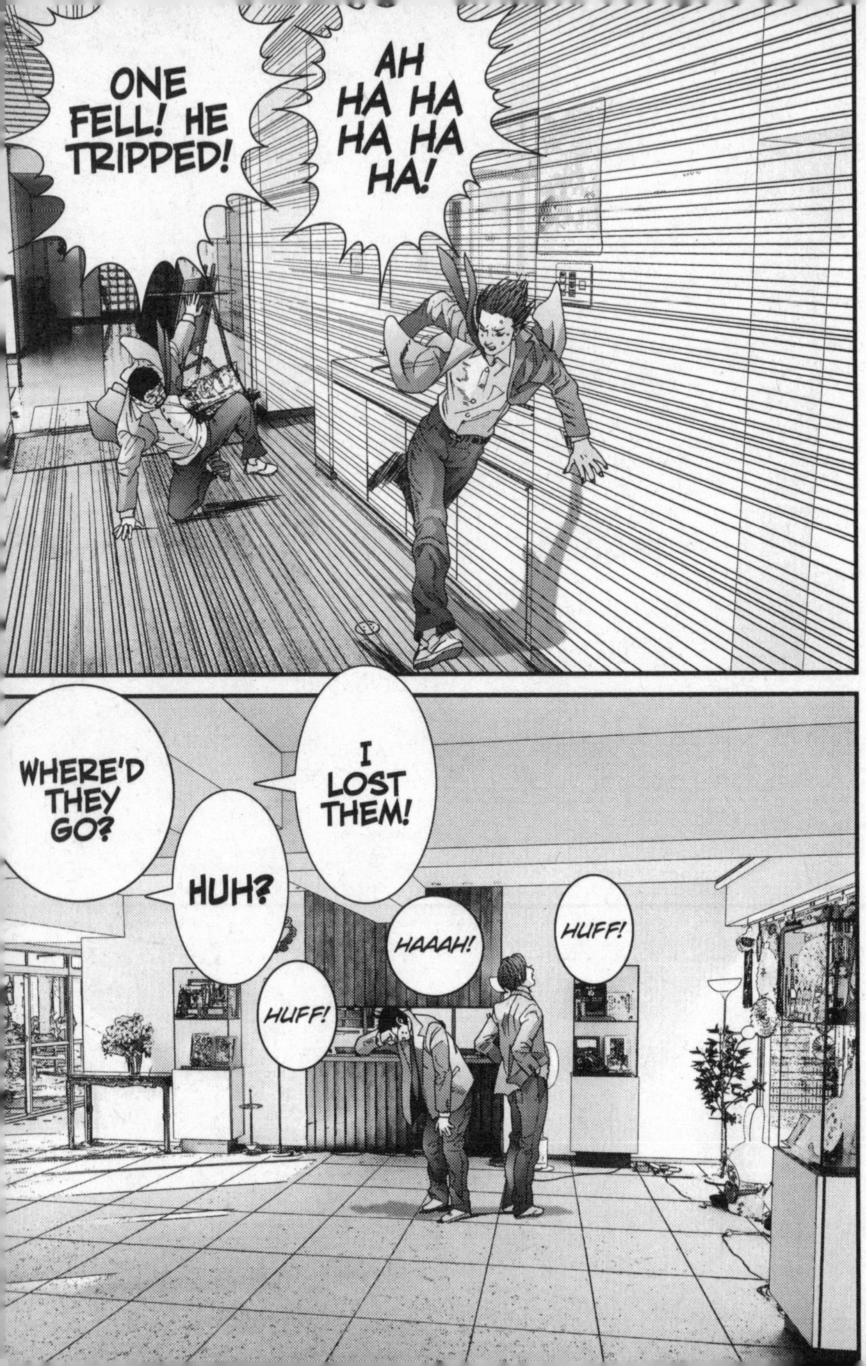
AH HA HA HA HA HA!
ONE FELL! HE TRIPPED!
I LOST THEM!
WHERE'D THEY GO?
HUFF!
HAAAH!
HUH?
HUFF!

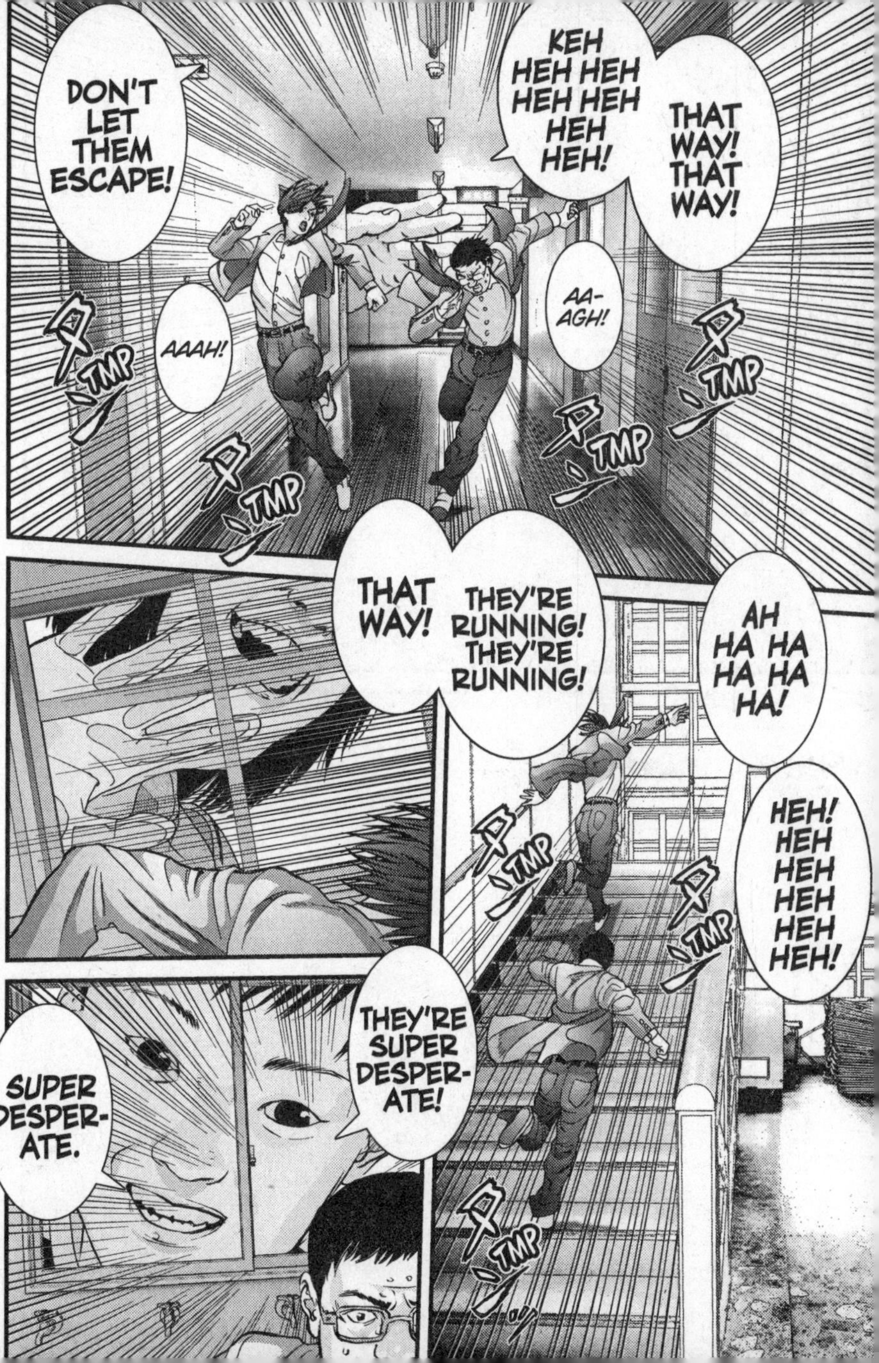
KEH HEH HEH HEH HEH HEH HEH!
THAT WAY! THAT WAY!
DON'T LET THEM ESCAPE!
AA-AGH!
TMP
TMP
AAAH!
TMP
TMP
AH HA HA HA HA HA!
THEY'RE RUNNING! THEY'RE RUNNING!
THAT WAY!
HEH! HEH HEH HEH HEH HEH!
TMP
TMP
TMP
THEY'RE SUPER DESPERATE!
SUPER DESPERATE.

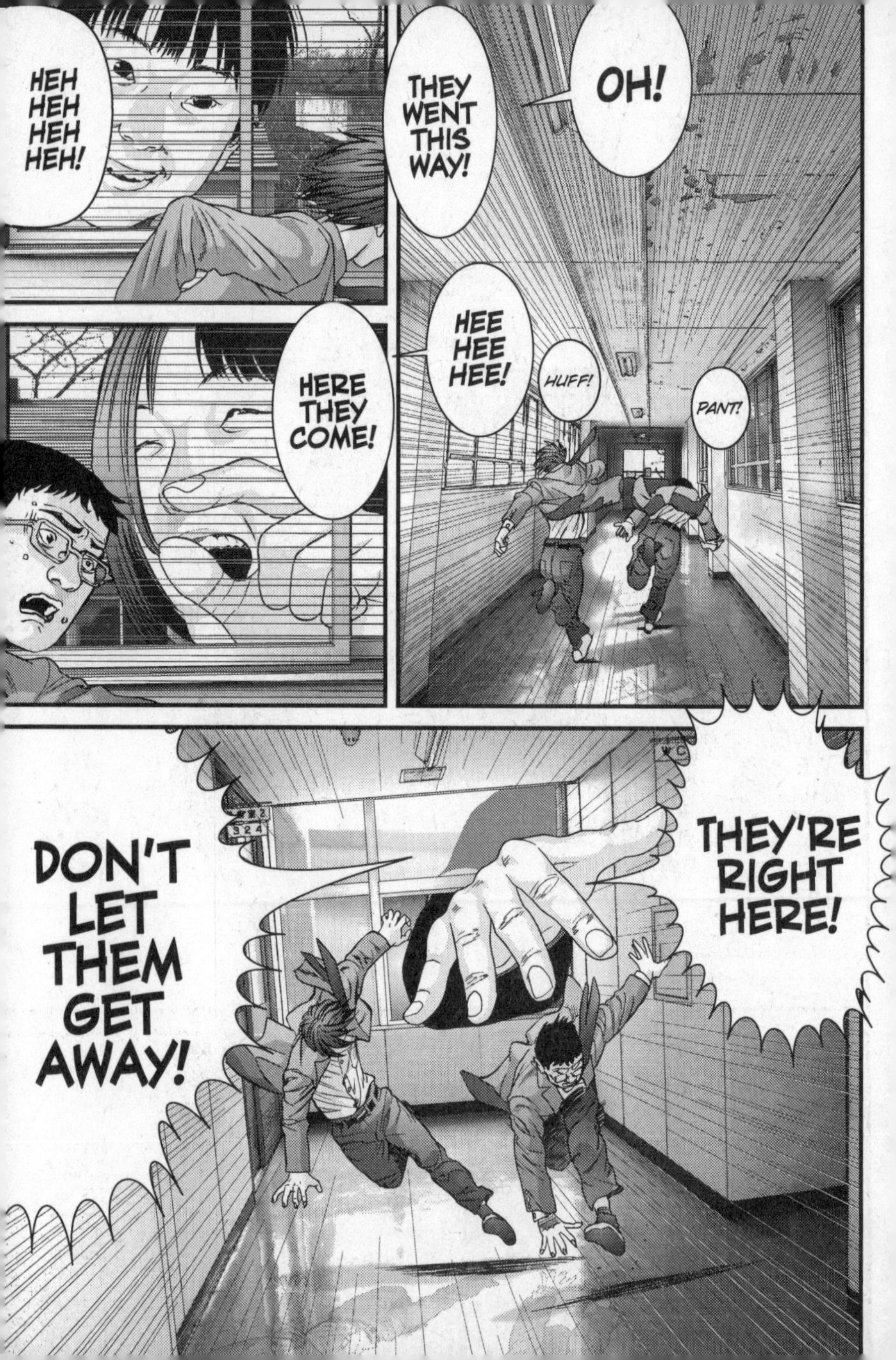

OH!
THEY WENT THIS WAY!
HEE HEE HEE!
PANT!
HUFF!
HEH HEH HEH HEH!
HERE THEY COME!
THEY'RE RIGHT HERE!
DON'T LET THEM GET AWAY!

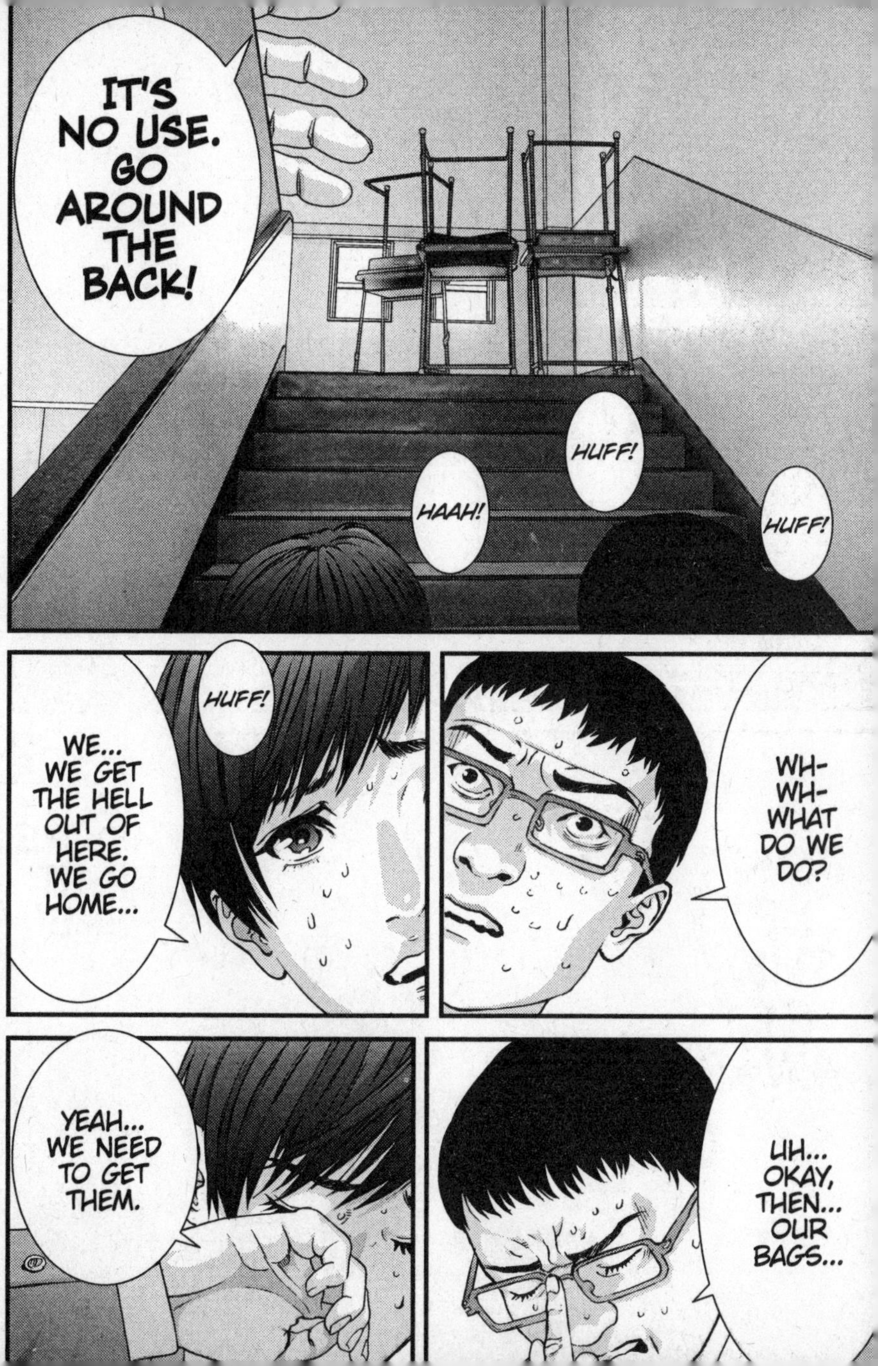
IT'S NO USE. GO AROUND THE BACK!
HUFF!
HUFF!
HAAH!
WH- WH- WHAT DO WE DO?
HUFF!
WE... WE GET THE HELL OUT OF HERE. WE GO HOME...
UH... OKAY, THEN... OUR BAGS...
YEAH... WE NEED TO GET THEM.

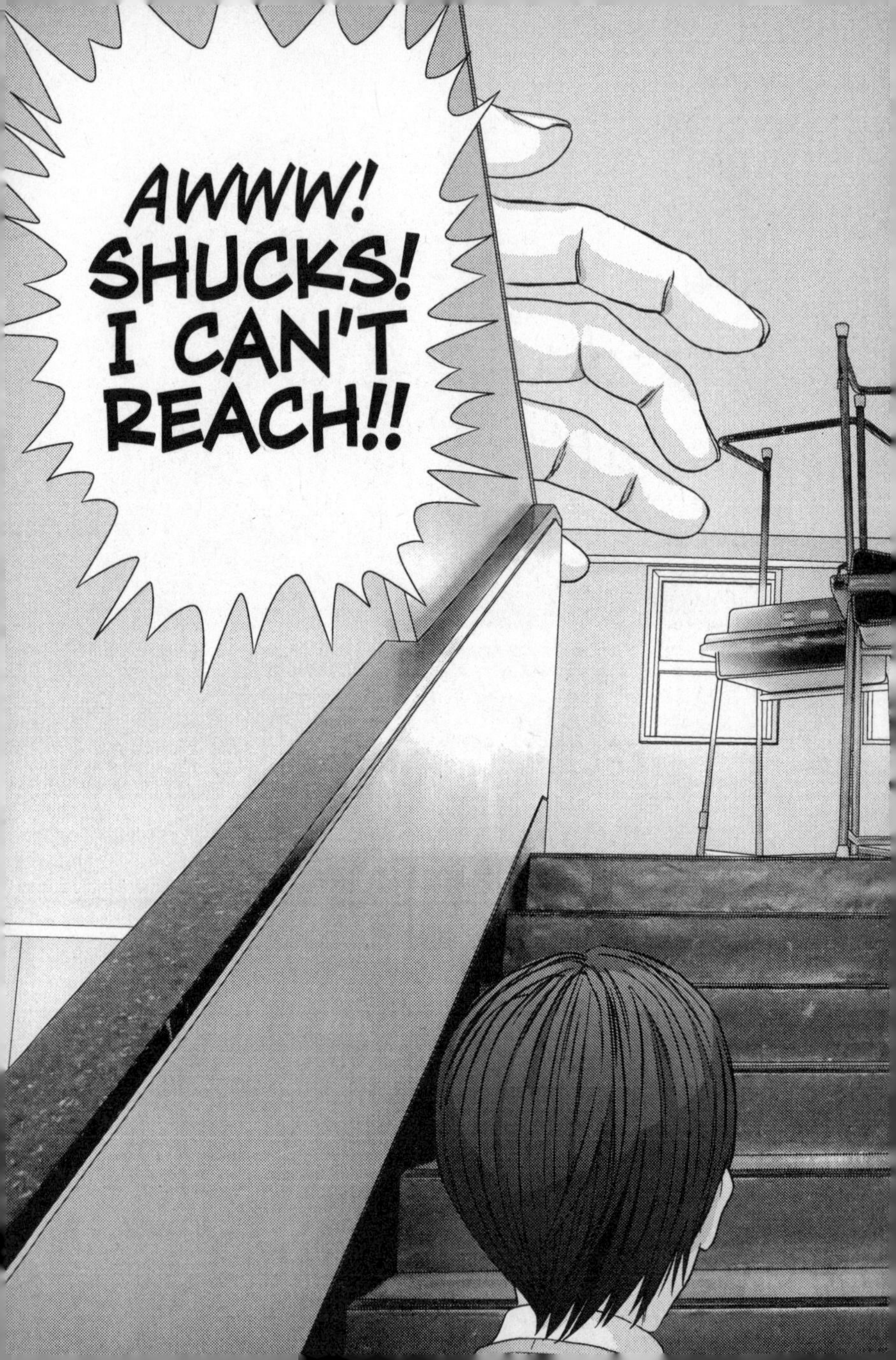
AWWW! SHUCKS! I CAN'T REACH!!

EPISODE 27: SUPER DESPERATE

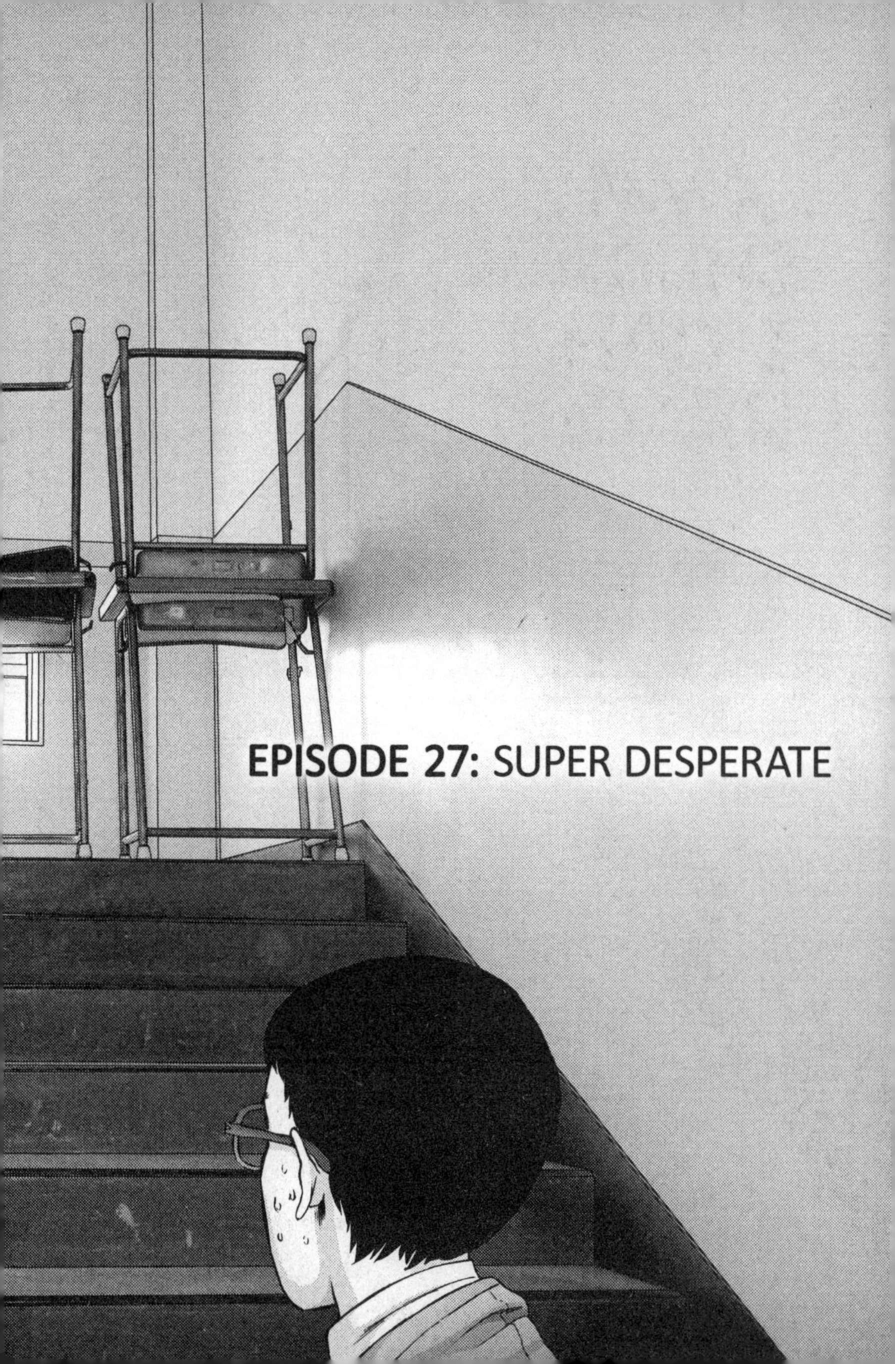

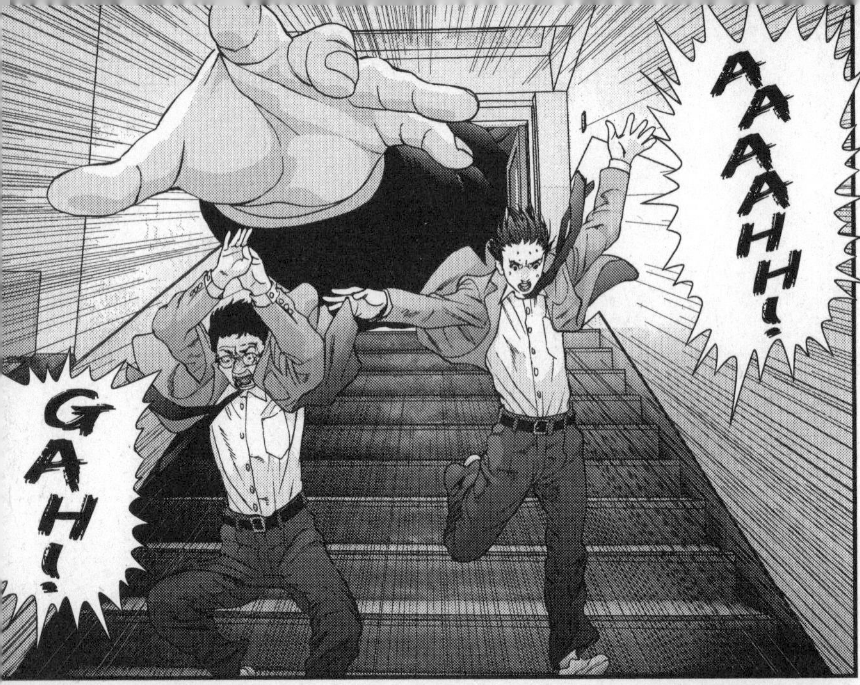
AAAAHH!
GAH!
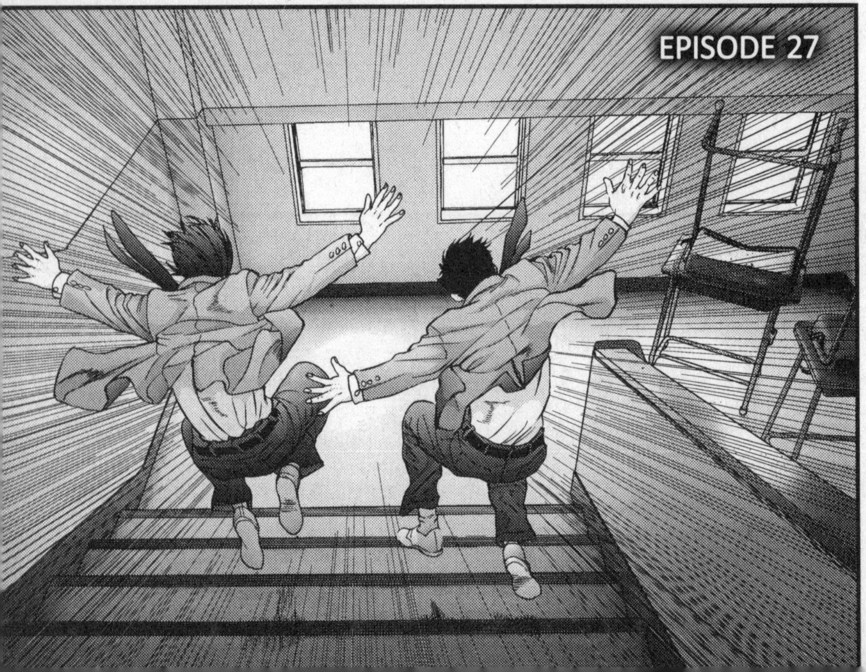
EPISODE 27

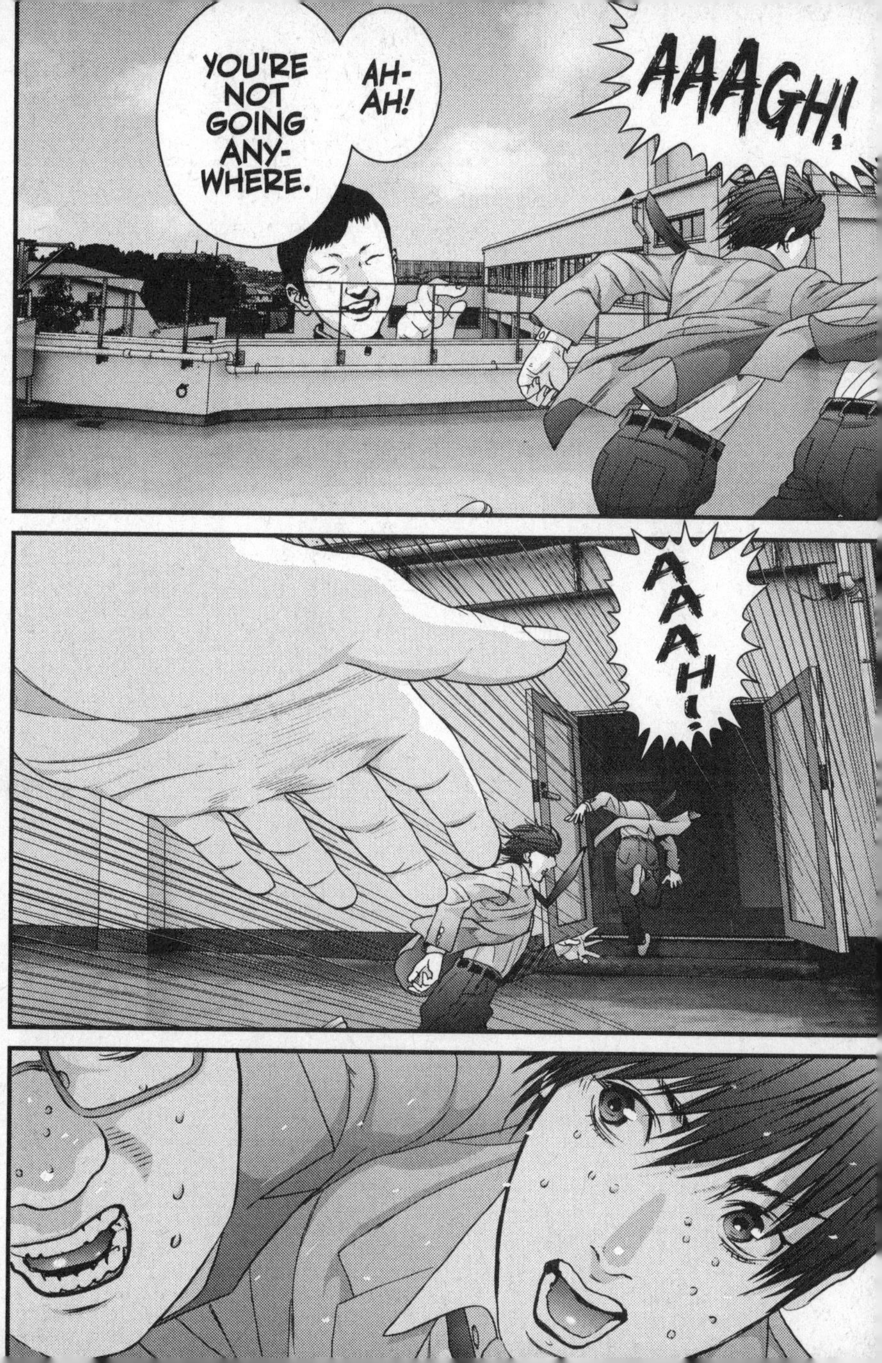
AAAGH!
AH-AH!
YOU'RE NOT GOING ANY-WHERE.
AAAH!

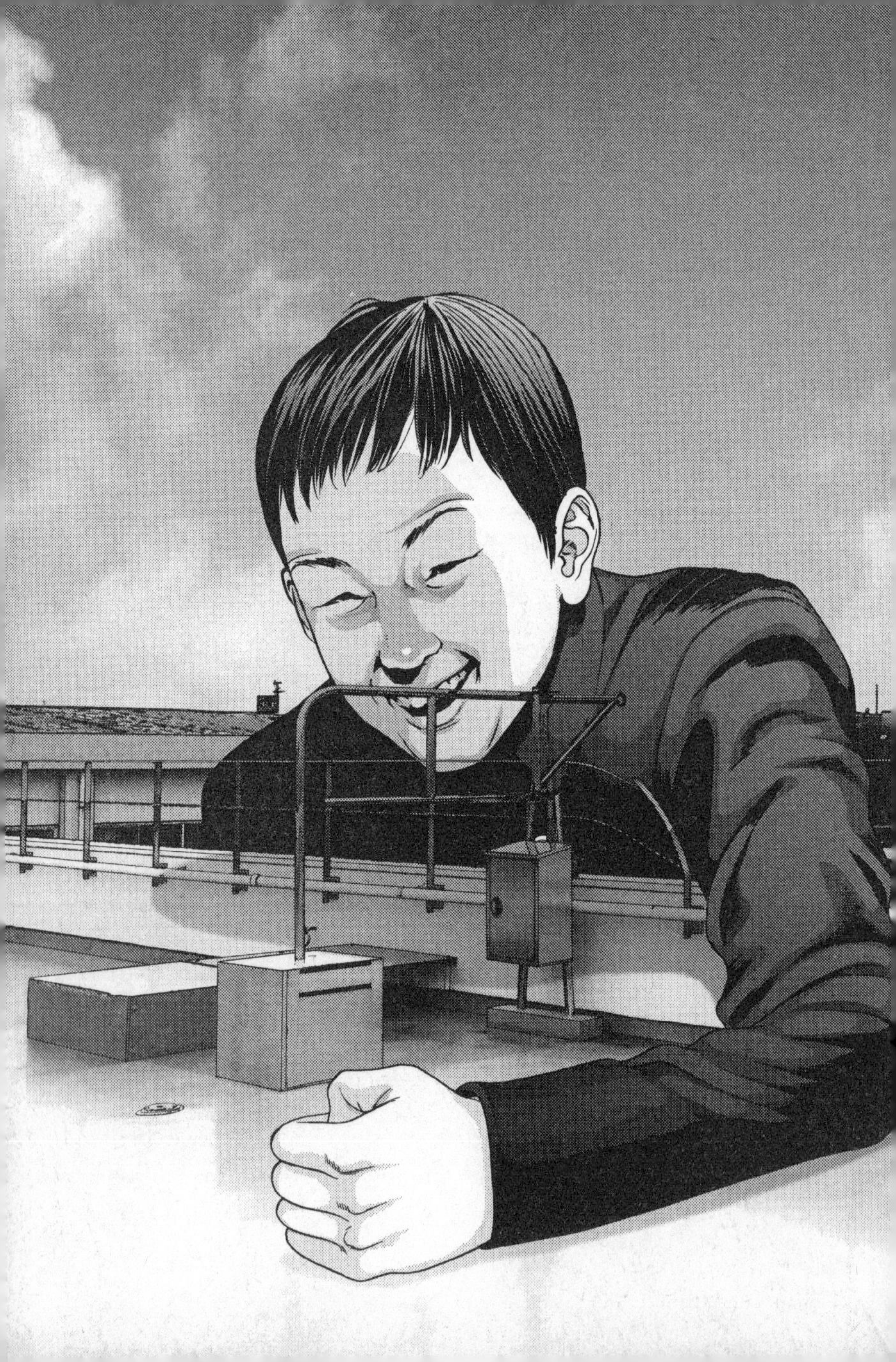

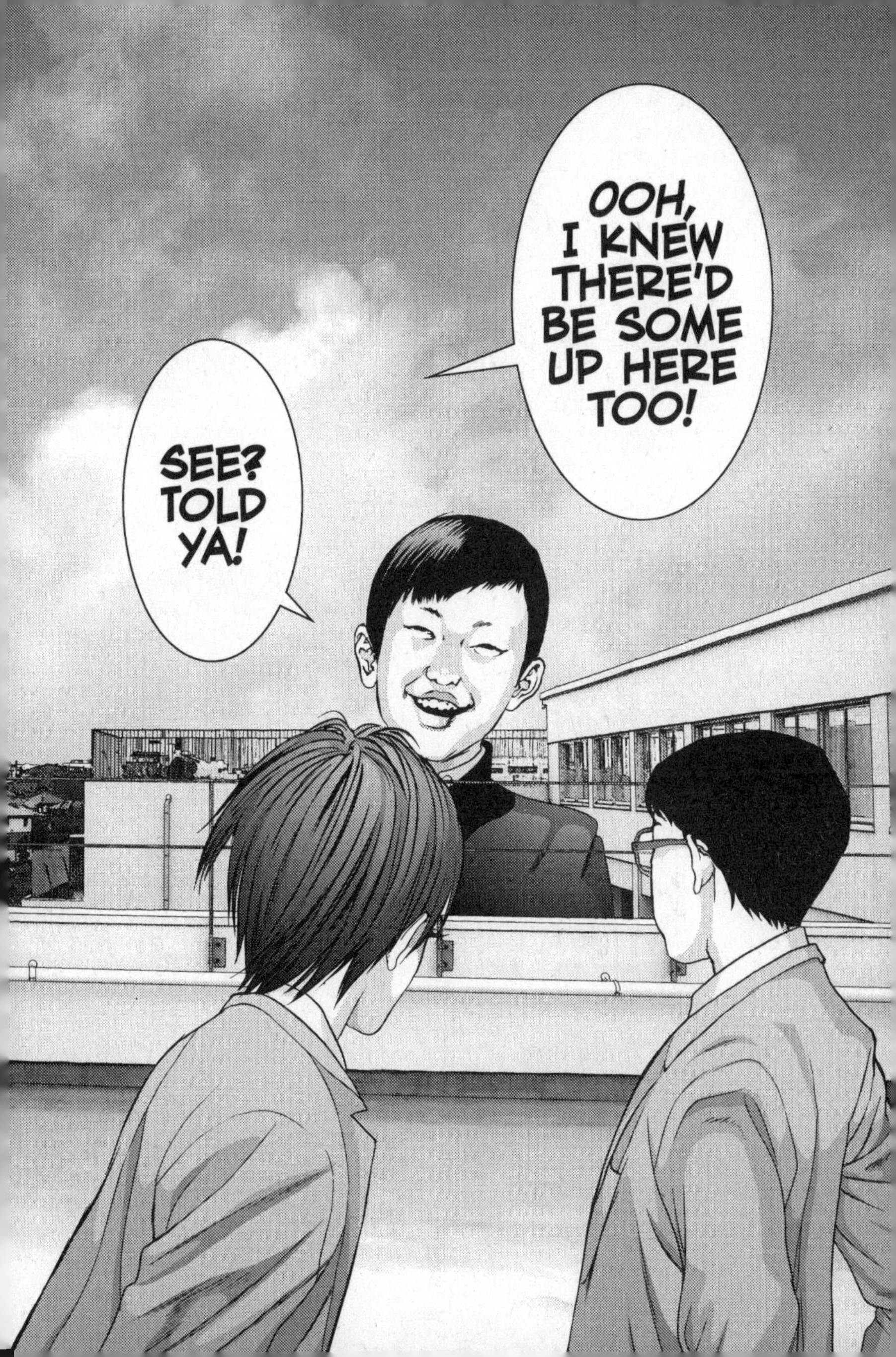
OOH, I KNEW THERE'D BE SOME UP HERE TOO!
SEE? TOLD YA!

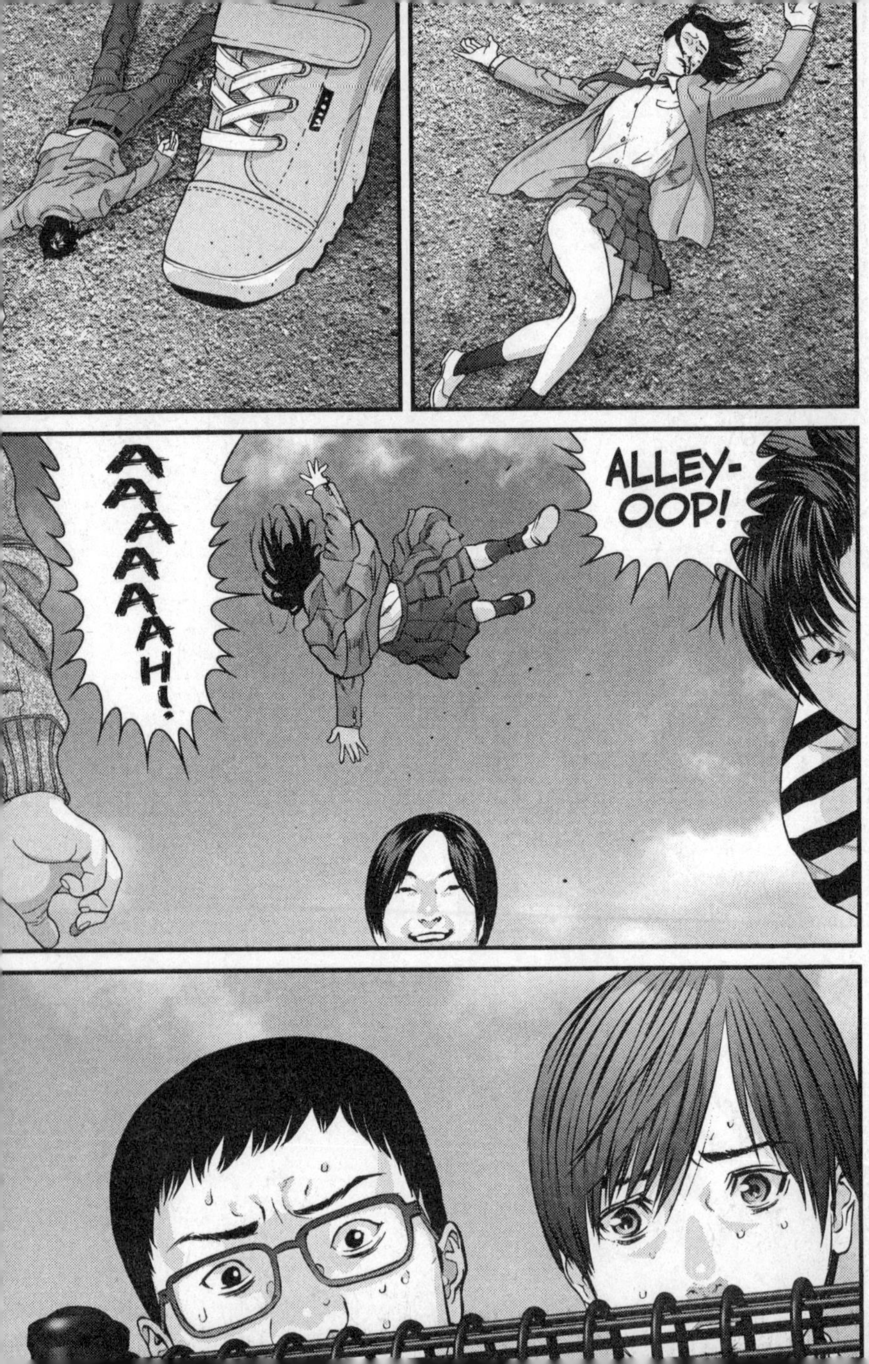
ALLEY-OOP!
AAAAAAH!

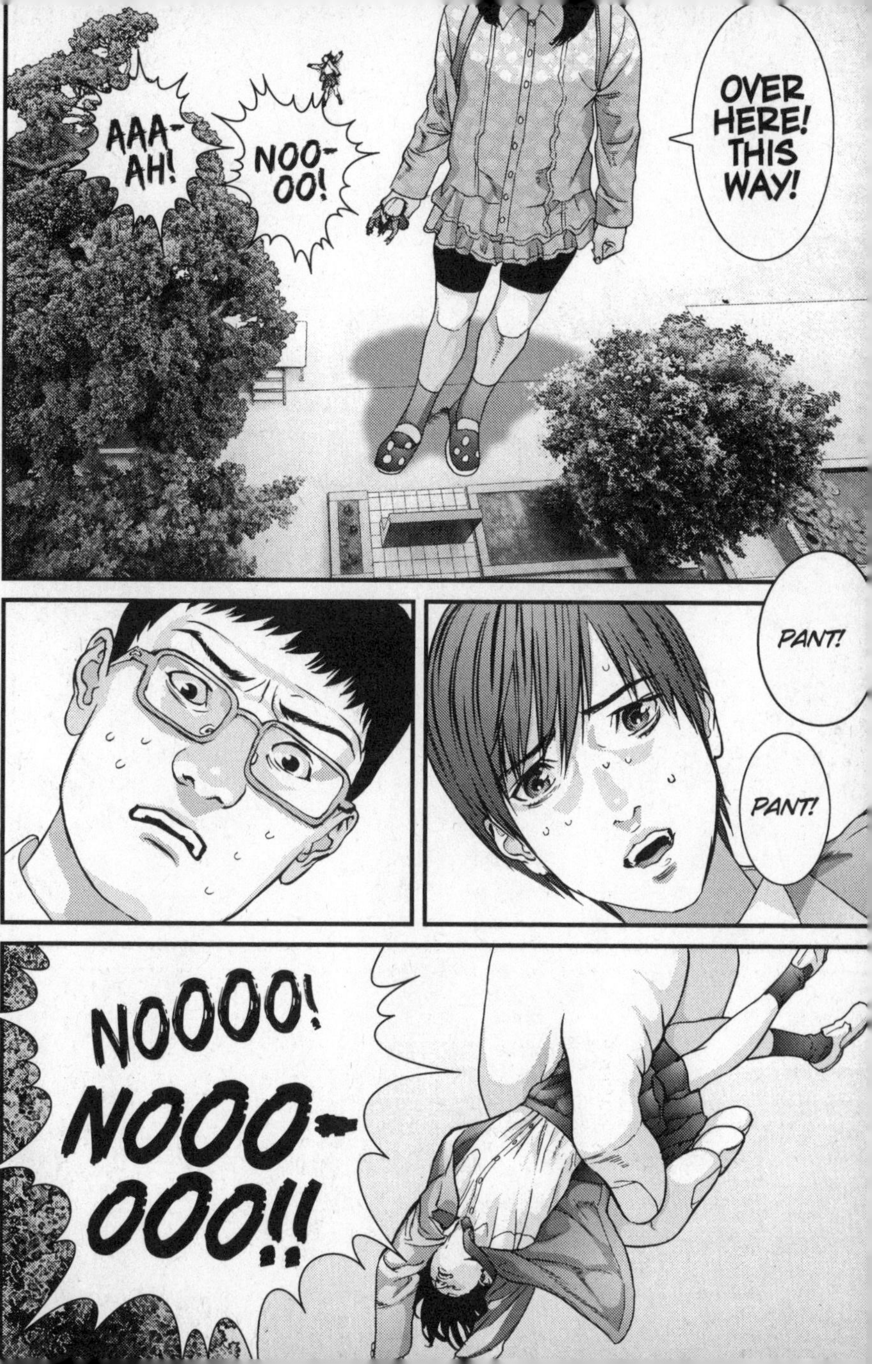
OVER HERE! THIS WAY!
NOO-OO!
AAA-AH!
PANT!
PANT!
NOOOO! NOOOO-OOO!!

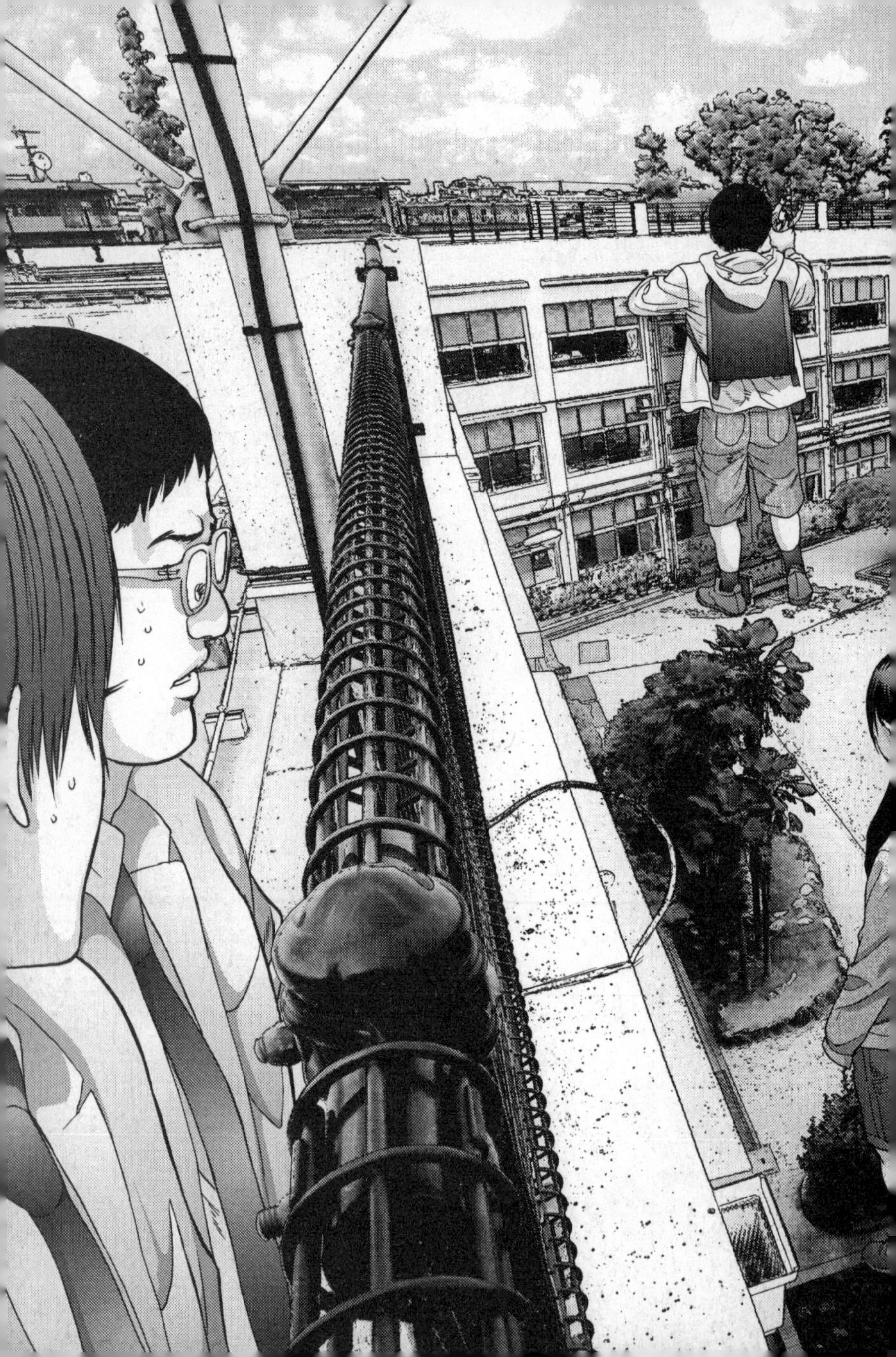

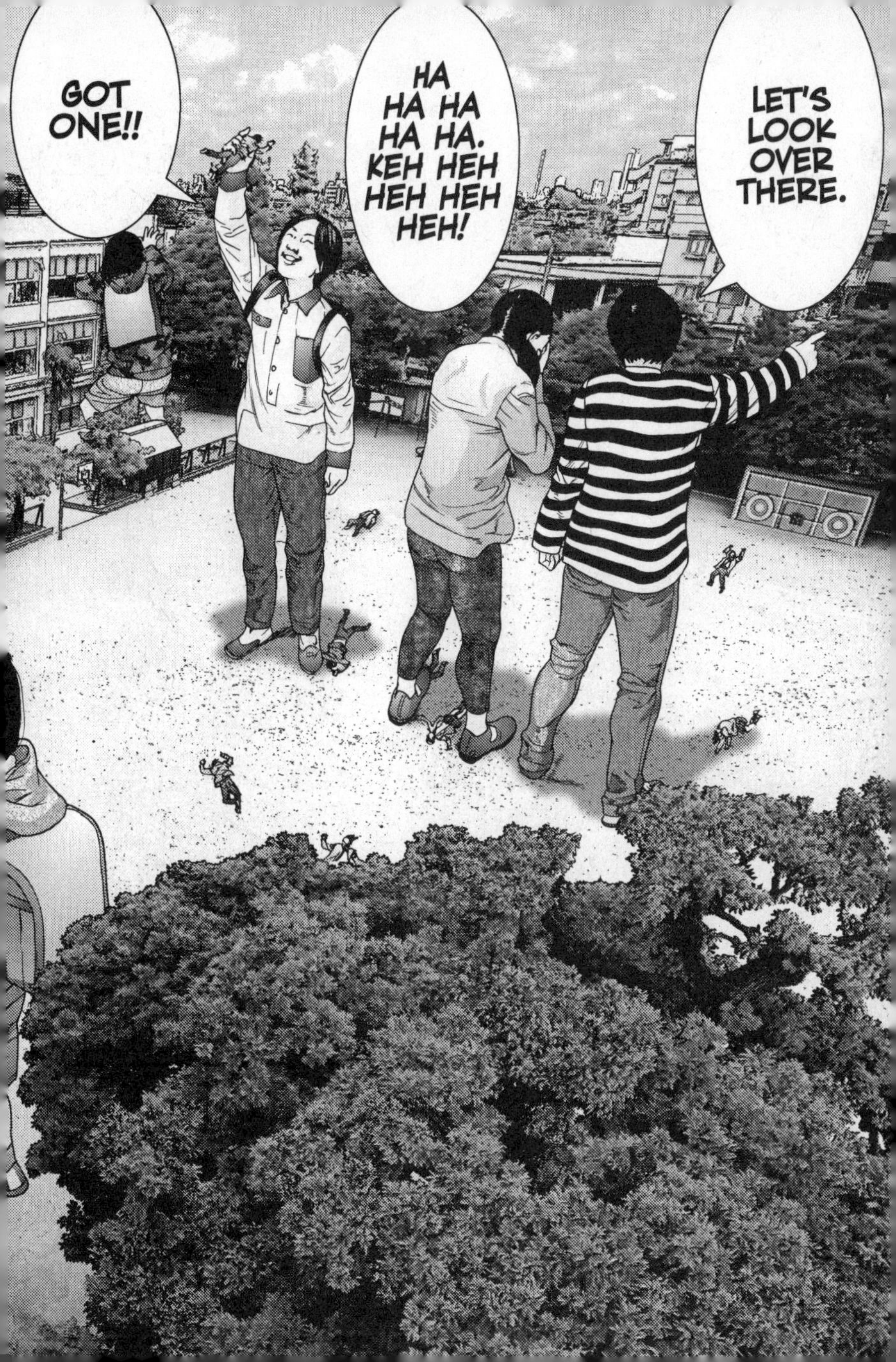
LET'S LOOK OVER THERE.
HA HA HA HA HA. KEH HEH HEH HEH HEH!
GOT ONE!!

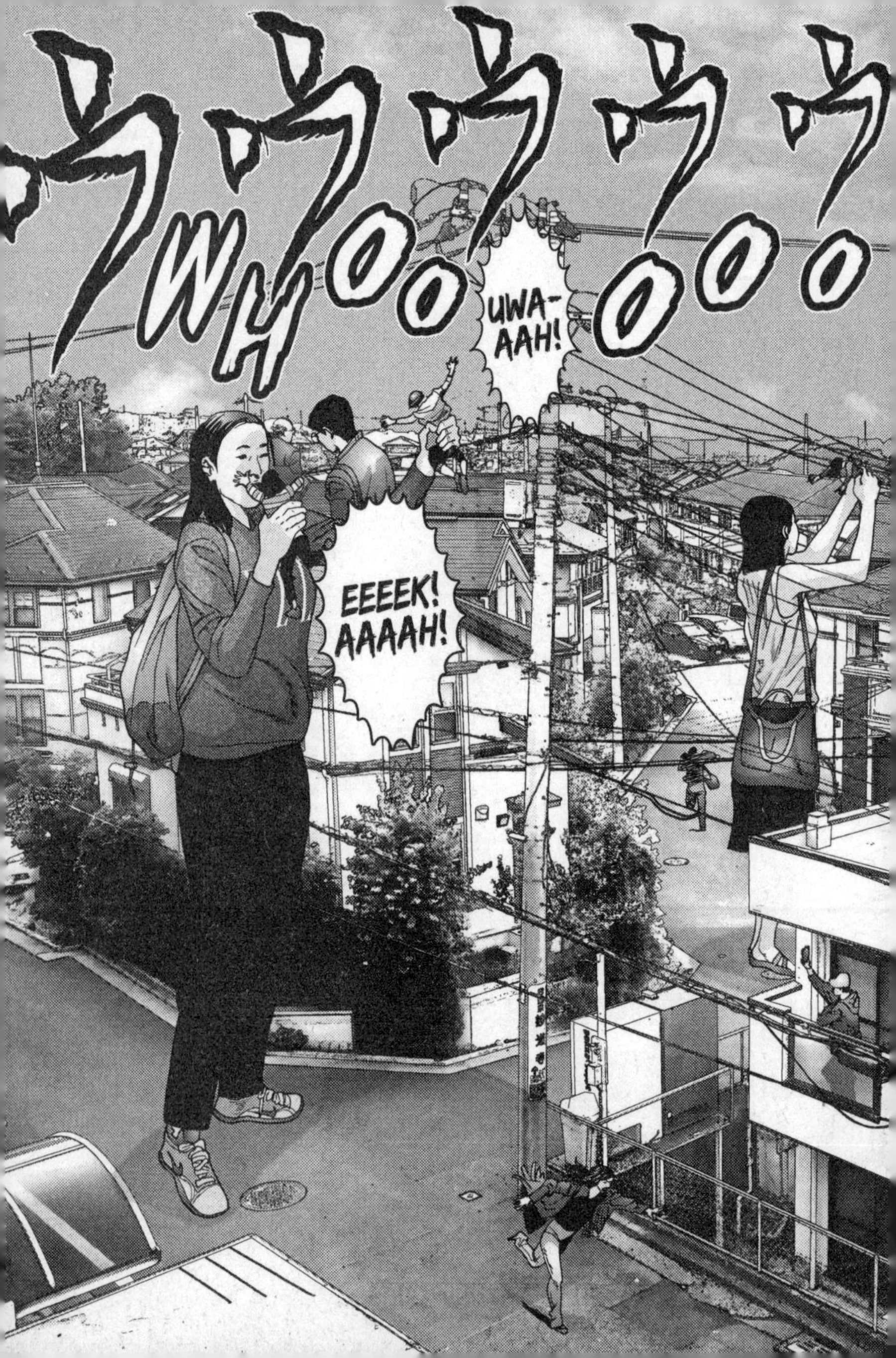
ウウウウウ
WHOOOOOO
UWA-AAH!
EEEEK! AAAAH!

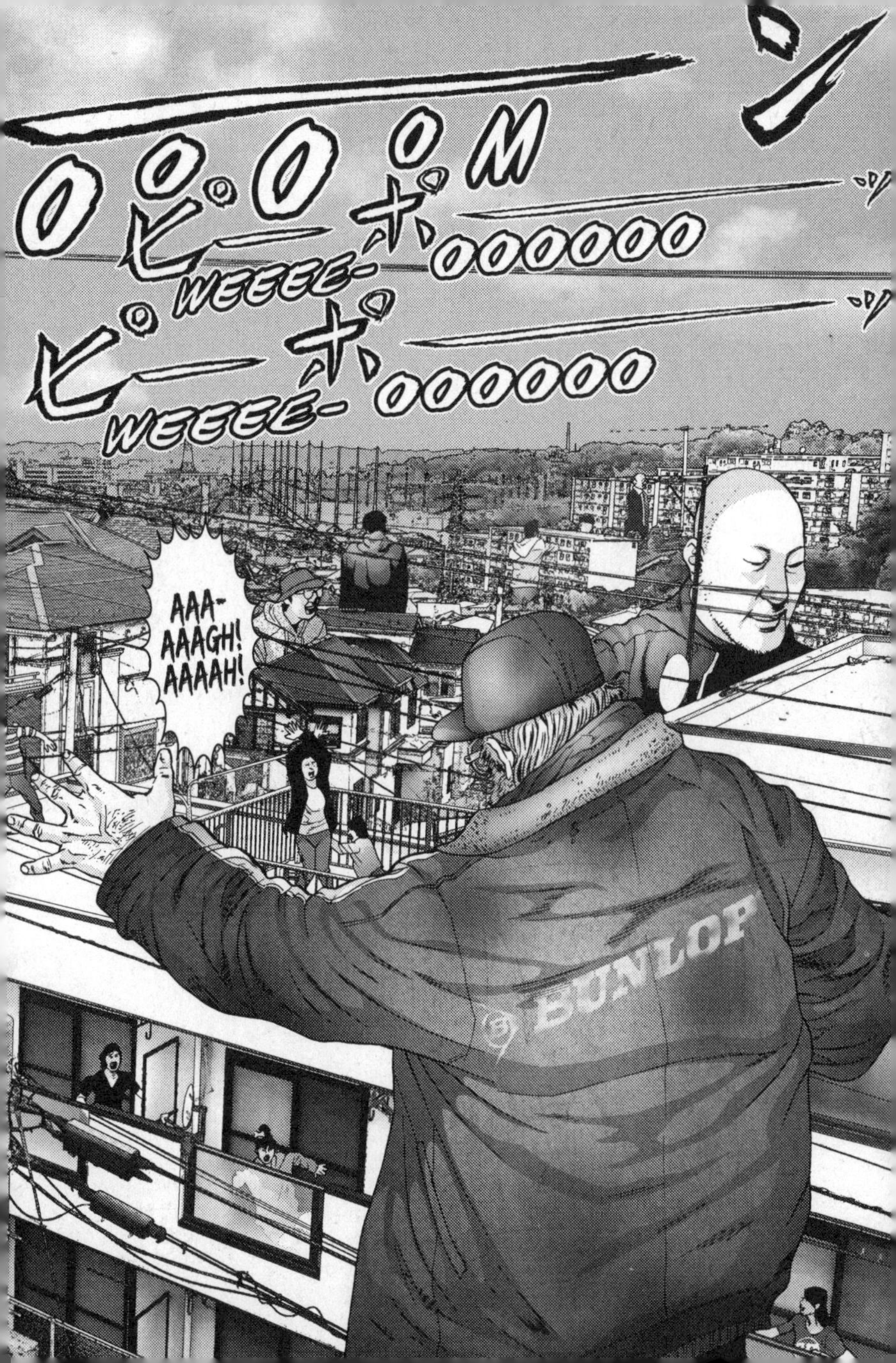
ン
OOOOM
ピーポー
WEEEE-OOOOOO
ピーポー
WEEEE-OOOOOO
AAA-AAAGH! AAAAH!
DUNLOP

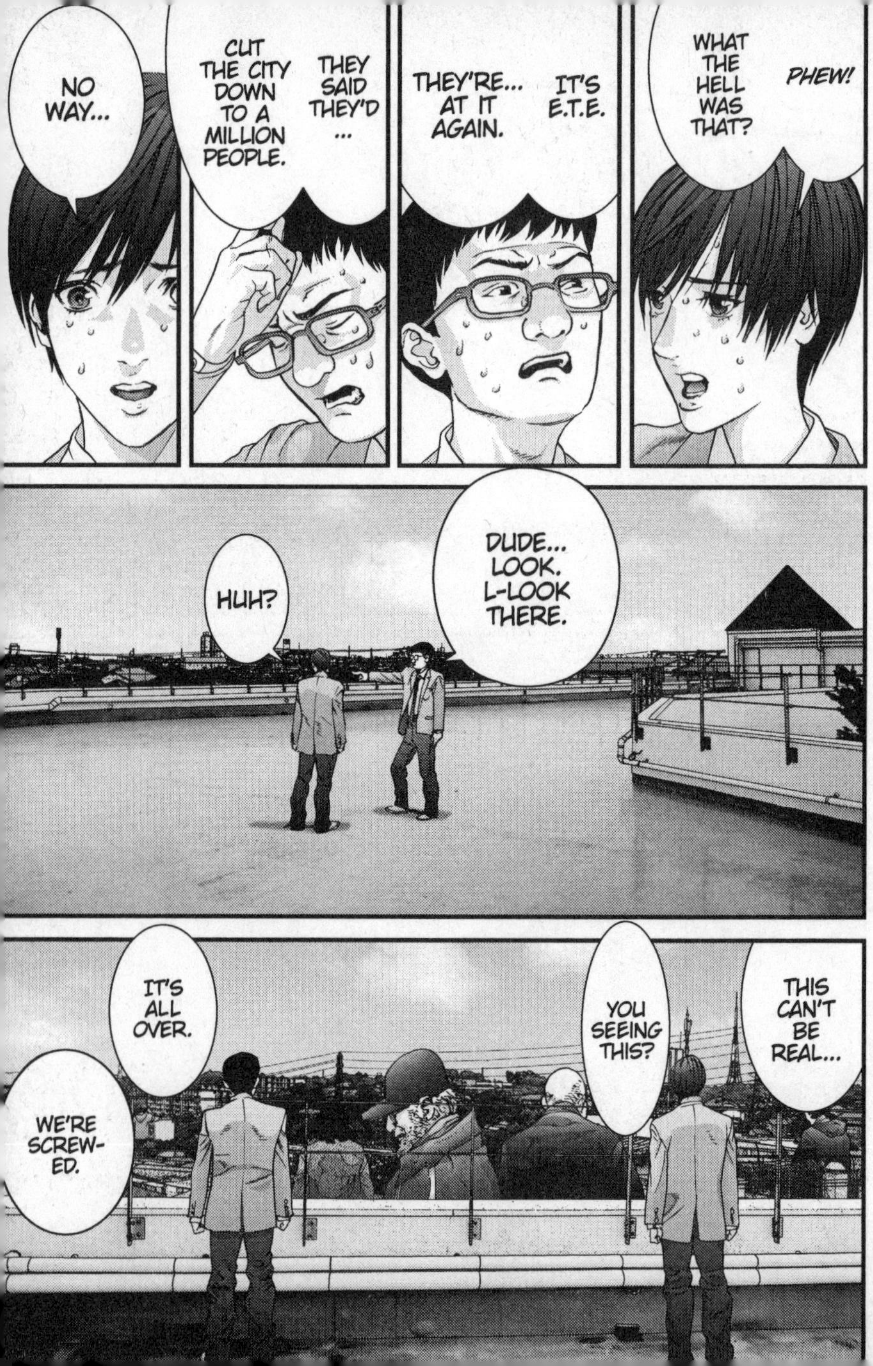
PHEW!
WHAT THE HELL WAS THAT?
IT'S E.T.E.
THEY'RE... AT IT AGAIN.
THEY SAID THEY'D ...
CUT THE CITY DOWN TO A MILLION PEOPLE.
NO WAY...
DUDE... LOOK. L-LOOK THERE.
HUH?
THIS CAN'T BE REAL...
YOU SEEING THIS?
IT'S ALL OVER.
WE'RE SCREW-ED.

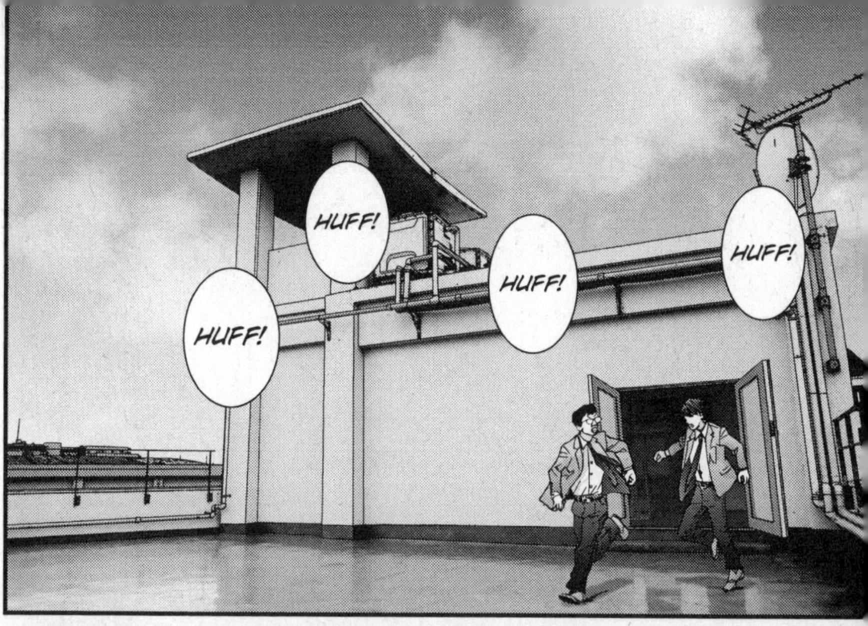
HUFF!
HUFF!
HUFF!
HUFF!

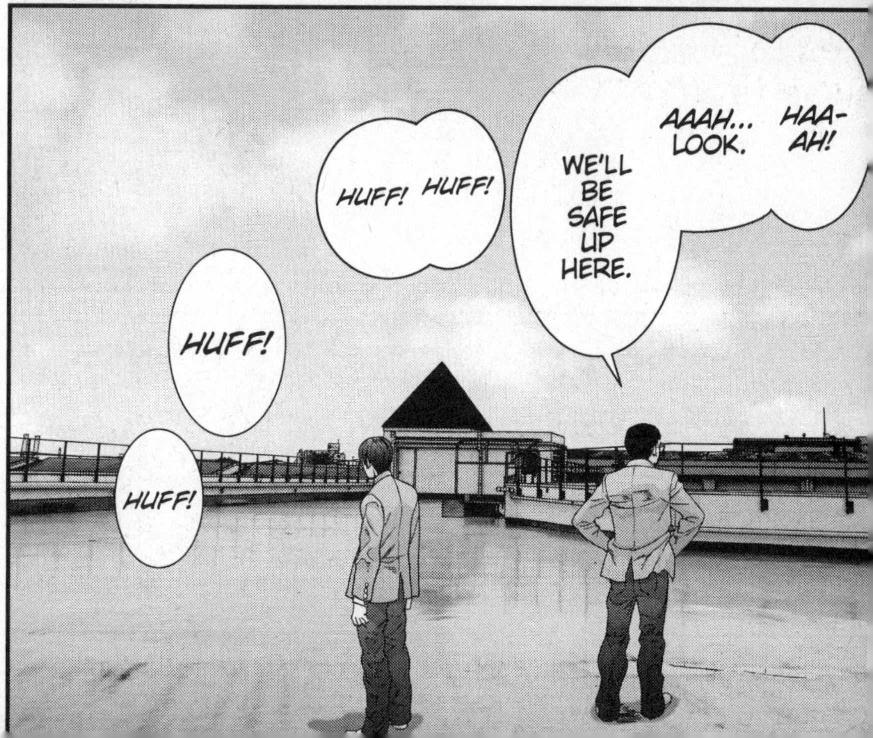
HAA-AH!
AAAH... LOOK.
WE'LL BE SAFE UP HERE.
HUFF! HUFF!
HUFF!
HUFF!

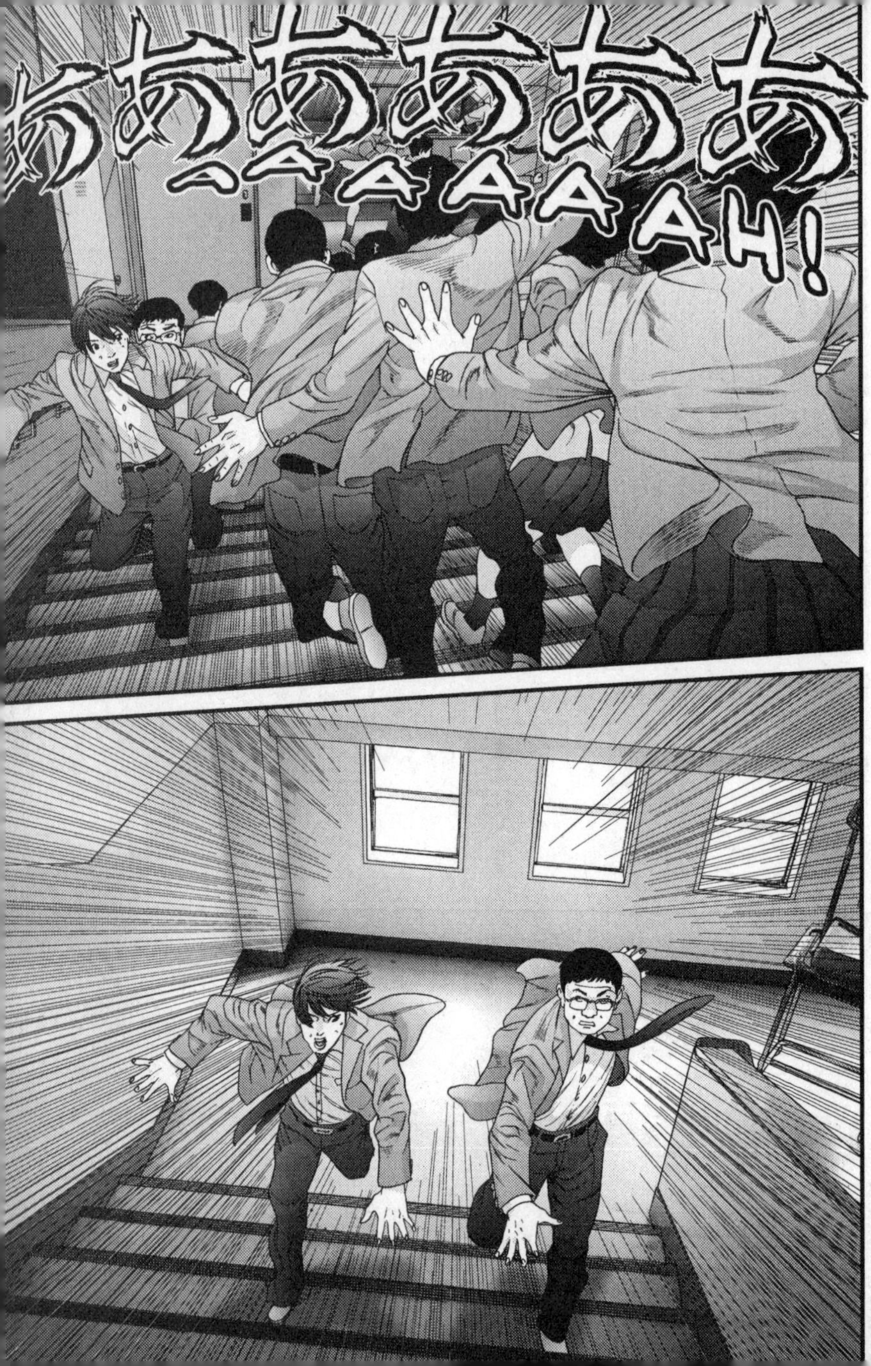
ああああああ
AAAAAAAH!

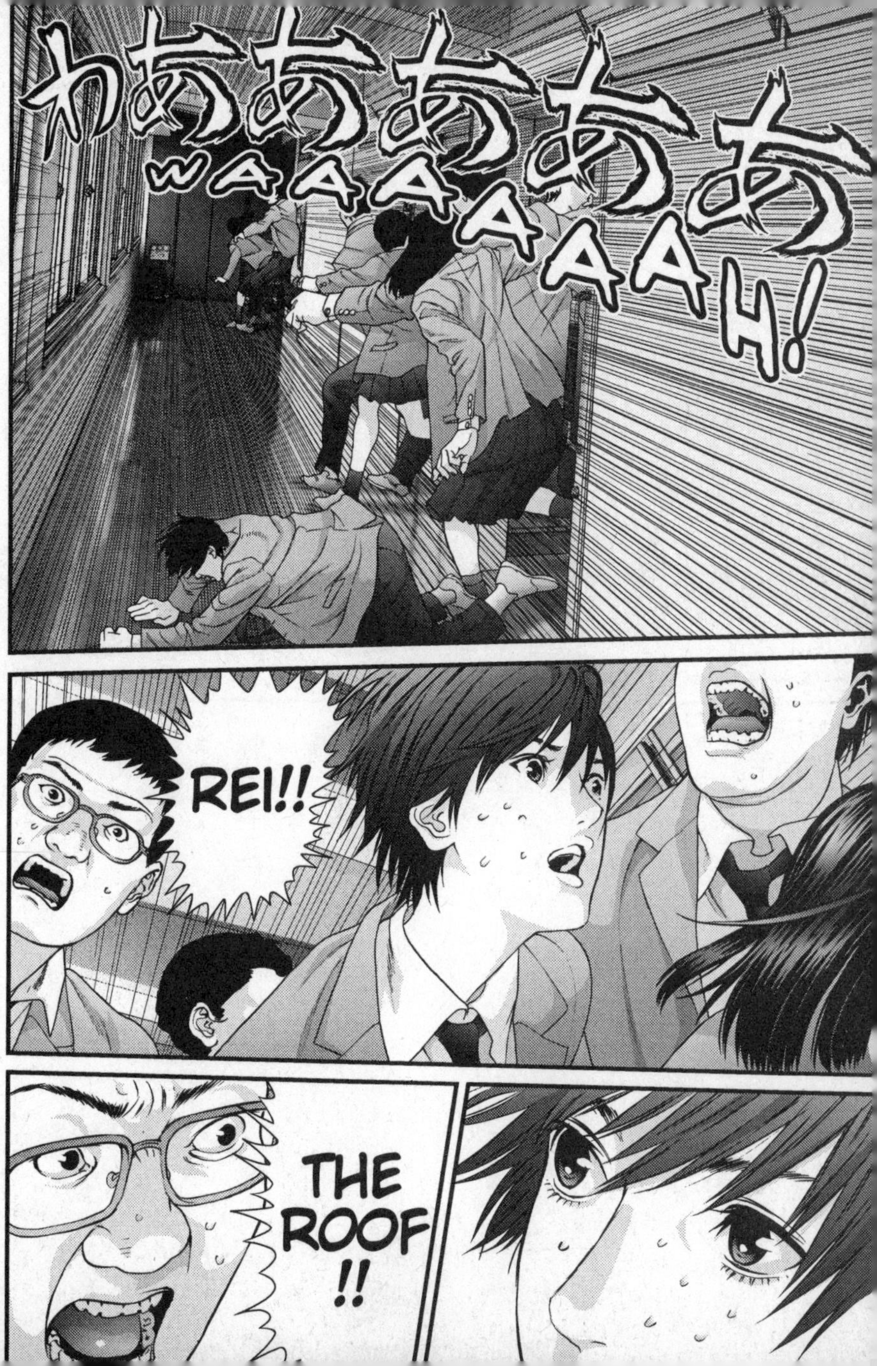
わあああああ
WAAAAAAAH!
REI!!
THE ROOF!!

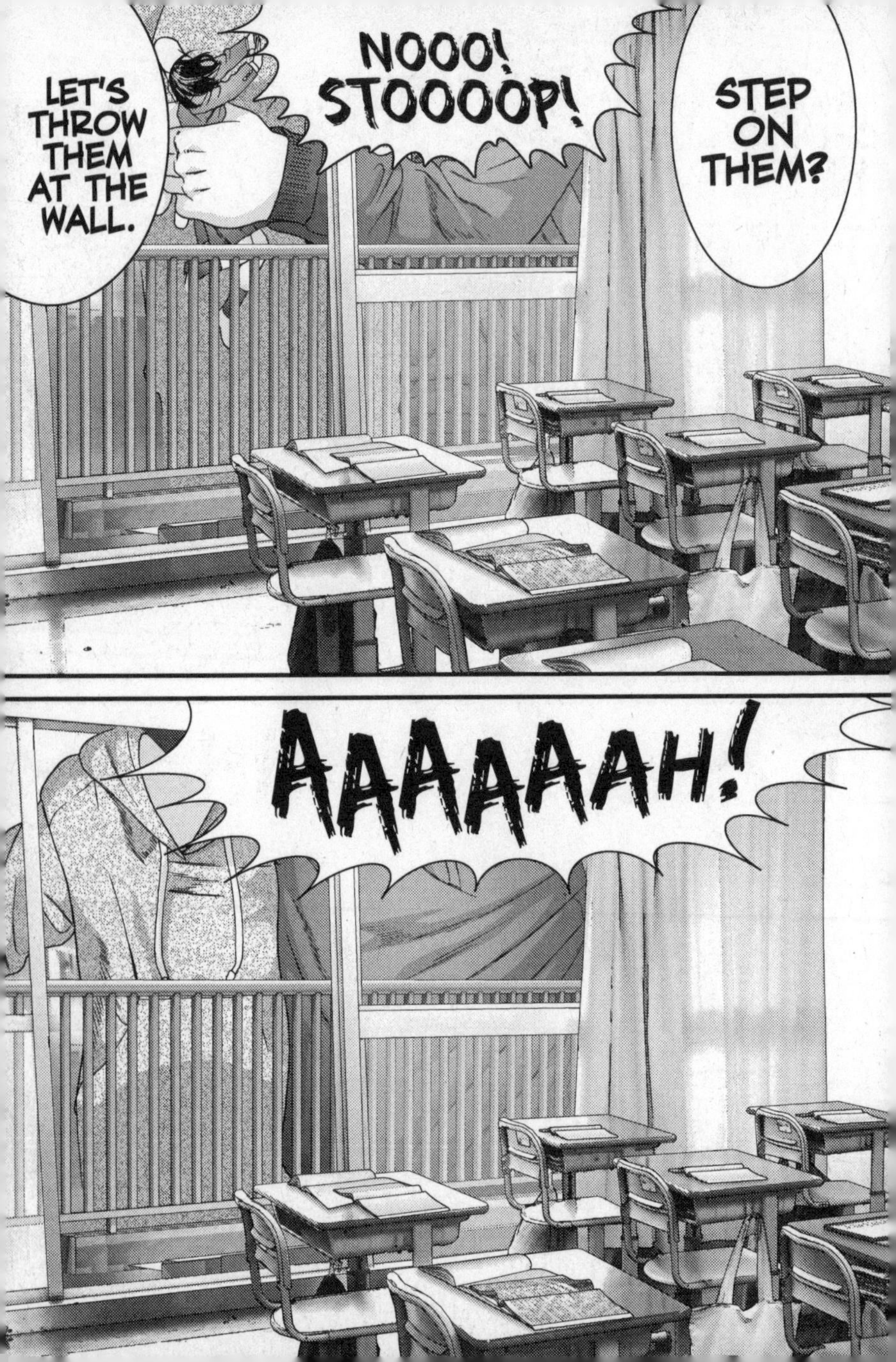
STEP ON THEM?
NOOO! STOOOOP!
LET'S THROW THEM AT THE WALL.
AAAAAAH!

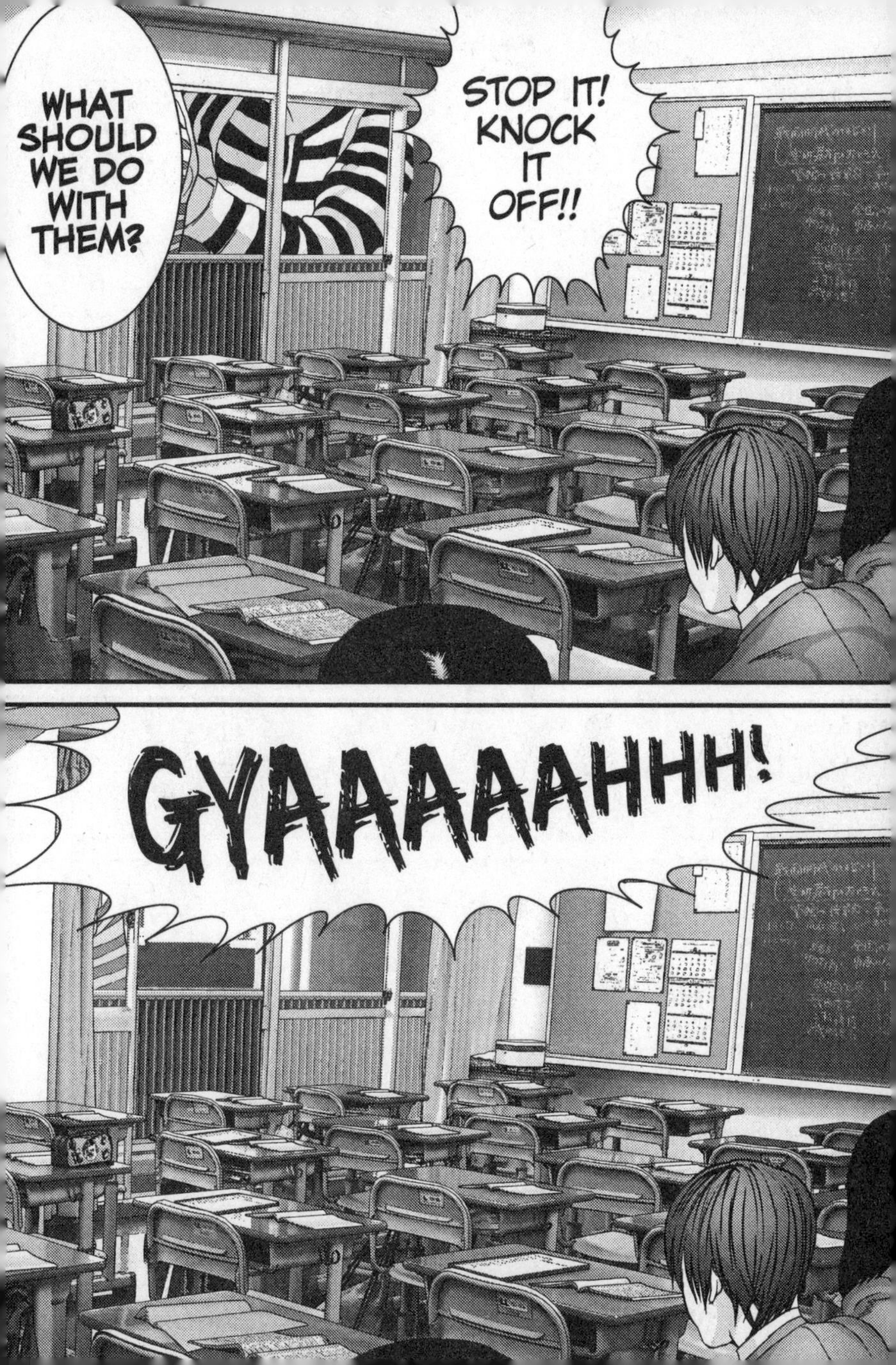
STOP IT! KNOCK IT OFF!!
WHAT SHOULD WE DO WITH THEM?
GYAAAAAHHH!

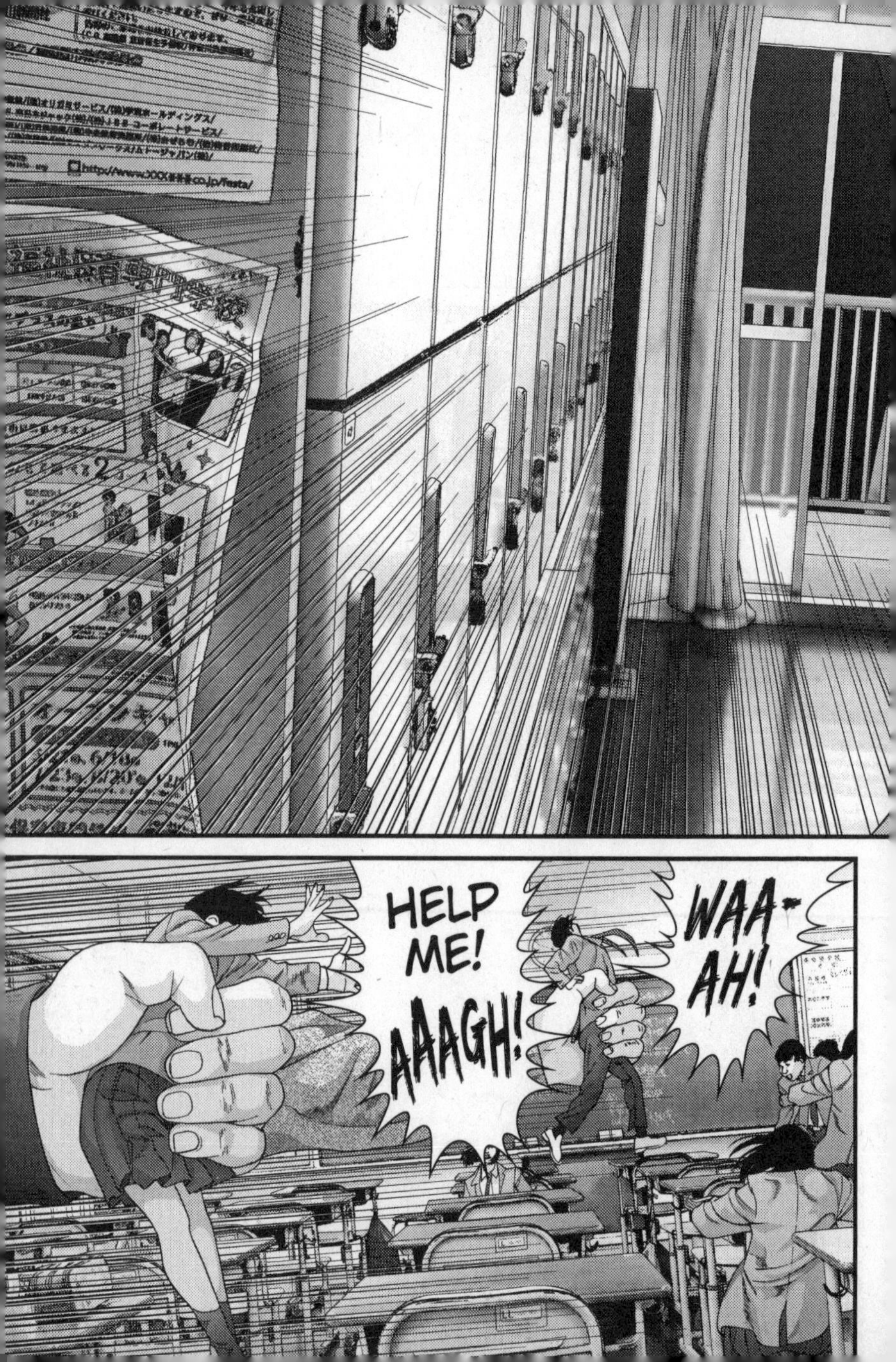
WAA-AH!
HELP ME!
AAAGH!

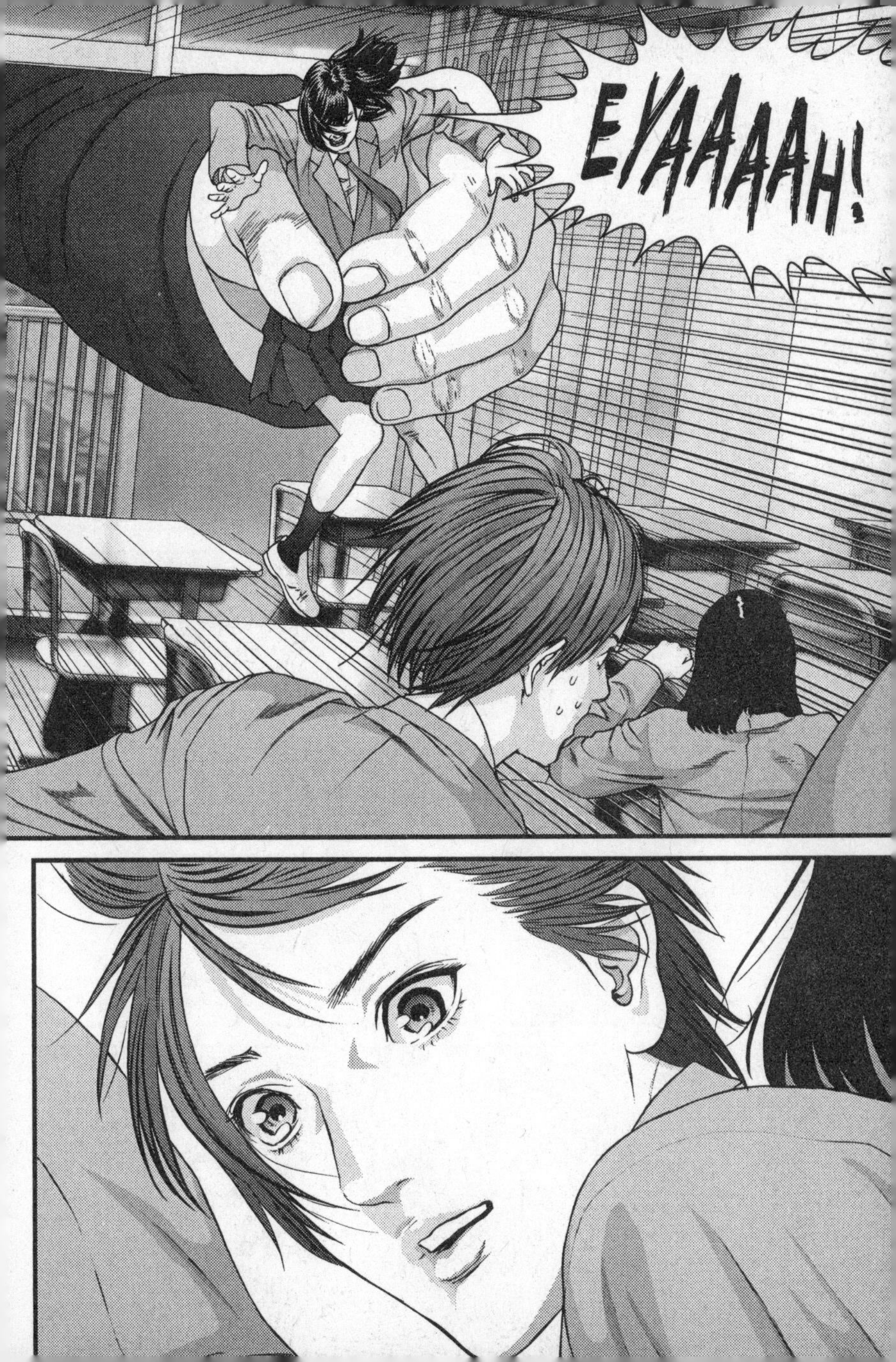
EYAAAAH!

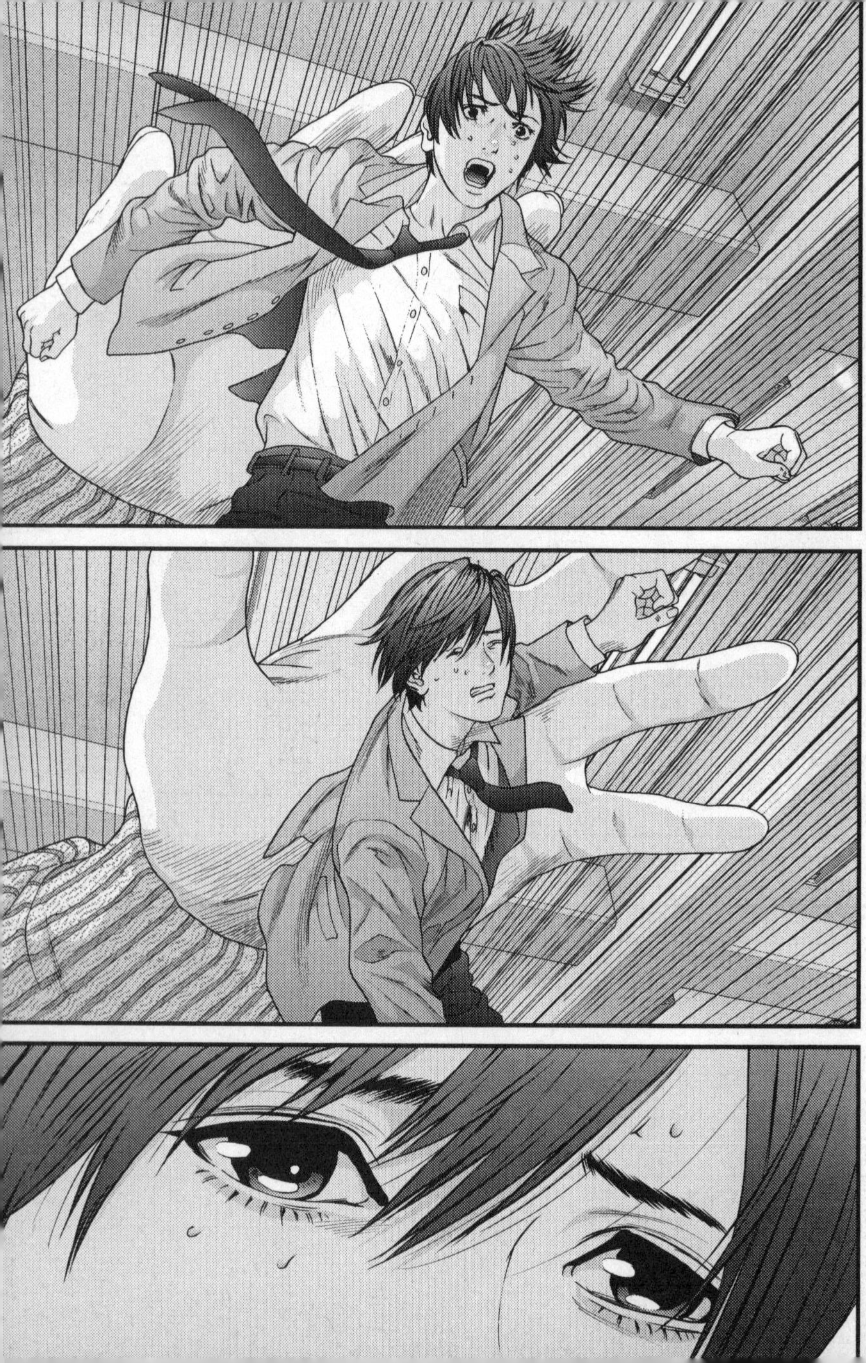

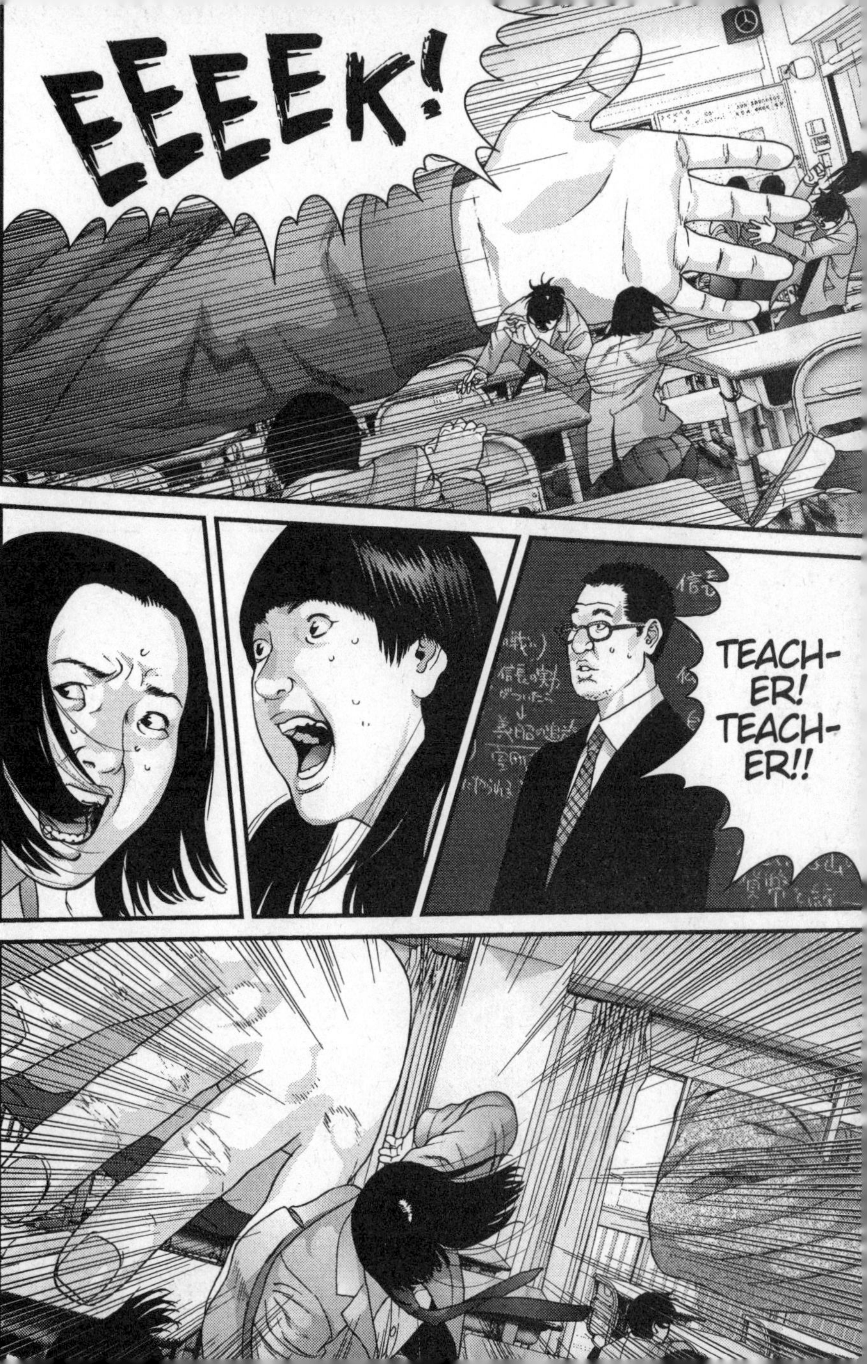
EEEEK!
TEACH-ER! TEACH-ER!!

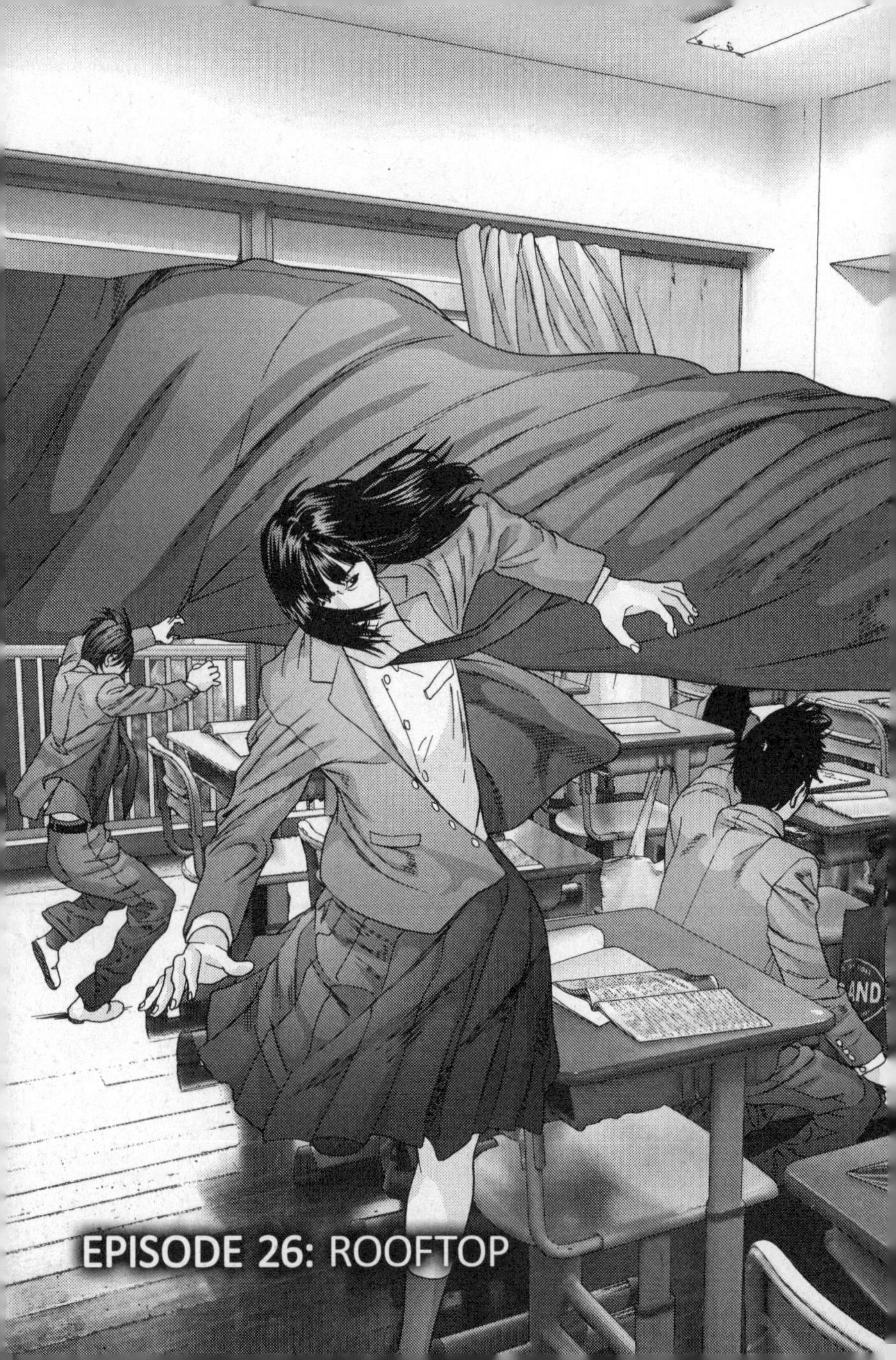

EPISODE 26: ROOFTOP

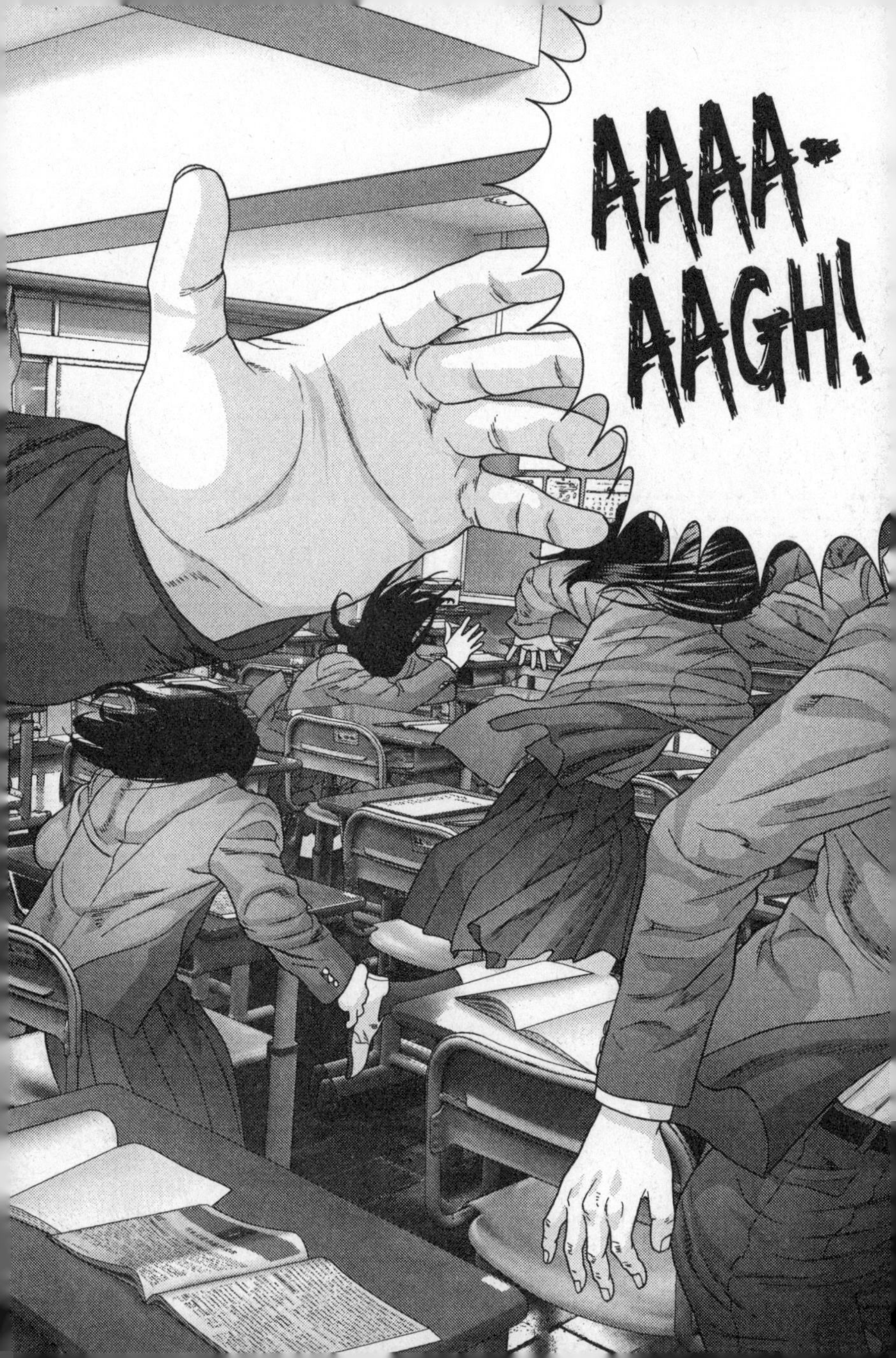
AAAA-AAGH!

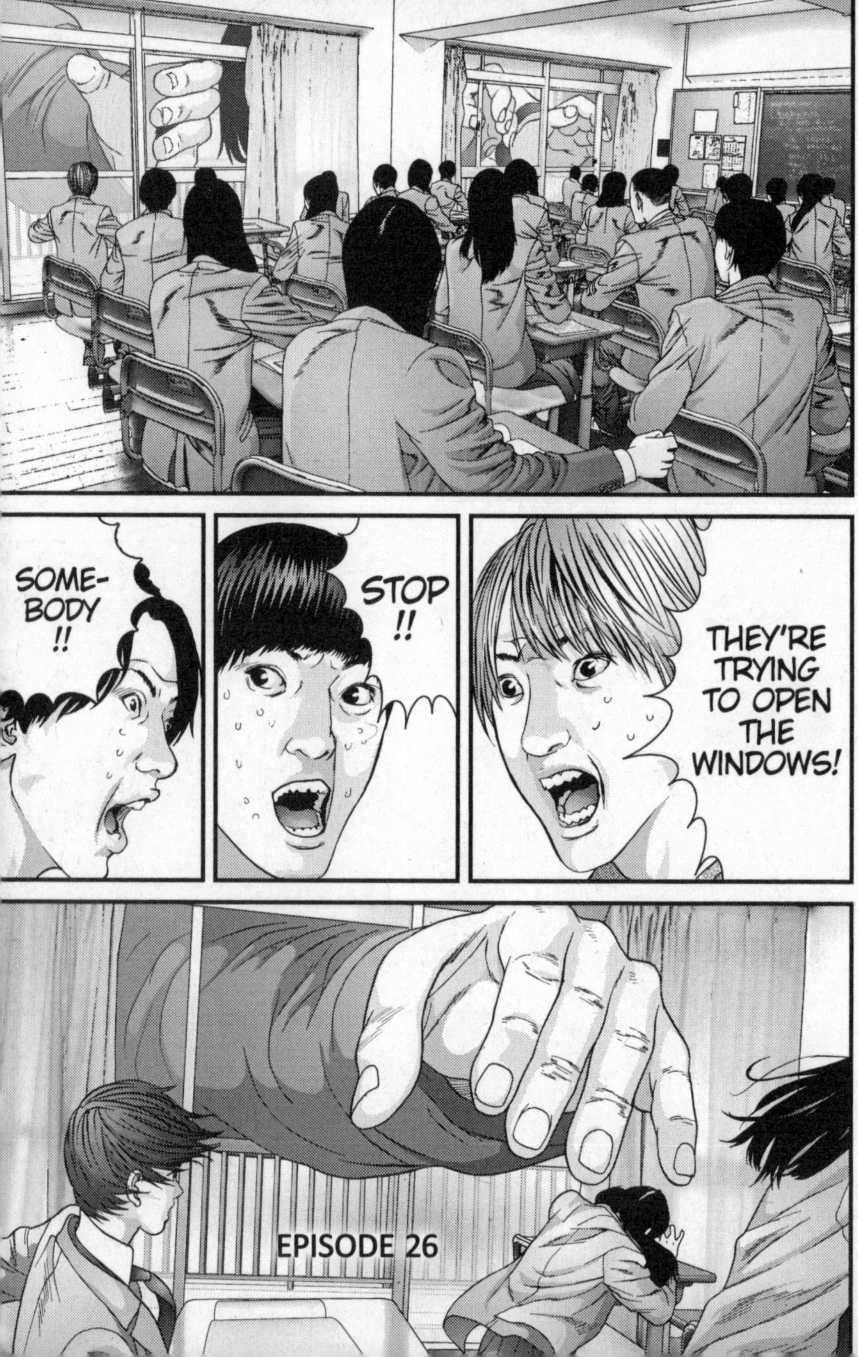
THEY'RE TRYING TO OPEN THE WINDOWS!
STOP !!
SOME-BODY !!
EPISODE 26

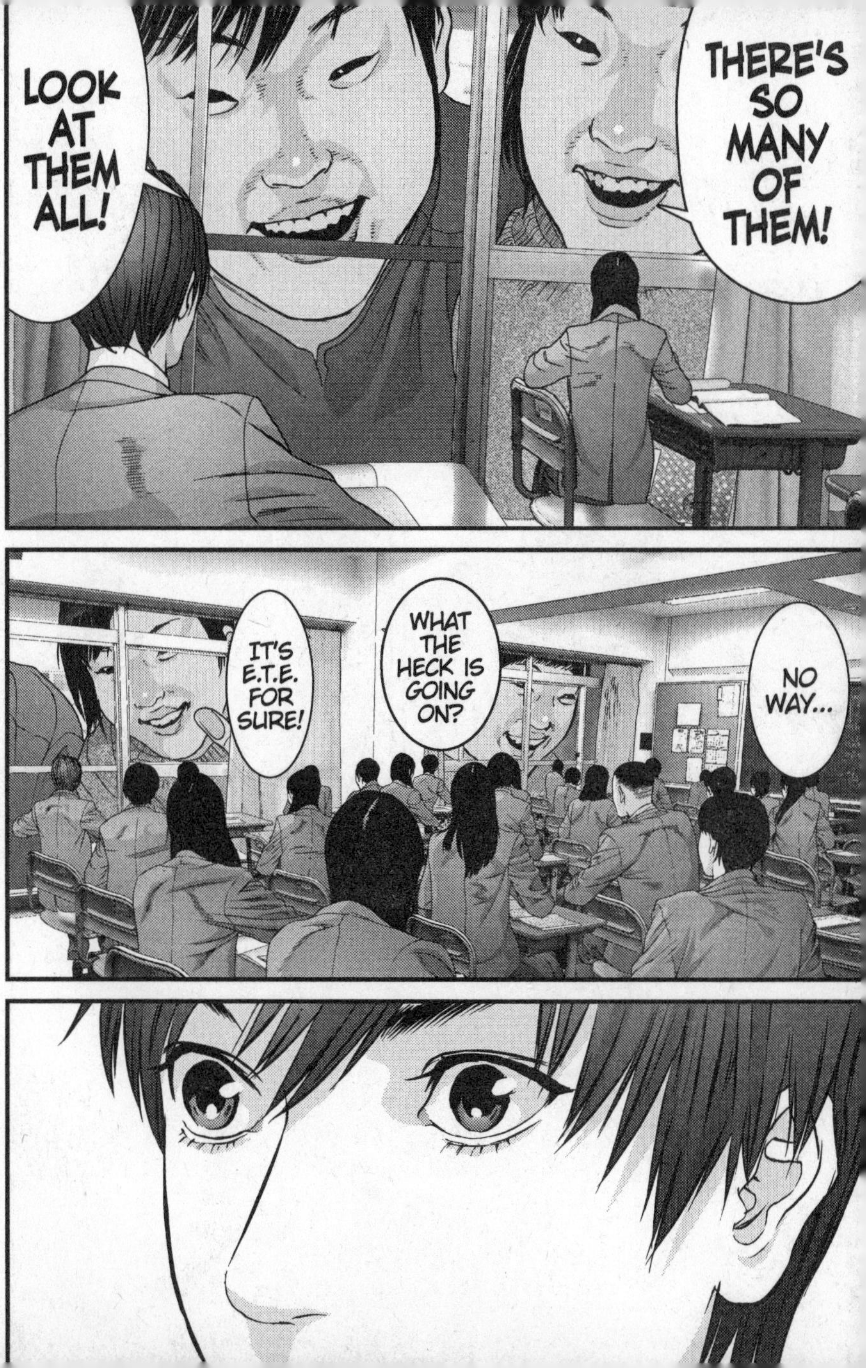
THERE'S SO MANY OF THEM!
LOOK AT THEM ALL!
NO WAY...
WHAT THE HECK IS GOING ON?
IT'S E.T.E. FOR SURE!

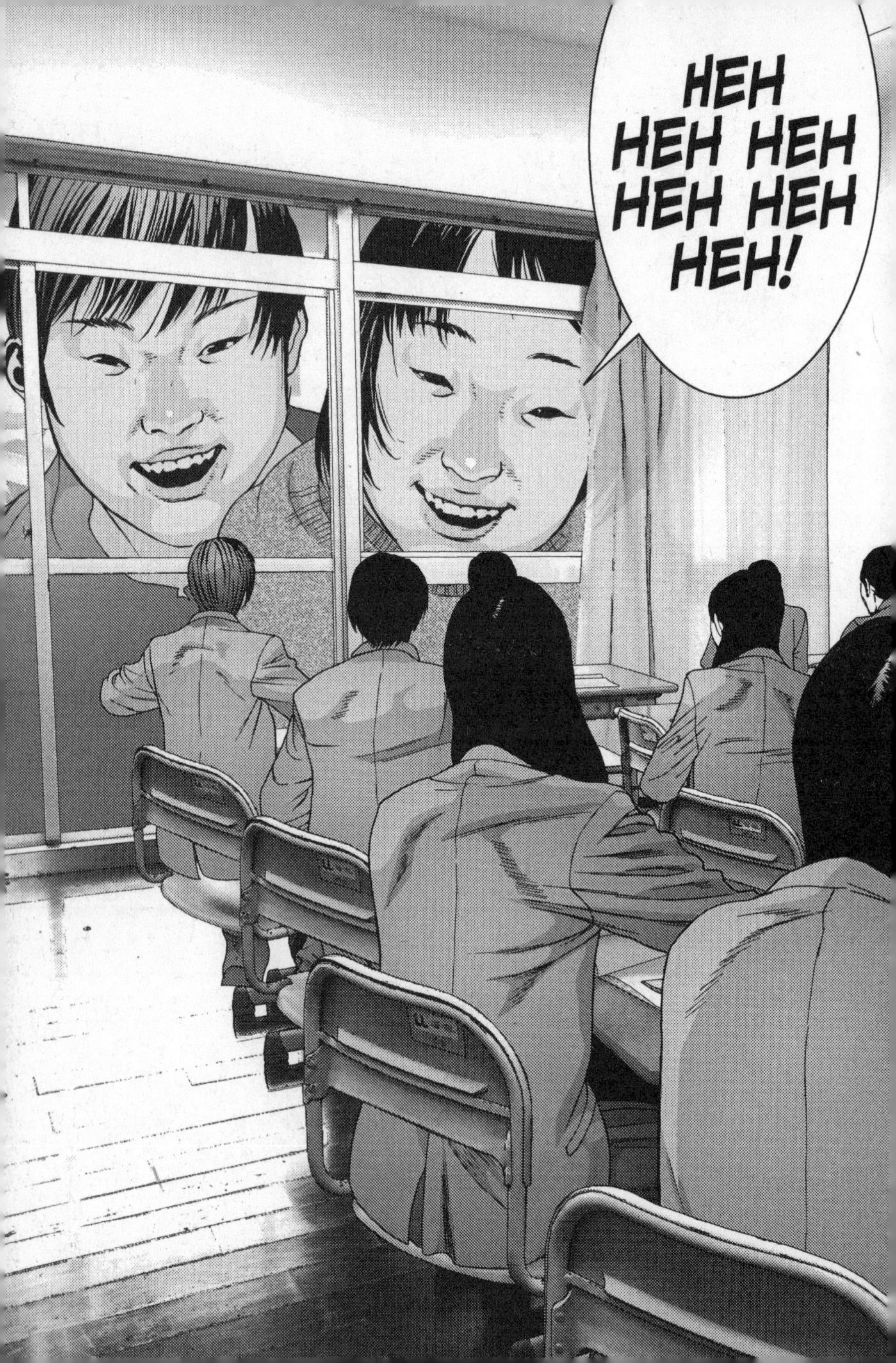
HEH HEH HEH HEH HEH HEH!

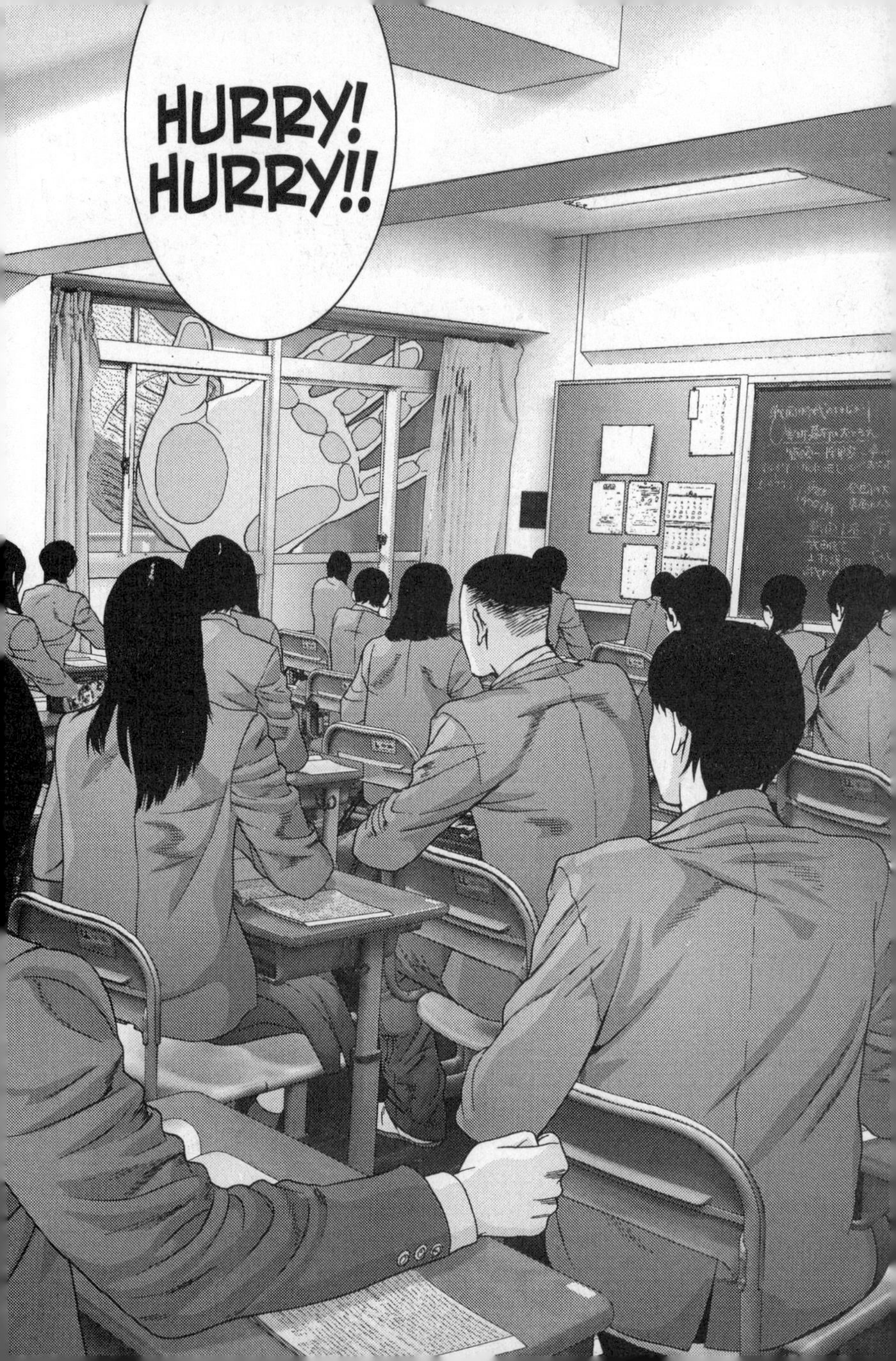
HURRY! HURRY!!

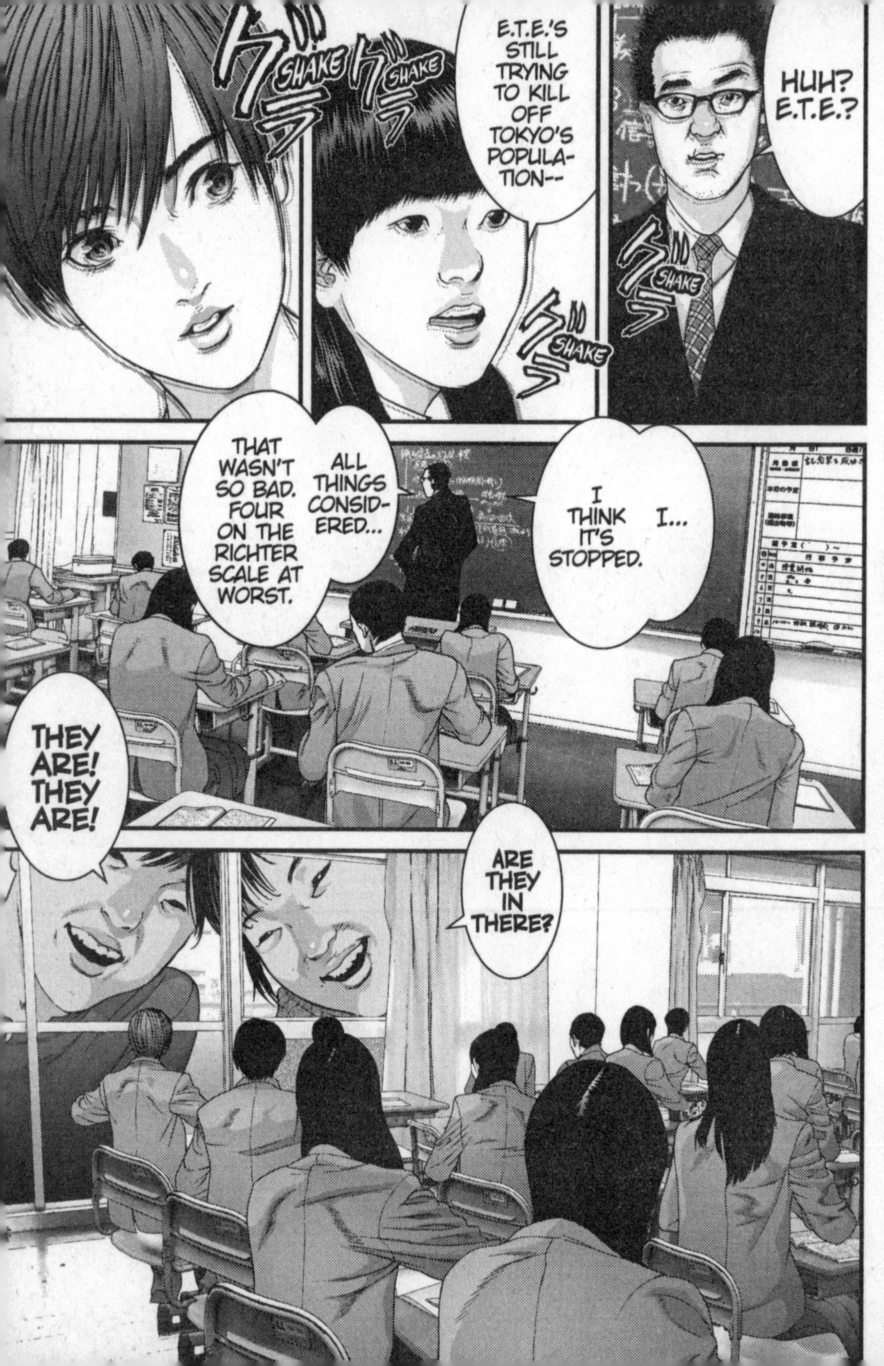
HUH? E.T.E.?
SHAKE
E.T.E.'S STILL TRYING TO KILL OFF TOKYO'S POPULATION--
SHAKE
SHAKE
SHAKE
I...
I THINK IT'S STOPPED.
ALL THINGS CONSIDERED...
THAT WASN'T SO BAD. FOUR ON THE RICHTER SCALE AT WORST.
ARE THEY IN THERE?
THEY ARE! THEY ARE!

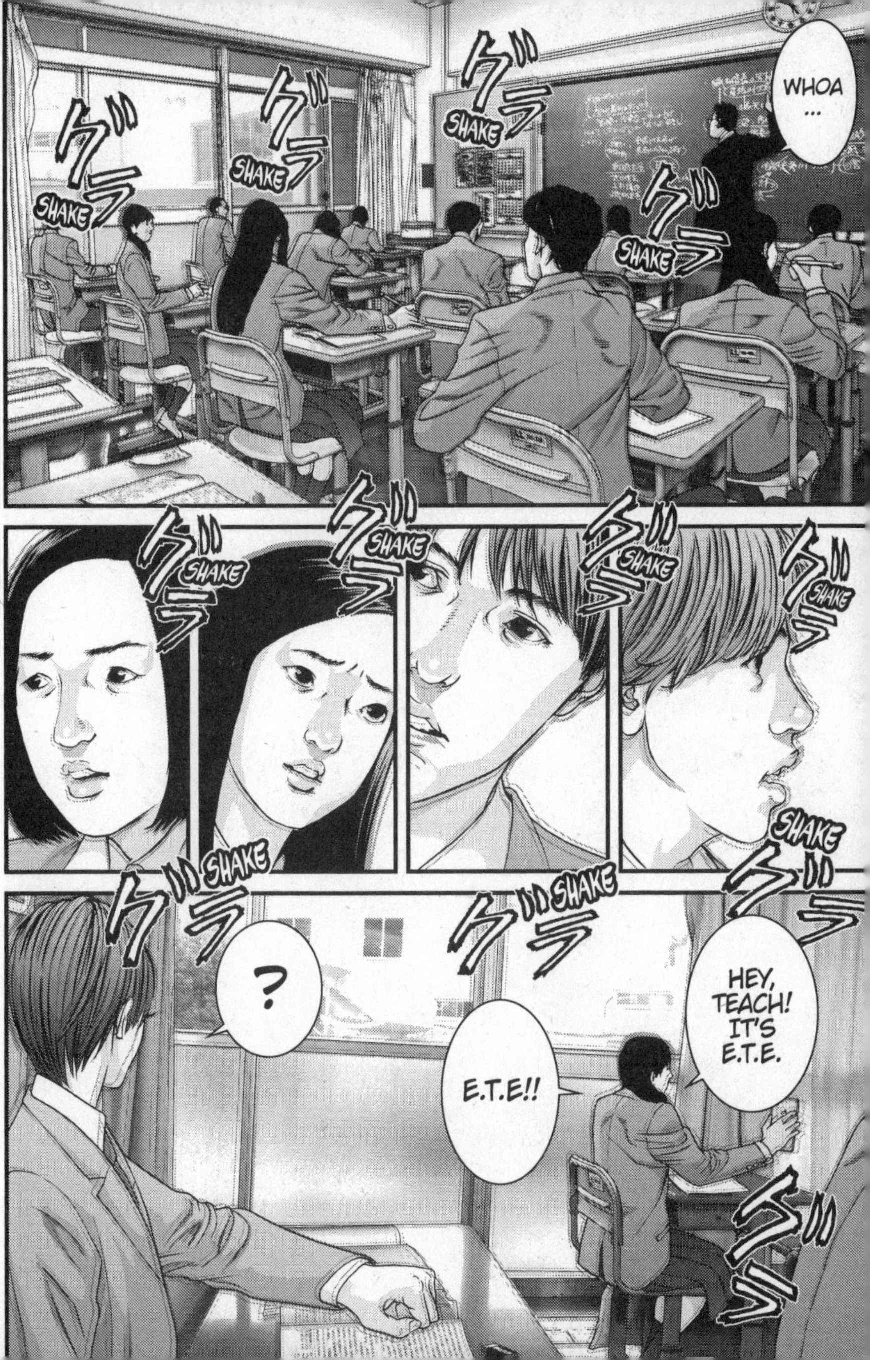
WHOA ...
SHAKE
SHAKE
SHAKE
SHAKE
SHAKE
SHAKE
SHAKE
SHAKE
SHAKE
SHAKE
SHAKE
HEY, TEACH! IT'S E.T.E.
E.T.E!!
?

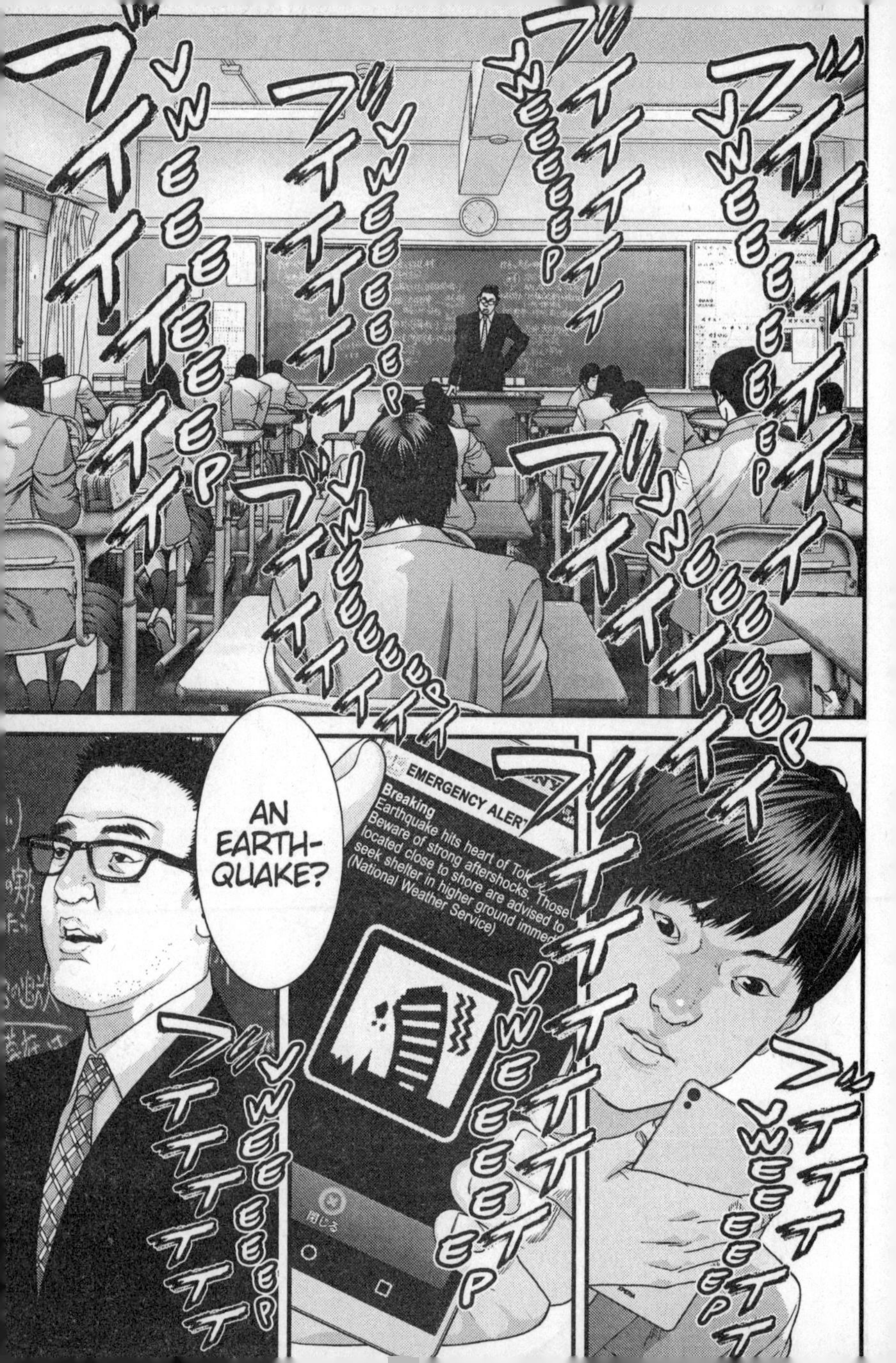
ブイイイイイイ
VWEEEEEP
ブイイイイ
VWEEEEEP
ブイイイイイ
VWEEEEEEEP
ブイイイイイ
VWEEEEEEP
ブイイイイ
VWEEEEEEEP
ブイイイイイ
VWEEEEEP
ブイイイイイ
VWEEEEEP
EMERGENCY ALER
Breaking
Earthquake hits heart of Tok
Beware of strong aftershocks. Those
located close to shore are advised to
seek shelter in higher ground immed
(National Weather Service)
閉じる
AN EARTH-QUAKE?
ブイイイイイ
VWEEEEEP
ブイイイイイ
VWEEEEEP

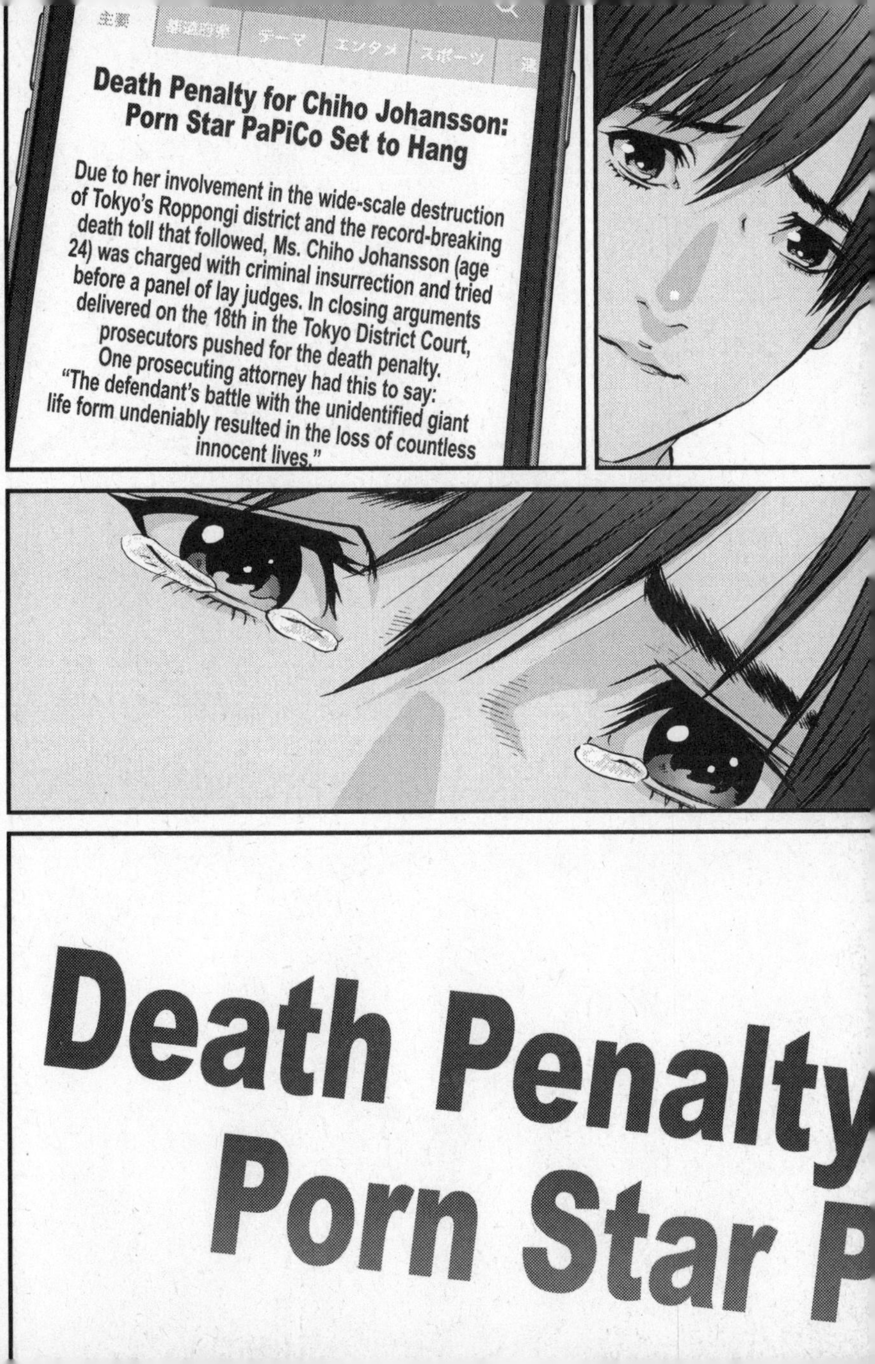
Death Penalty for Chiho Johansson: Porn Star PaPiCo Set to Hang
Due to her involvement in the wide-scale destruction of Tokyo's Roppongi district and the record-breaking death toll that followed, Ms. Chiho Johansson (age 24) was charged with criminal insurrection and tried before a panel of lay judges. In closing arguments delivered on the 18th in the Tokyo District Court, prosecutors pushed for the death penalty. One prosecuting attorney had this to say: "The defendant's battle with the unidentified giant life form undeniably resulted in the loss of countless innocent lives."
Death Penalty
Porn Star P

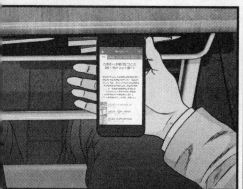

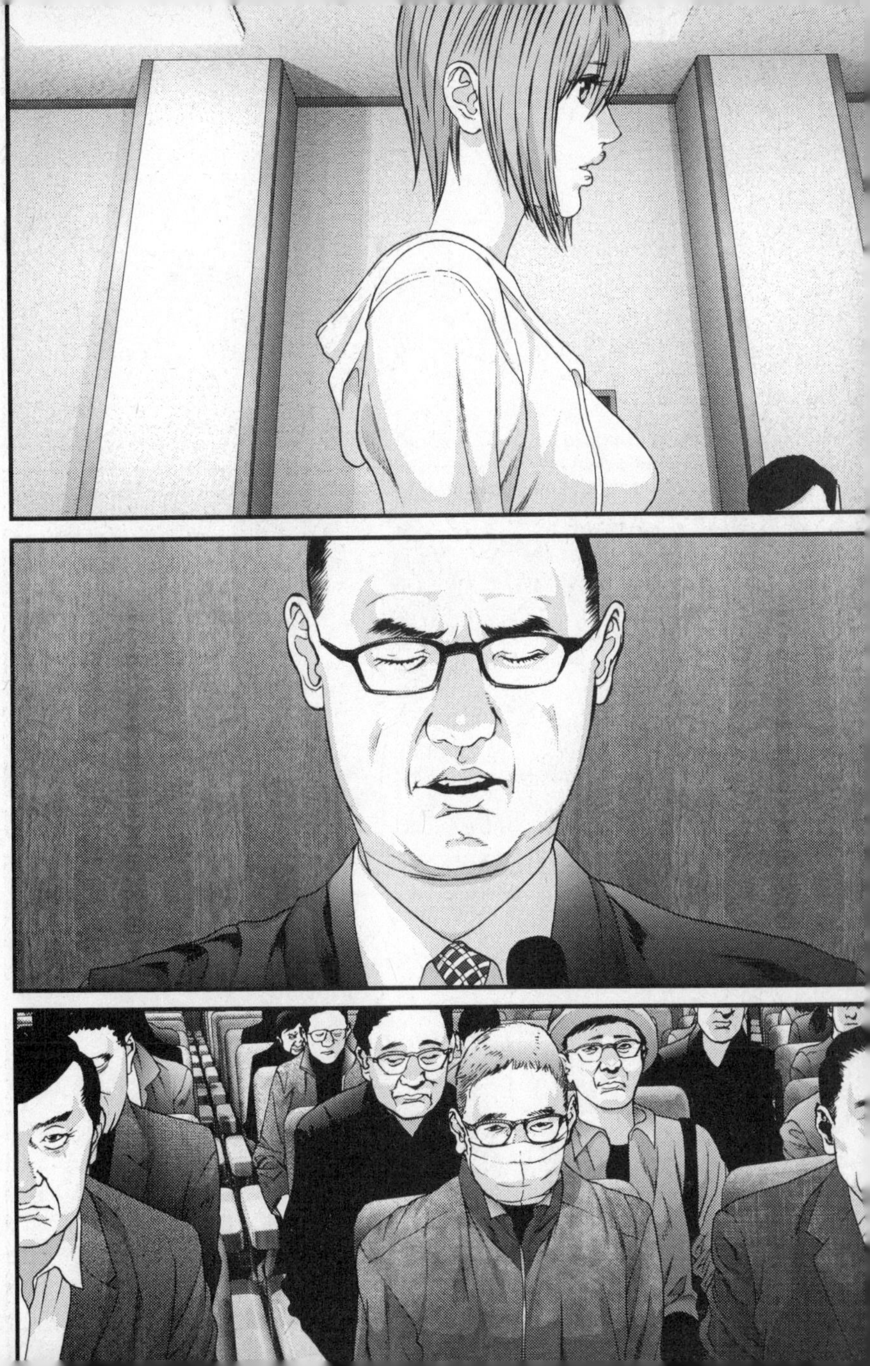

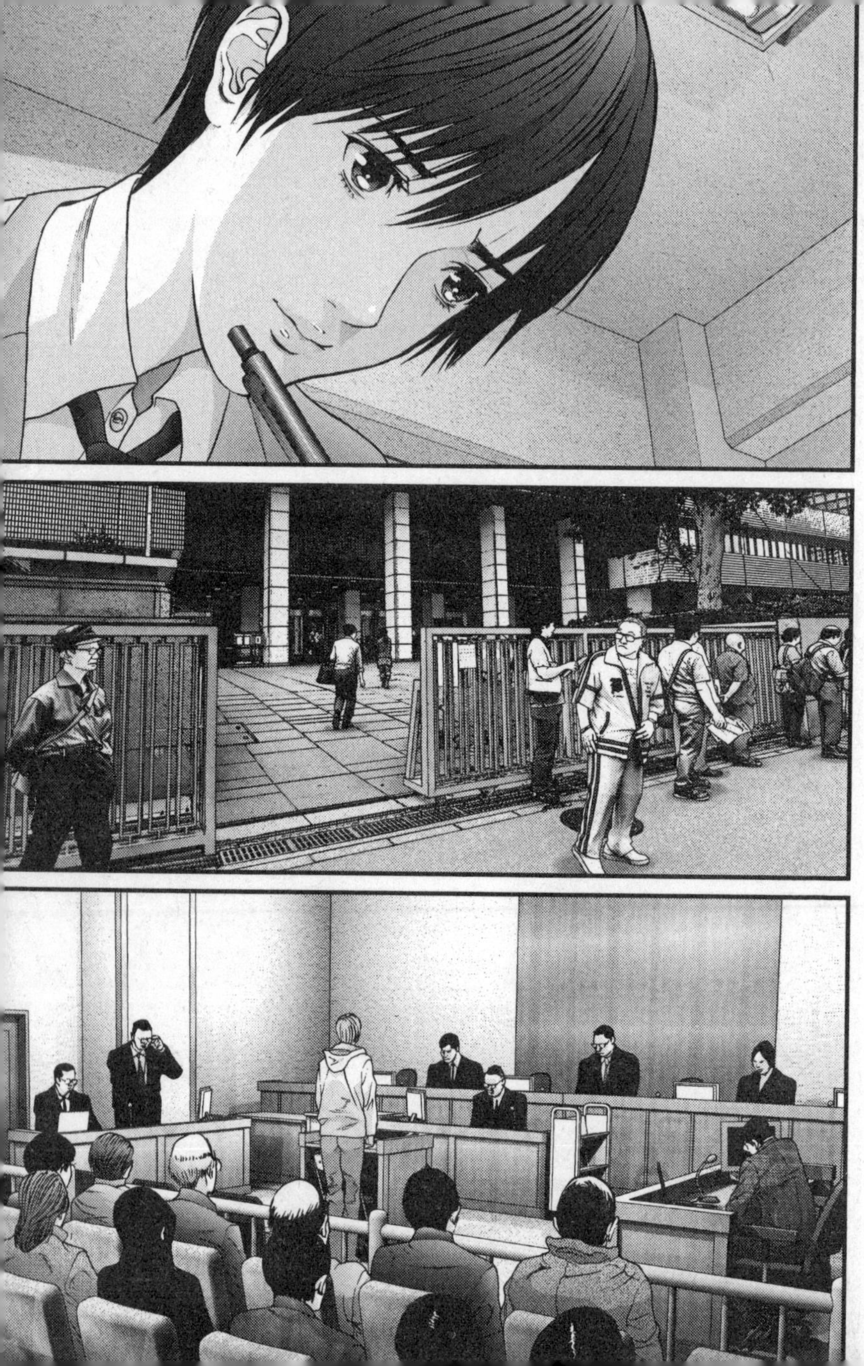

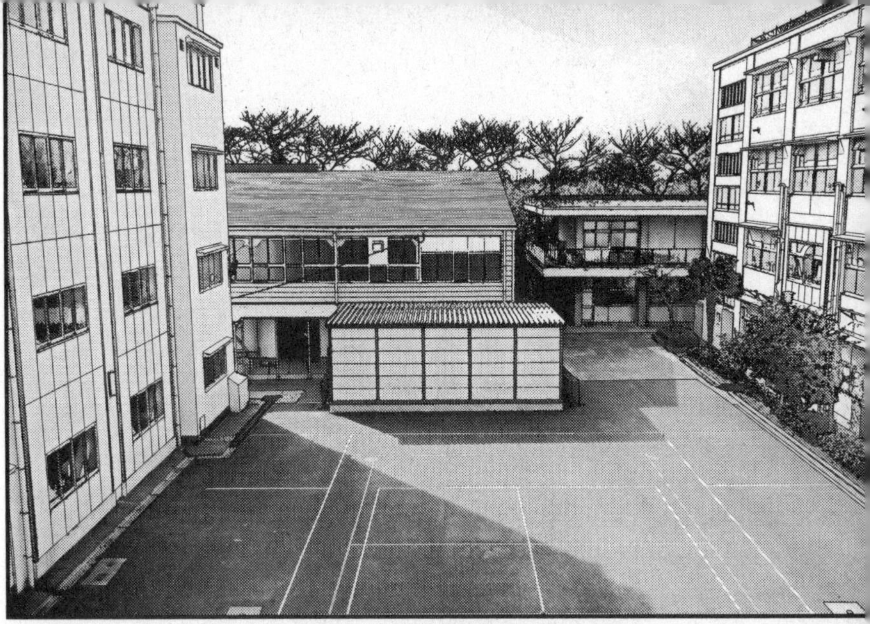
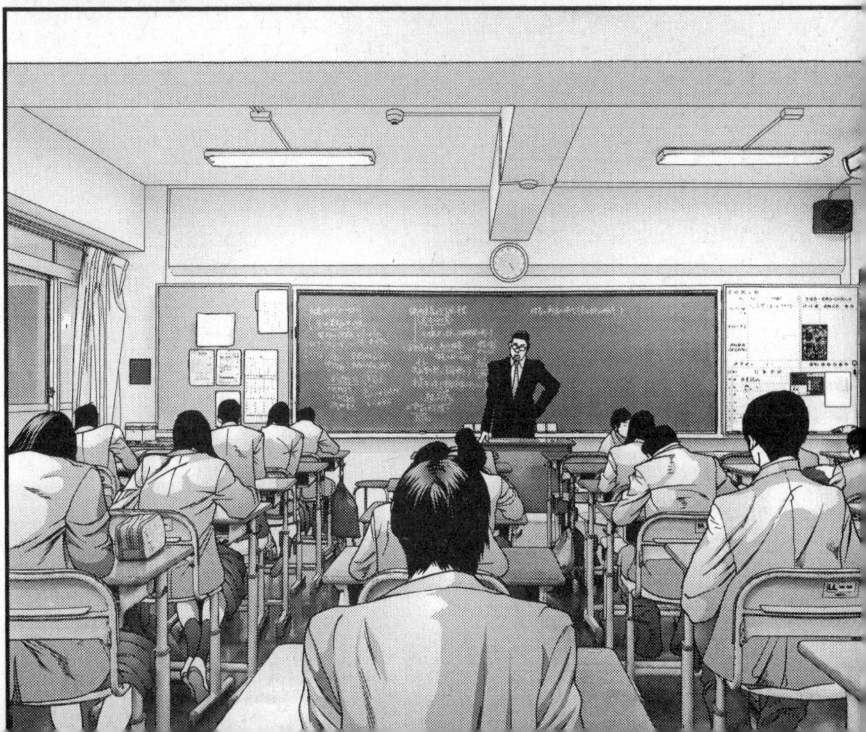

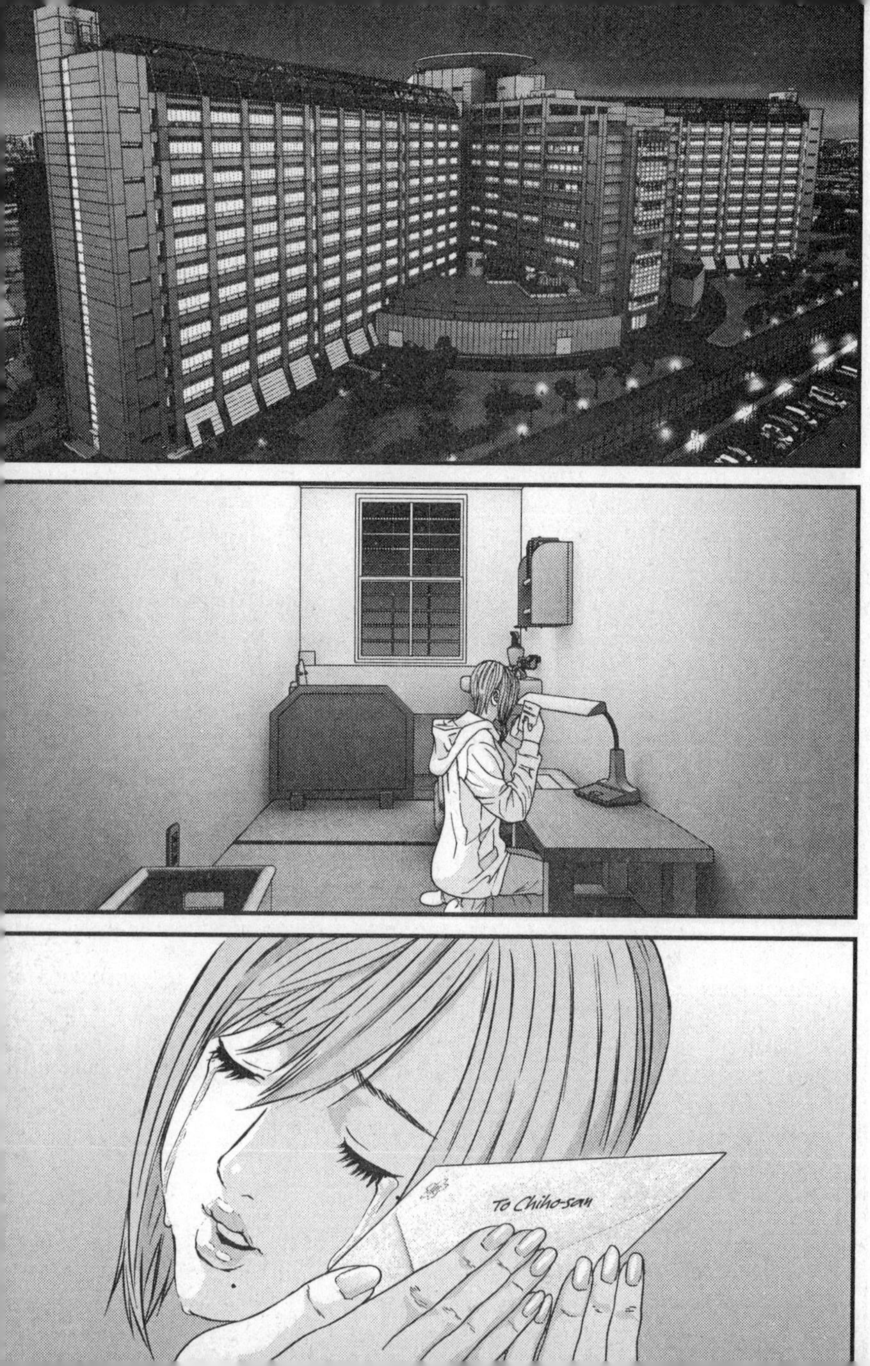
To Chiho-san

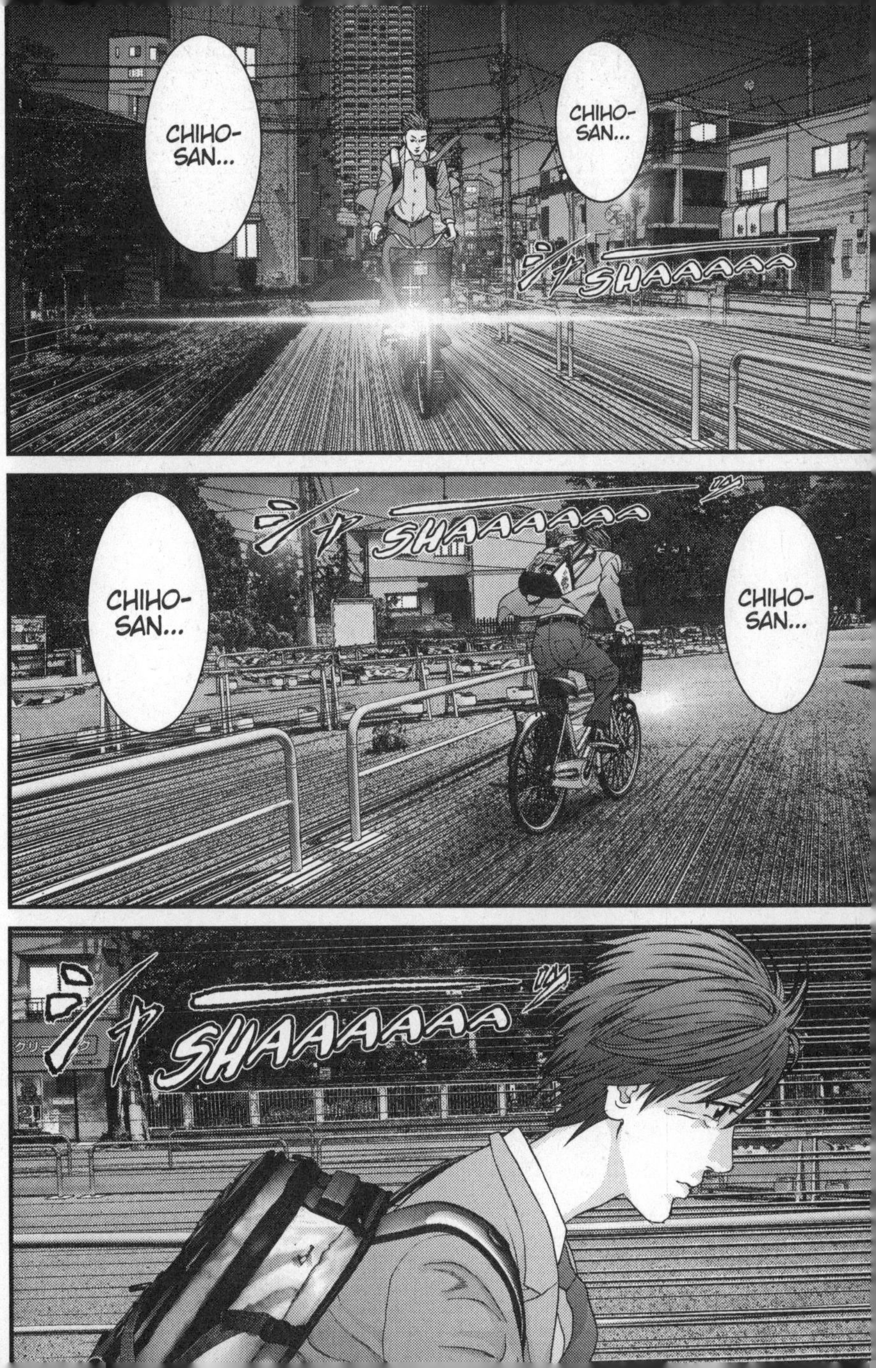
CHIHO-SAN...
SHAAAAA
CHIHO-SAN...
CHIHO-SAN...
SHAAAAAA
CHIHO-SAN...
SHAAAAAA

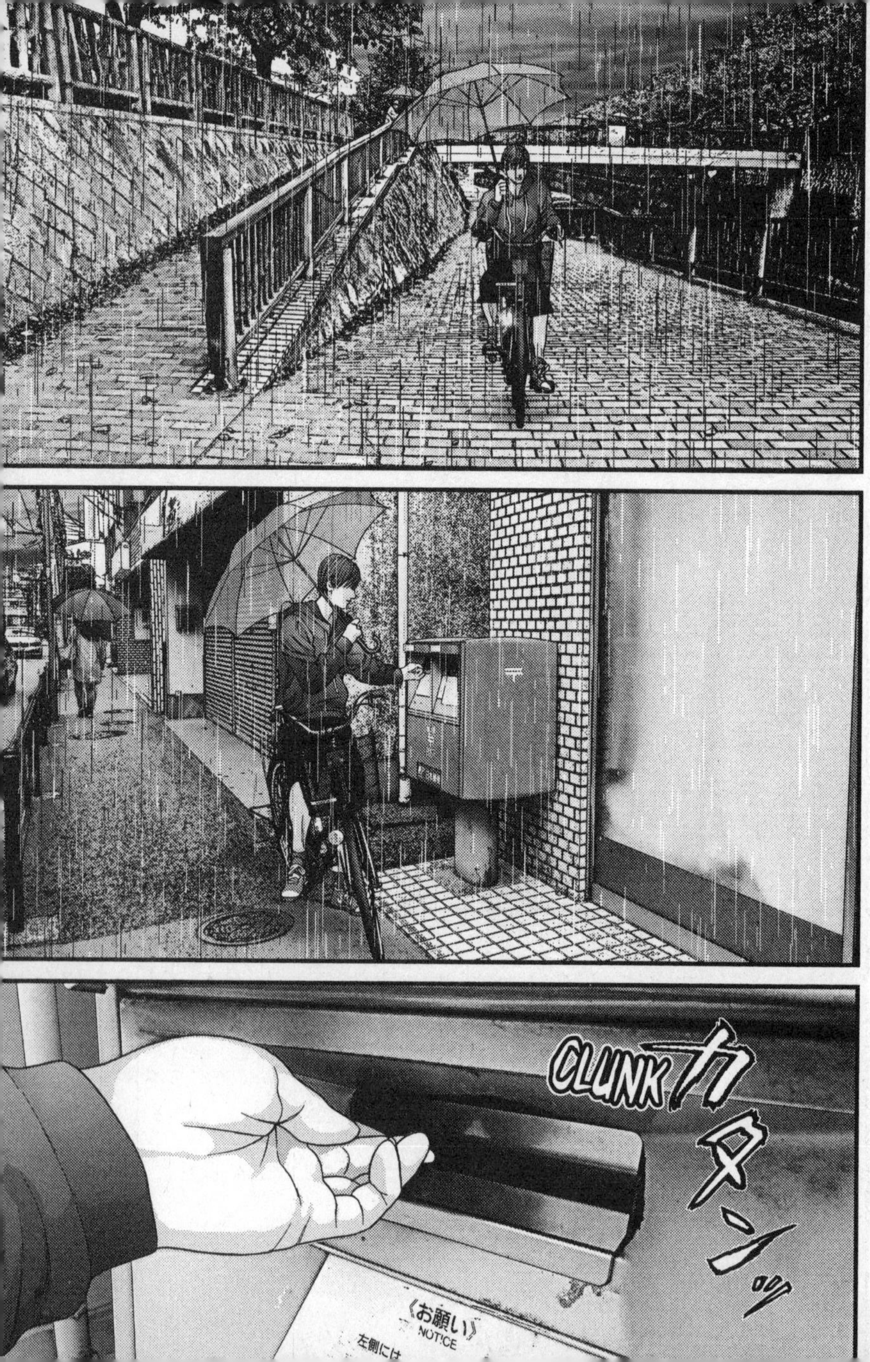
CLUNK
カターンッ
《お願い》
NOTICE
左側には

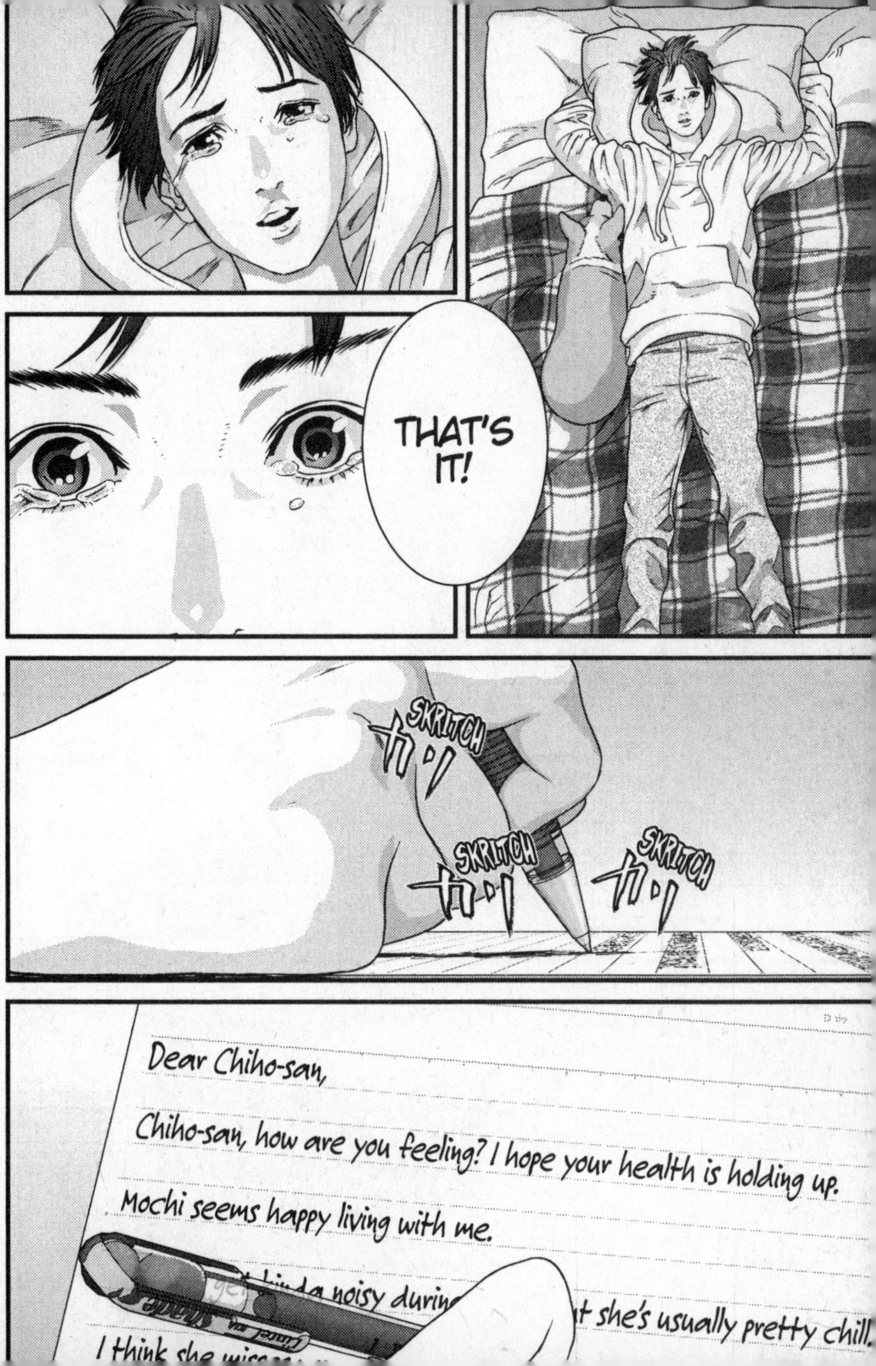
THAT'S IT!
SKRITCH
カリ
SKRITCH
カリ
SKRITCH
カリ
Dear Chiho-san,
Chiho-san, how are you feeling? I hope your health is holding up.
Mochi seems happy living with me.
she's usually pretty chill.

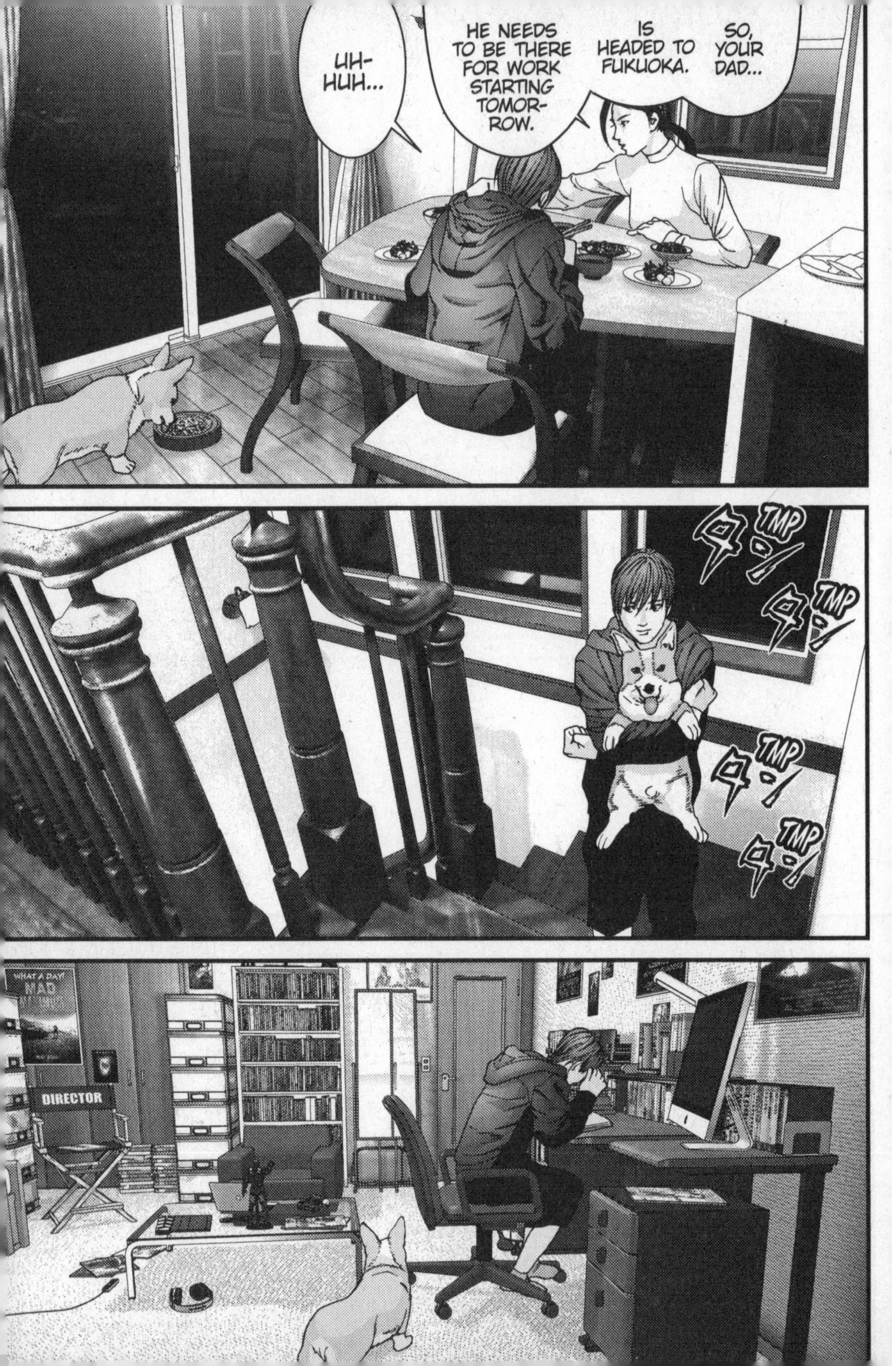
SO, YOUR DAD...
IS HEADED TO FUKUOKA.
HE NEEDS TO BE THERE FOR WORK STARTING TOMORROW.
UH-HUH...
TMP
TMP
TMP
TMP
WHAT A DAY!
MAD
DIRECTOR

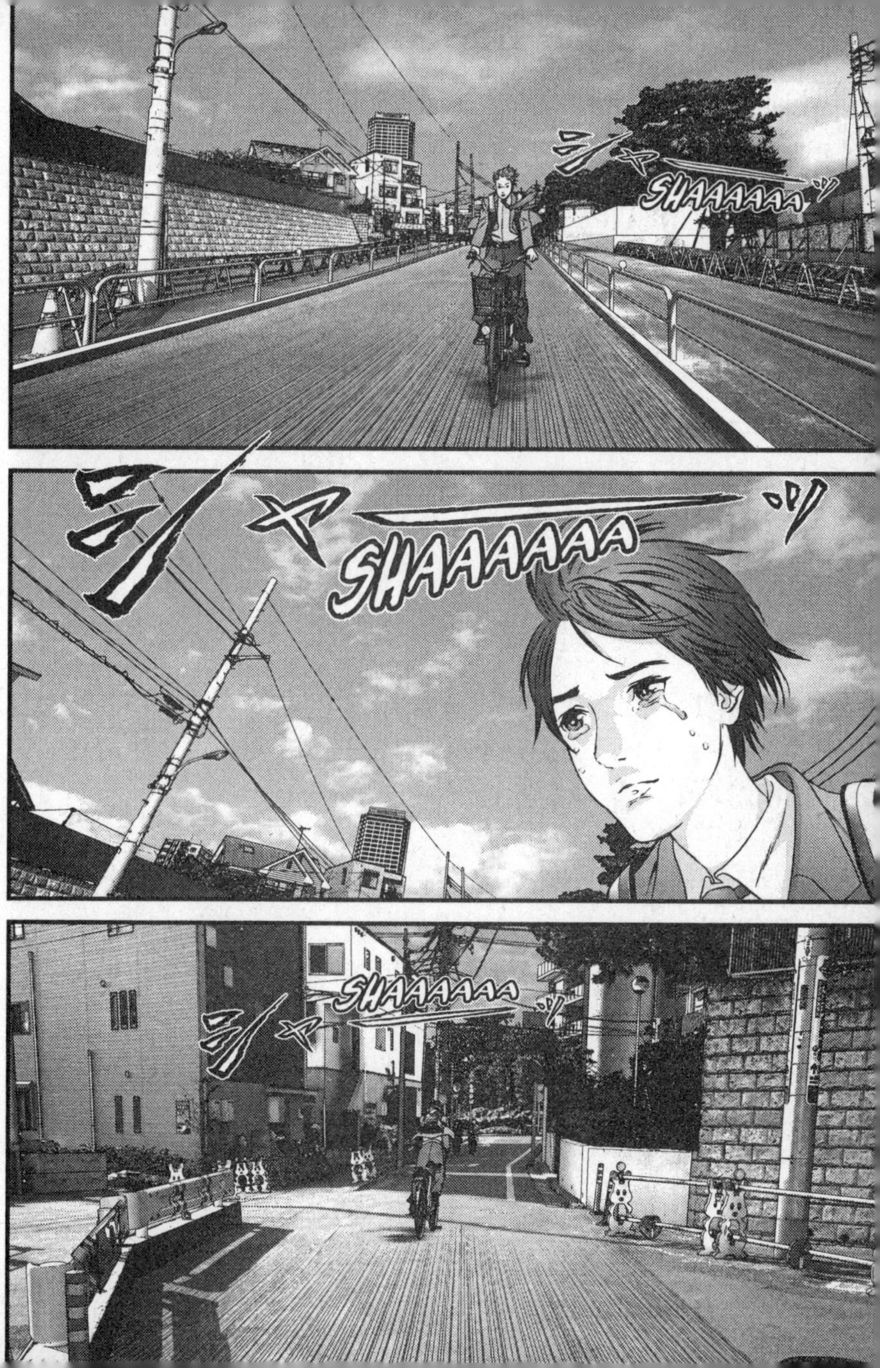

シャーッ
SHAAAAAA
シャーッ
SHAAAAAAA
シャーッ
SHAAAAAA

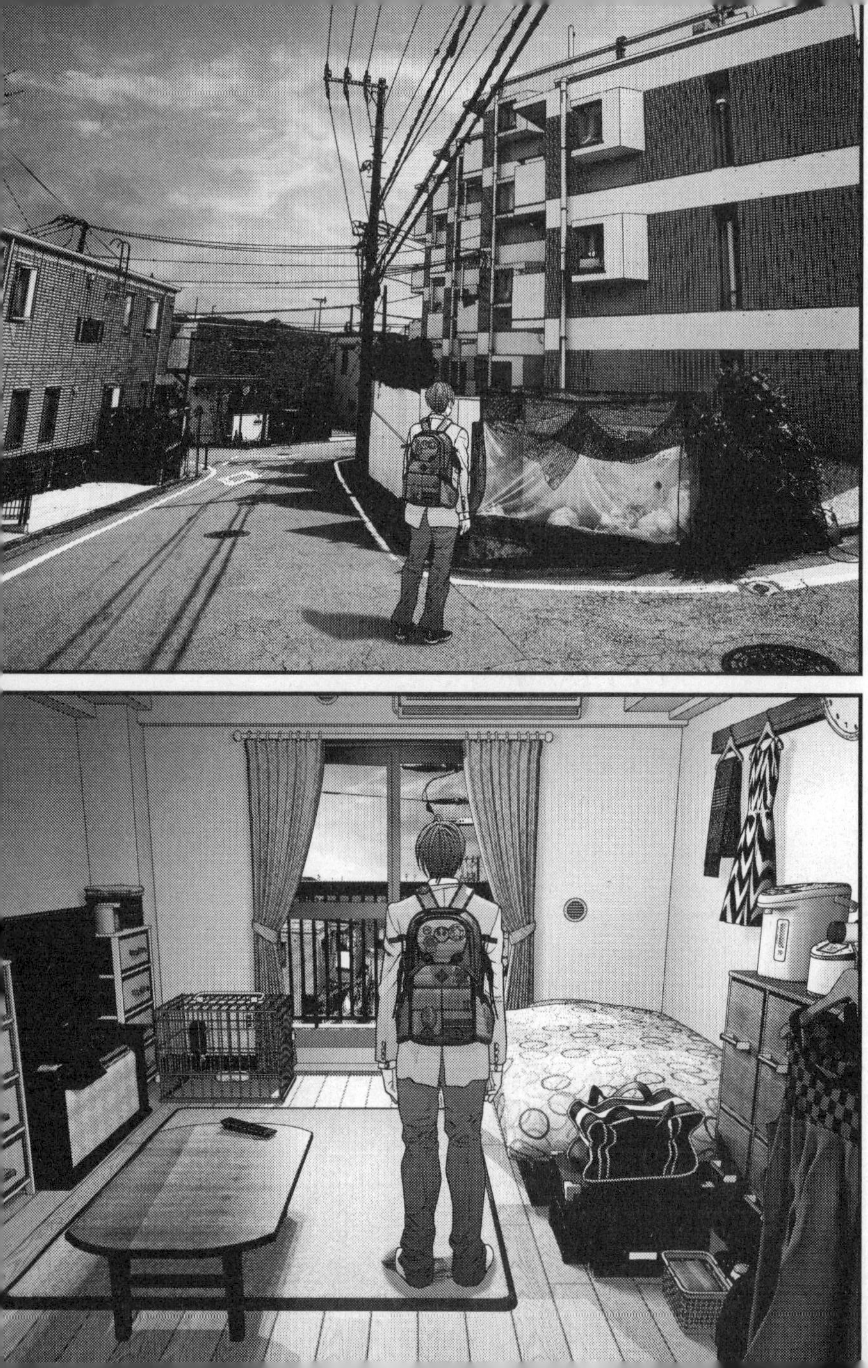

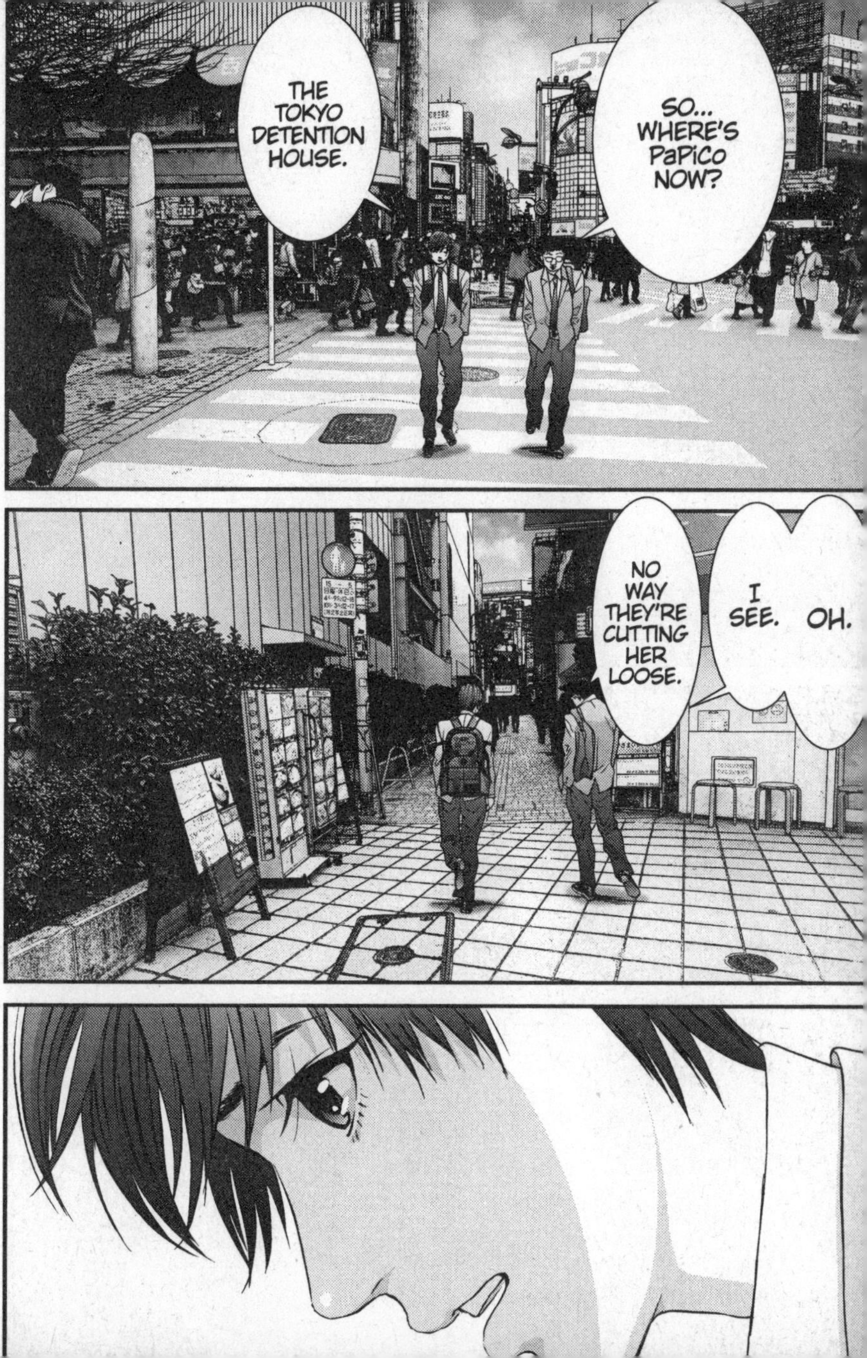

SO... WHERE'S PaPiCo NOW?
THE TOKYO DETENTION HOUSE.
OH.
I SEE.
NO WAY THEY'RE CUTTING HER LOOSE.

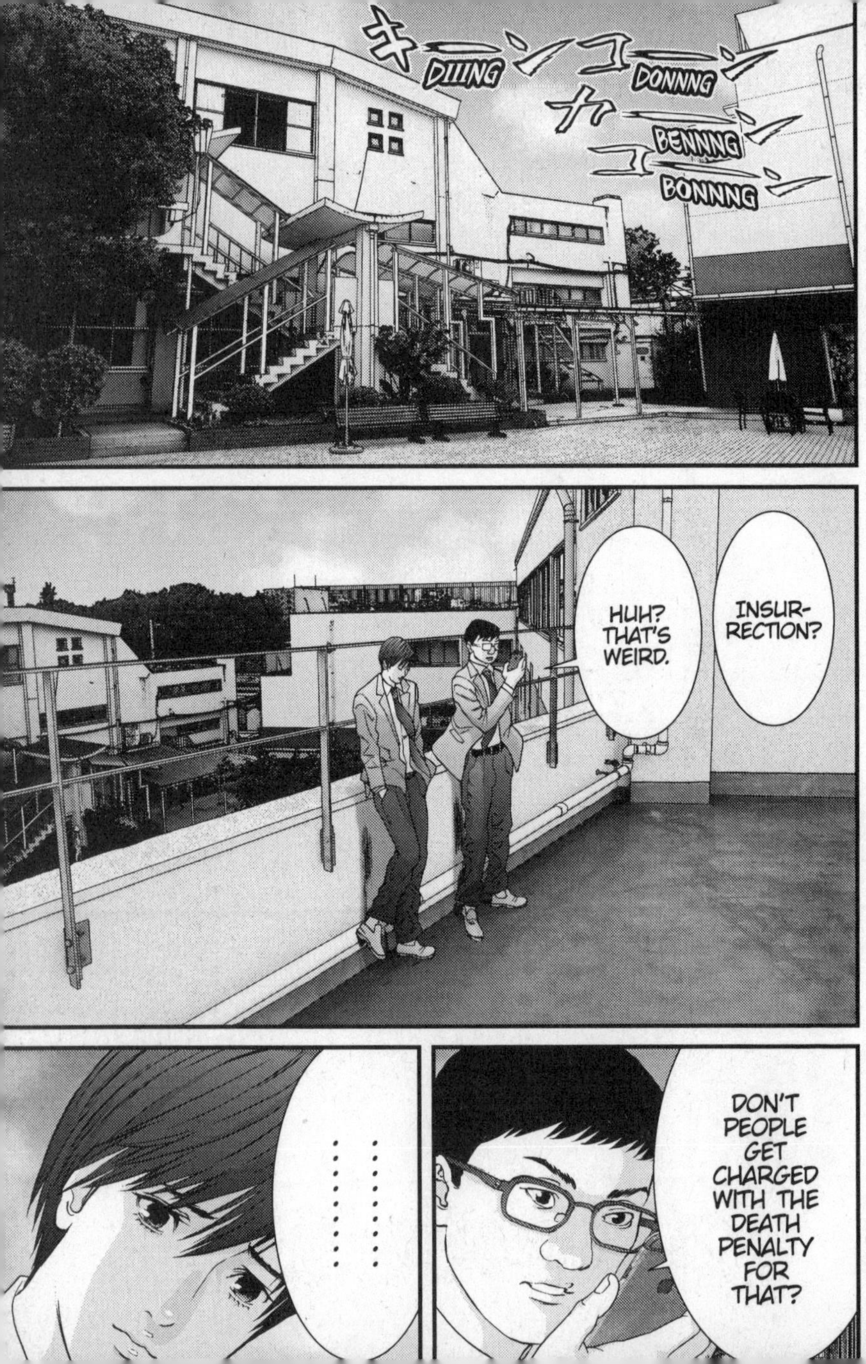
キーンコーン
DIIING
DONNNG
カーン
BENNNG
コーン
BONNNG
INSUR-RECTION?
HUH? THAT'S WEIRD.
DON'T PEOPLE GET CHARGED WITH THE DEATH PENALTY FOR THAT?
……

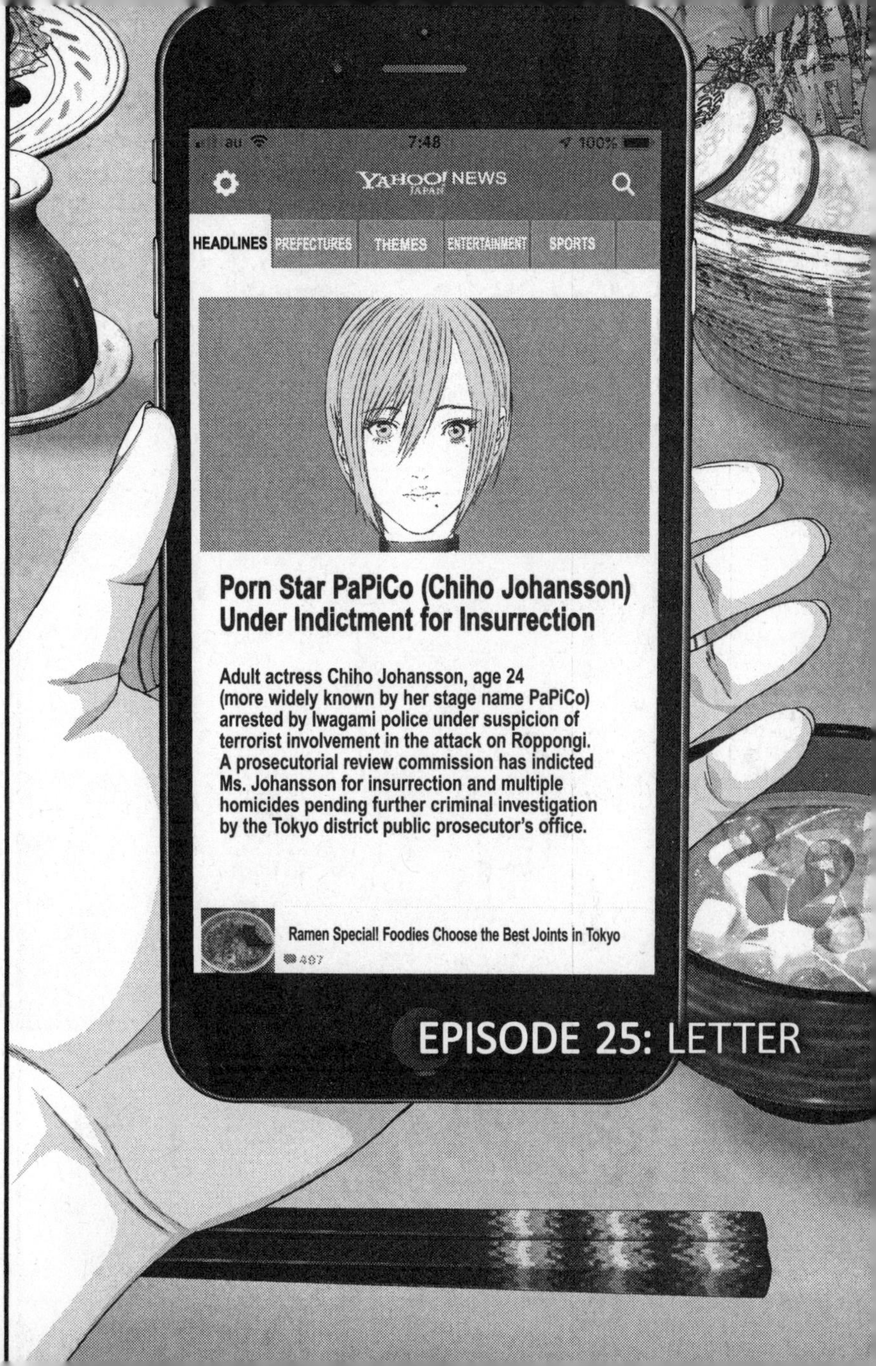

au 7:48 100%
YAHOO! JAPAN NEWS
HEADLINES
PREFECTURES
THEMES
ENTERTAINMENT
SPORTS
Porn Star PaPiCo (Chiho Johansson) Under Indictment for Insurrection
Adult actress Chiho Johansson, age 24 (more widely known by her stage name PaPiCo) arrested by Iwagami police under suspicion of terrorist involvement in the attack on Roppongi. A prosecutorial review commission has indicted Ms. Johansson for insurrection and multiple homicides pending further criminal investigation by the Tokyo district public prosecutor's office.
Ramen Special! Foodies Choose the Best Joints in Tokyo
497
EPISODE 25: LETTER

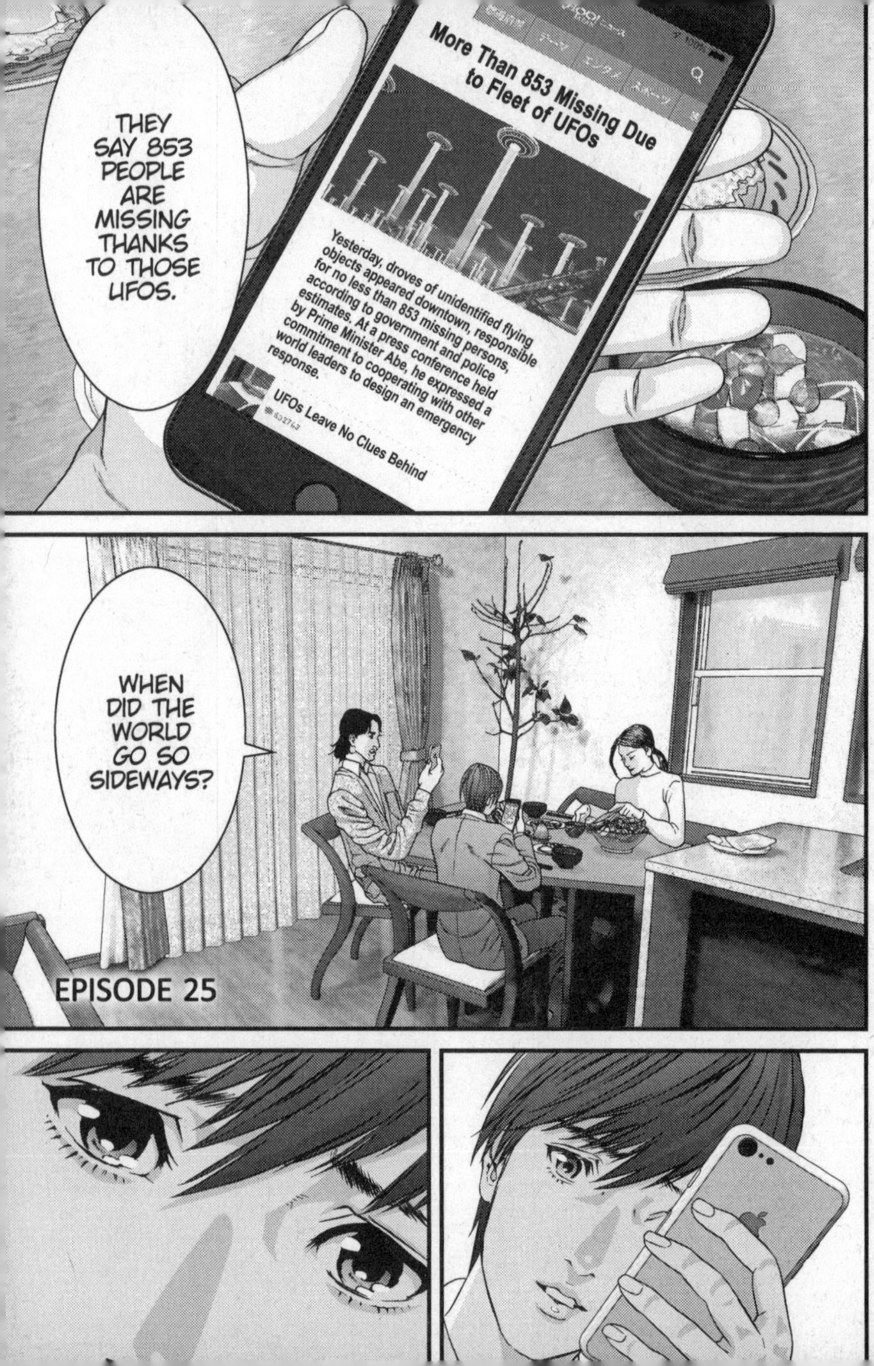
More Than 853 Missing Due to Fleet of UFOs
Yesterday, droves of unidentified flying objects appeared downtown, responsible for no less than 853 missing persons, according to government and police estimates. At a press conference held by Prime Minister Abe, he expressed a commitment to cooperating with other world leaders to design an emergency response.
UFOs Leave No Clues Behind
THEY SAY 853 PEOPLE ARE MISSING THANKS TO THOSE UFOS.
WHEN DID THE WORLD GO SO SIDEWAYS?
EPISODE 25

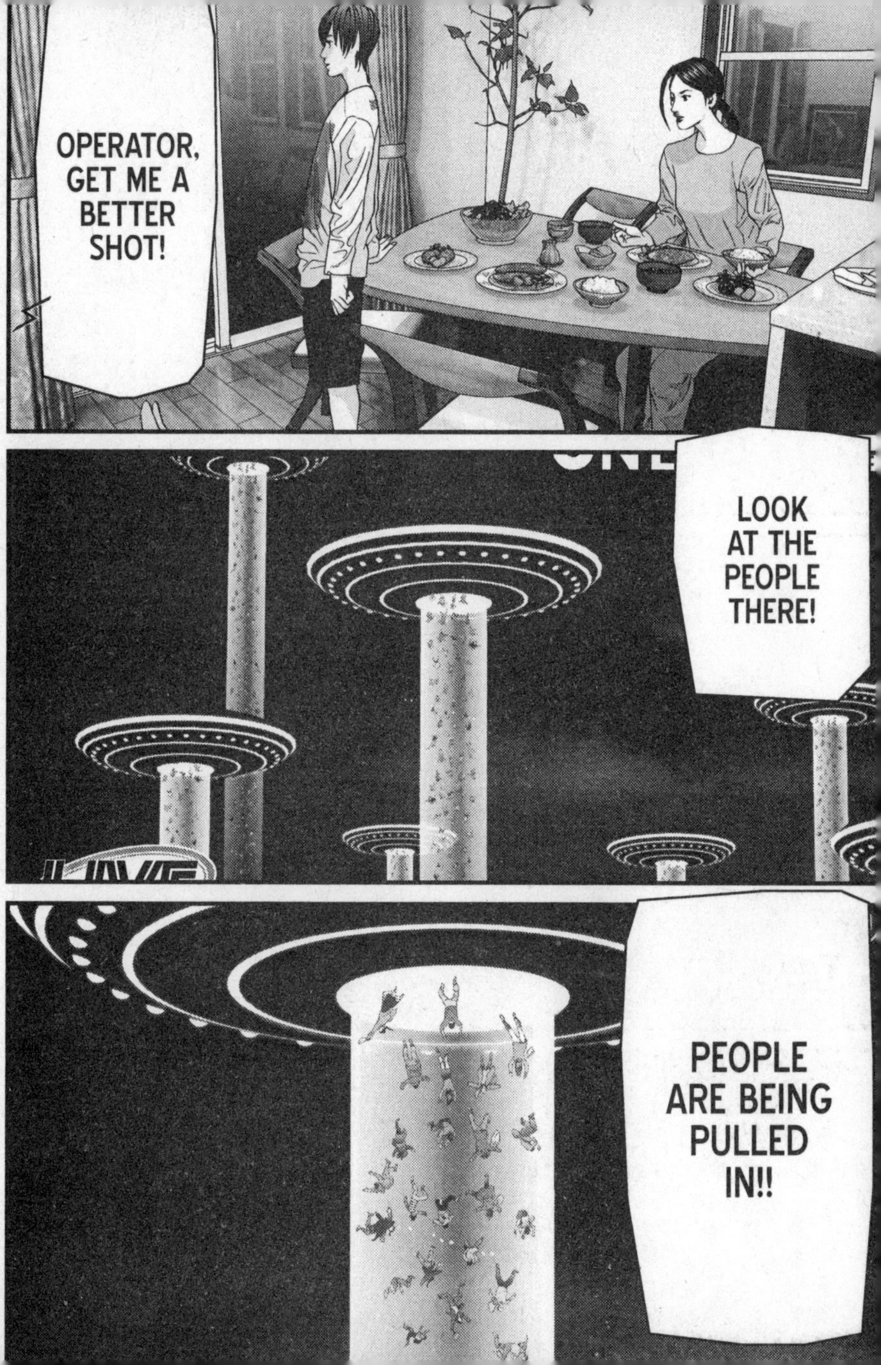
OPERATOR, GET ME A BETTER SHOT!
LOOK AT THE PEOPLE THERE!
PEOPLE ARE BEING PULLED IN!!

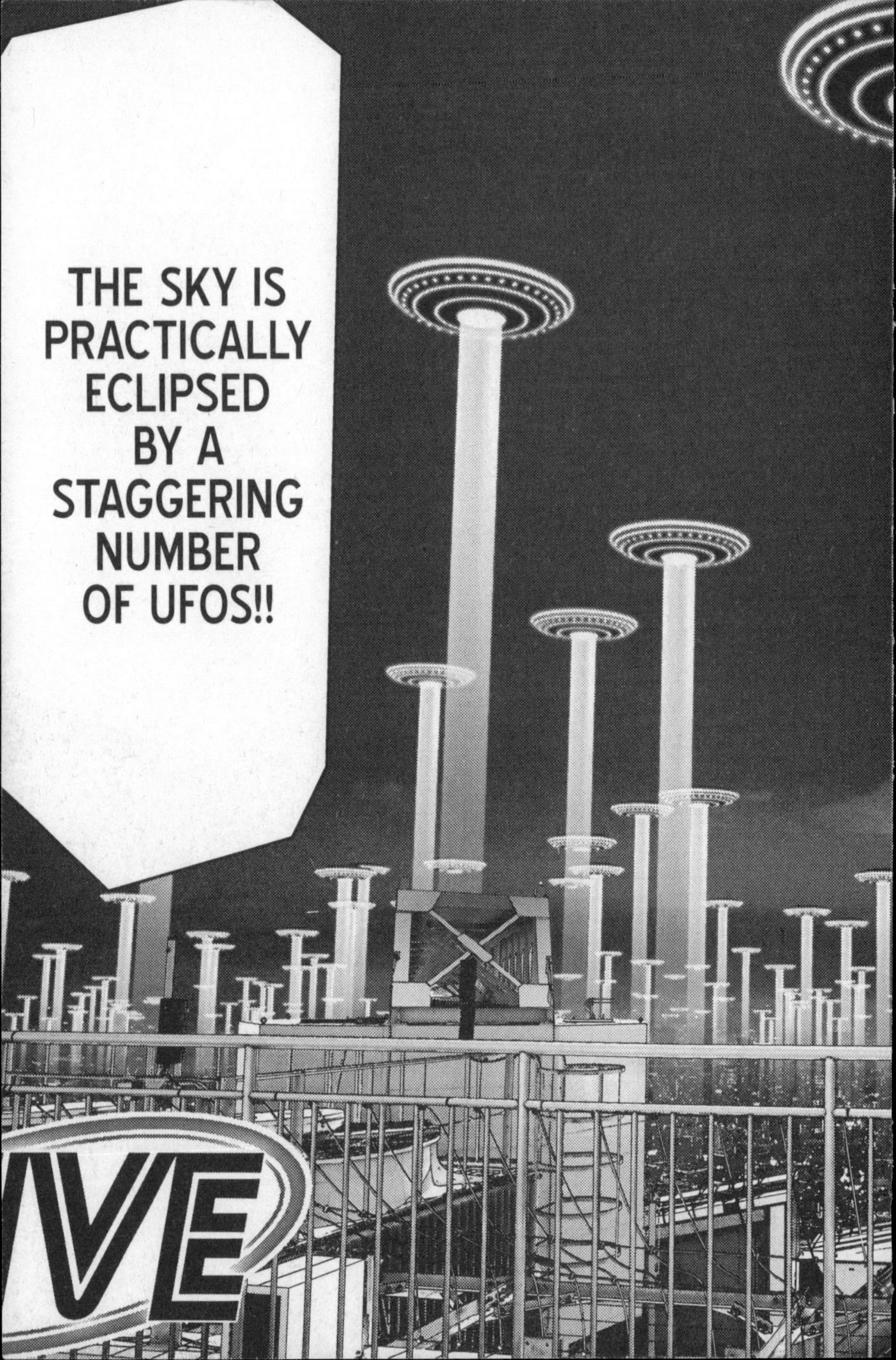
THE SKY IS PRACTICALLY ECLIPSED BY A STAGGERING NUMBER OF UFOS!!
VE

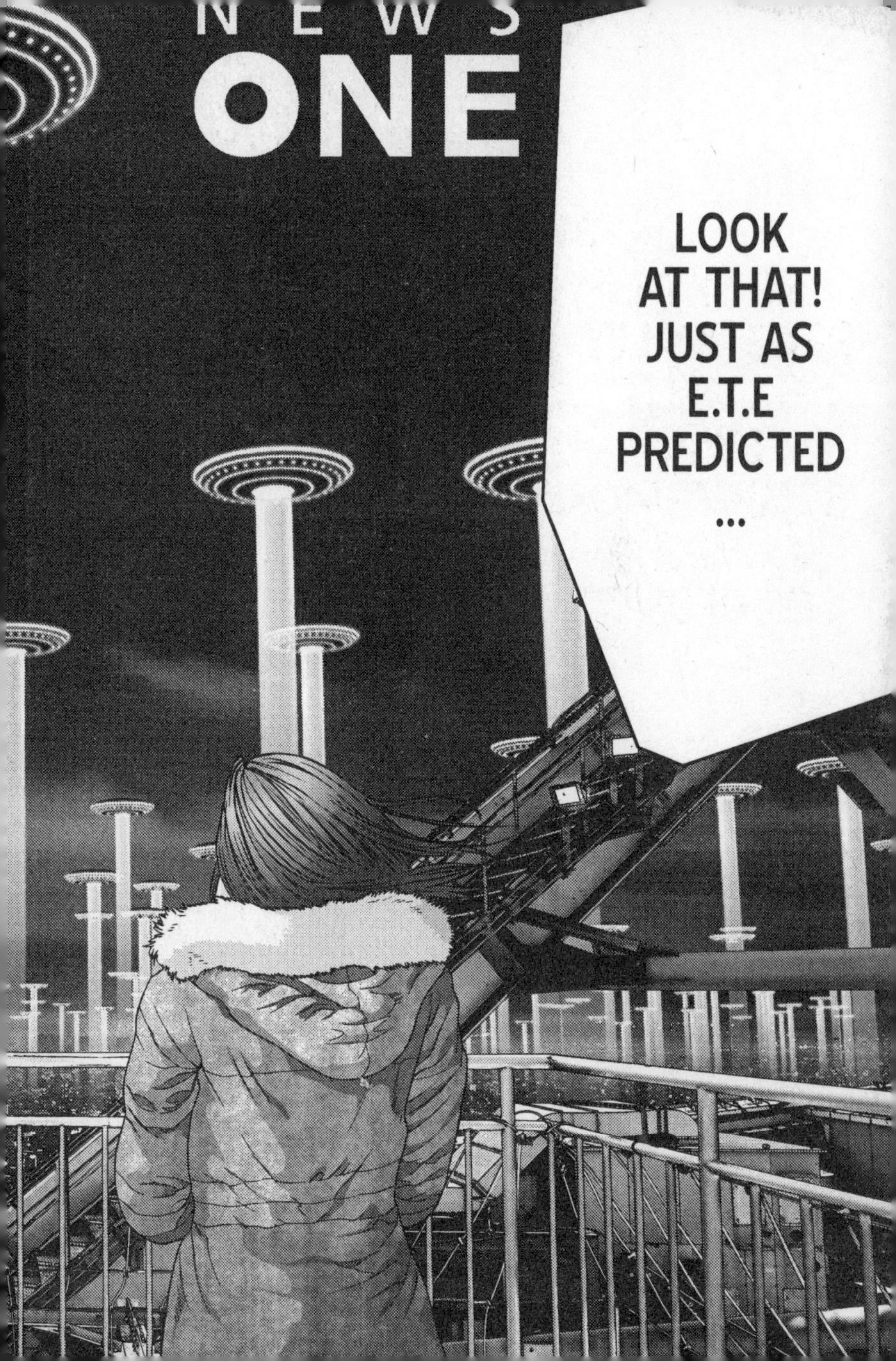
NEWS
ONE
LOOK AT THAT! JUST AS E.T.E PREDICTED ...

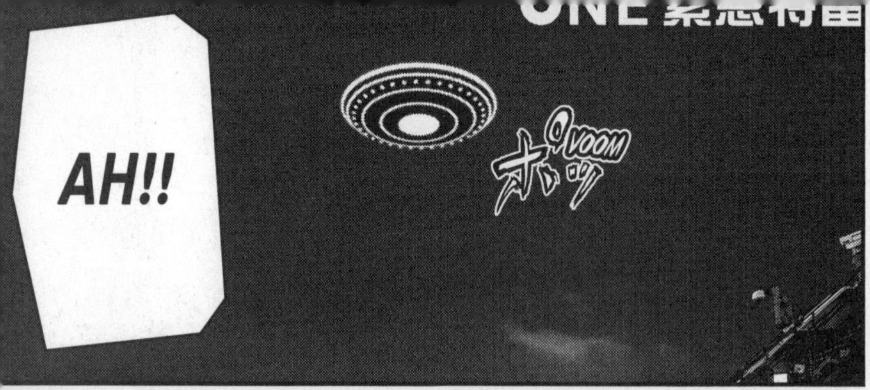
VOOM
AH!!

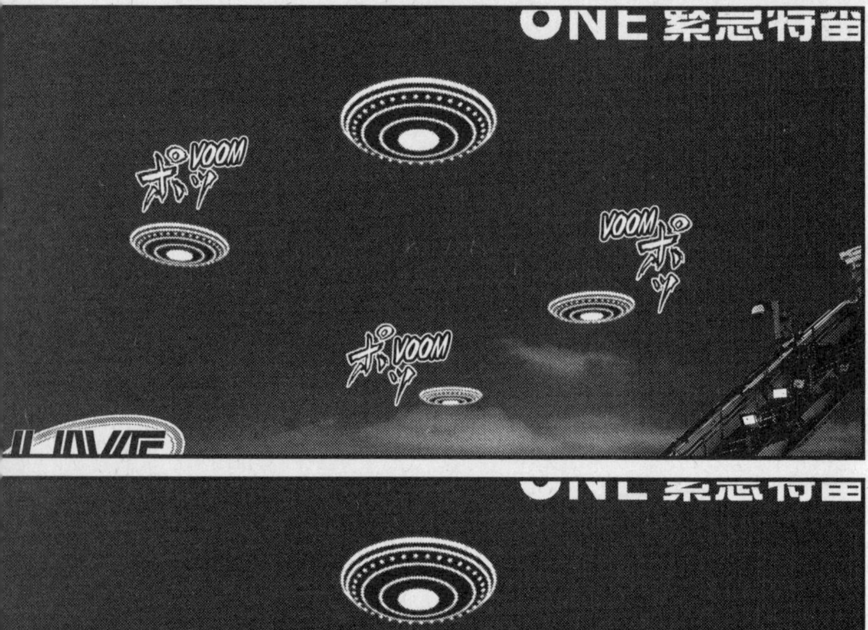
ONE 緊急特番
VOOM
VOOM
VOOM
VOOM

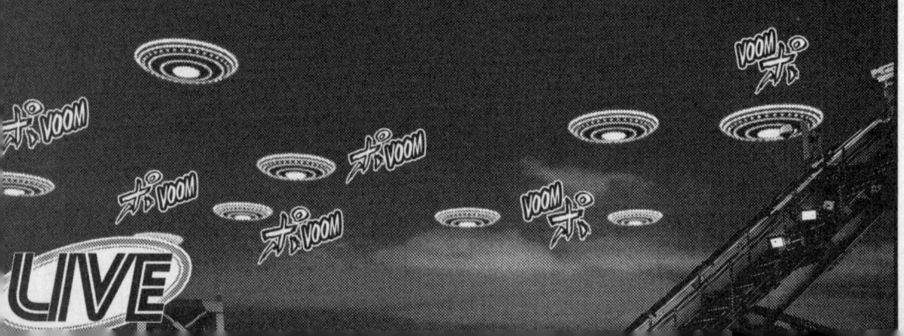
VOOM
VOOM
VOOM
VOOM
VOOM
VOOM
LIVE

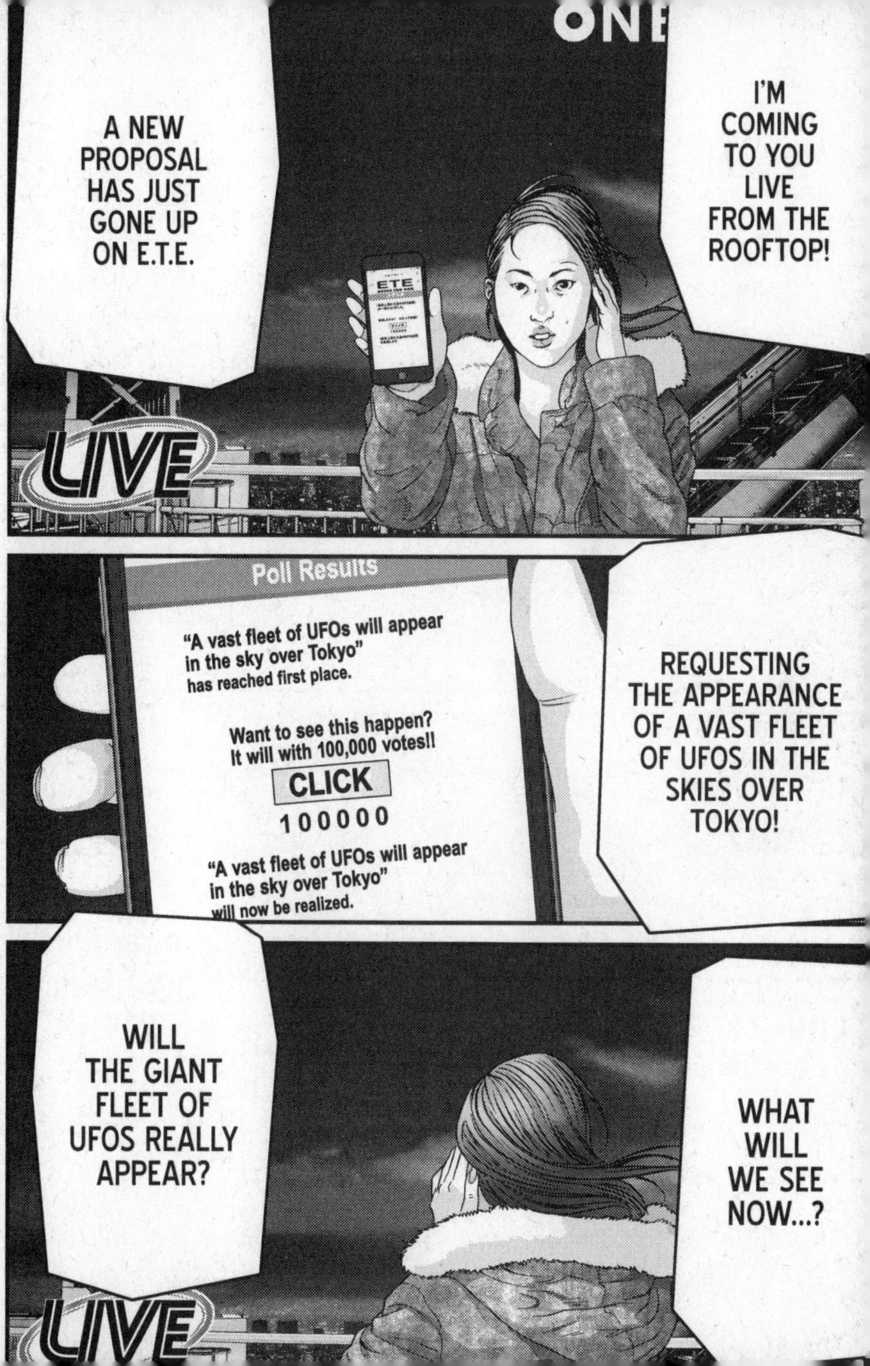
ONE
I'M COMING TO YOU LIVE FROM THE ROOFTOP!
A NEW PROPOSAL HAS JUST GONE UP ON E.T.E.
ETE
LIVE
REQUESTING THE APPEARANCE OF A VAST FLEET OF UFOS IN THE SKIES OVER TOKYO!
Poll Results
"A vast fleet of UFOs will appear in the sky over Tokyo" has reached first place.
Want to see this happen? It will with 100,000 votes!!
CLICK
100000
"A vast fleet of UFOs will appear in the sky over Tokyo" will now be realized.
WHAT WILL WE SEE NOW...?
WILL THE GIANT FLEET OF UFOS REALLY APPEAR?
LIVE

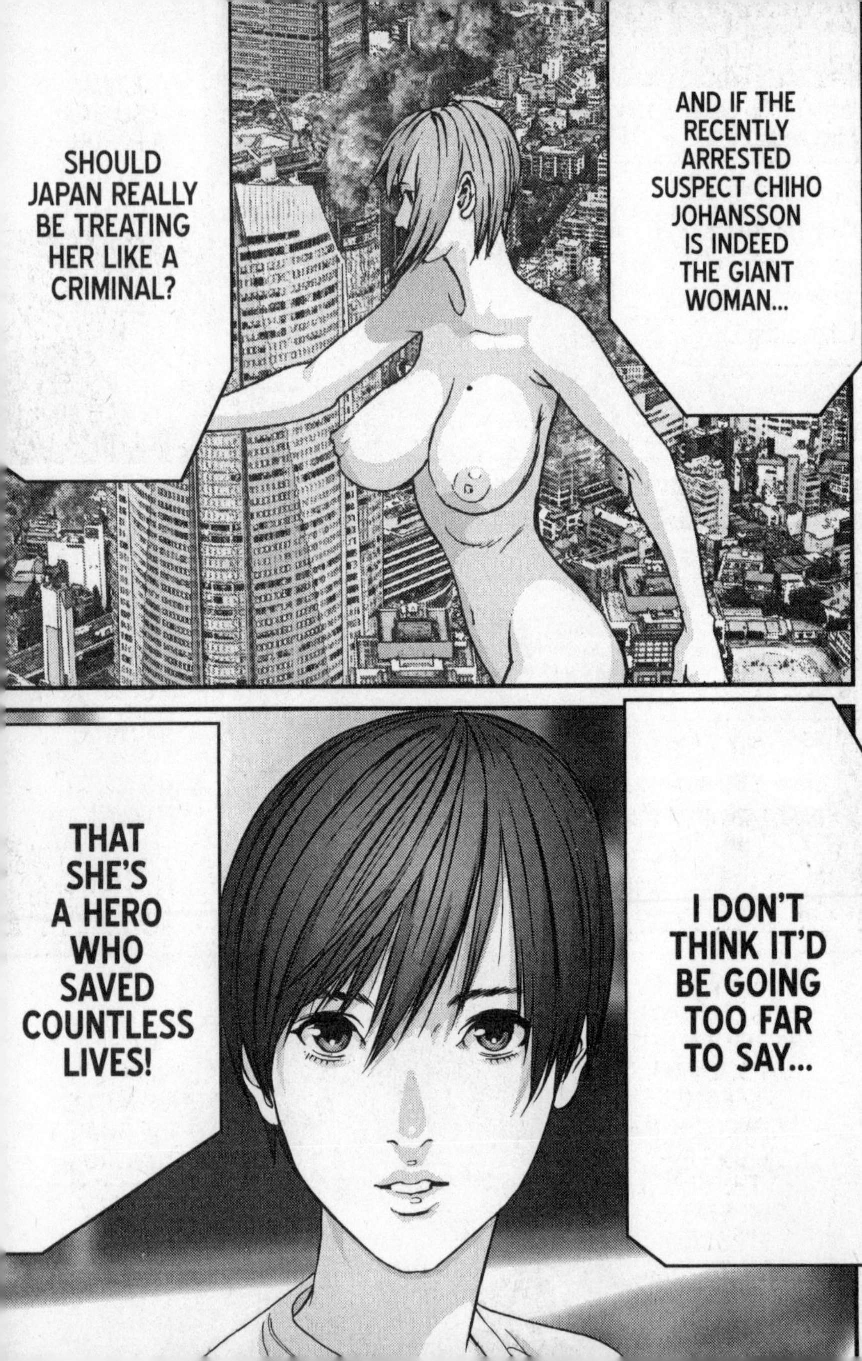
AND IF THE RECENTLY ARRESTED SUSPECT CHIHO JOHANSSON IS INDEED THE GIANT WOMAN...
SHOULD JAPAN REALLY BE TREATING HER LIKE A CRIMINAL?
I DON'T THINK IT'D BE GOING TOO FAR TO SAY...
THAT SHE'S A HERO WHO SAVED COUNTLESS LIVES!

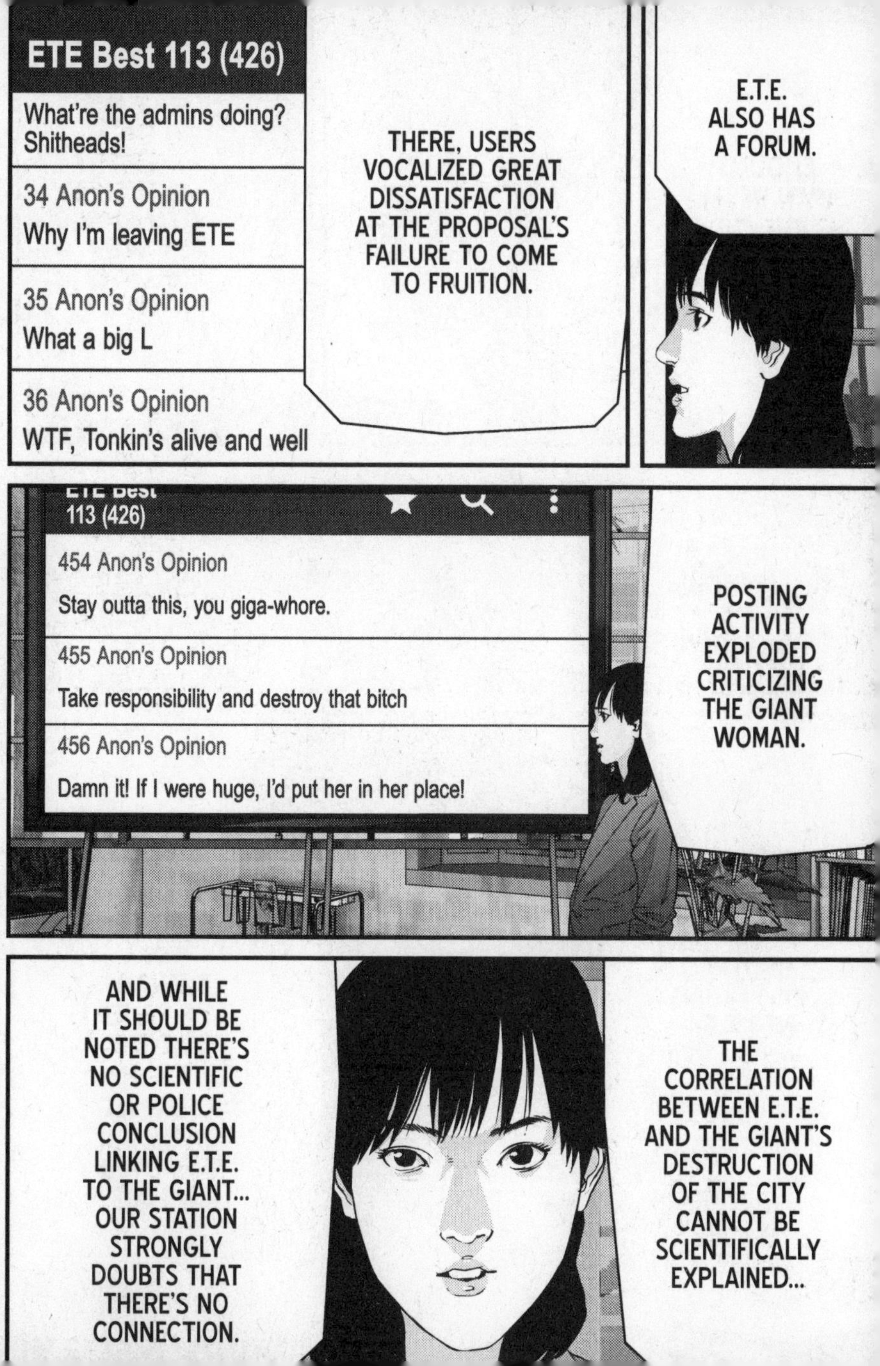

E.T.E. ALSO HAS A FORUM.
THERE, USERS VOCALIZED GREAT DISSATISFACTION AT THE PROPOSAL'S FAILURE TO COME TO FRUITION.
ETE Best 113 (426)
What're the admins doing? Shitheads!
34 Anon's Opinion
Why I'm leaving ETE
35 Anon's Opinion
What a big L
36 Anon's Opinion
WTF, Tonkin's alive and well
POSTING ACTIVITY EXPLODED CRITICIZING THE GIANT WOMAN.
113 (426)
454 Anon's Opinion
Stay outta this, you giga-whore.
455 Anon's Opinion
Take responsibility and destroy that bitch
456 Anon's Opinion
Damn it! If I were huge, I'd put her in her place!
THE CORRELATION BETWEEN E.T.E. AND THE GIANT'S DESTRUCTION OF THE CITY CANNOT BE SCIENTIFICALLY EXPLAINED...
AND WHILE IT SHOULD BE NOTED THERE'S NO SCIENTIFIC OR POLICE CONCLUSION LINKING E.T.E. TO THE GIANT... OUR STATION STRONGLY DOUBTS THAT THERE'S NO CONNECTION.

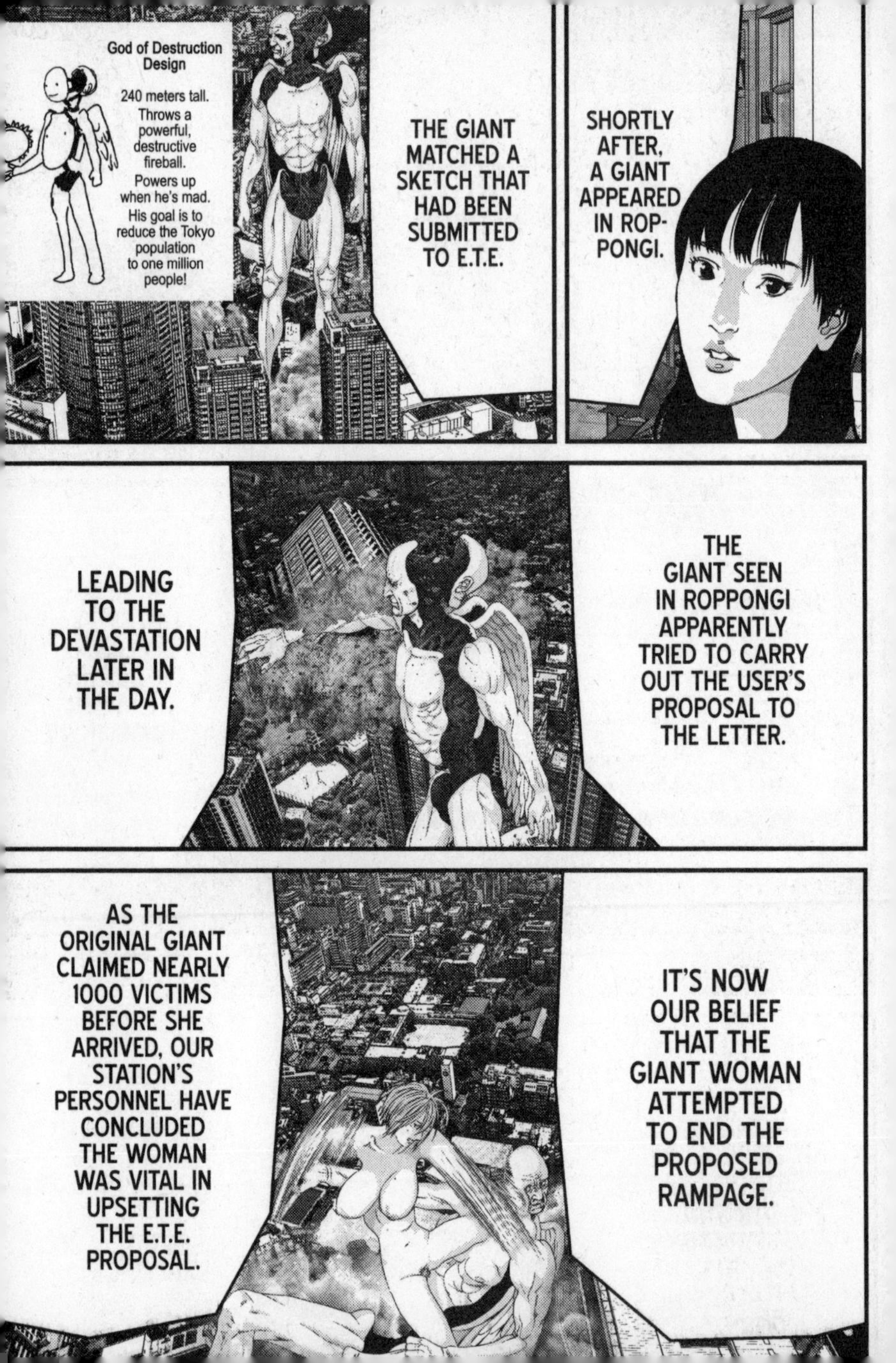
SHORTLY AFTER, A GIANT APPEARED IN ROPPONGI.
THE GIANT MATCHED A SKETCH THAT HAD BEEN SUBMITTED TO E.T.E.
God of Destruction Design
240 meters tall. Throws a powerful, destructive fireball. Powers up when he's mad. His goal is to reduce the Tokyo population to one million people!
THE GIANT SEEN IN ROPPONGI APPARENTLY TRIED TO CARRY OUT THE USER'S PROPOSAL TO THE LETTER.
LEADING TO THE DEVASTATION LATER IN THE DAY.
IT'S NOW OUR BELIEF THAT THE GIANT WOMAN ATTEMPTED TO END THE PROPOSED RAMPAGE.
AS THE ORIGINAL GIANT CLAIMED NEARLY 1000 VICTIMS BEFORE SHE ARRIVED, OUR STATION'S PERSONNEL HAVE CONCLUDED THE WOMAN WAS VITAL IN UPSETTING THE E.T.E. PROPOSAL.

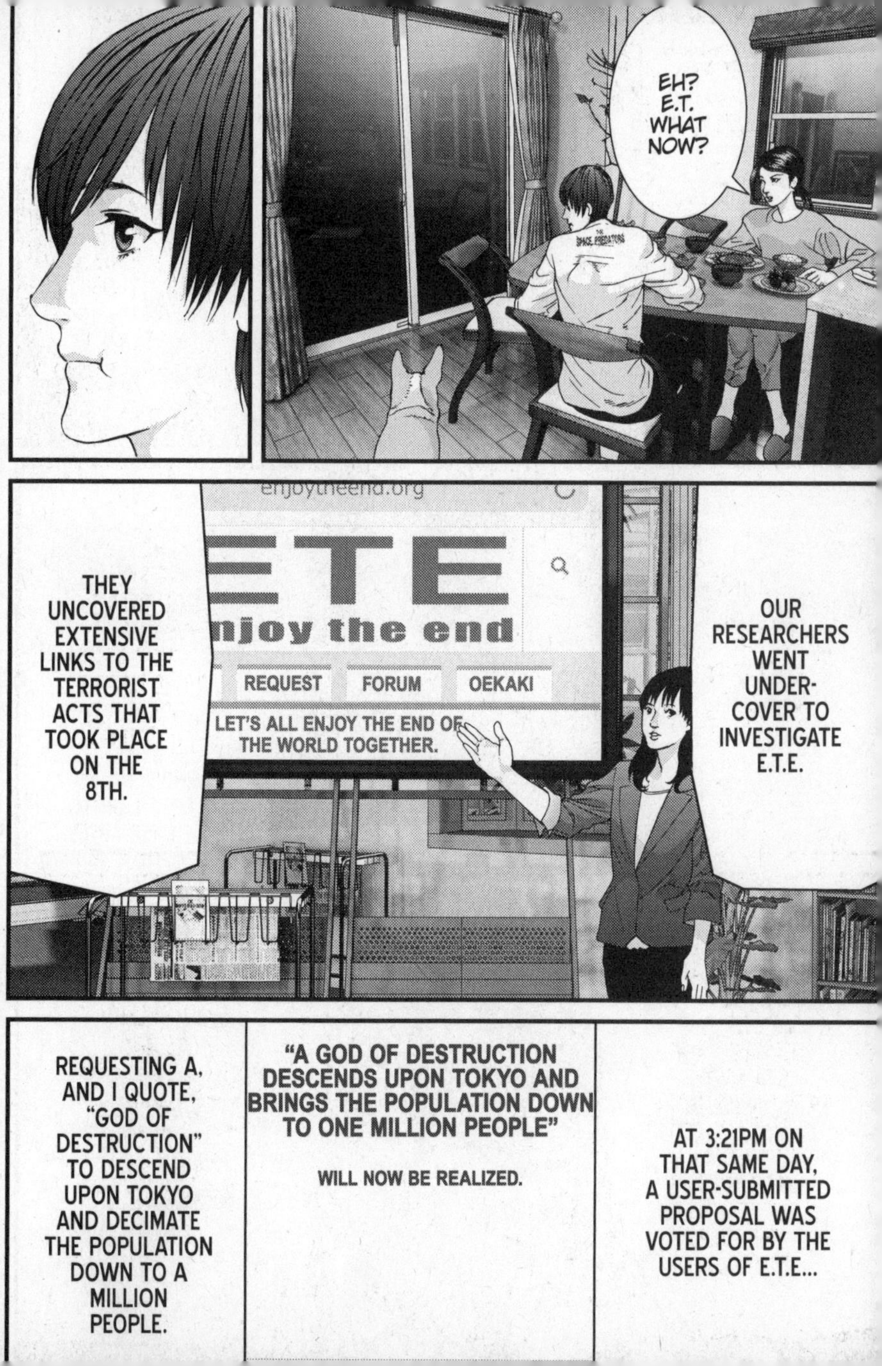
EH? E.T. WHAT NOW?
OUR RESEARCHERS WENT UNDER-COVER TO INVESTIGATE E.T.E.
enjoytheend.org
ETE
njoy the end
REQUEST
FORUM
OEKAKI
LET'S ALL ENJOY THE END OF THE WORLD TOGETHER.
THEY UNCOVERED EXTENSIVE LINKS TO THE TERRORIST ACTS THAT TOOK PLACE ON THE 8TH.
AT 3:21PM ON THAT SAME DAY, A USER-SUBMITTED PROPOSAL WAS VOTED FOR BY THE USERS OF E.T.E...
"A GOD OF DESTRUCTION DESCENDS UPON TOKYO AND BRINGS THE POPULATION DOWN TO ONE MILLION PEOPLE"
WILL NOW BE REALIZED.
REQUESTING A, AND I QUOTE, "GOD OF DESTRUCTION" TO DESCEND UPON TOKYO AND DECIMATE THE POPULATION DOWN TO A MILLION PEOPLE.

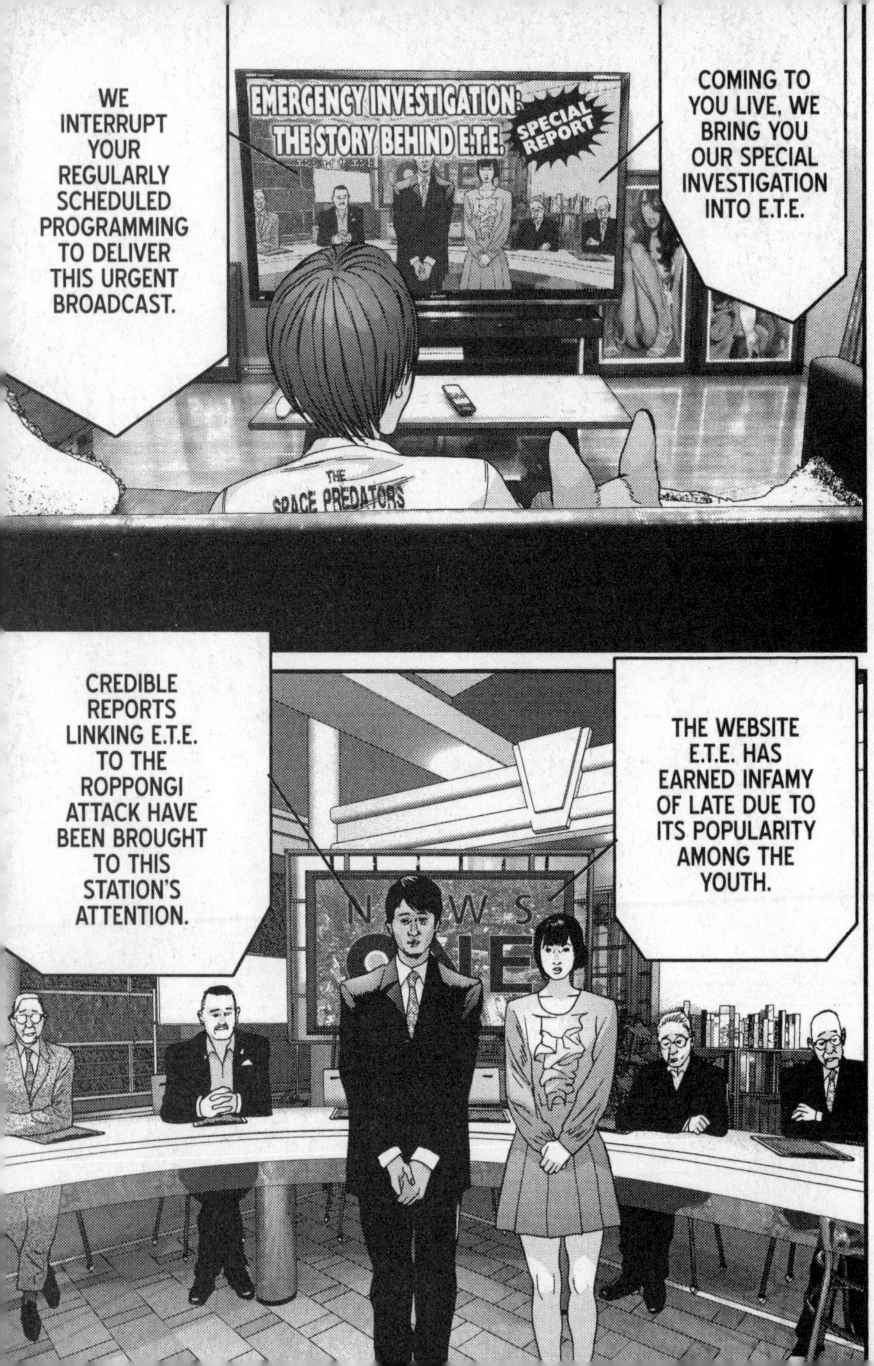
EMERGENCY INVESTIGATION: THE STORY BEHIND E.T.E.
SPECIAL REPORT
COMING TO YOU LIVE, WE BRING YOU OUR SPECIAL INVESTIGATION INTO E.T.E.
WE INTERRUPT YOUR REGULARLY SCHEDULED PROGRAMMING TO DELIVER THIS URGENT BROADCAST.
THE SPACE PREDATORS
THE WEBSITE E.T.E. HAS EARNED INFAMY OF LATE DUE TO ITS POPULARITY AMONG THE YOUTH.
CREDIBLE REPORTS LINKING E.T.E. TO THE ROPPONGI ATTACK HAVE BEEN BROUGHT TO THIS STATION'S ATTENTION.
NEWS

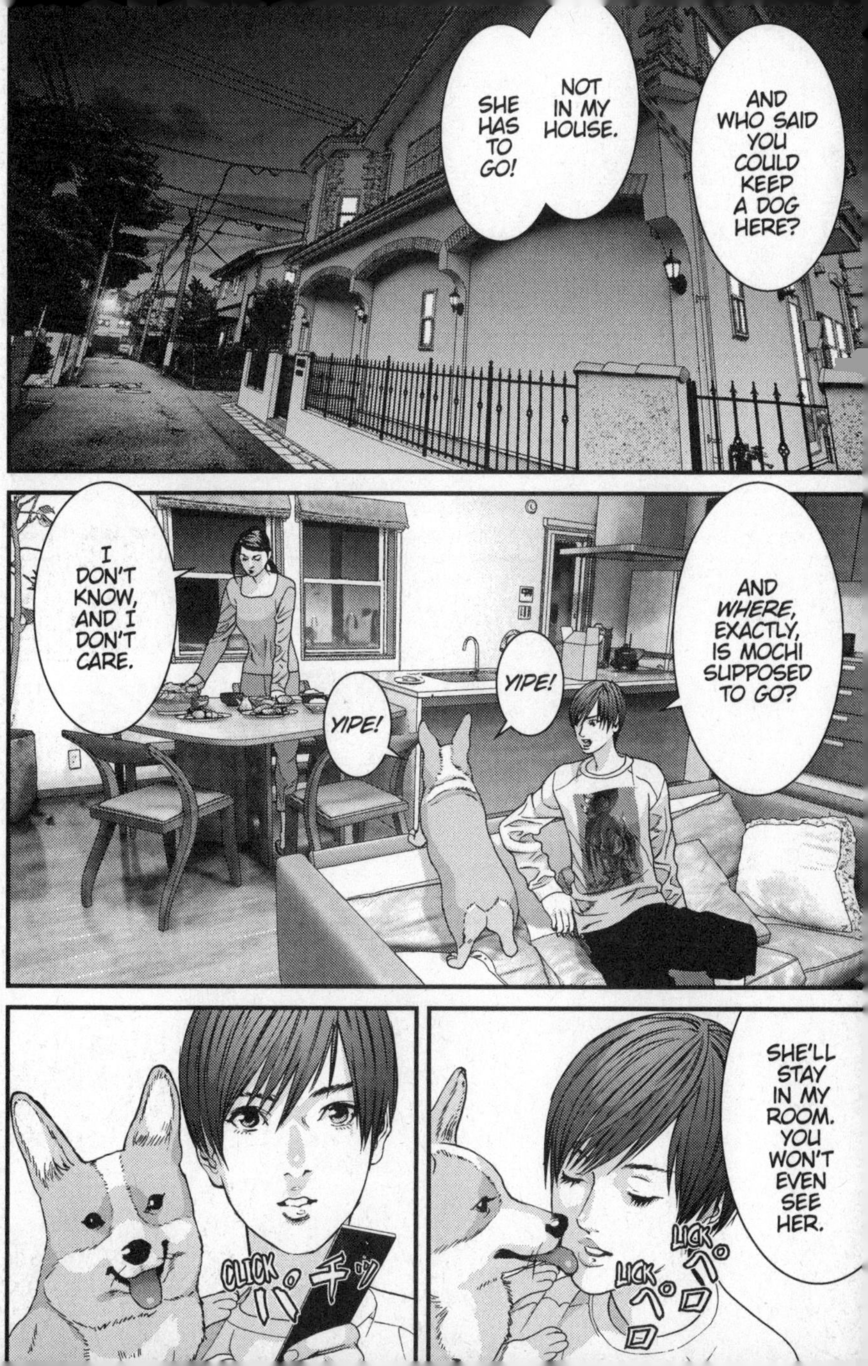
AND WHO SAID YOU COULD KEEP A DOG HERE?
NOT IN MY HOUSE.
SHE HAS TO GO!
AND WHERE, EXACTLY, IS MOCHI SUPPOSED TO GO?
YIPE!
YIPE!
I DON'T KNOW, AND I DON'T CARE.
SHE'LL STAY IN MY ROOM. YOU WON'T EVEN SEE HER.
LICK
ペロ
LICK
ペロ
CLICK
パチッ

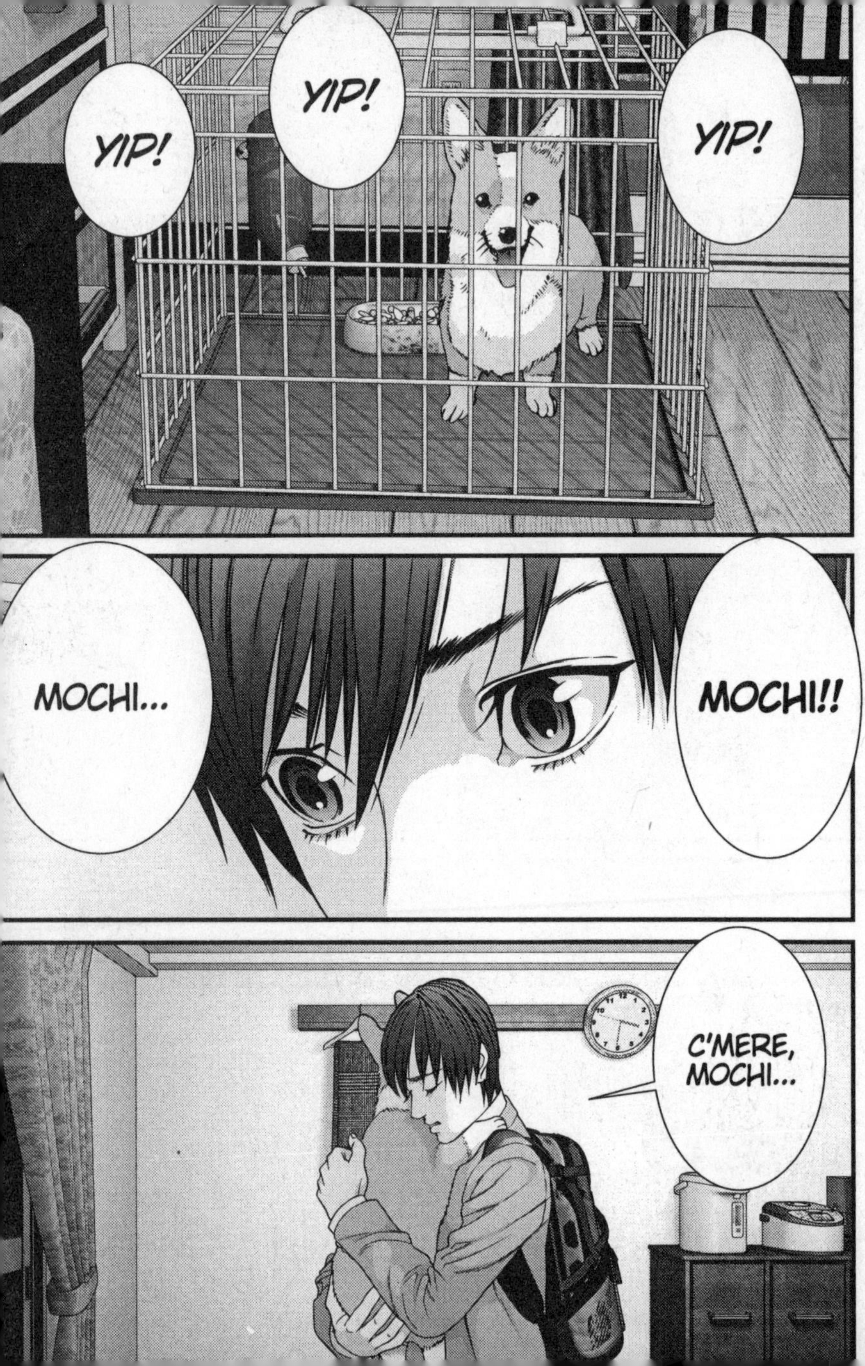
YIP!
YIP!
YIP!
MOCHI!!
MOCHI...
C'MERE, MOCHI...

CREAK
ギィ
RATTLE
ガチ
RATTLE
ャガチャ

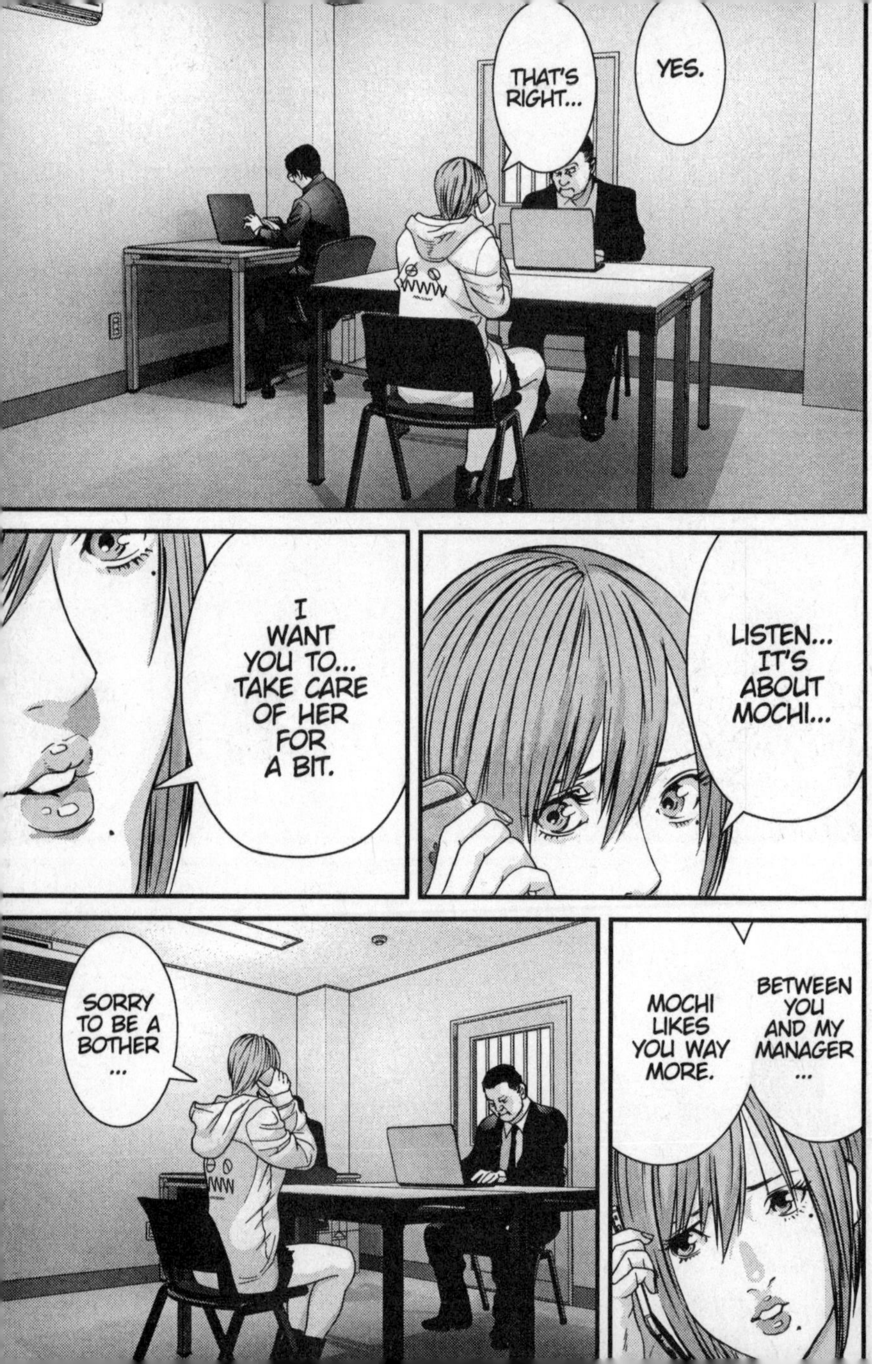
YES.
THAT'S RIGHT...
LISTEN... IT'S ABOUT MOCHI...
I WANT YOU TO... TAKE CARE OF HER FOR A BIT.
BETWEEN YOU AND MY MANAGER ...
MOCHI LIKES YOU WAY MORE.
SORRY TO BE A BOTHER ...

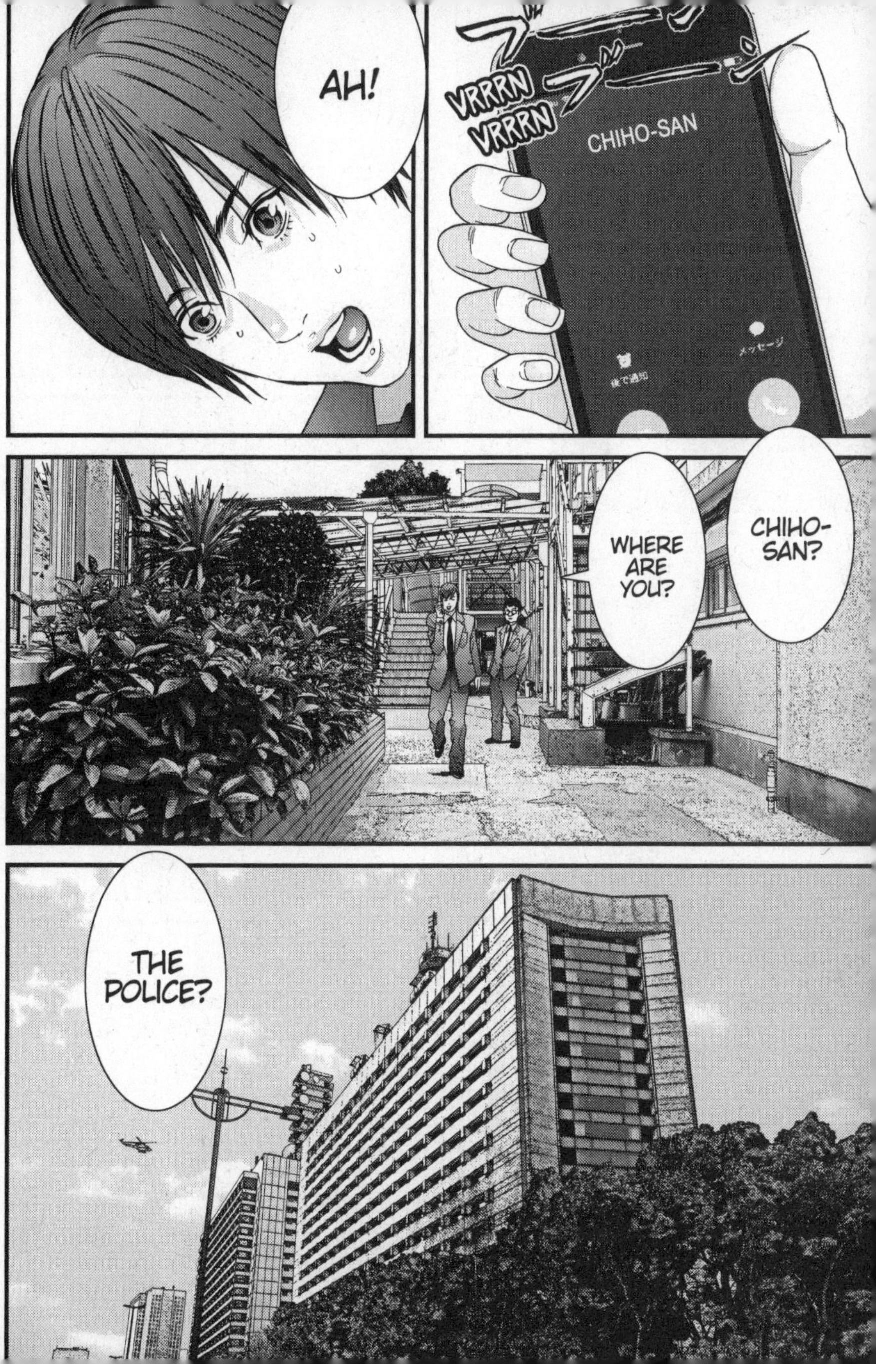
VRRRN
VRRRN
CHIHO-SAN
後で通知
メッセージ
AH!
CHIHO-SAN?
WHERE ARE YOU?
THE POLICE?

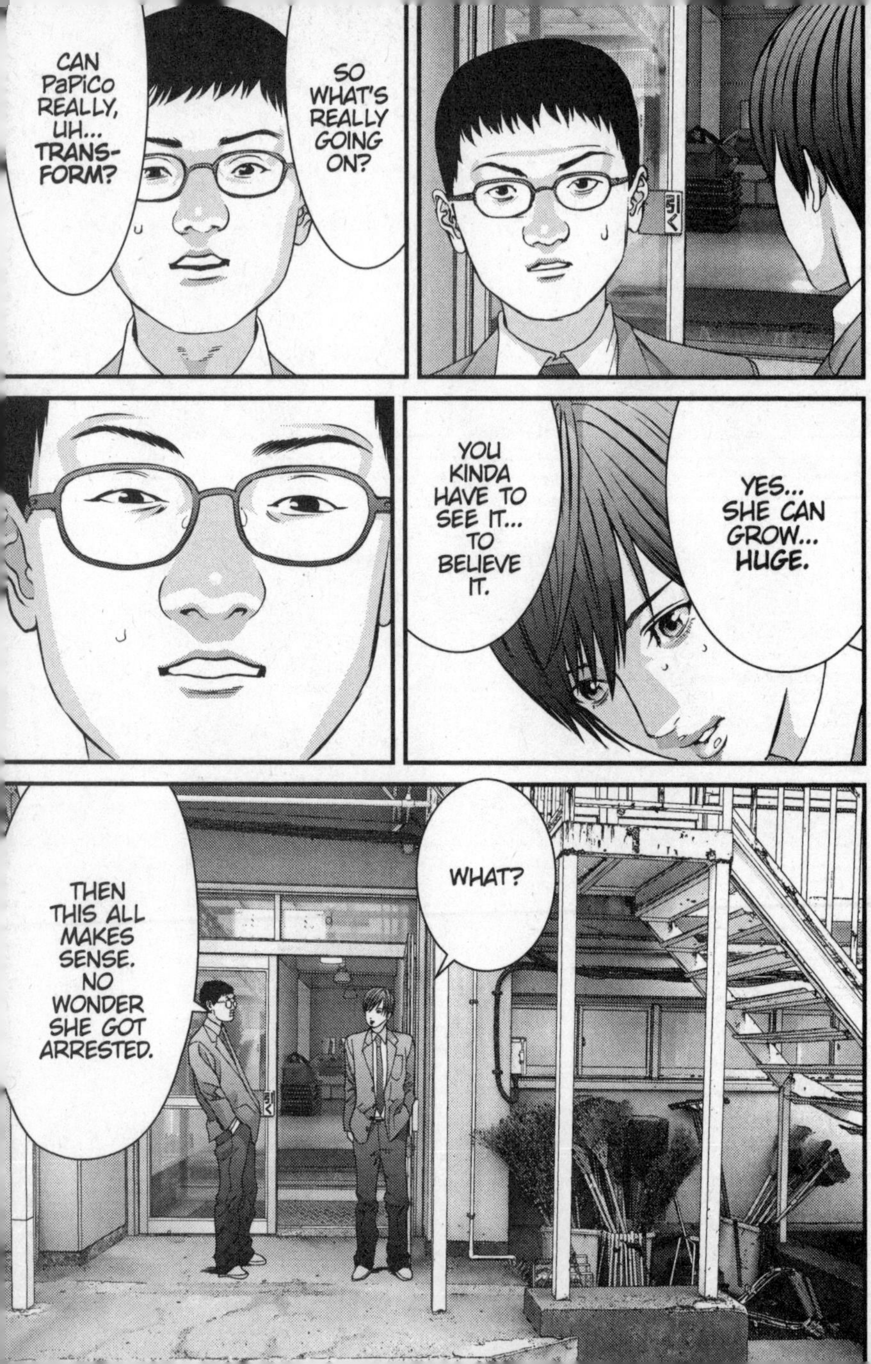
SO WHAT'S REALLY GOING ON?
CAN PaPiCo REALLY, UH... TRANS-FORM?
YES... SHE CAN GROW... HUGE.
YOU KINDA HAVE TO SEE IT... TO BELIEVE IT.
WHAT?
THEN THIS ALL MAKES SENSE. NO WONDER SHE GOT ARRESTED.

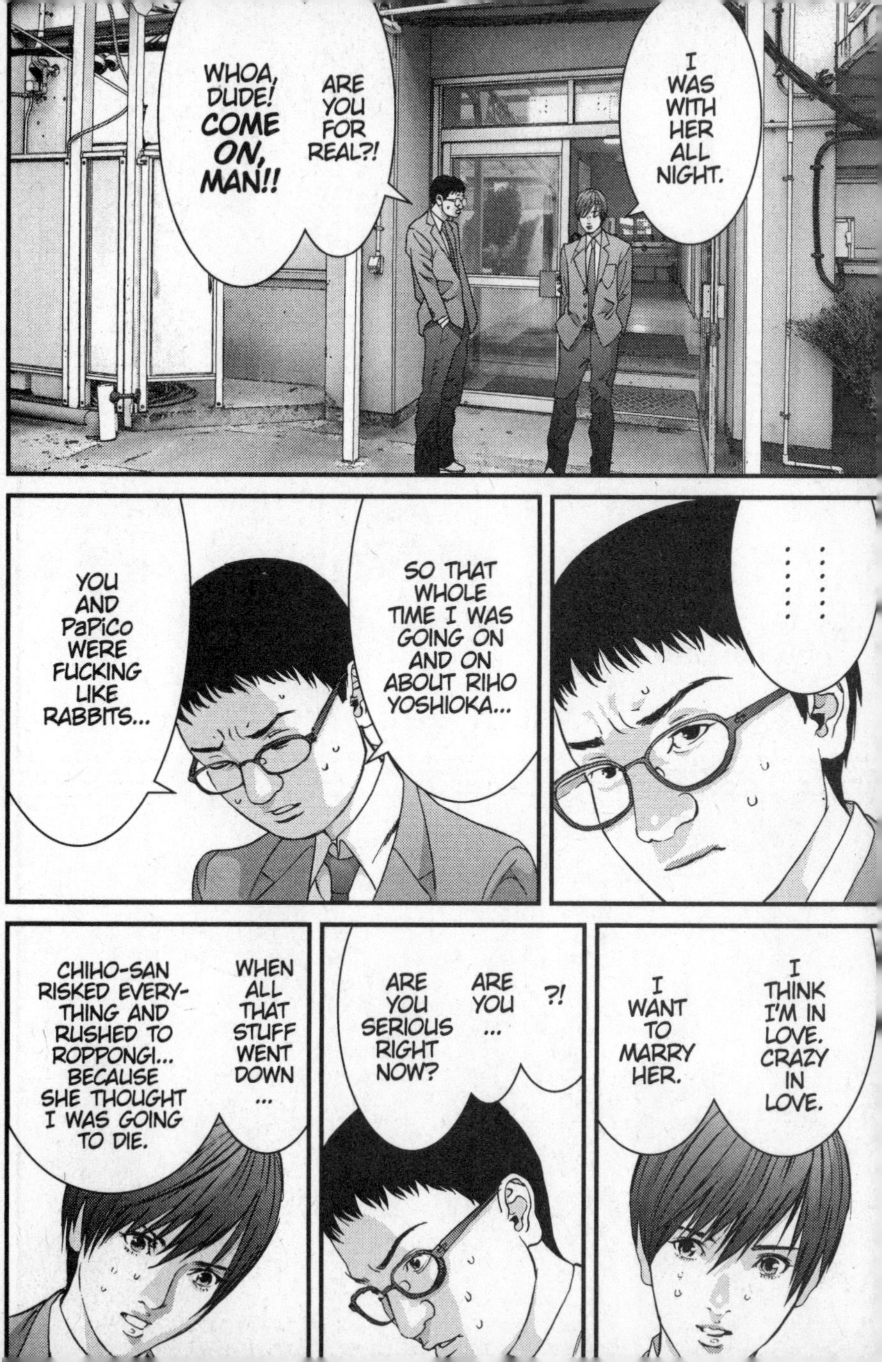
I WAS WITH HER ALL NIGHT.
WHOA, DUDE! COME ON, MAN!! ARE YOU FOR REAL?!
......
SO THAT WHOLE TIME I WAS GOING ON AND ON ABOUT RIHO YOSHIOKA...
YOU AND PaPiCo WERE FUCKING LIKE RABBITS...
I THINK I'M IN LOVE. CRAZY IN LOVE.
I WANT TO MARRY HER.
?!
ARE YOU ...
ARE YOU SERIOUS RIGHT NOW?
WHEN ALL THAT STUFF WENT DOWN ...
CHIHO-SAN RISKED EVERY-THING AND RUSHED TO ROPPONGI... BECAUSE SHE THOUGHT I WAS GOING TO DIE.

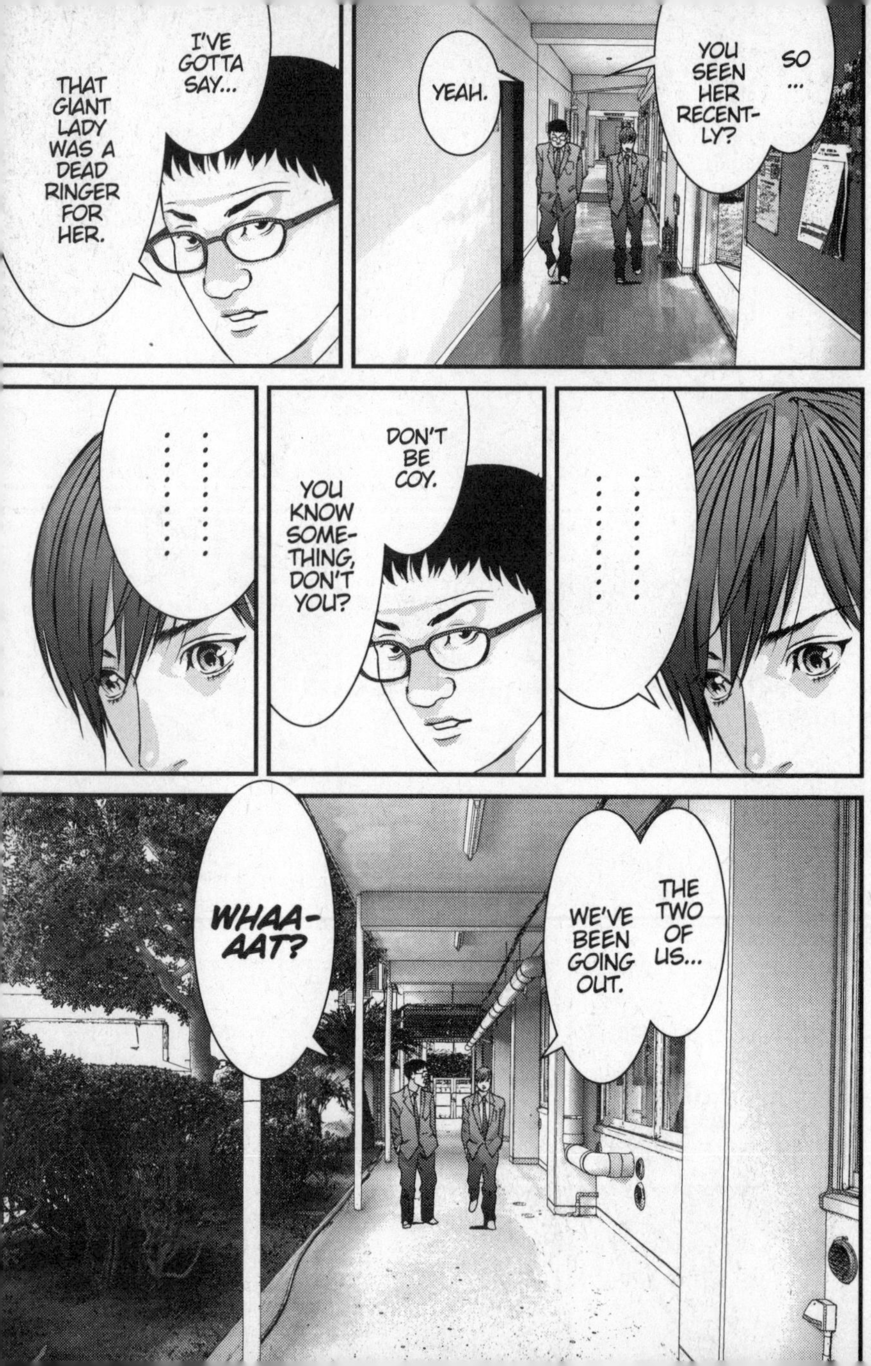
SO ... YOU SEEN HER RECENT-LY?
YEAH.
I'VE GOTTA SAY... THAT GIANT LADY WAS A DEAD RINGER FOR HER.
......
DON'T BE COY. YOU KNOW SOME-THING, DON'T YOU?
......
THE TWO OF US... WE'VE BEEN GOING OUT.
WHAA-AAT?

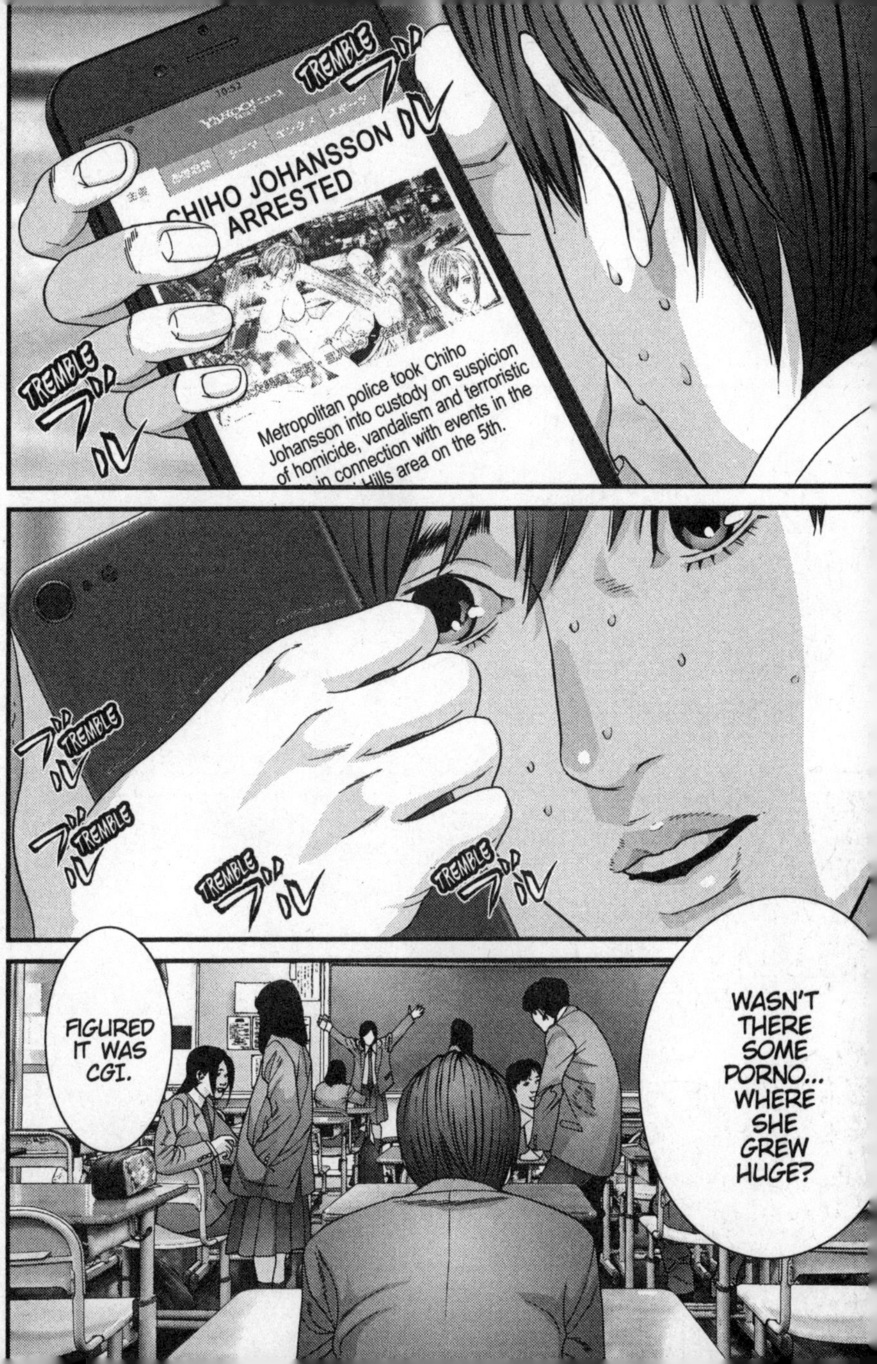
TREMBLE
CHIHO JOHANSSON ARRESTED
Metropolitan police took Chiho Johansson into custody on suspicion of homicide, vandalism and terroristic
in connection with events in the
Hills area on the 5th.
TREMBLE
TREMBLE
TREMBLE
TREMBLE
TREMBLE
WASN'T THERE SOME PORNO... WHERE SHE GREW HUGE?
FIGURED IT WAS CGI.

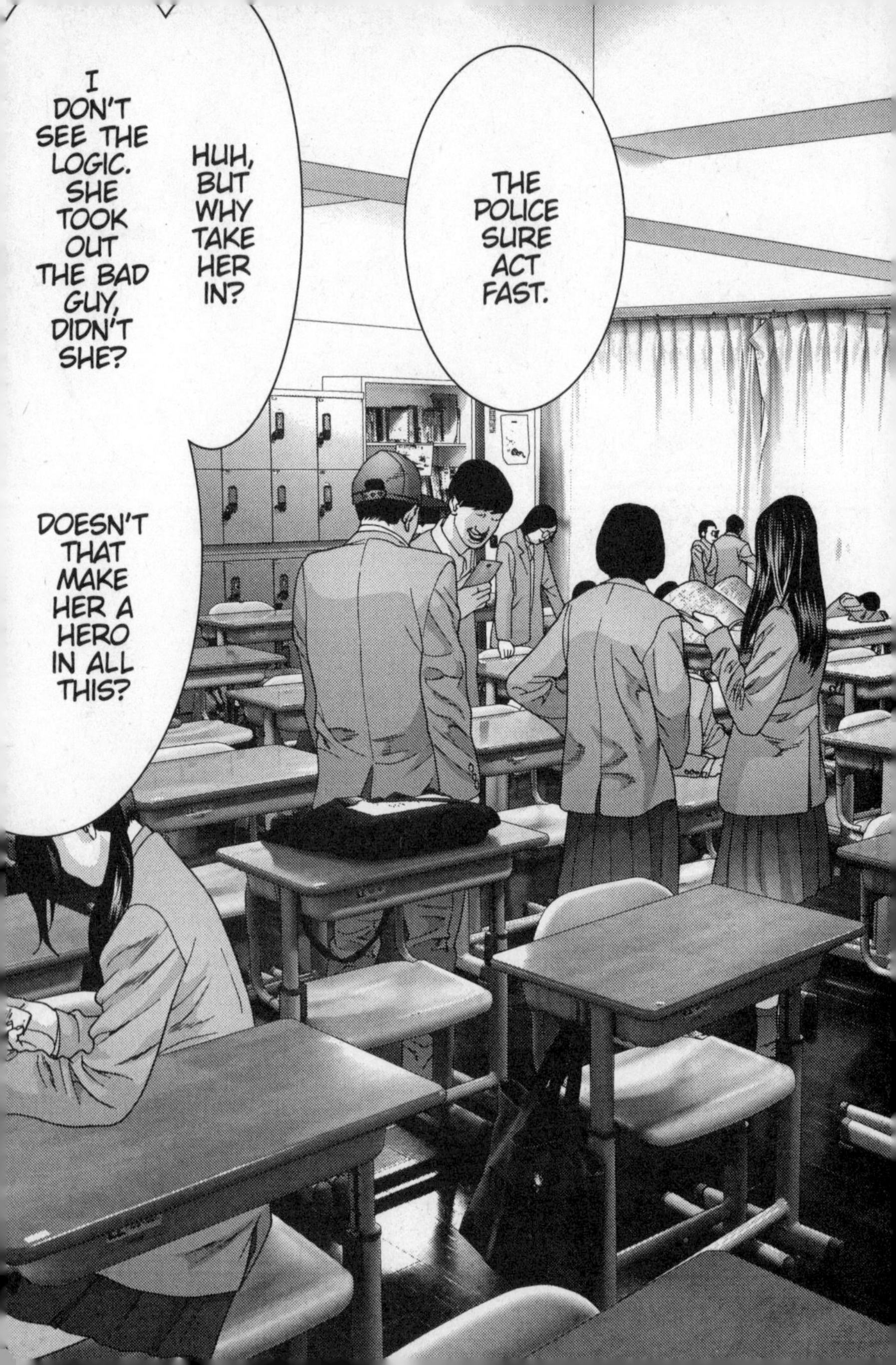
THE POLICE SURE ACT FAST.
HUH, BUT WHY TAKE HER IN?
I DON'T SEE THE LOGIC. SHE TOOK OUT THE BAD GUY, DIDN'T SHE?
DOESN'T THAT MAKE HER A HERO IN ALL THIS?

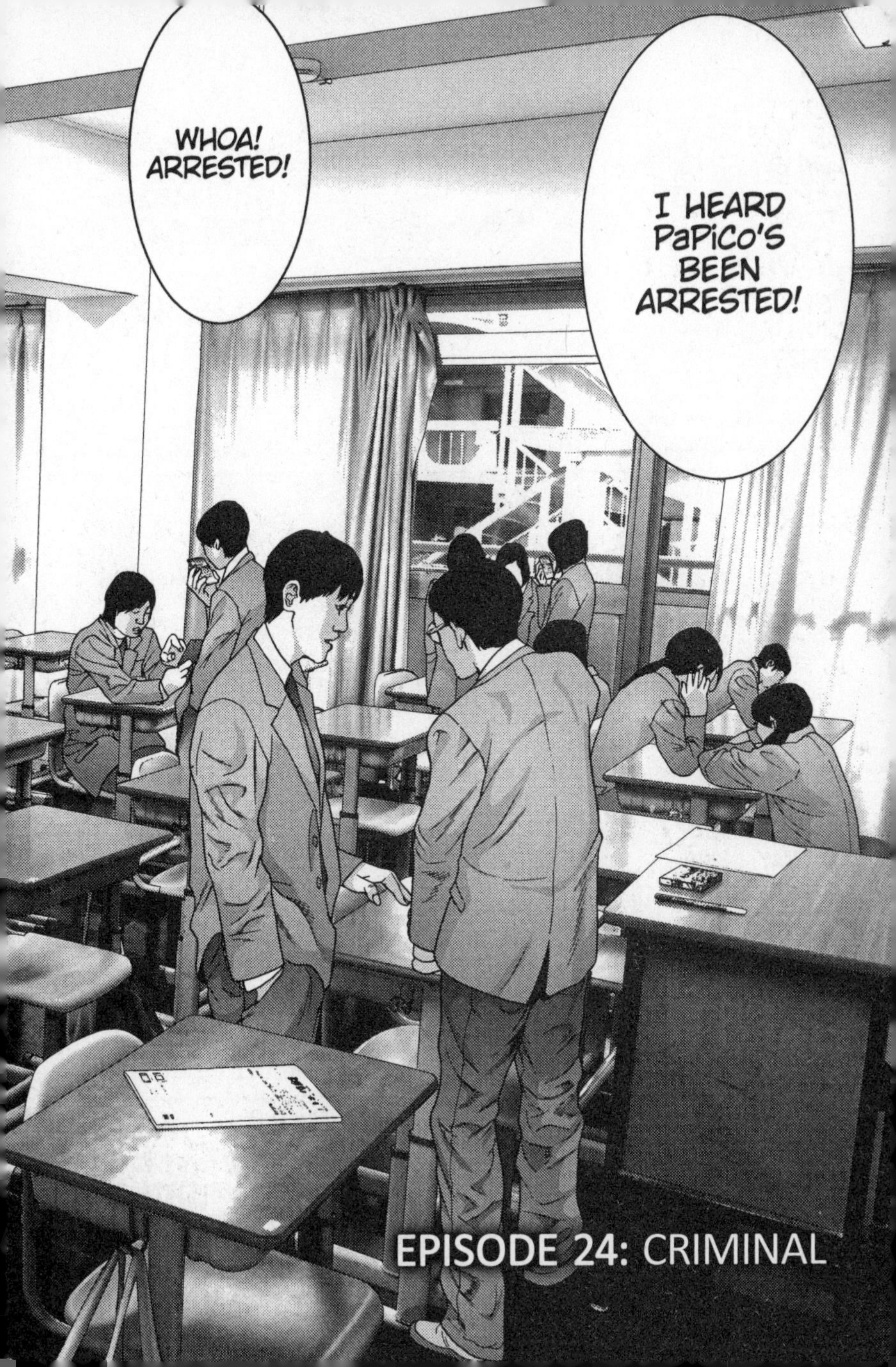
I HEARD PaPiCo'S BEEN ARRESTED!
WHOA! ARRESTED!
EPISODE 24: CRIMINAL

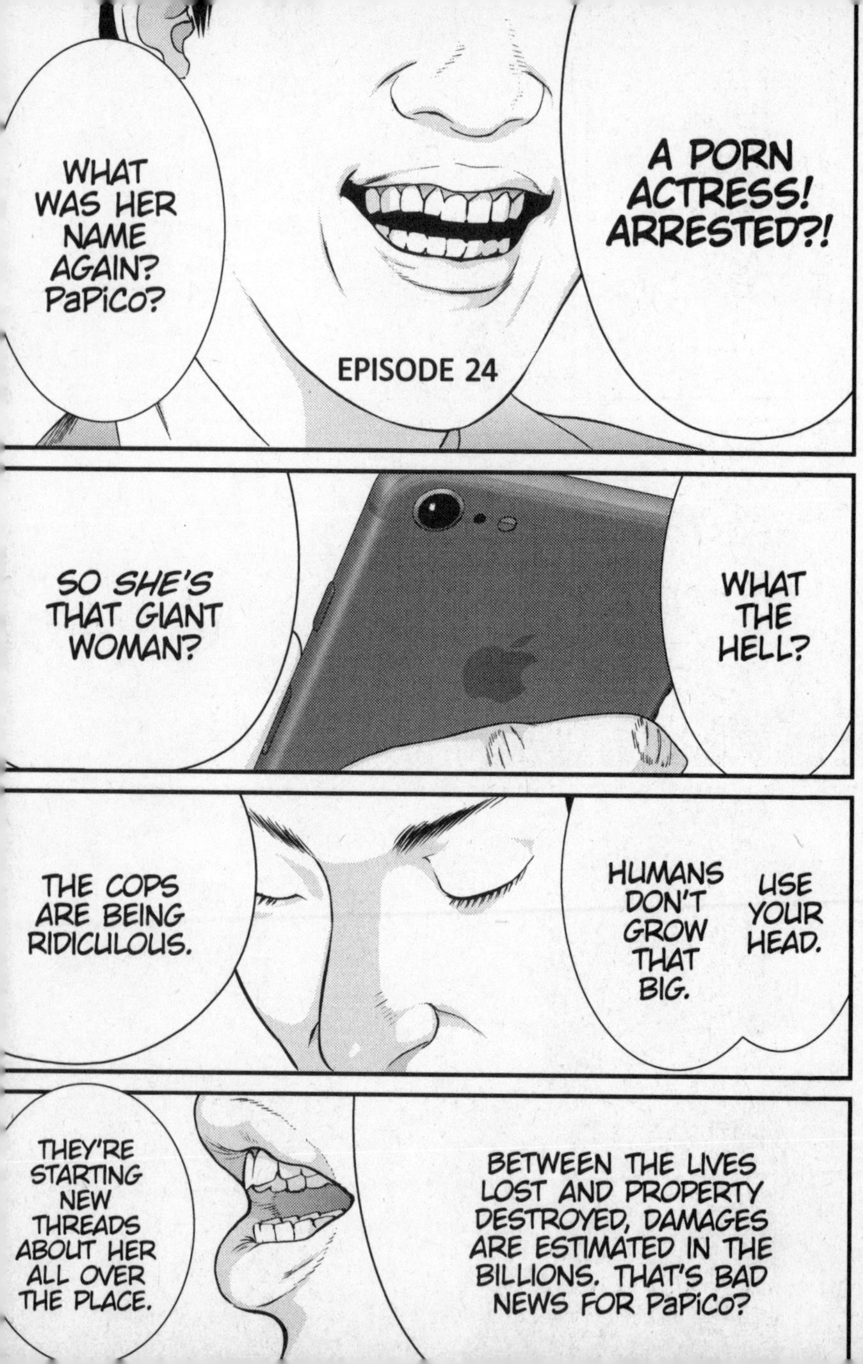
A PORN ACTRESS! ARRESTED?!
WHAT WAS HER NAME AGAIN? PaPiCo?
EPISODE 24
WHAT THE HELL?
SO SHE'S THAT GIANT WOMAN?
USE YOUR HEAD.
HUMANS DON'T GROW THAT BIG.
THE COPS ARE BEING RIDICULOUS.
BETWEEN THE LIVES LOST AND PROPERTY DESTROYED, DAMAGES ARE ESTIMATED IN THE BILLIONS. THAT'S BAD NEWS FOR PaPiCo?
THEY'RE STARTING NEW THREADS ABOUT HER ALL OVER THE PLACE.

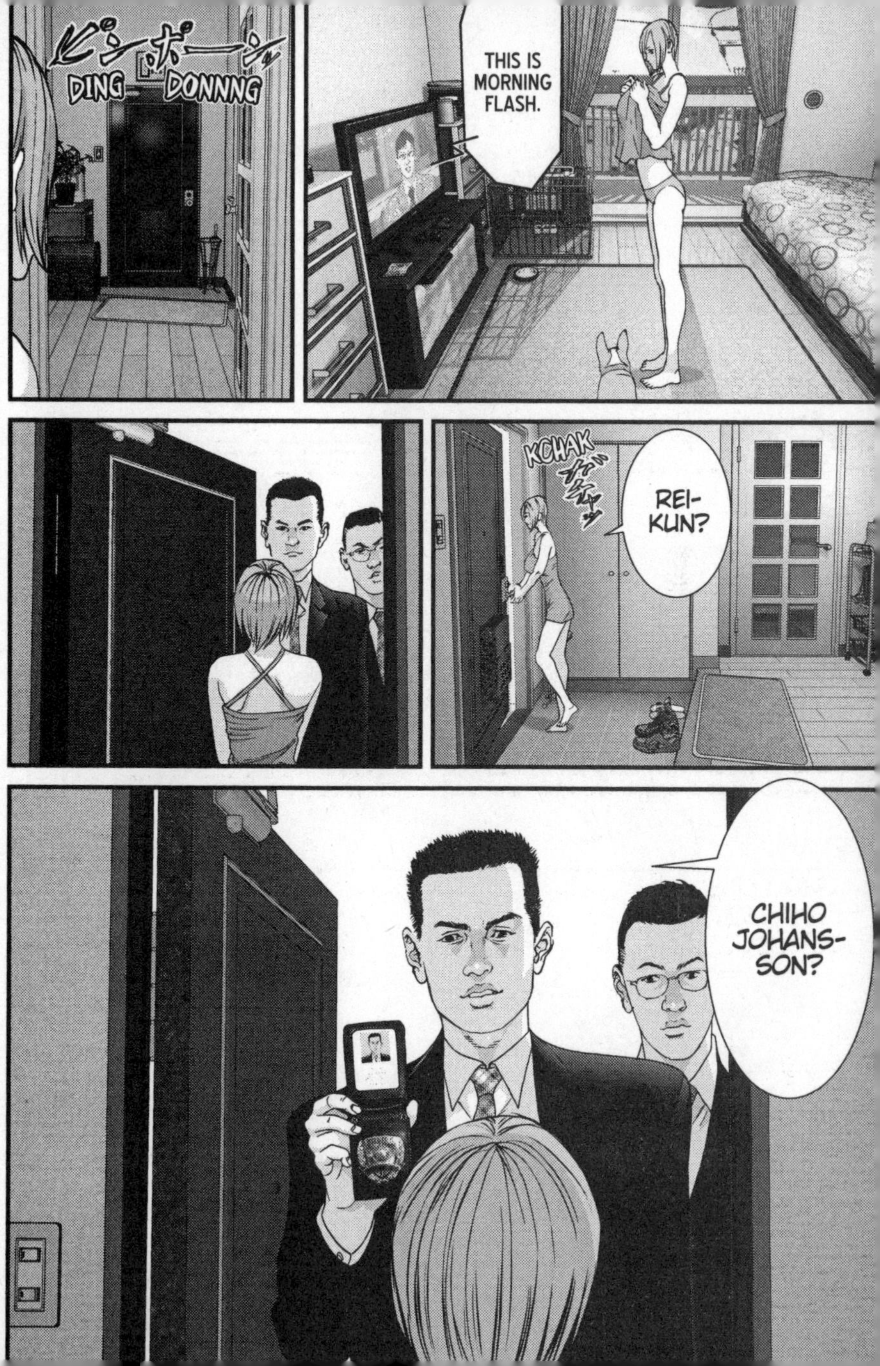
THIS IS MORNING FLASH.
ピンポーン
DING DONNNG
KCHAK
REI-KUN?
CHIHO JOHANSSON?

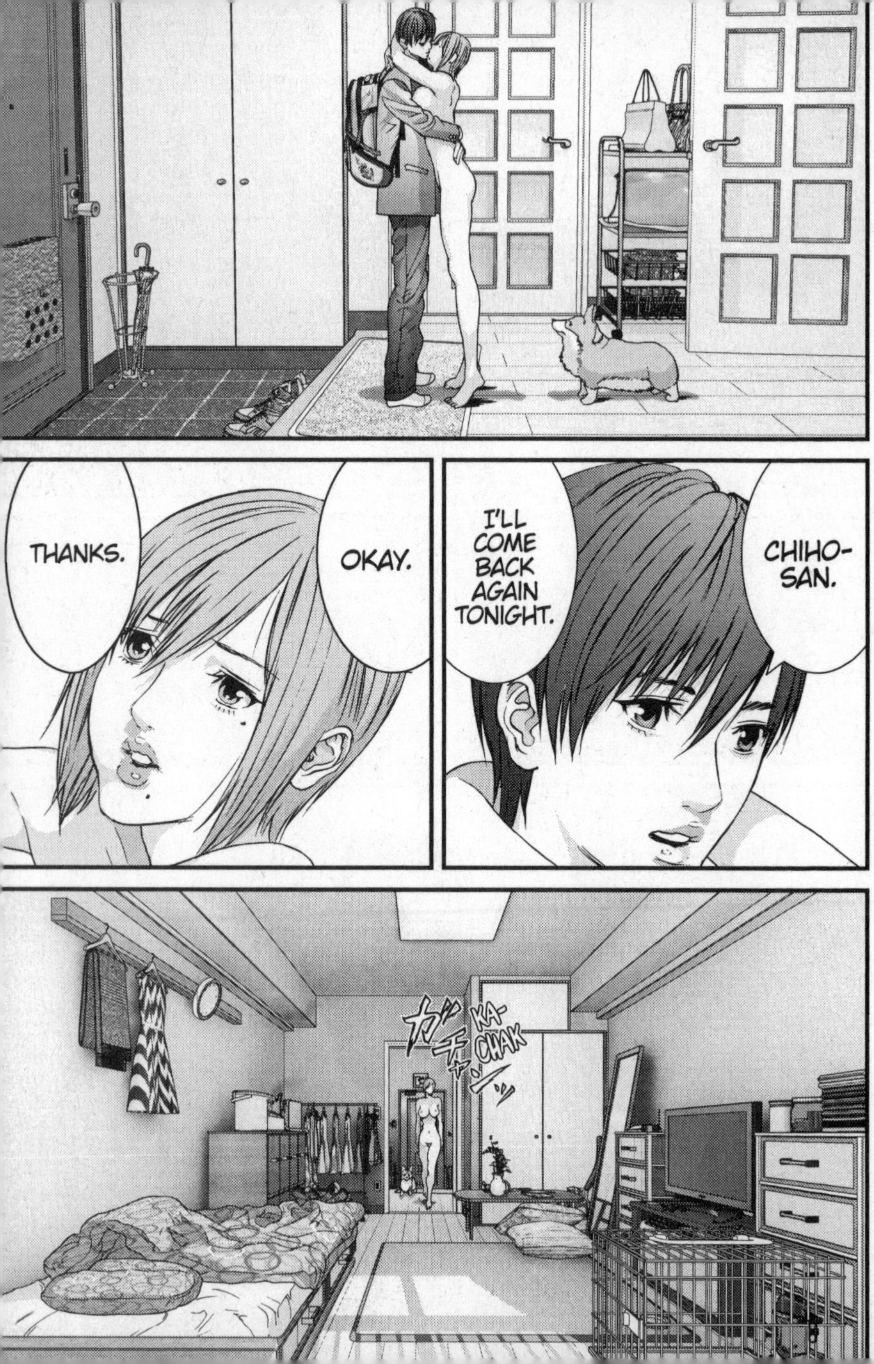
CHIHO-SAN.
I'LL COME BACK AGAIN TONIGHT.
OKAY.
THANKS.
KA-CHAK

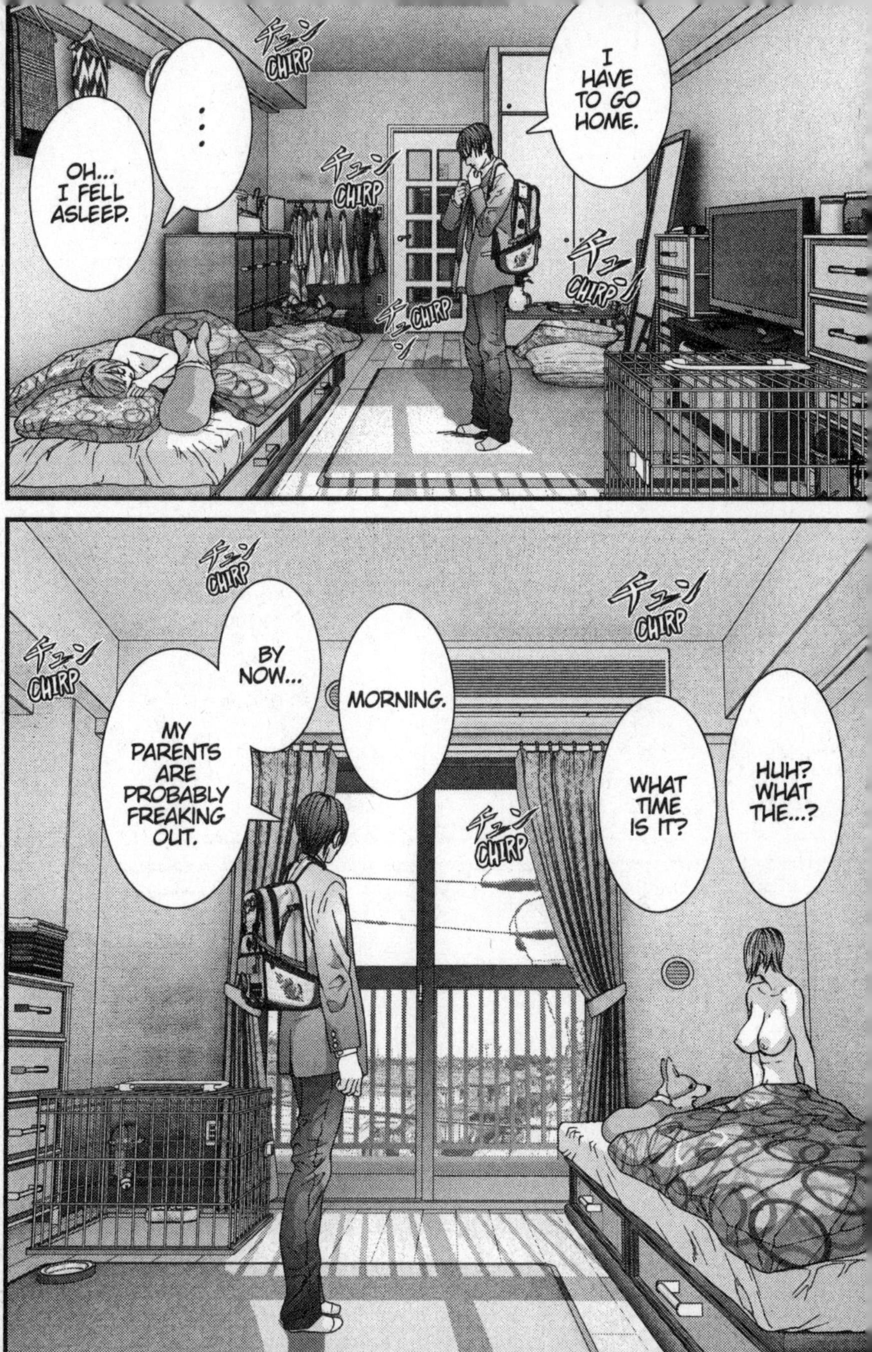
I HAVE TO GO HOME.
チュン
CHIRP
チュン
CHIRP
チュン
CHIRP
チュン
CHIRP
チュン
CHIRP
...
OH... I FELL ASLEEP.
チュン
CHIRP
HUH? WHAT THE...?
WHAT TIME IS IT?
チュン
CHIRP
MORNING.
BY NOW...
MY PARENTS ARE PROBABLY FREAKING OUT.
チュン
CHIRP
チュン
CHIRP

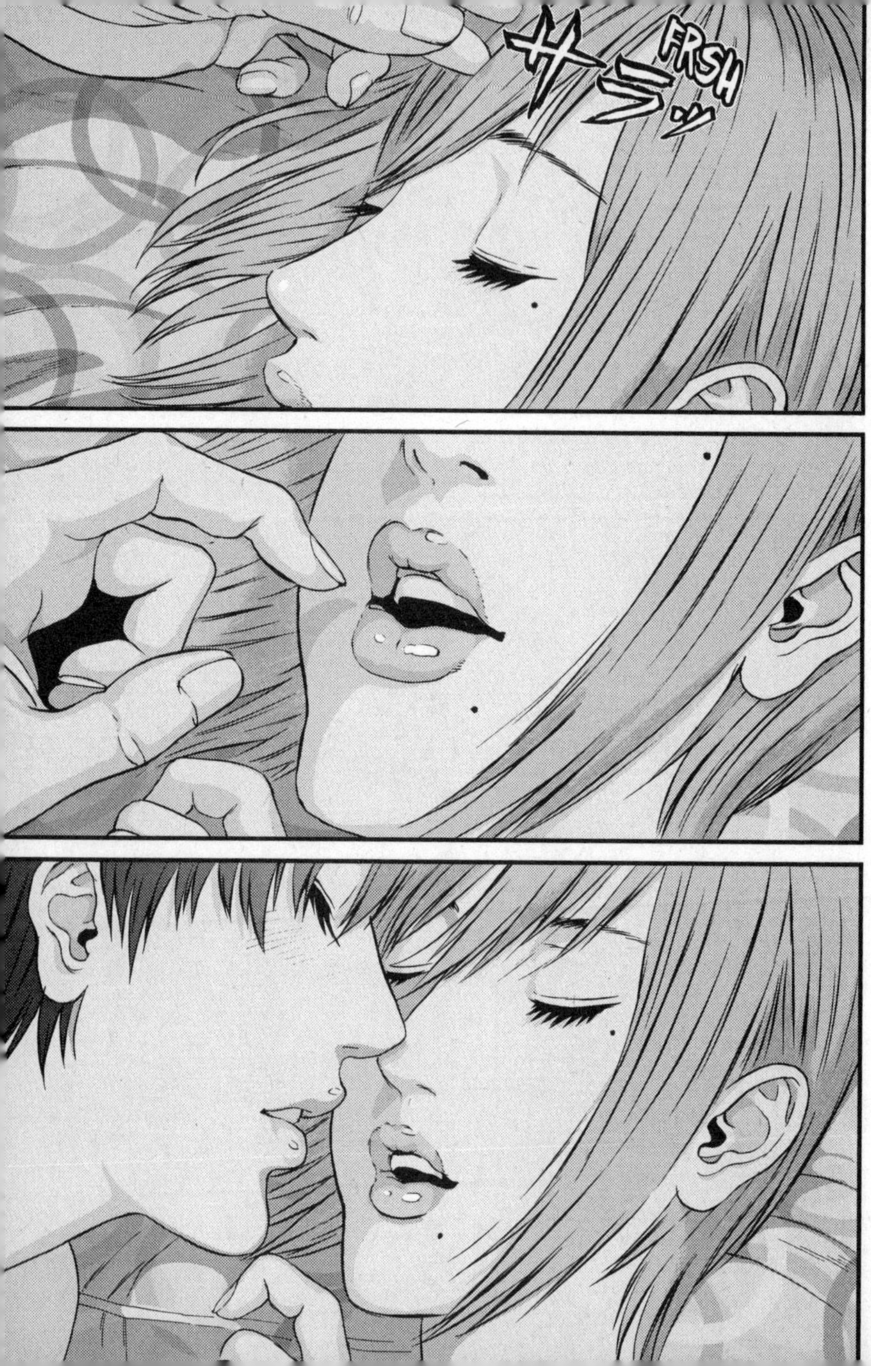
サラッ
FRSH

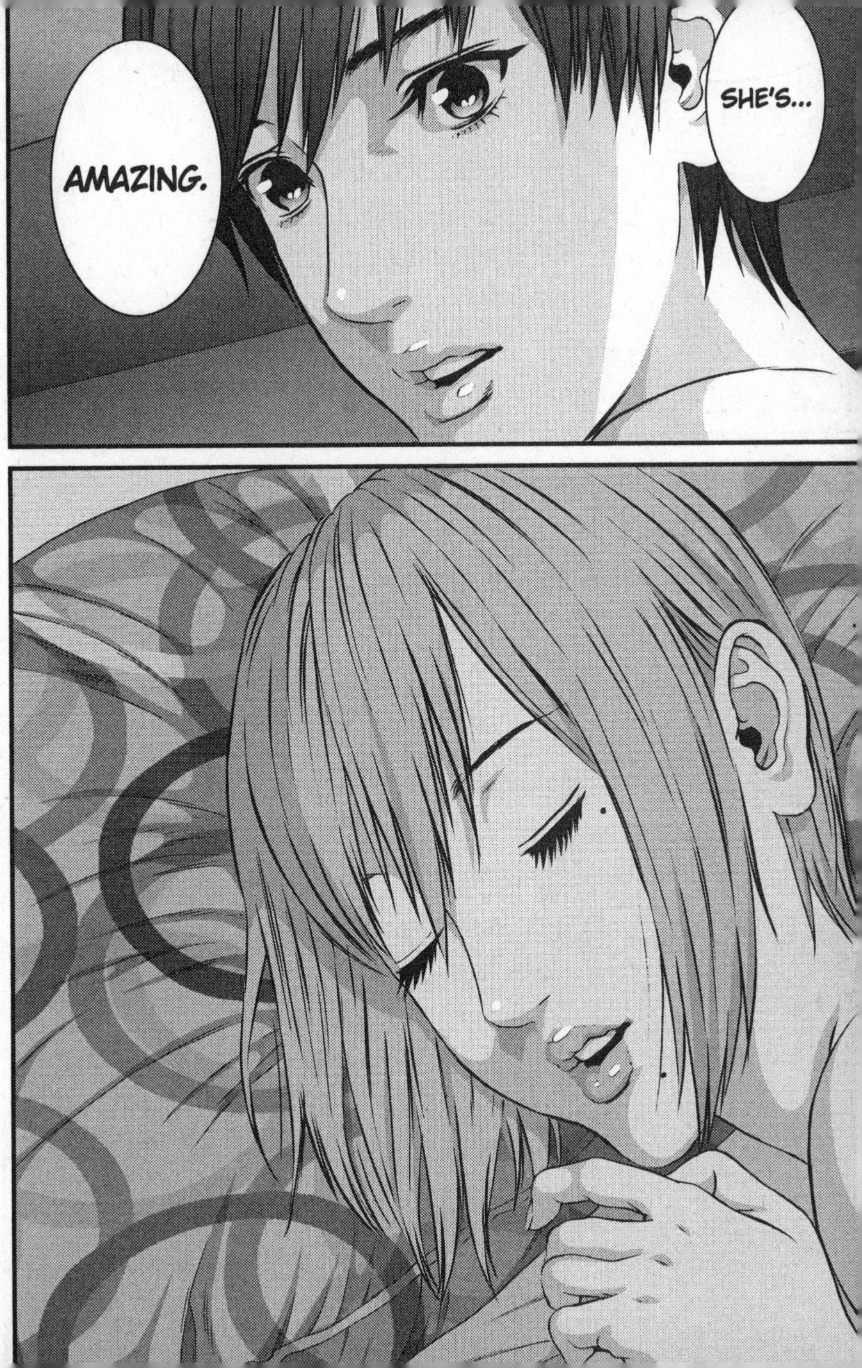
SHE'S...
AMAZING.

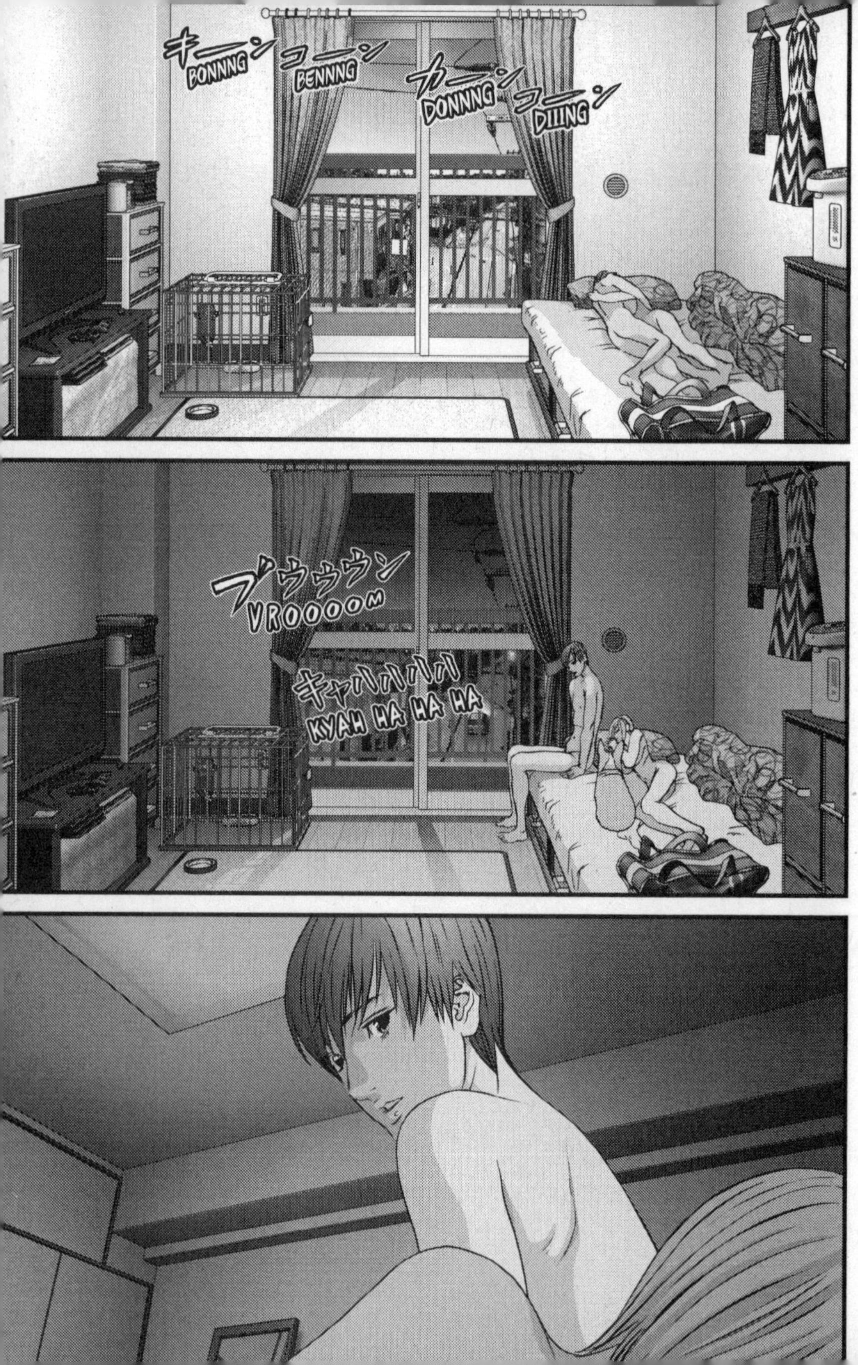
キーン BONNNG
コーン BENNNG
カーン DONNNG
コーン DIIING
ブウウウン VROOOOM
キャハハハ KYAH HA HA HA

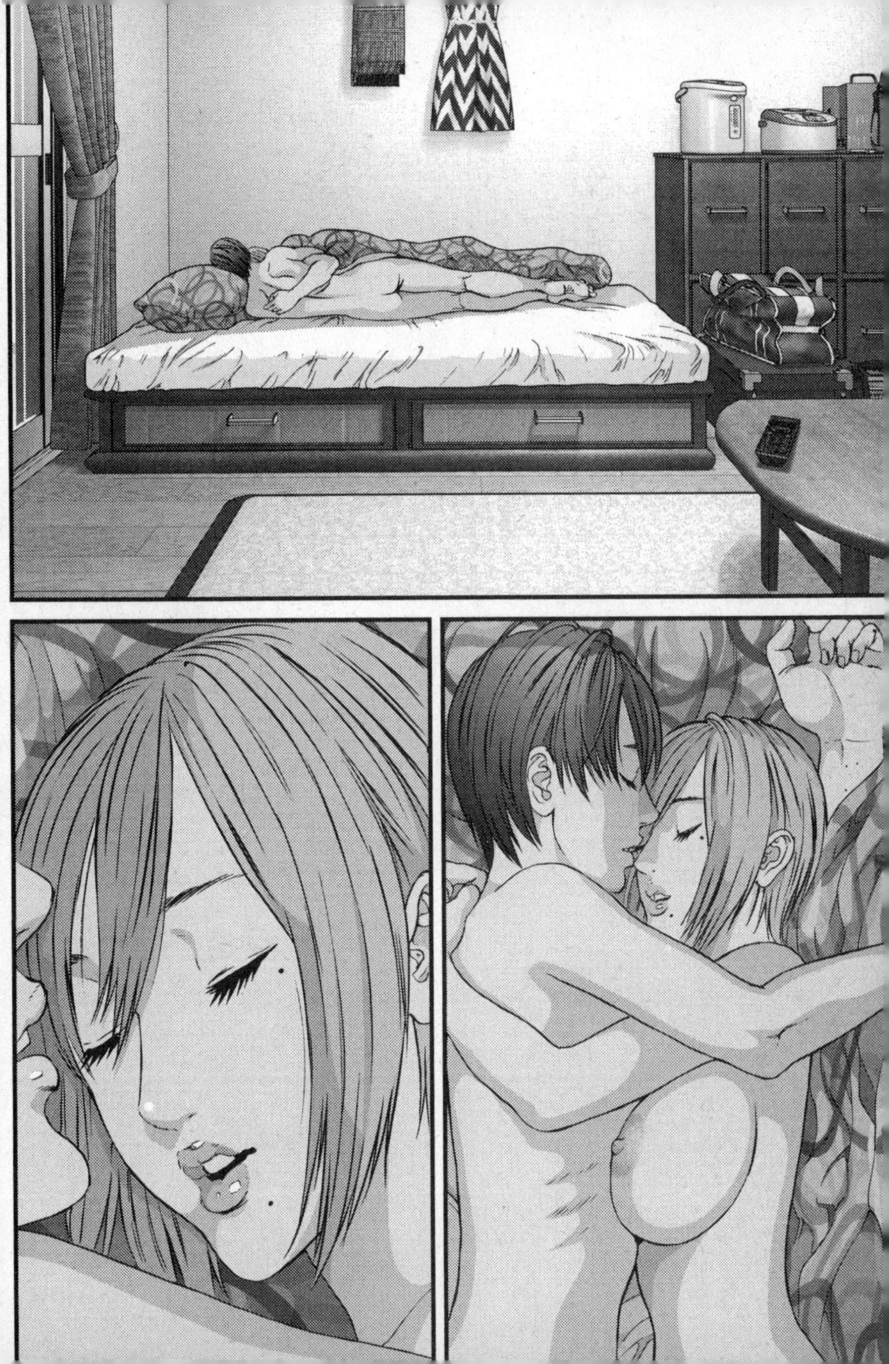

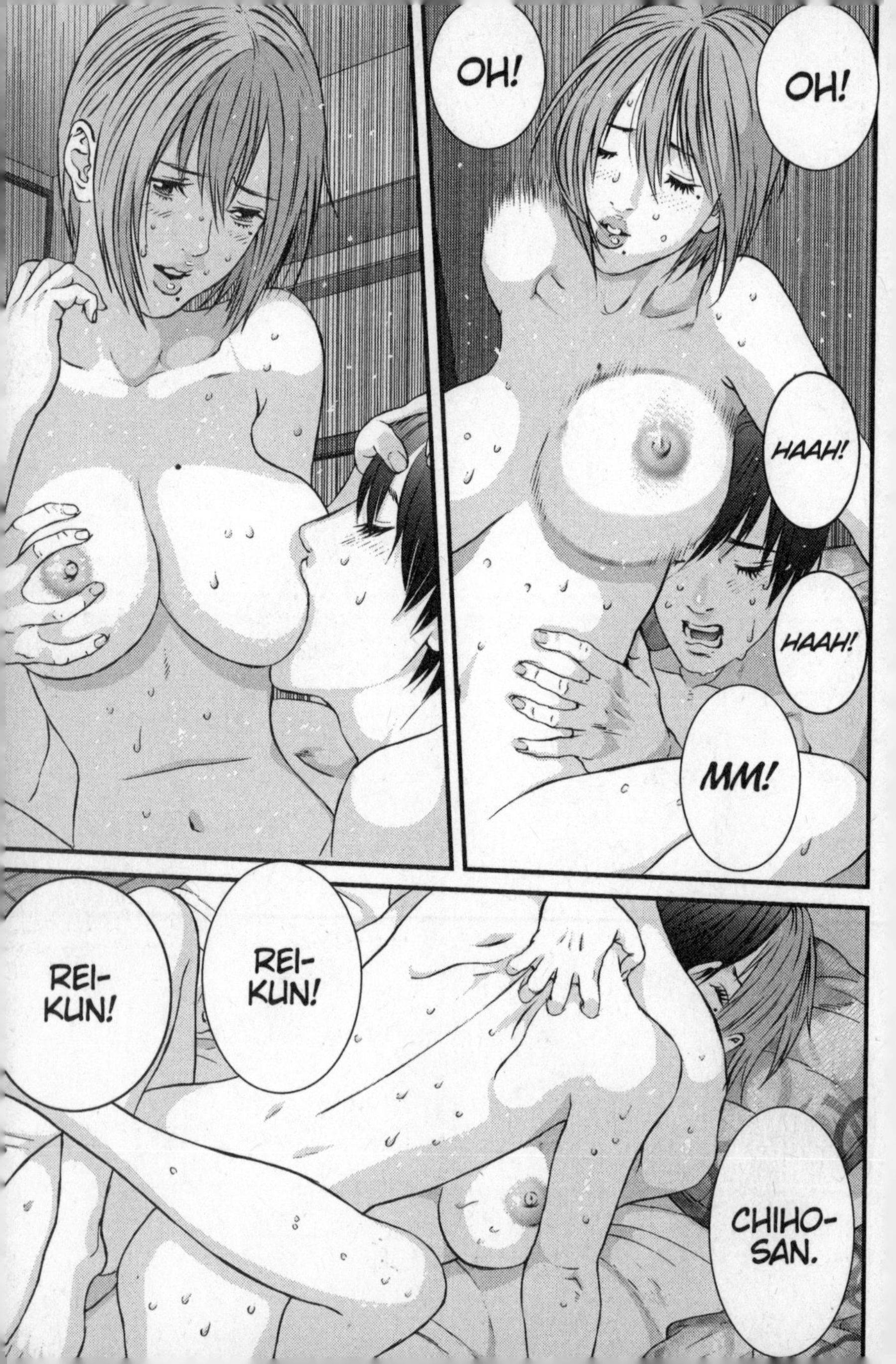
OH!
OH!
HAAH!
HAAH!
MM!
REI-KUN!
REI-KUN!
CHIHO-SAN.

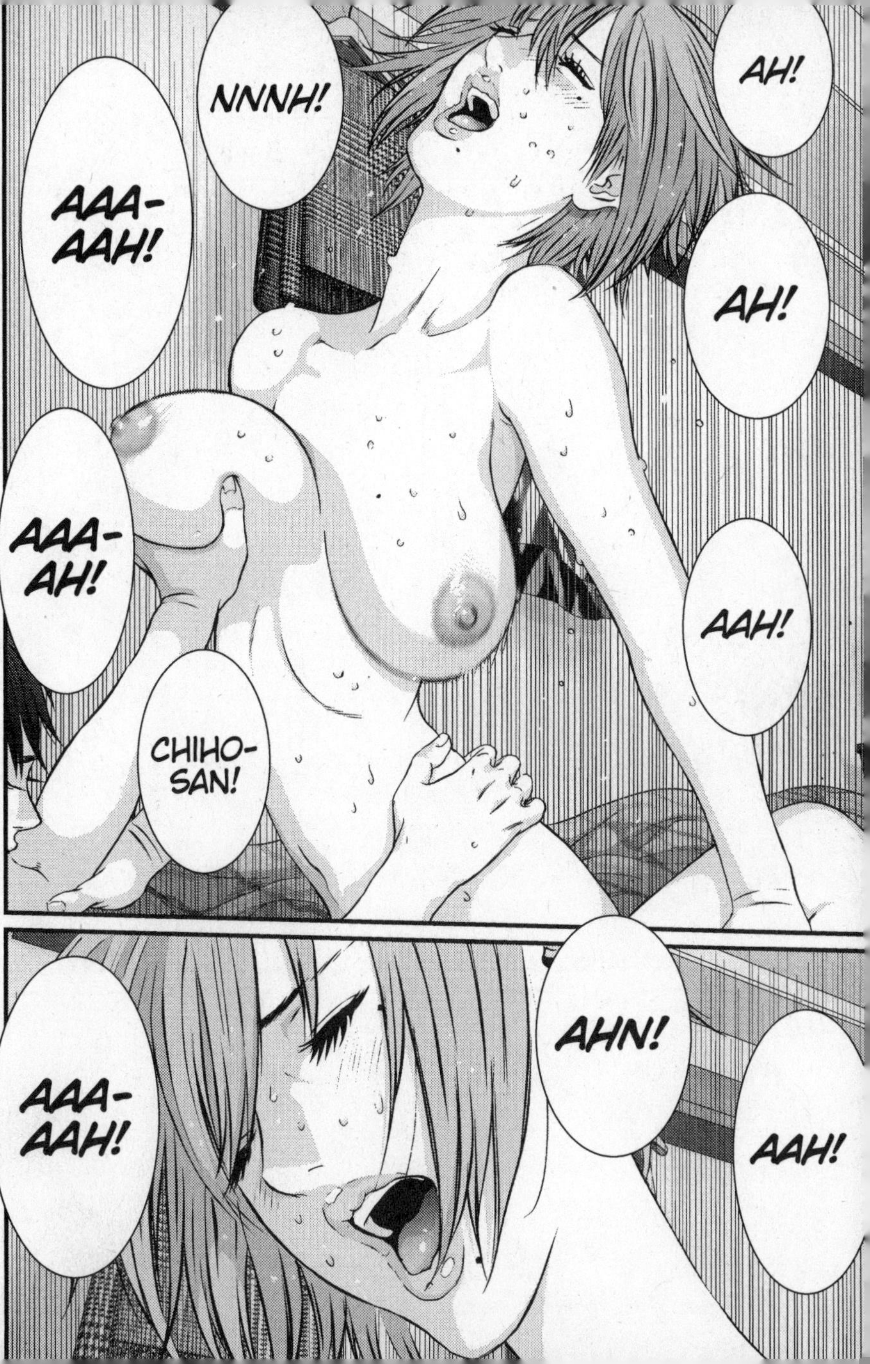
AH!
NNNH!
AH!
AAA-
AAH!
AAH!
AAA-
AH!
CHIHO-
SAN!
AAH!
AHN!
AAA-
AAH!

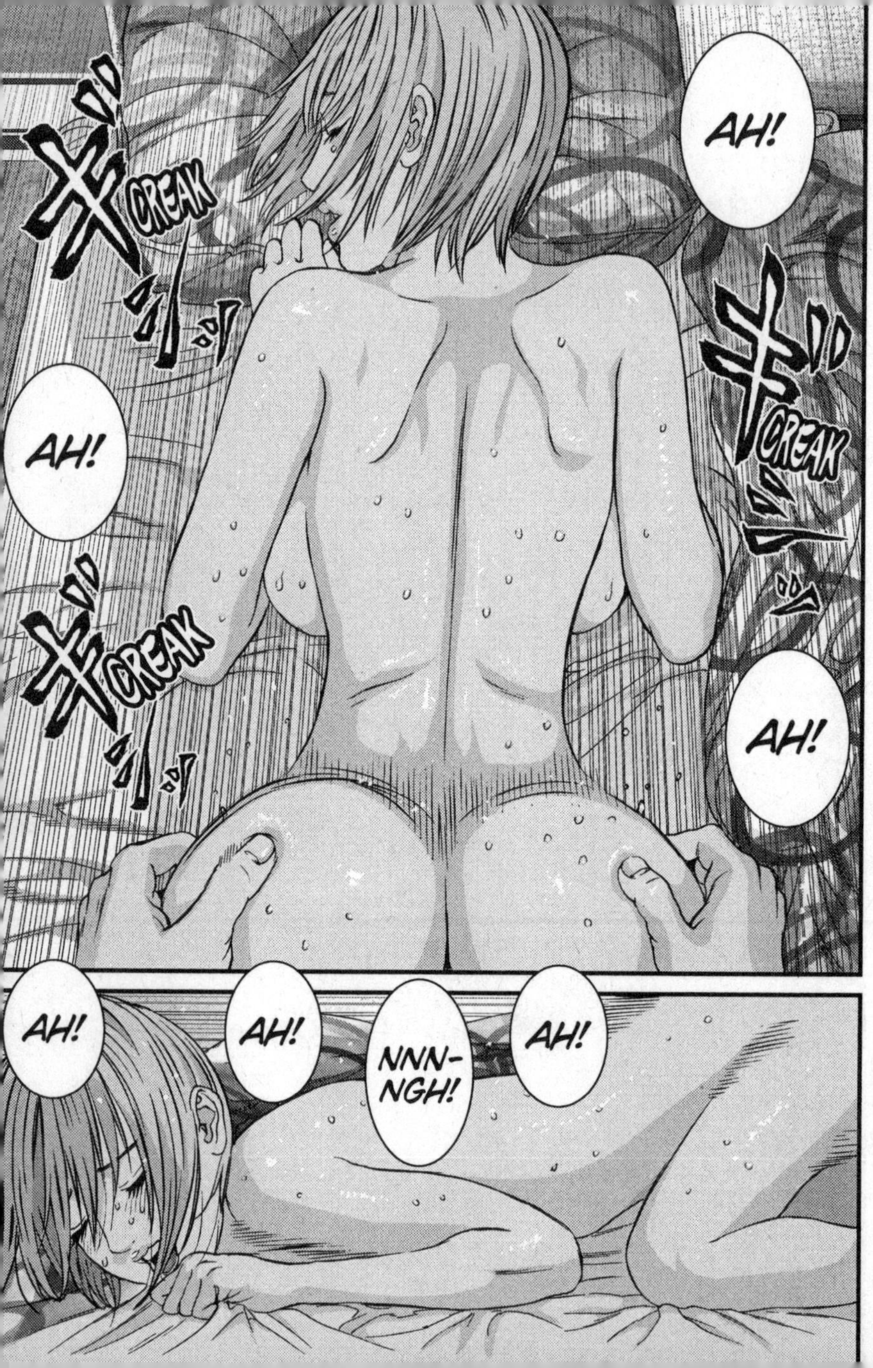
AH!
CREAK
CREAK
AH!
CREAK
AH!
AH!
NNNN-NGH!
AH!
AH!

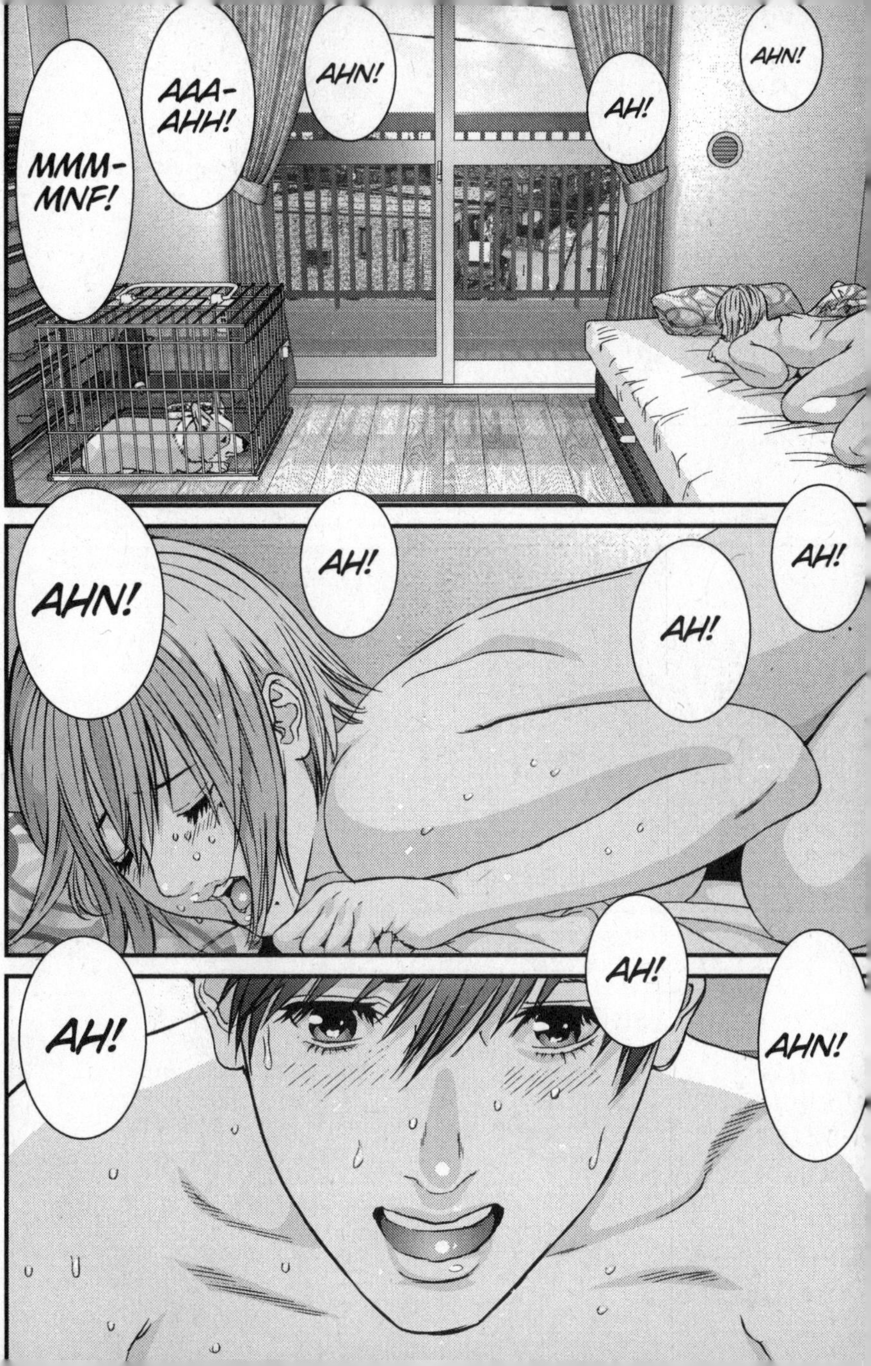
AHN!
AH!
AHN!
AAA-AHH!
MMMM-MNF!
AH!
AH!
AH!
AHN!
AHN!
AH!
AH!

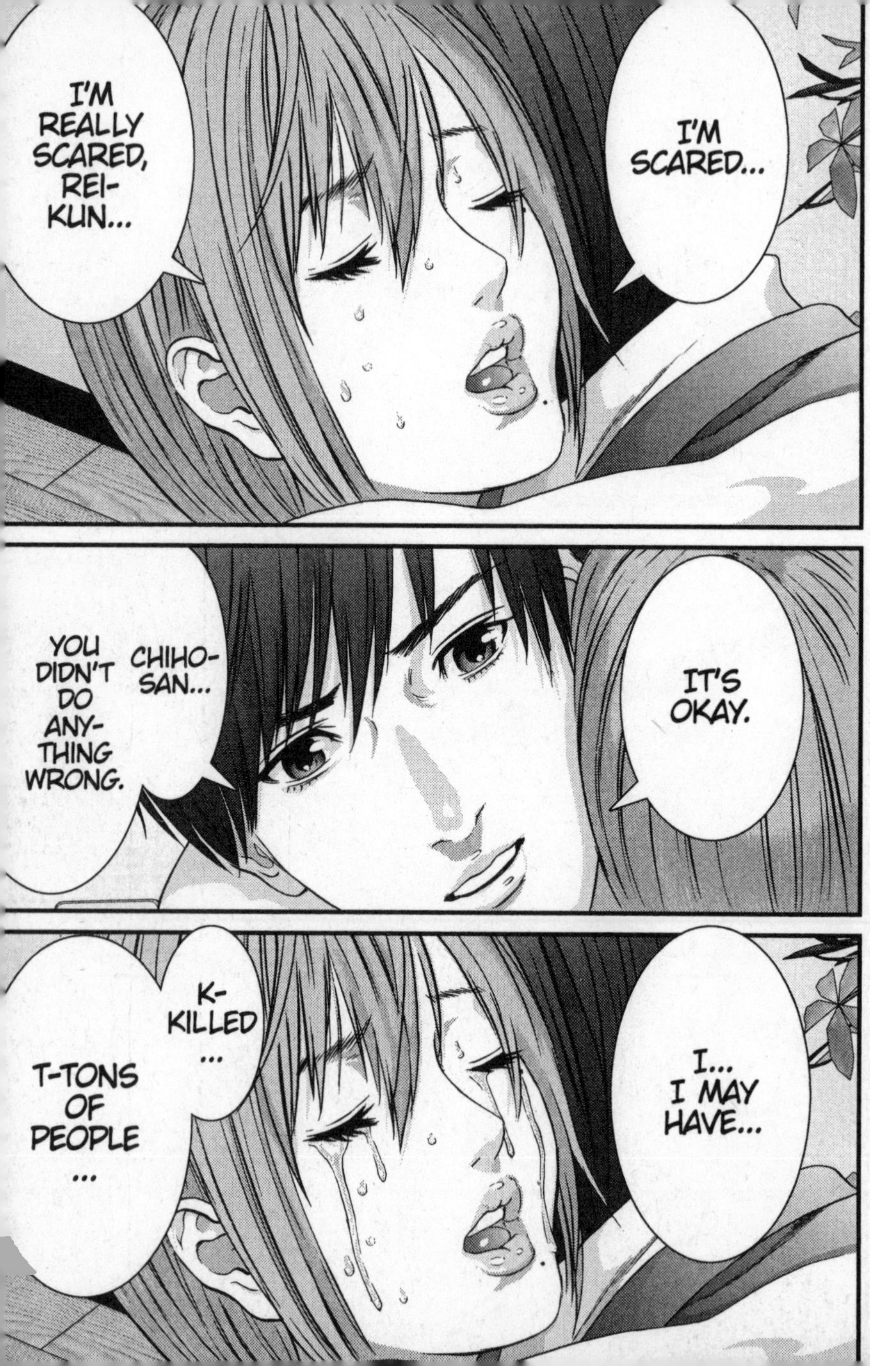
I'M SCARED...
I'M REALLY SCARED, REI-KUN...
IT'S OKAY.
CHIHO-SAN...
YOU DIDN'T DO ANY-THING WRONG.
I... I MAY HAVE...
K-KILLED...
T-TONS OF PEOPLE...

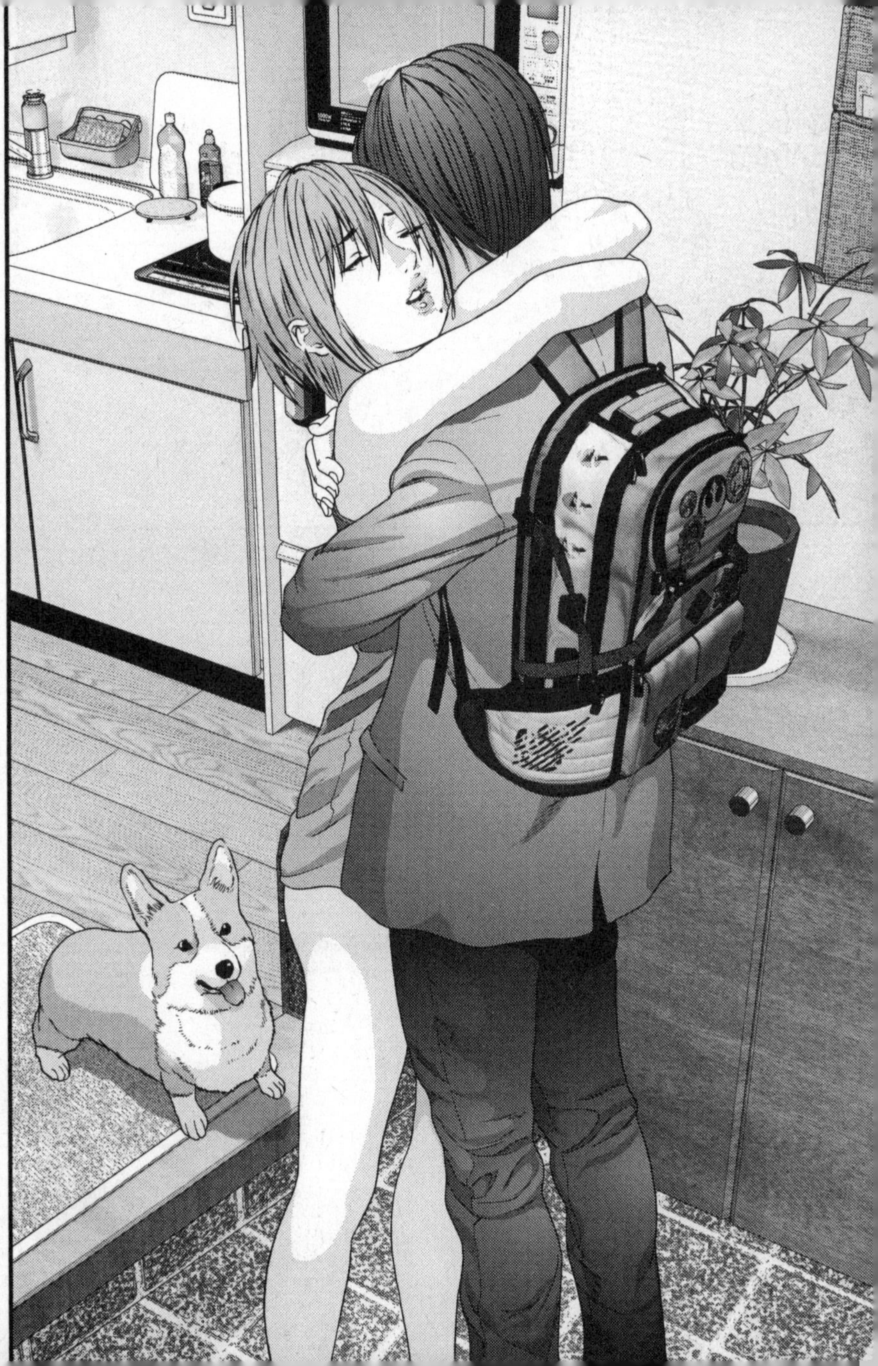

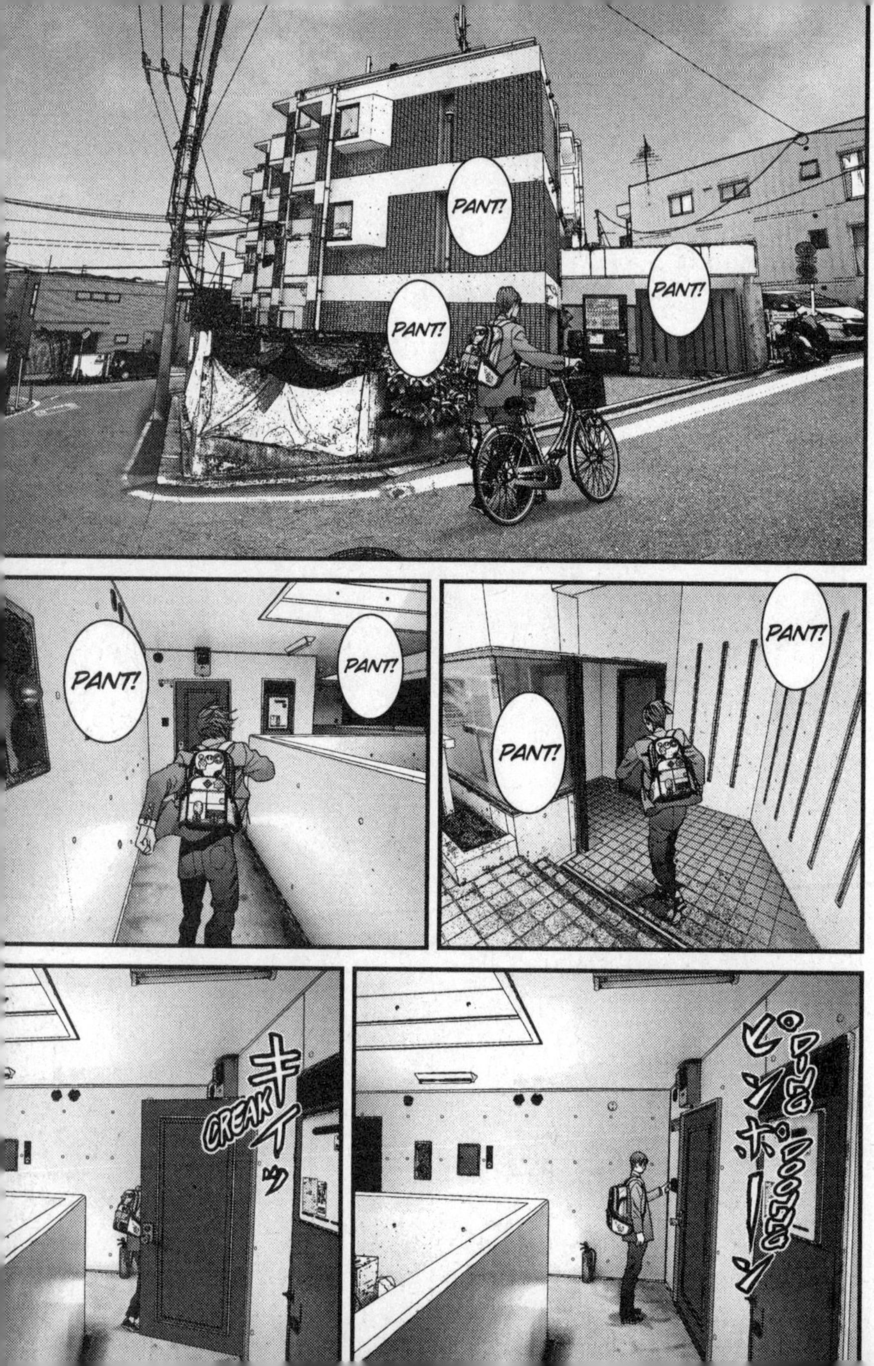
PANT!
PANT!
PANT!
PANT!
PANT!
PANT!
PANT!
ピンポーン
DING DOOONG
キイッ
CREAK

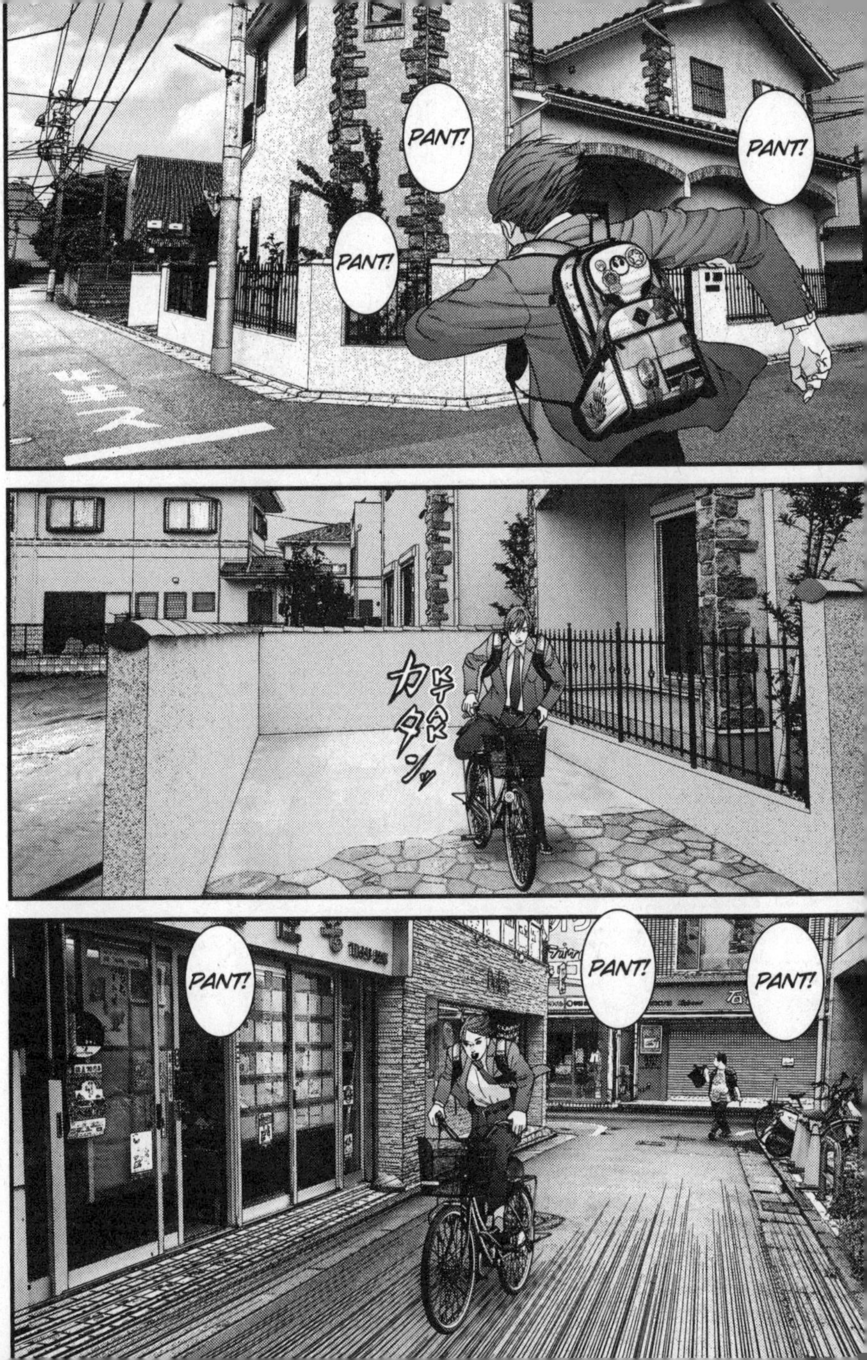
PANT!
PANT!
PANT!
カタッ
PANT!
PANT!
PANT!

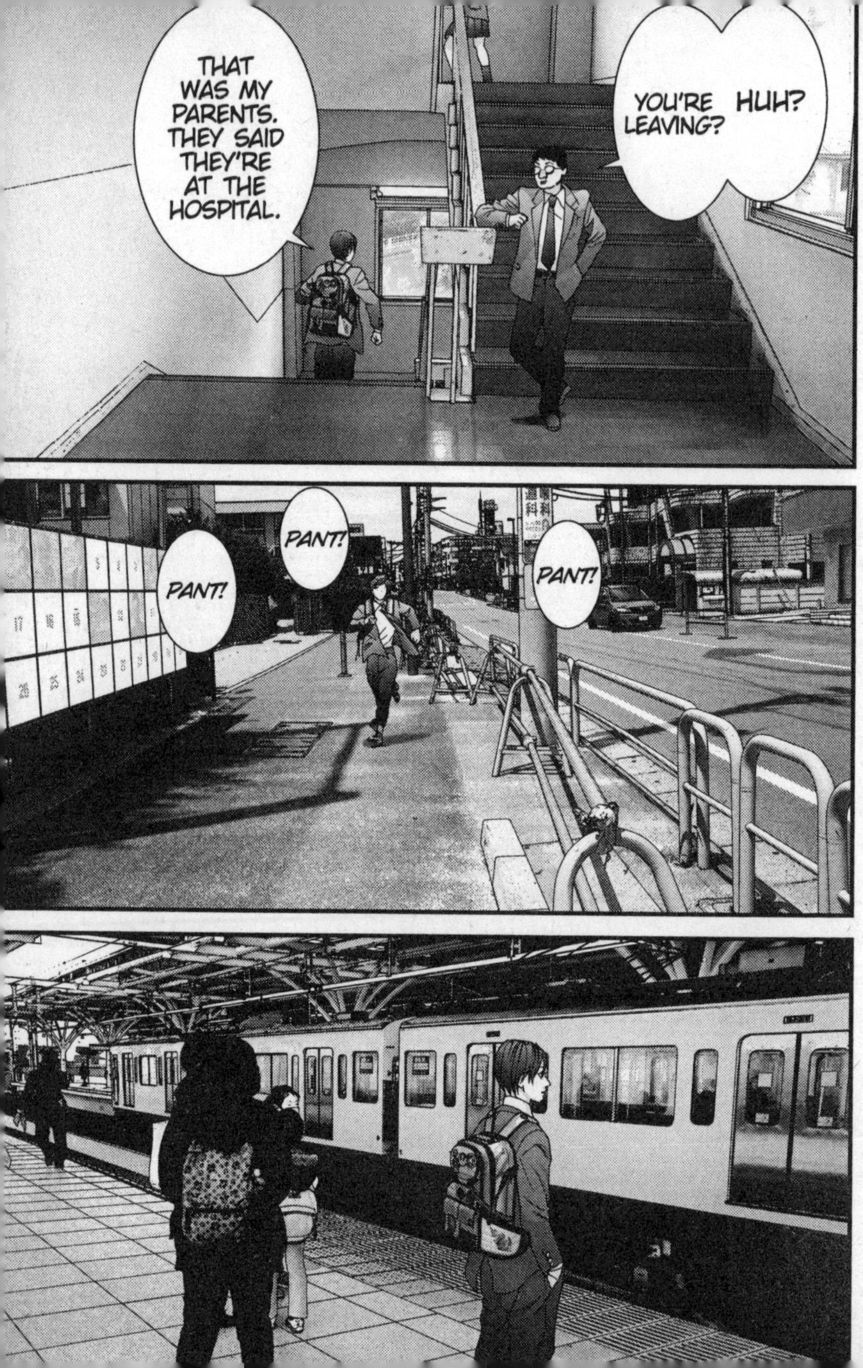
HUH?
YOU'RE LEAVING?
THAT WAS MY PARENTS. THEY SAID THEY'RE AT THE HOSPITAL.
PANT!
PANT!
PANT!

IF YOU'RE IN TROUBLE, JUST LET ME KNOW.

IT'S FINE. YOU CAN HIT ME UP ANYTIME.

I'M SORRY FOR CALLING YOU AT SCHOOL.

CHIHO-SAN, ARE YOU OKAY?

REI-KUN... I MISS YOU. I WANT TO SEE YOU.

RIGHT AWAY.

I'LL COME ...

I MISS YOU TOO.

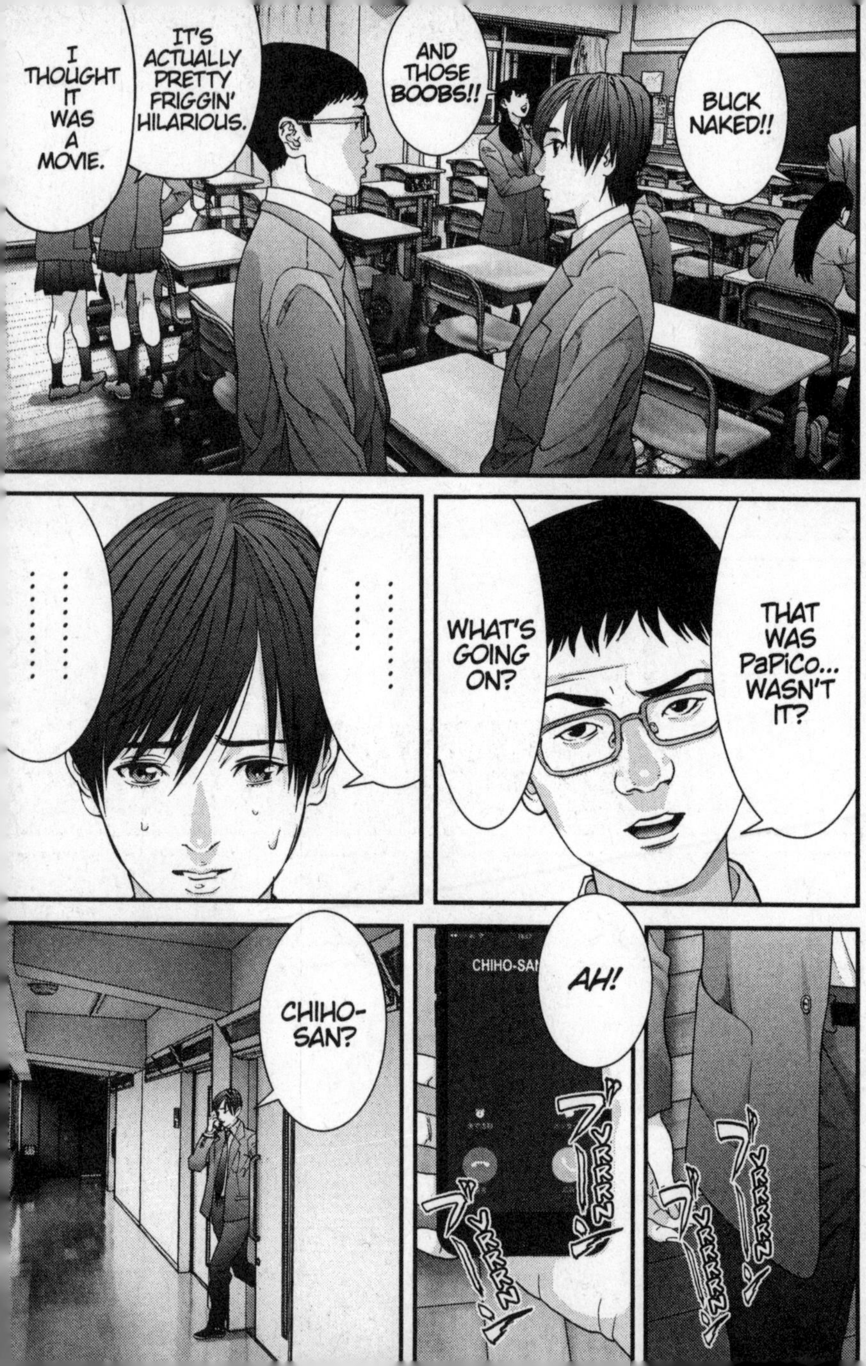

BUCK NAKED!!
AND THOSE BOOBS!!
IT'S ACTUALLY PRETTY FRIGGIN' HILARIOUS.
I THOUGHT IT WAS A MOVIE.
THAT WAS PaPiCo... WASN'T IT?
WHAT'S GOING ON?
......
......
AH!
CHIHO-SAN
VRRRRN
VRRRRN
VRRRRN
VRRRRN
CHIHO-SAN?

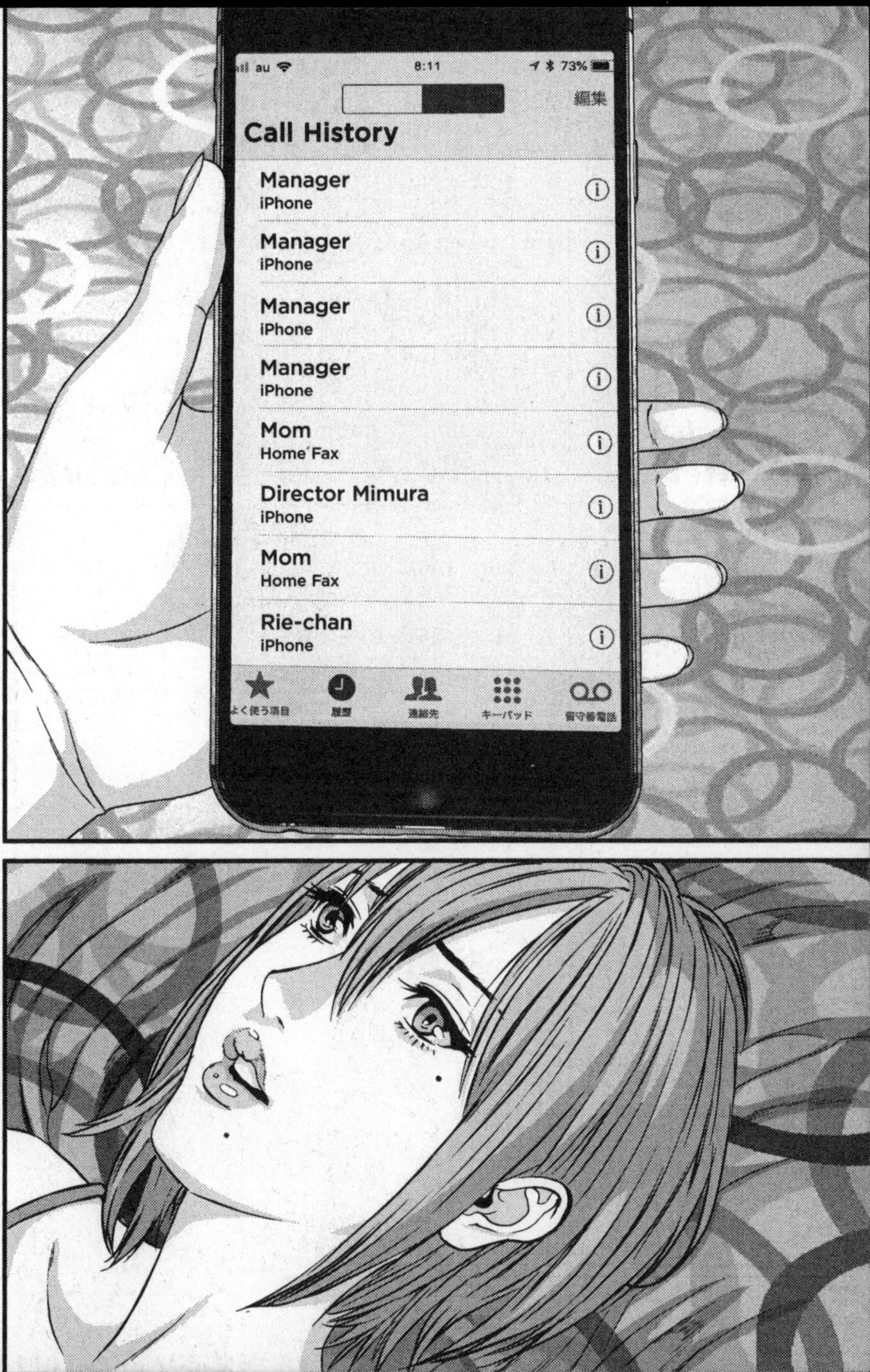
au
8:11
73%
編集
Call History
Manager
iPhone
Manager
iPhone
Manager
iPhone
Manager
iPhone
Mom
Home Fax
Director Mimura
iPhone
Mom
Home Fax
Rie-chan
iPhone
よく使う項目
履歴
連絡先
キーパッド
留守番電話

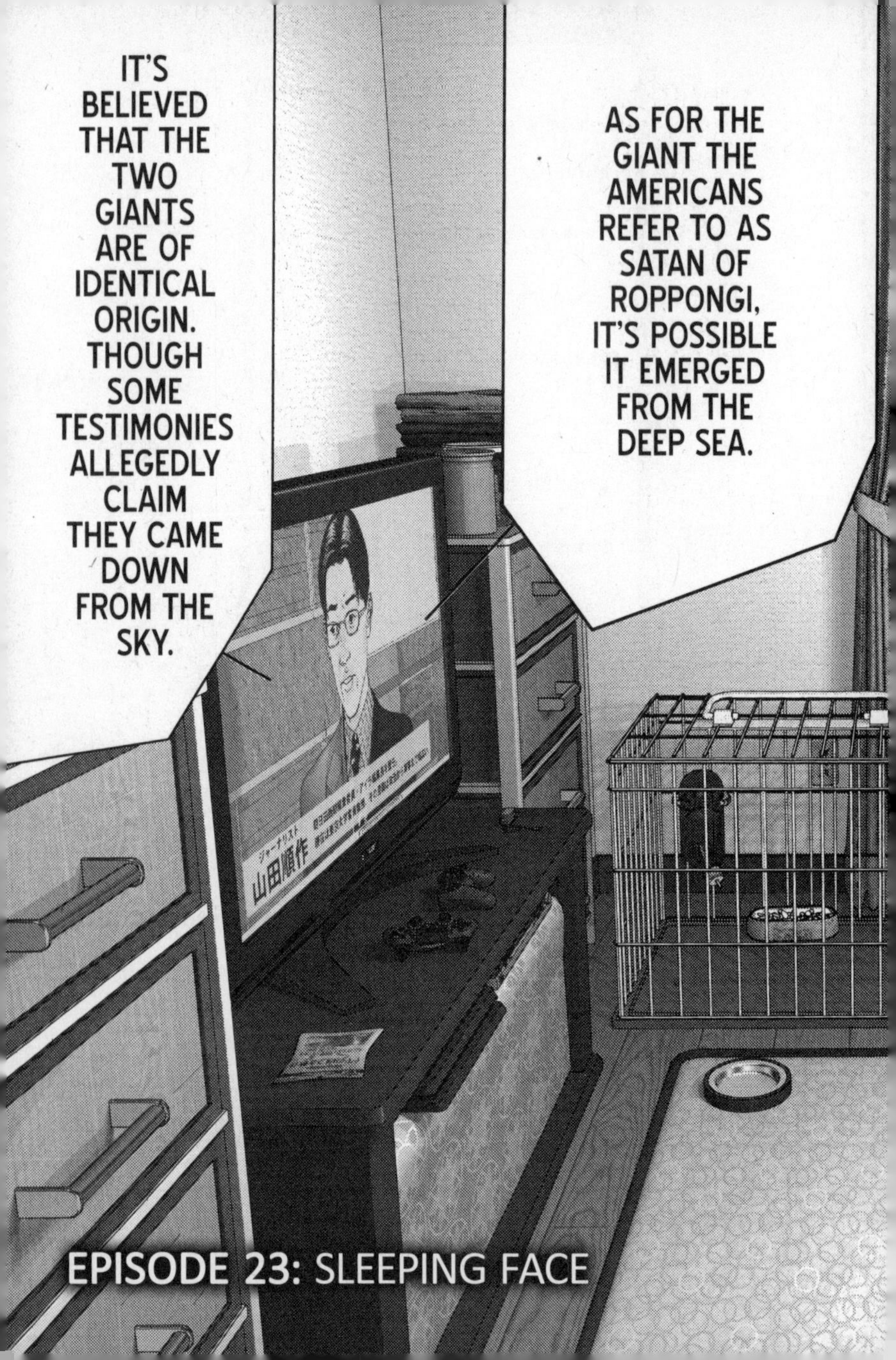
AS FOR THE GIANT THE AMERICANS REFER TO AS SATAN OF ROPPONGI, IT'S POSSIBLE IT EMERGED FROM THE DEEP SEA.
IT'S BELIEVED THAT THE TWO GIANTS ARE OF IDENTICAL ORIGIN. THOUGH SOME TESTIMONIES ALLEGEDLY CLAIM THEY CAME DOWN FROM THE SKY.
ジャーナリスト
山田順作
EPISODE 23: SLEEPING FACE

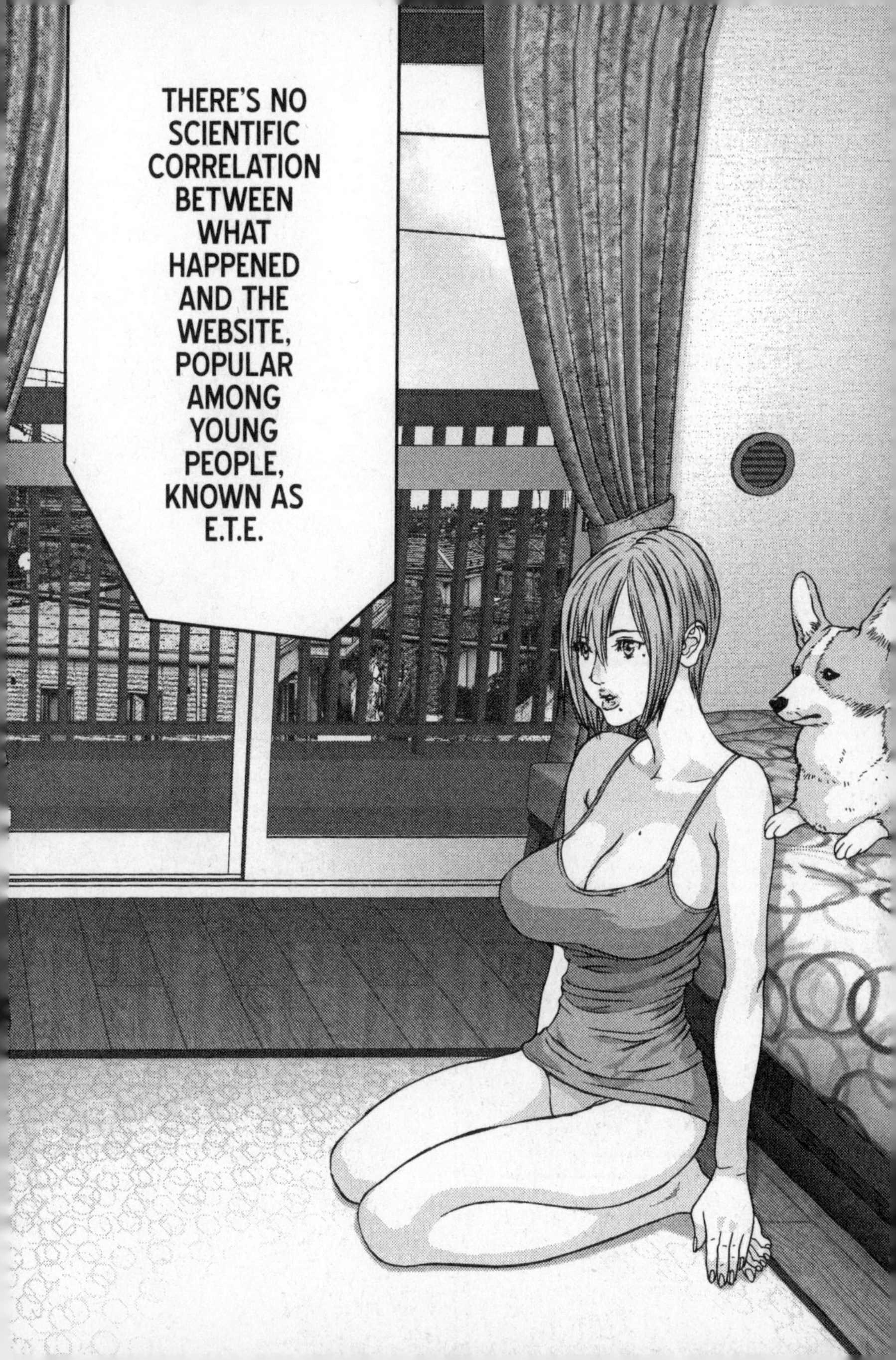
THERE'S NO SCIENTIFIC CORRELATION BETWEEN WHAT HAPPENED AND THE WEBSITE, POPULAR AMONG YOUNG PEOPLE, KNOWN AS E.T.E.

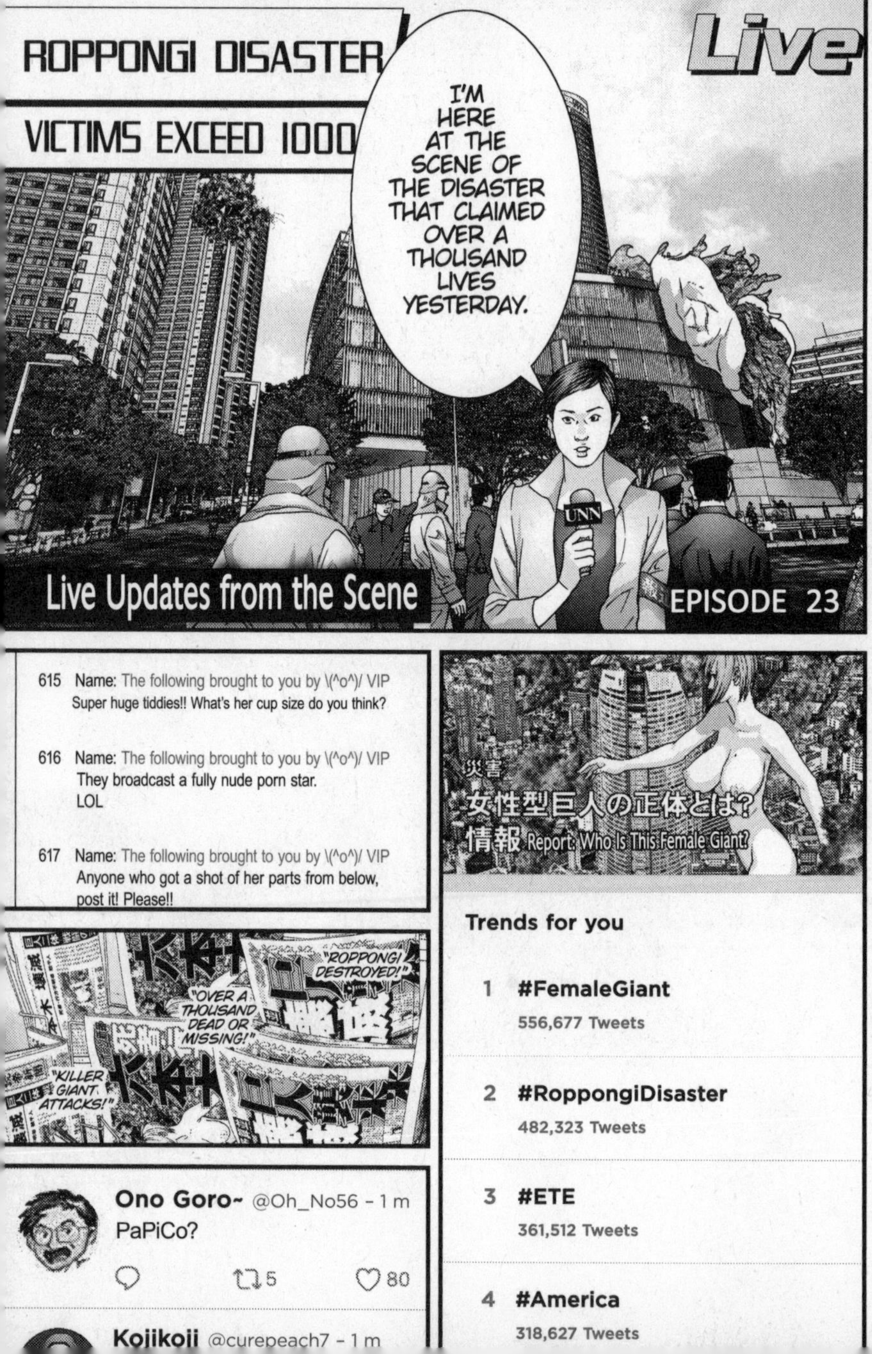

Live
ROPPONGI DISASTER
VICTIMS EXCEED 1000
I'M HERE AT THE SCENE OF THE DISASTER THAT CLAIMED OVER A THOUSAND LIVES YESTERDAY.
UNN
Live Updates from the Scene
EPISODE 23
災害
女性型巨人の正体とは?
情報 Report: Who Is This Female Giant?
Trends for you
1 #FemaleGiant
556,677 Tweets
2 #RoppongiDisaster
482,323 Tweets
3 #ETE
361,512 Tweets
4 #America
318,627 Tweets
615 Name: The following brought to you by \(^o^)/ VIP
Super huge tiddies!! What's her cup size do you think?
616 Name: The following brought to you by \(^o^)/ VIP
They broadcast a fully nude porn star.
LOL
617 Name: The following brought to you by \(^o^)/ VIP
Anyone who got a shot of her parts from below, post it! Please!!
"ROPPONGI DESTROYED!"
"OVER A THOUSAND DEAD OR MISSING!"
"KILLER GIANT ATTACKS!"
Ono Goro~ @Oh_No56 - 1 m
PaPiCo?
5
80
Kojikoji @curepeach7 - 1 m

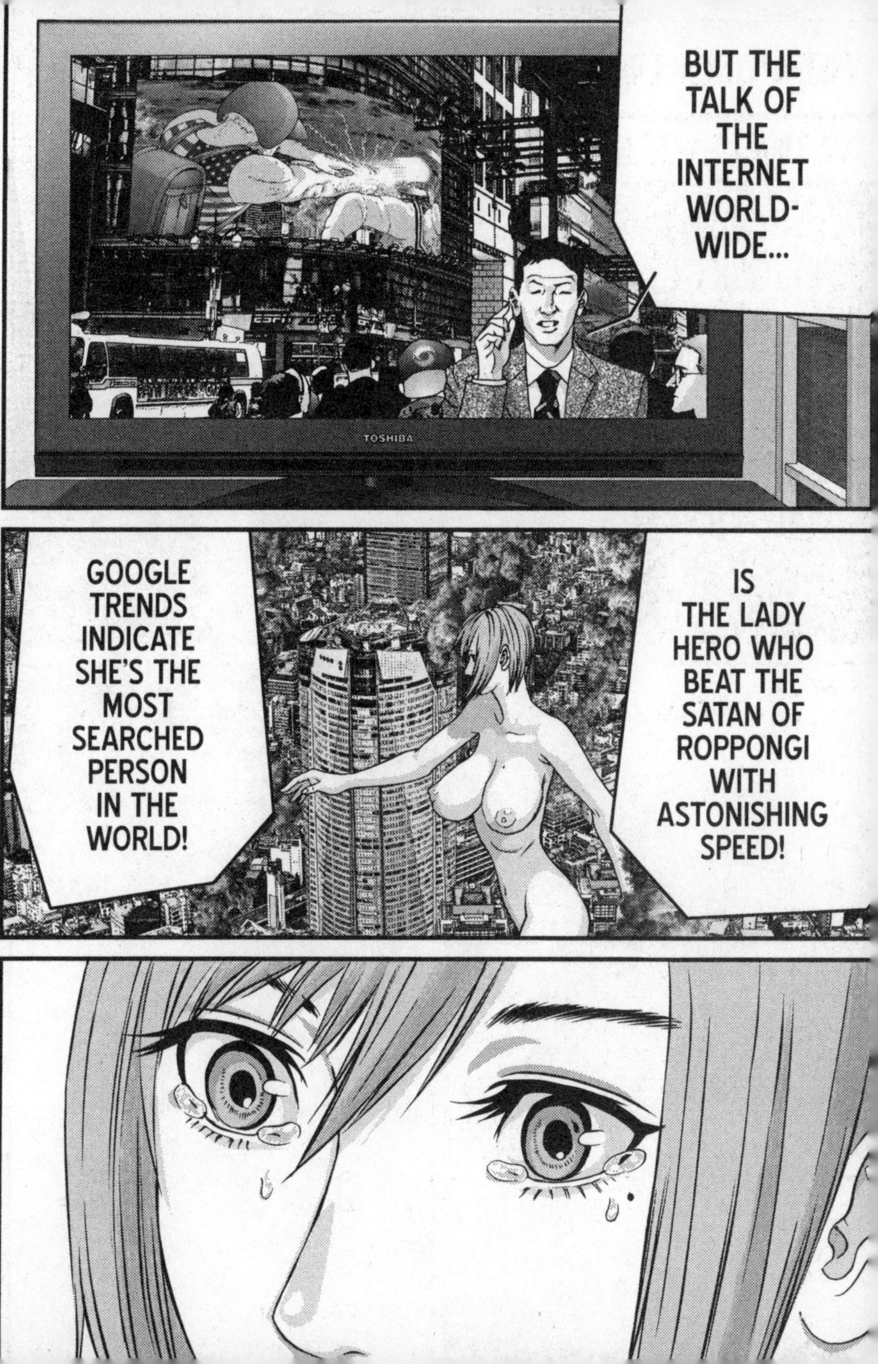
BUT THE TALK OF THE INTERNET WORLD-WIDE...
TOSHIBA
IS THE LADY HERO WHO BEAT THE SATAN OF ROPPONGI WITH ASTONISHING SPEED!
GOOGLE TRENDS INDICATE SHE'S THE MOST SEARCHED PERSON IN THE WORLD!

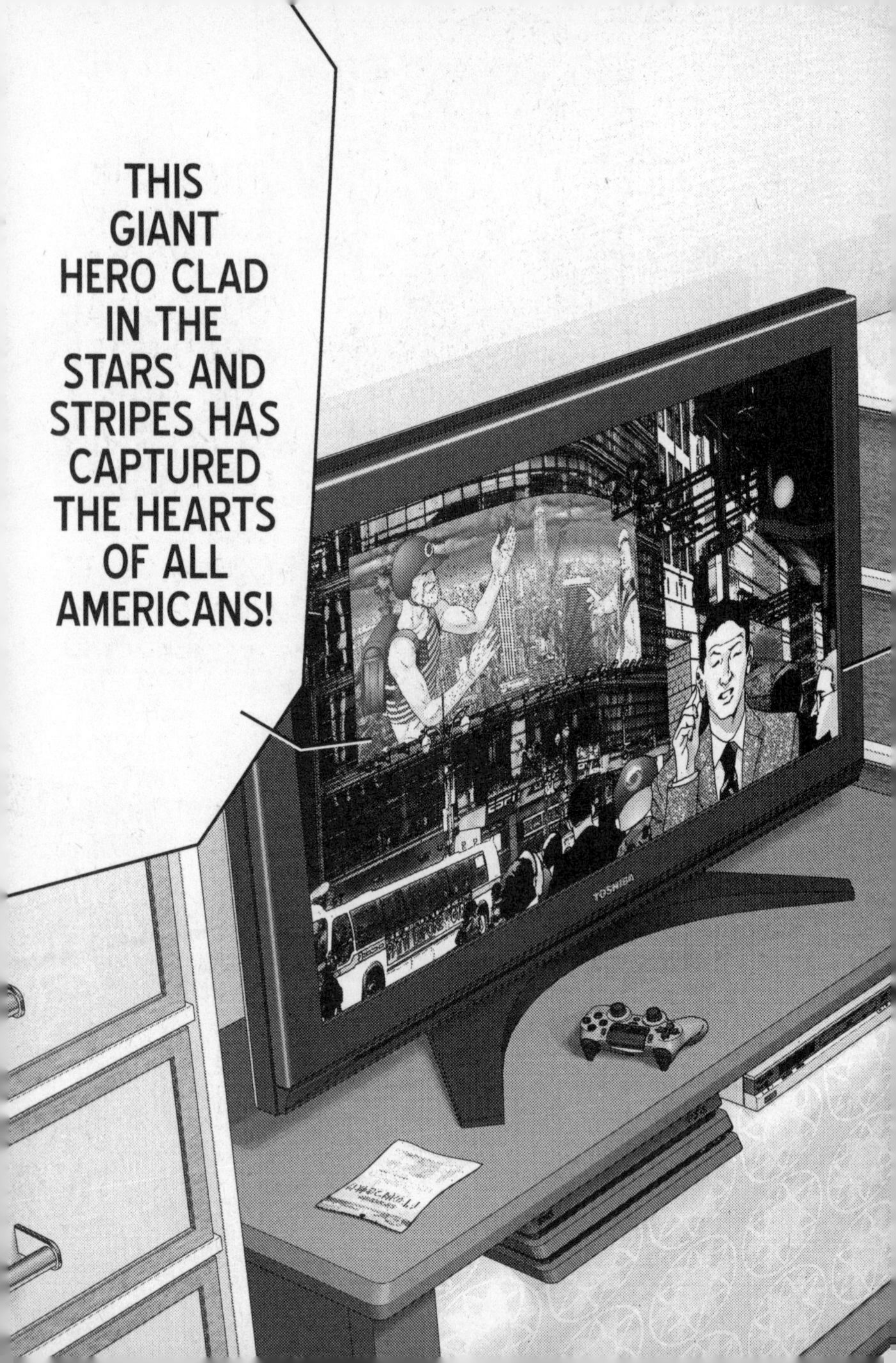
THIS GIANT HERO CLAD IN THE STARS AND STRIPES HAS CAPTURED THE HEARTS OF ALL AMERICANS!
TOSHIBA

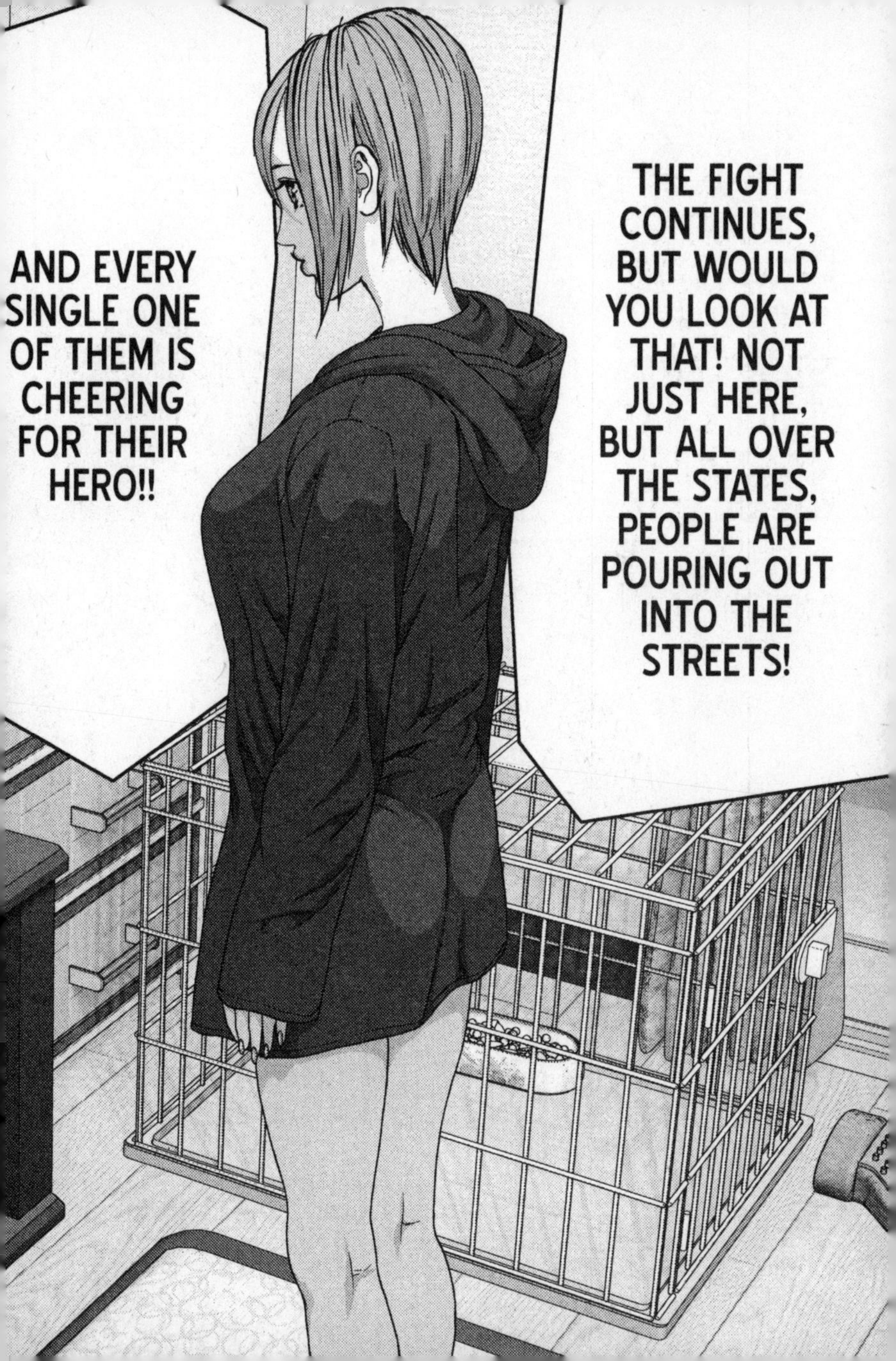
THE FIGHT CONTINUES, BUT WOULD YOU LOOK AT THAT! NOT JUST HERE, BUT ALL OVER THE STATES, PEOPLE ARE POURING OUT INTO THE STREETS!
AND EVERY SINGLE ONE OF THEM IS CHEERING FOR THEIR HERO!!

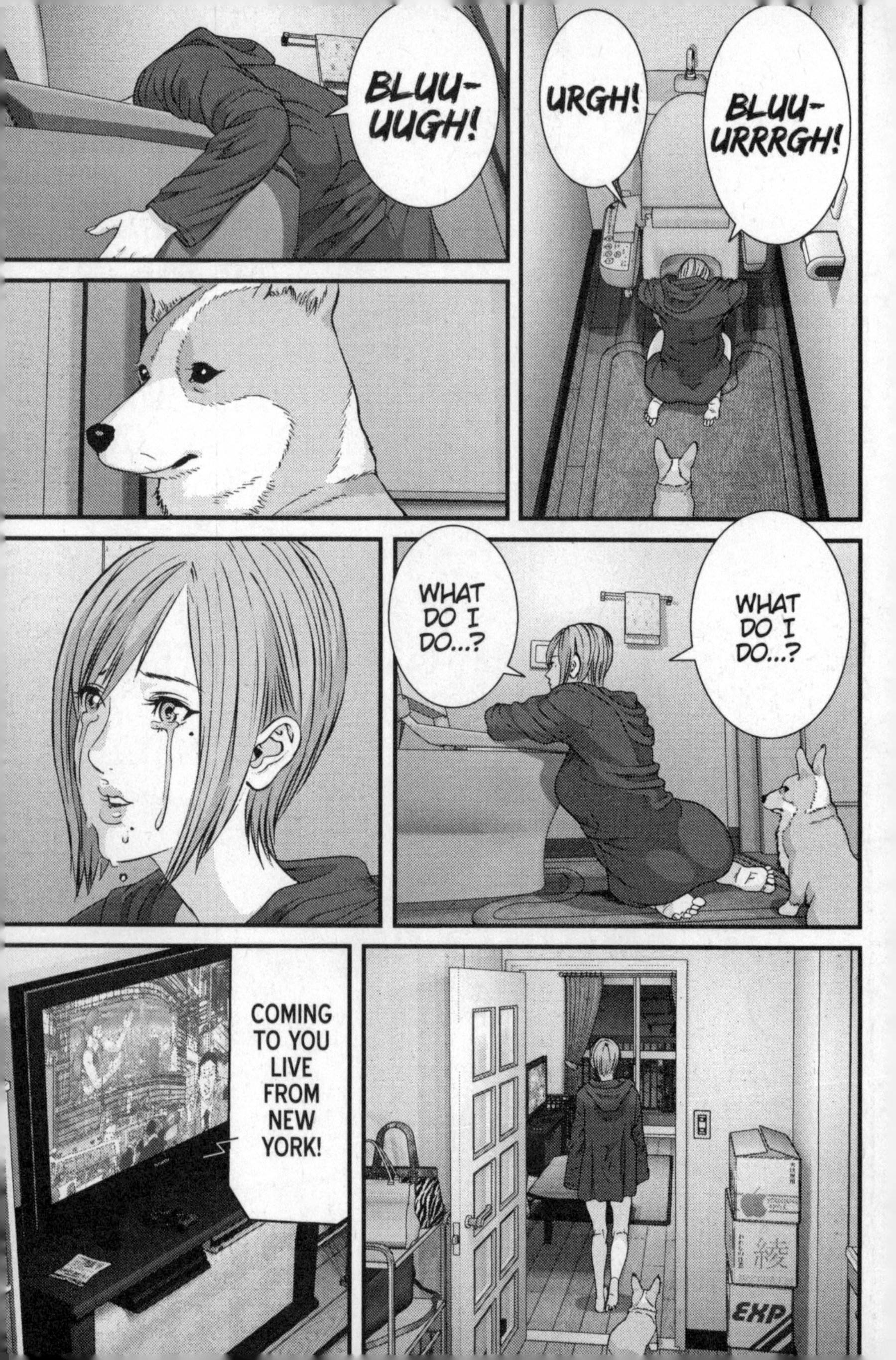
BLUU-URRRGH!
URGH!
BLUU-UUGH!
WHAT DO I DO...?
WHAT DO I DO...?
綾
EXP
COMING TO YOU LIVE FROM NEW YORK!

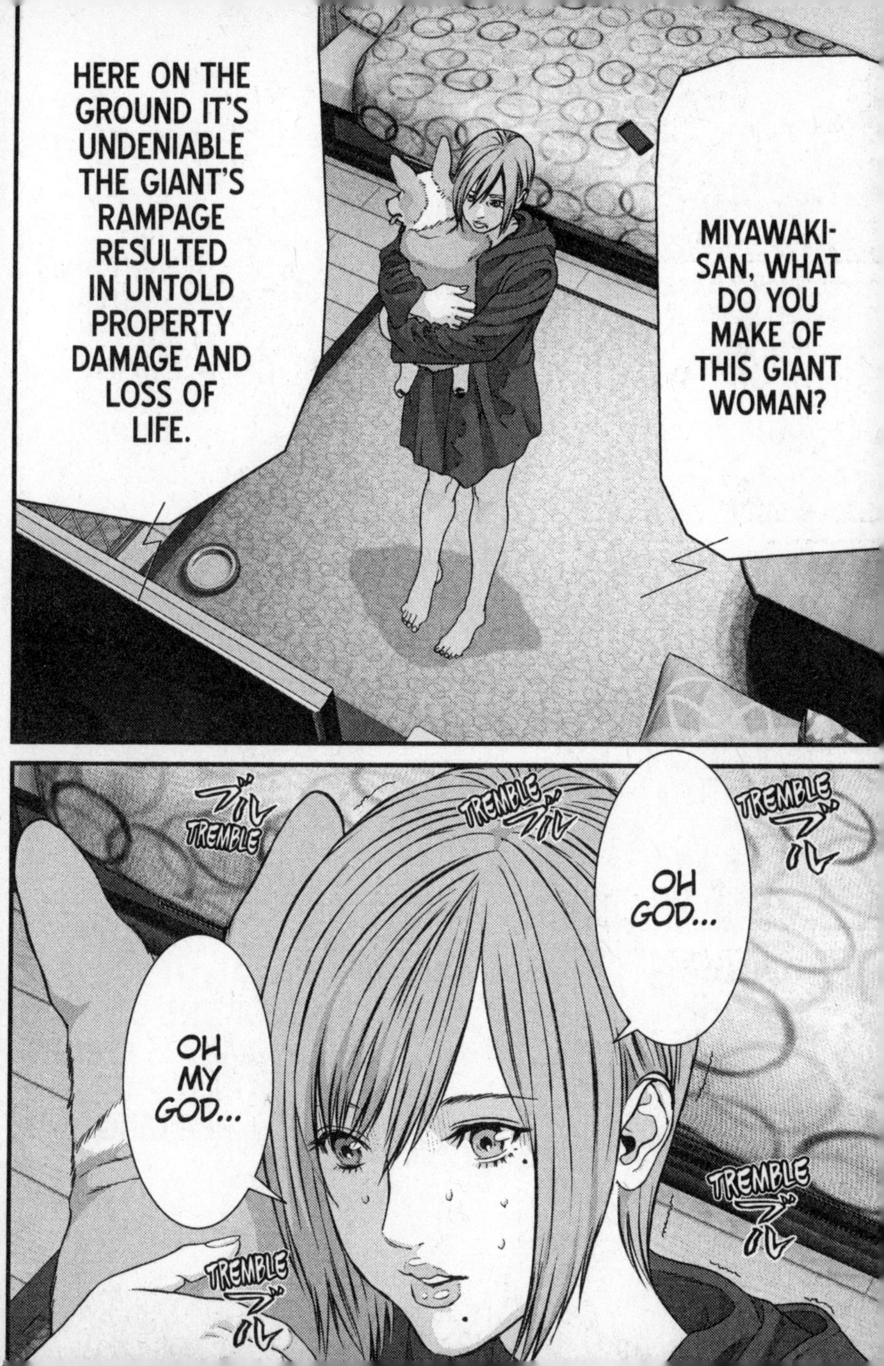
MIYAWAKI-SAN, WHAT DO YOU MAKE OF THIS GIANT WOMAN?
HERE ON THE GROUND IT'S UNDENIABLE THE GIANT'S RAMPAGE RESULTED IN UNTOLD PROPERTY DAMAGE AND LOSS OF LIFE.
TREMBLE ブル
OH GOD...
TREMBLE ブル
ブル TREMBLE
OH MY GOD...
TREMBLE ブル
TREMBLE ブル

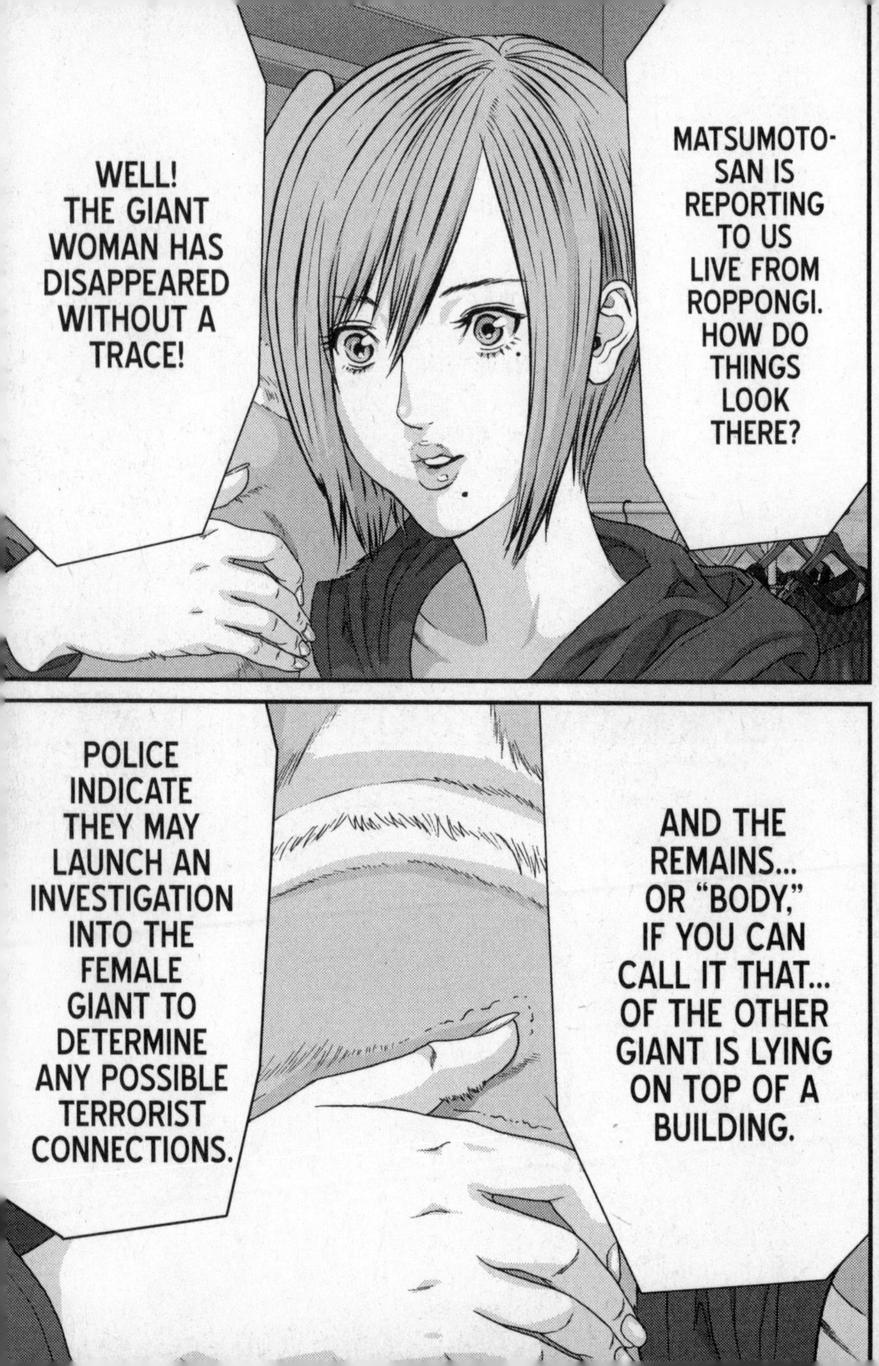
MATSUMOTO-SAN IS REPORTING TO US LIVE FROM ROPPONGI. HOW DO THINGS LOOK THERE?
WELL! THE GIANT WOMAN HAS DISAPPEARED WITHOUT A TRACE!
AND THE REMAINS... OR "BODY," IF YOU CAN CALL IT THAT... OF THE OTHER GIANT IS LYING ON TOP OF A BUILDING.
POLICE INDICATE THEY MAY LAUNCH AN INVESTIGATION INTO THE FEMALE GIANT TO DETERMINE ANY POSSIBLE TERRORIST CONNECTIONS.

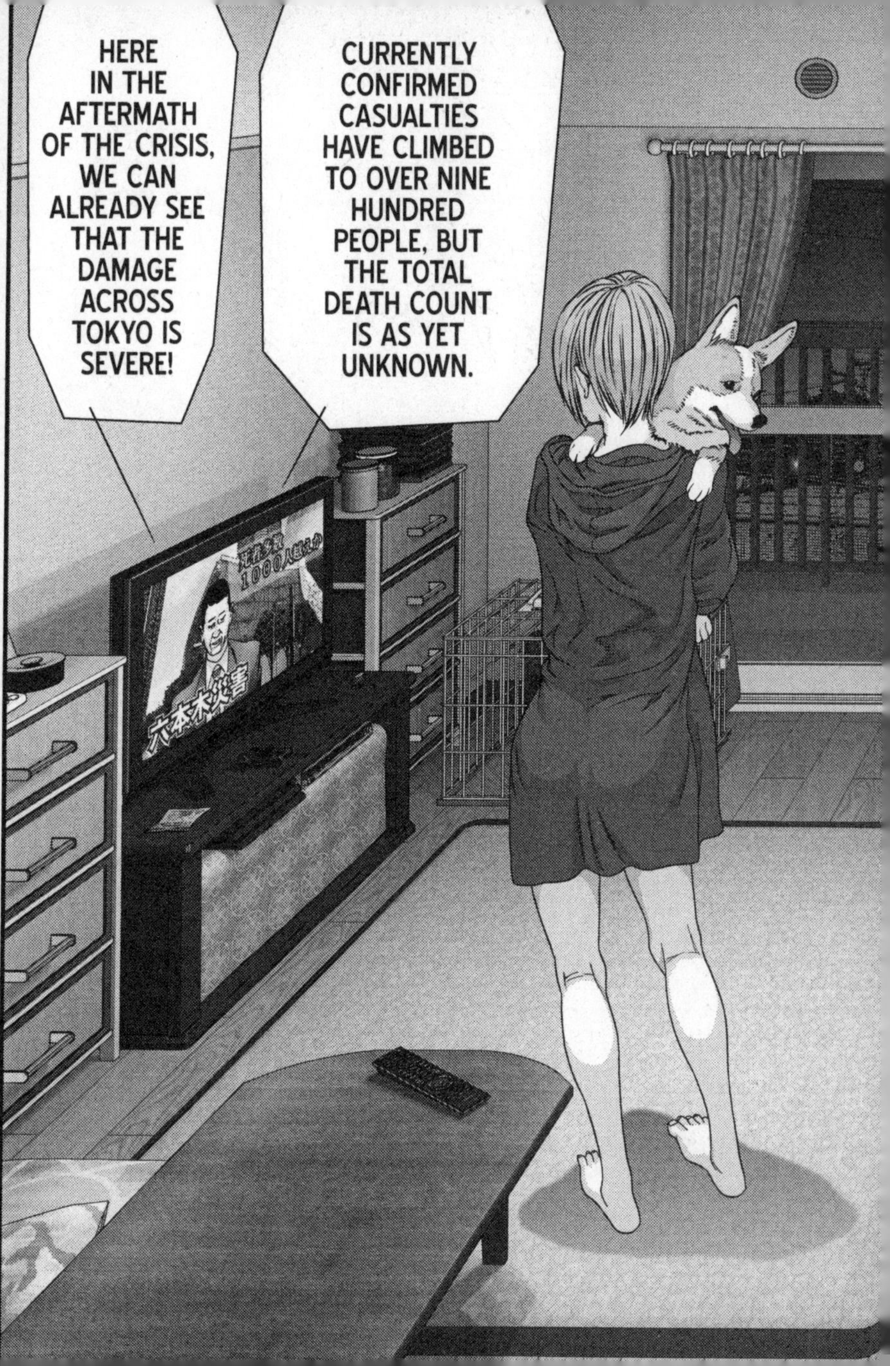
CURRENTLY CONFIRMED CASUALTIES HAVE CLIMBED TO OVER NINE HUNDRED PEOPLE, BUT THE TOTAL DEATH COUNT IS AS YET UNKNOWN.
HERE IN THE AFTERMATH OF THE CRISIS, WE CAN ALREADY SEE THAT THE DAMAGE ACROSS TOKYO IS SEVERE!
六本木災害

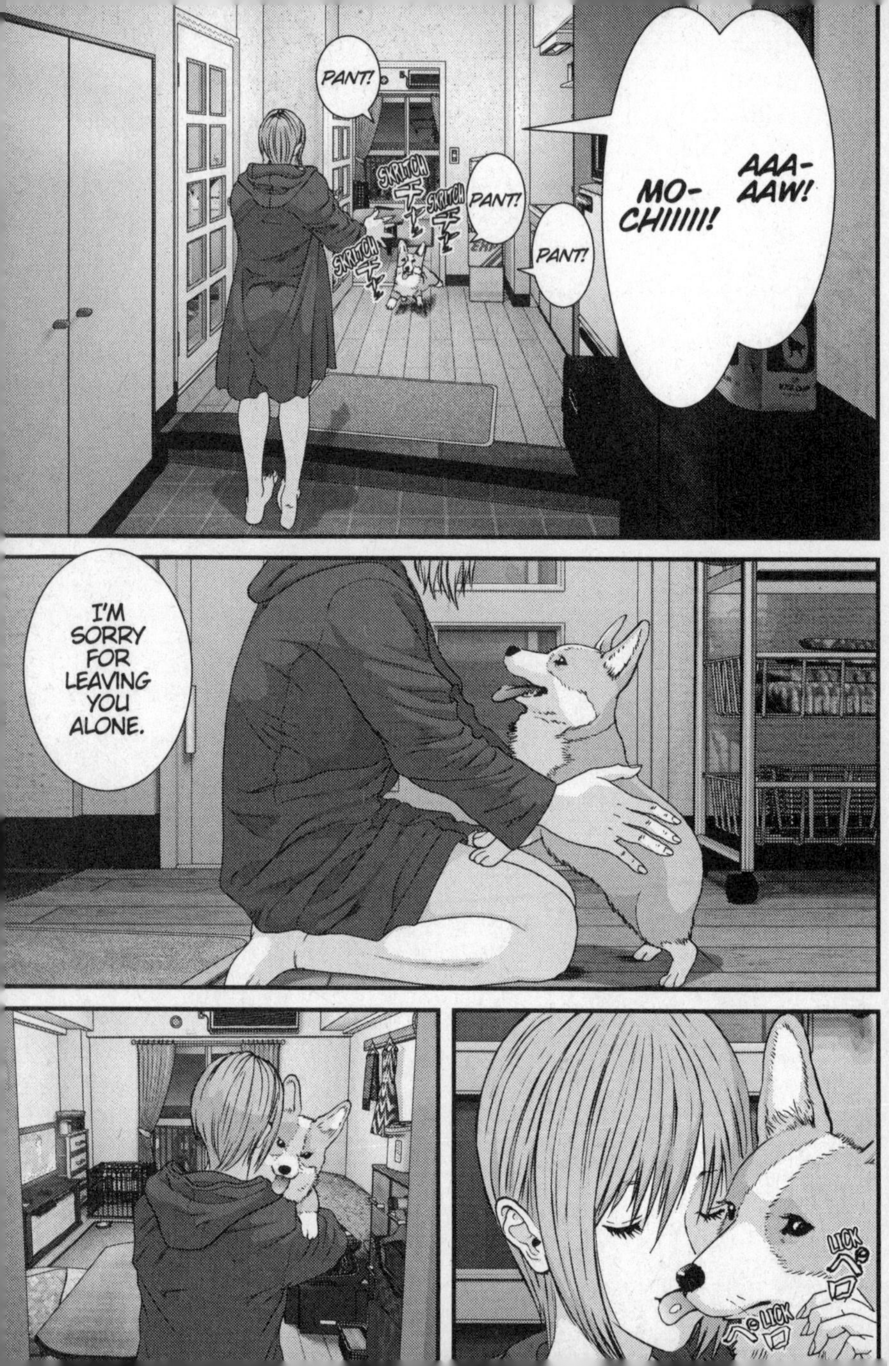

AAA-AAW! MO-CHIIIIII!
PANT!
PANT!
SKRITCH
SKRITCH
SKRITCH
PANT!
I'M SORRY FOR LEAVING YOU ALONE.
LICK
LICK

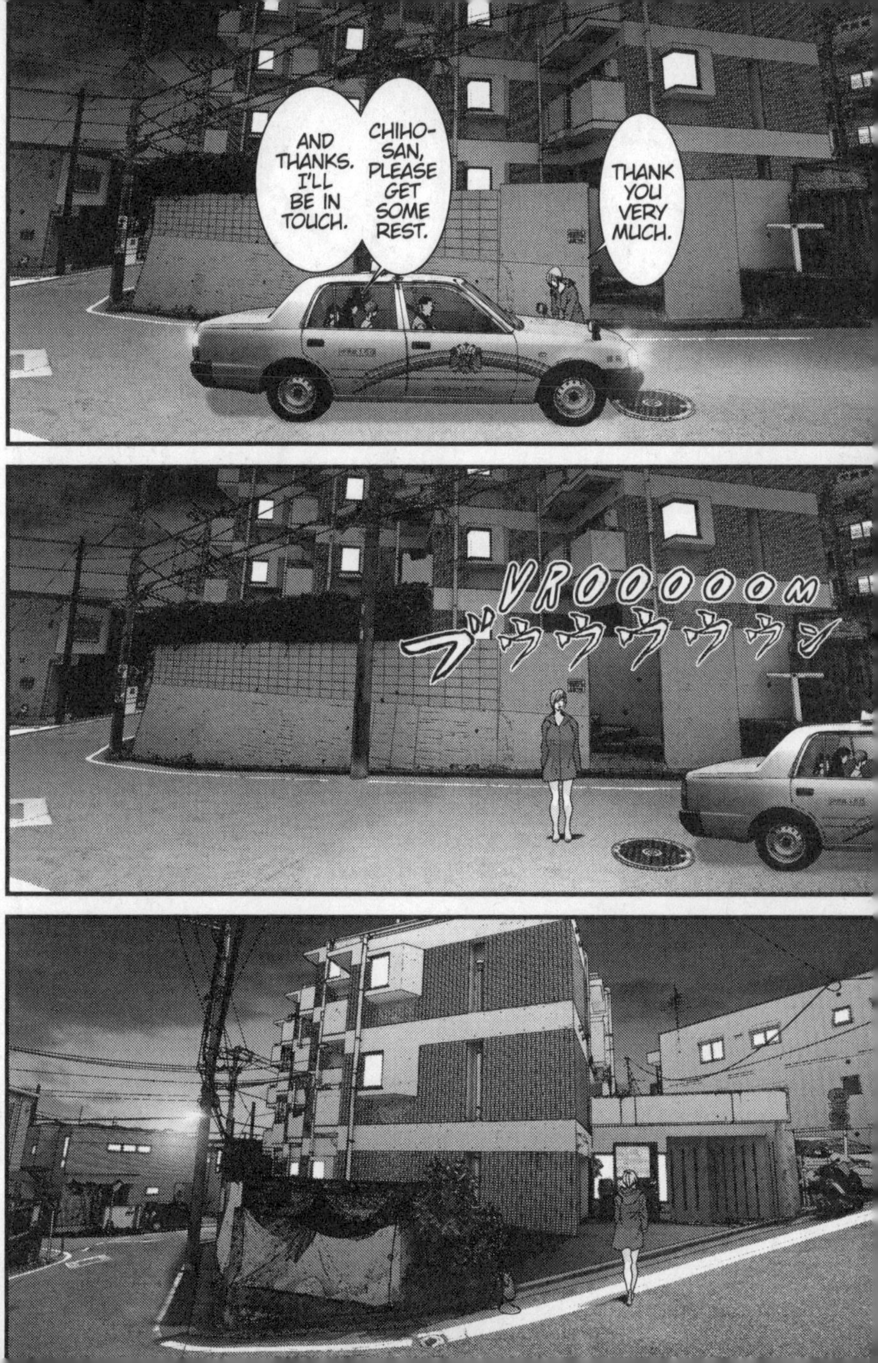
THANK YOU VERY MUCH.
CHIHO-SAN, PLEASE GET SOME REST.
AND THANKS. I'LL BE IN TOUCH.
VROOOOOOM
ブウウウウウン

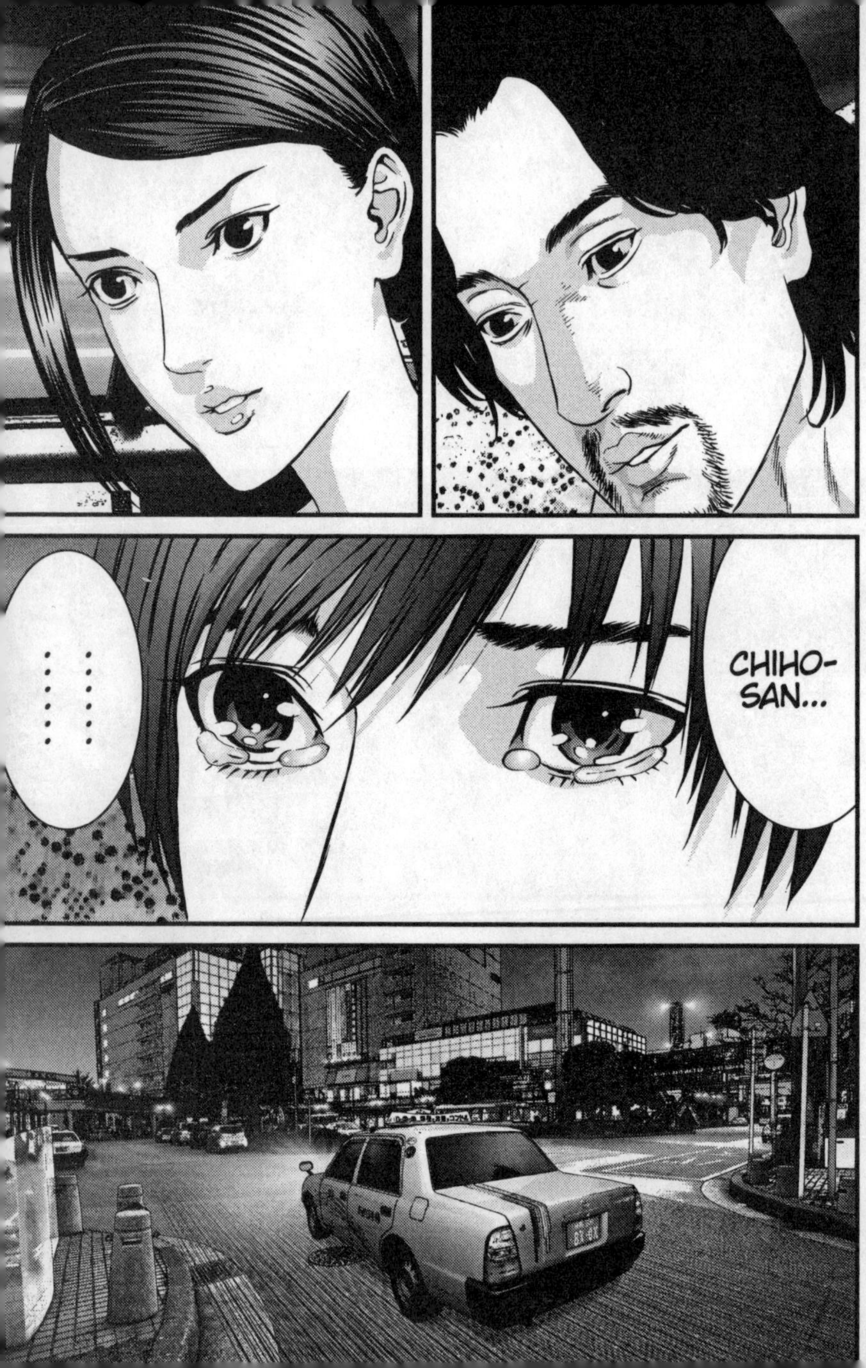
CHIHO-SAN...
......
......

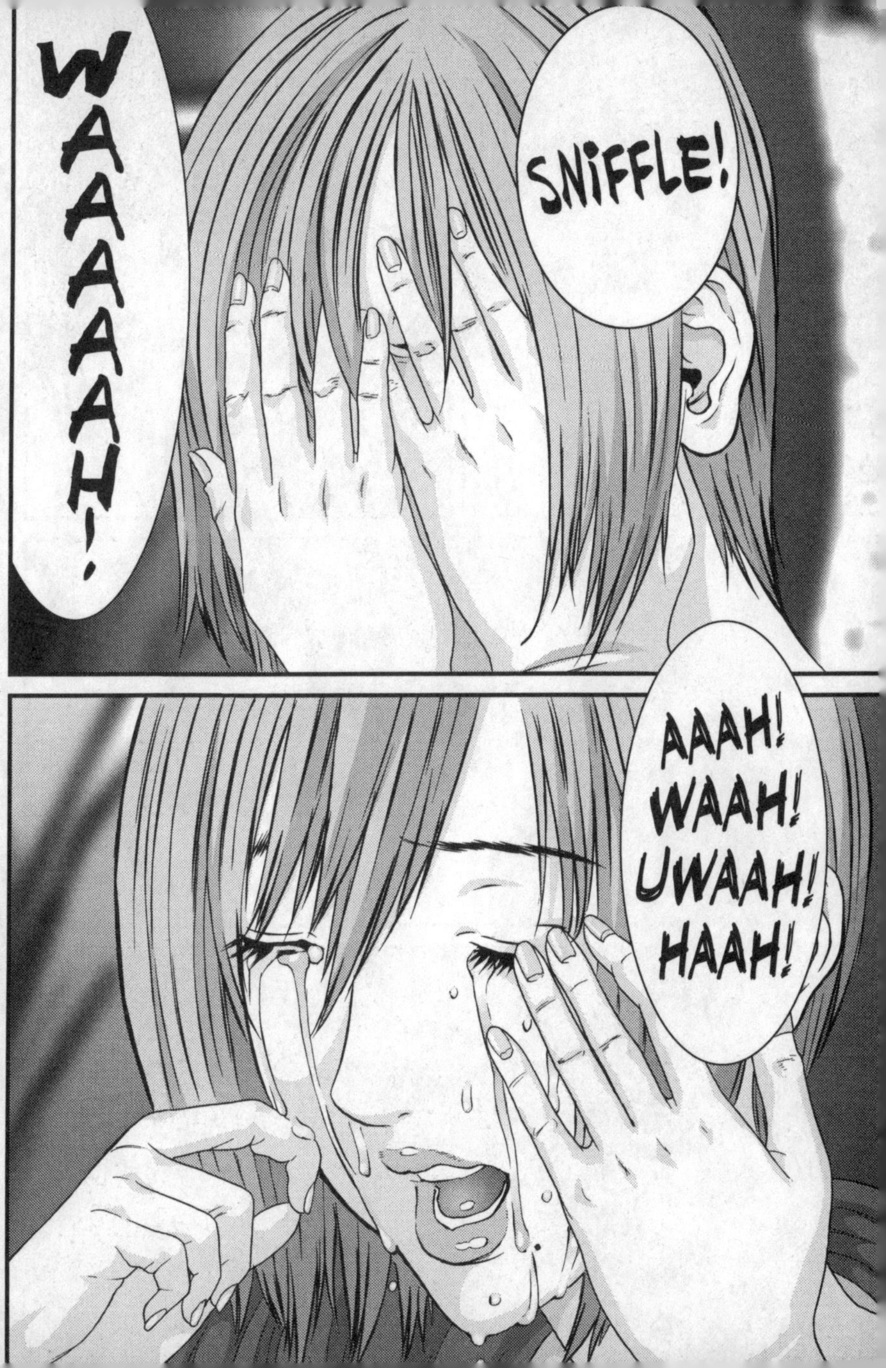
SNIFFLE!
WAAAAAAH!
AAAH! WAAH! UWAAH! HAAH!

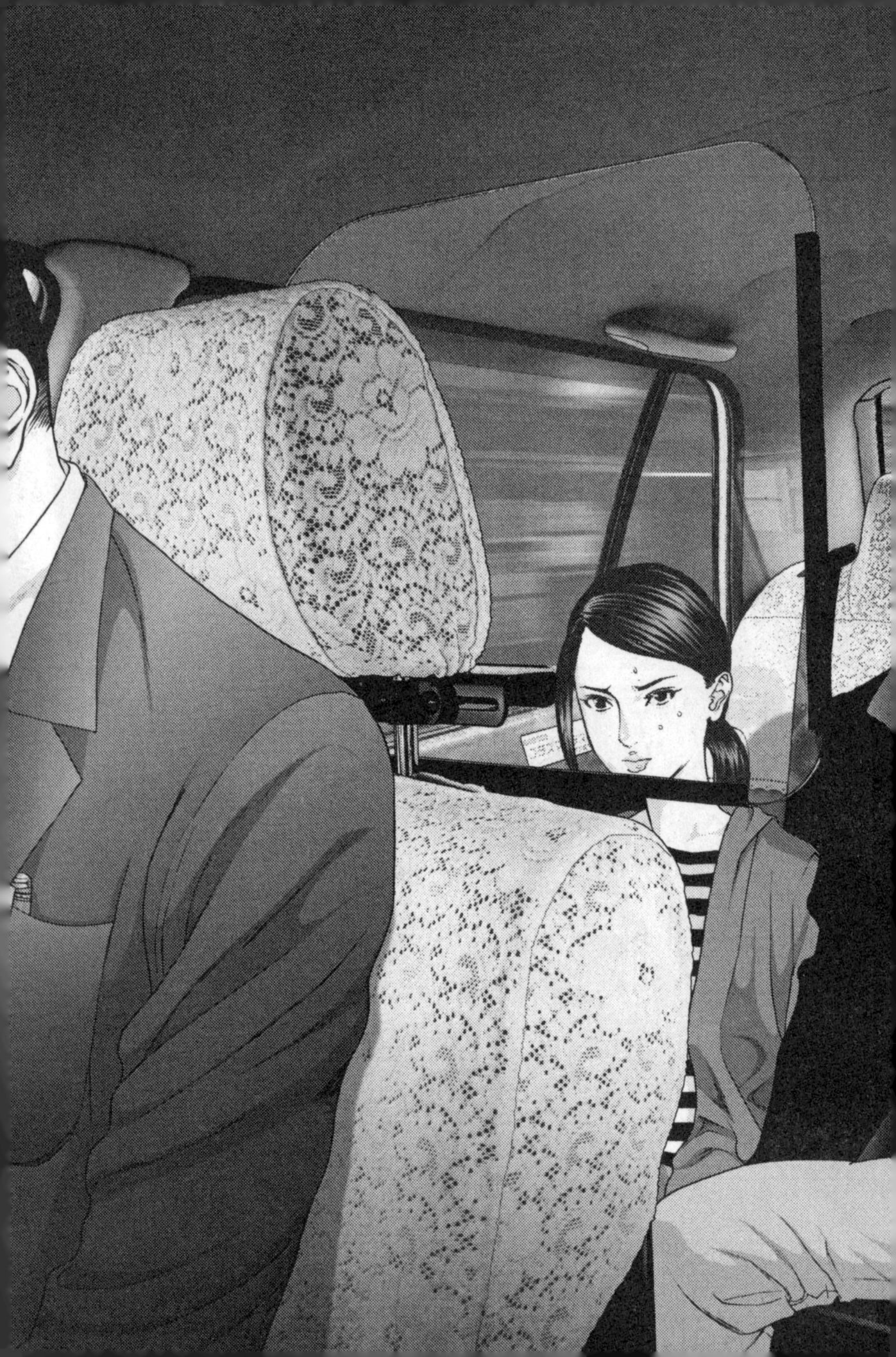

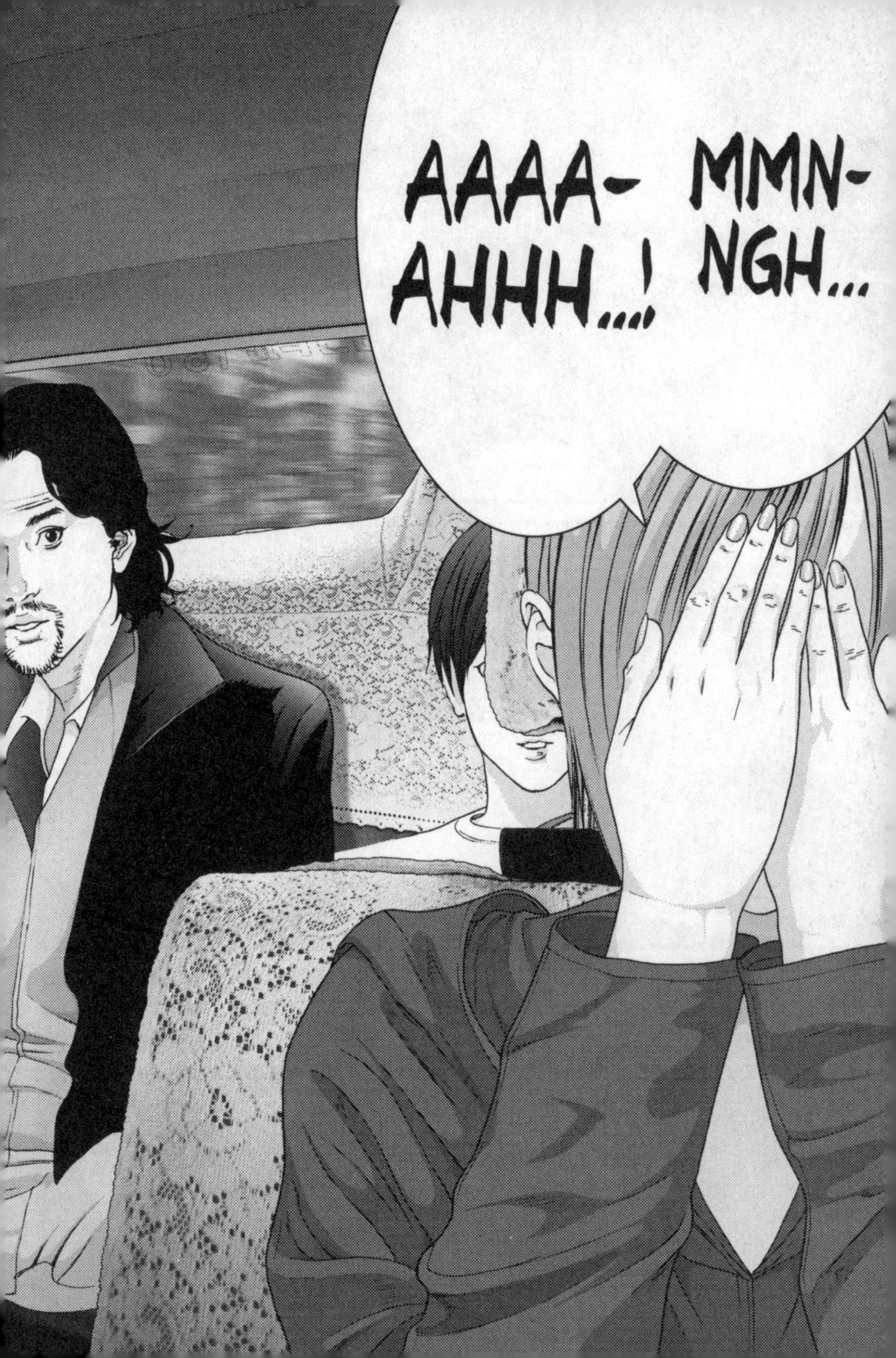
AAAA-AHHH...!
MMN-NGH...

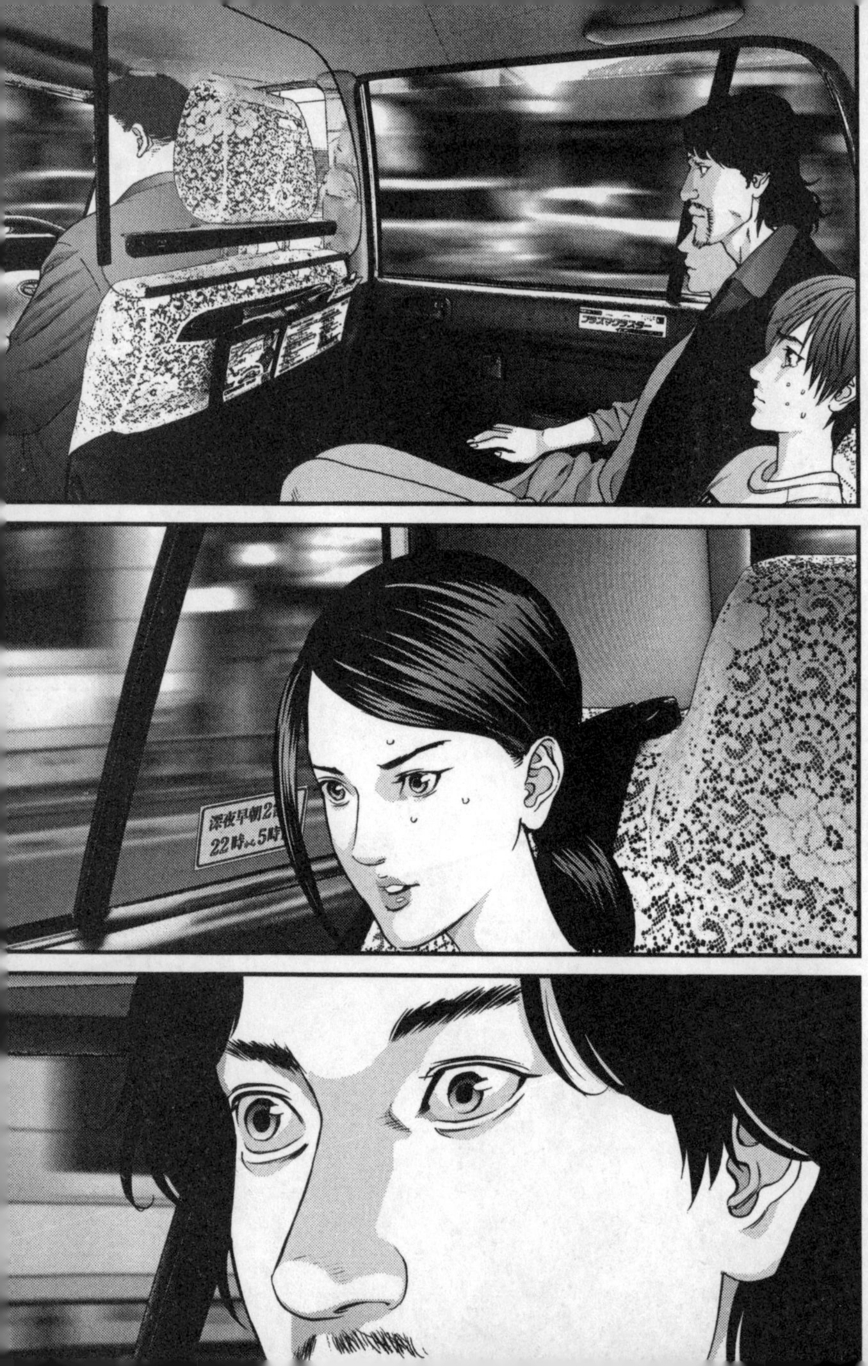
プラズマクラスター
深夜早朝2
22時～5時

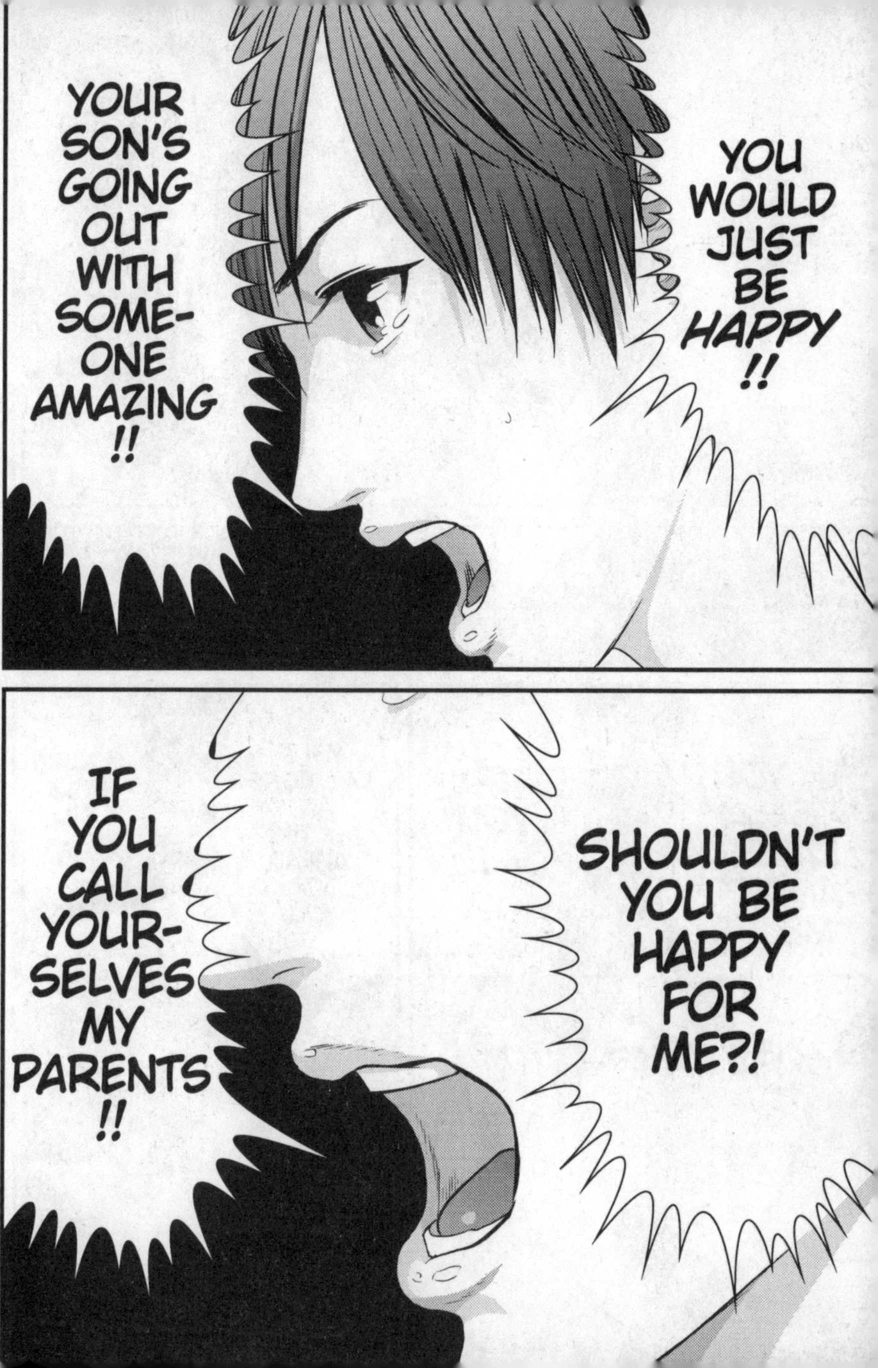
YOU WOULD JUST BE HAPPY!!
YOUR SON'S GOING OUT WITH SOME-ONE AMAZING!!
SHOULDN'T YOU BE HAPPY FOR ME?!
IF YOU CALL YOUR-SELVES MY PARENTS!!

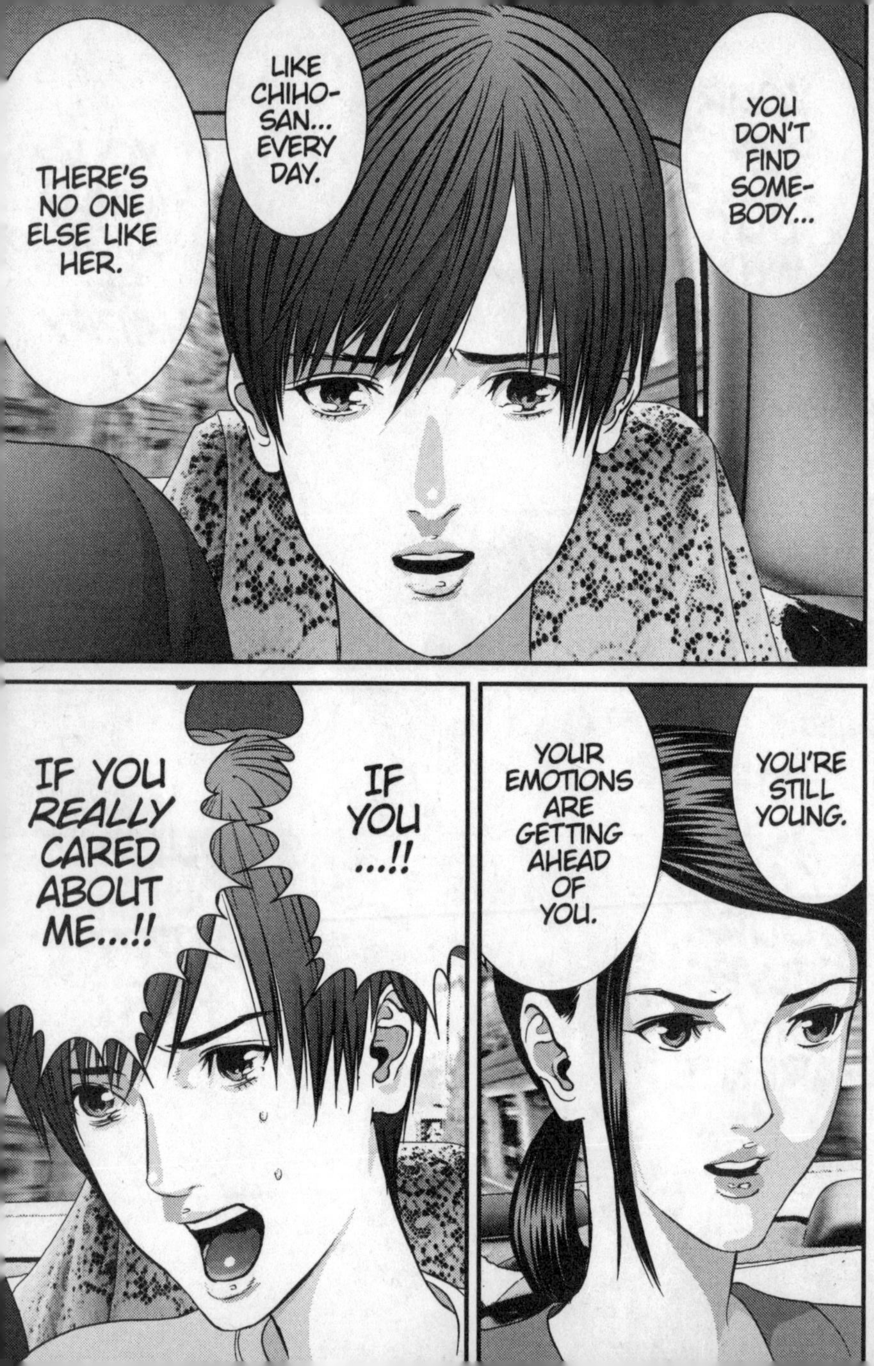
YOU DON'T FIND SOME-BODY...
LIKE CHIHO-SAN... EVERY DAY.
THERE'S NO ONE ELSE LIKE HER.
YOU'RE STILL YOUNG.
YOUR EMOTIONS ARE GETTING AHEAD OF YOU.
IF YOU ...!!
IF YOU *REALLY* CARED ABOUT ME...!!

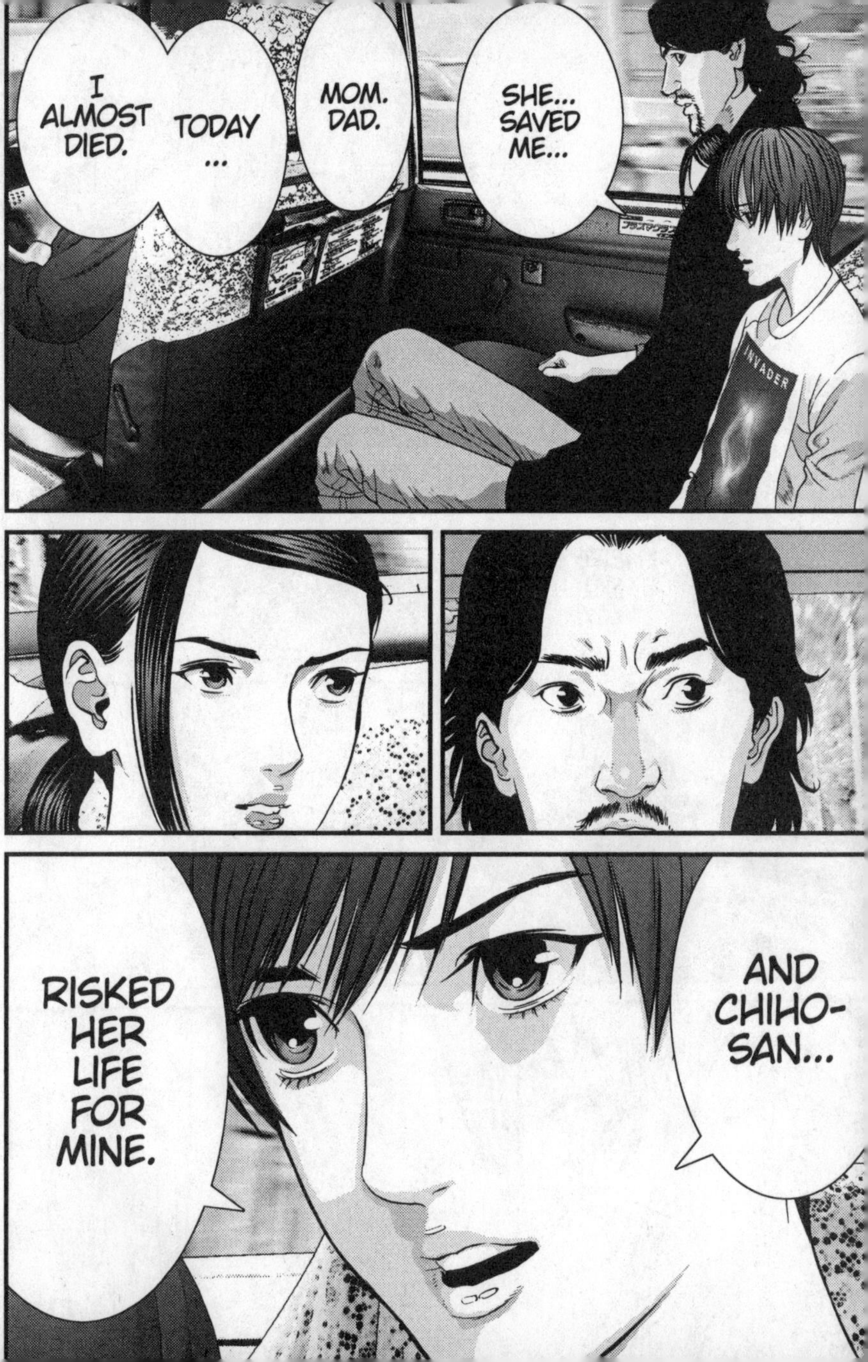
SHE... SAVED ME...
MOM. DAD.
TODAY ...
I ALMOST DIED.
AND CHIHO-SAN...
RISKED HER LIFE FOR MINE.

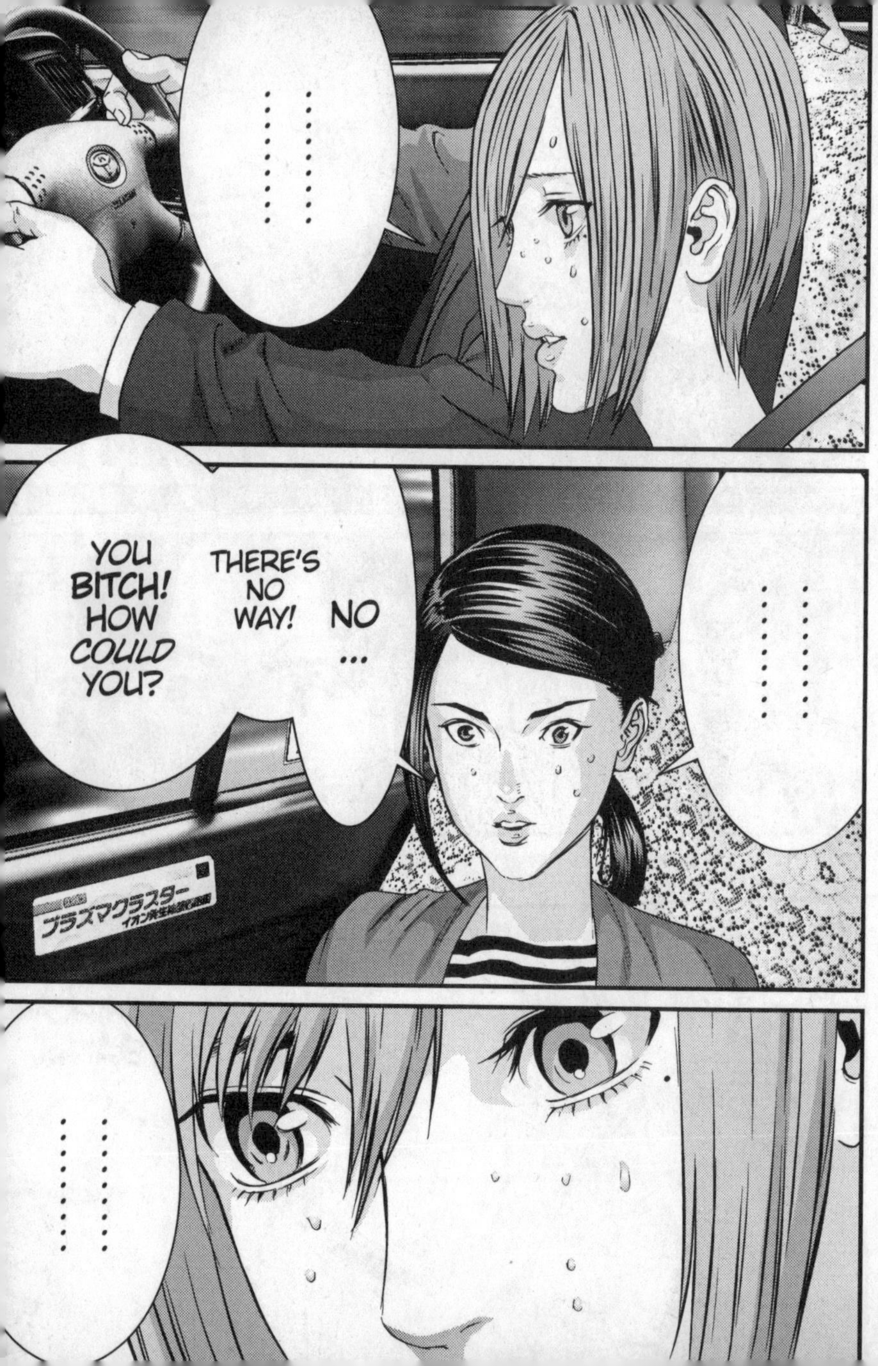
......
......
NO ...
THERE'S NO WAY!
YOU BITCH! HOW COULD YOU?
プラズマクラスター
......

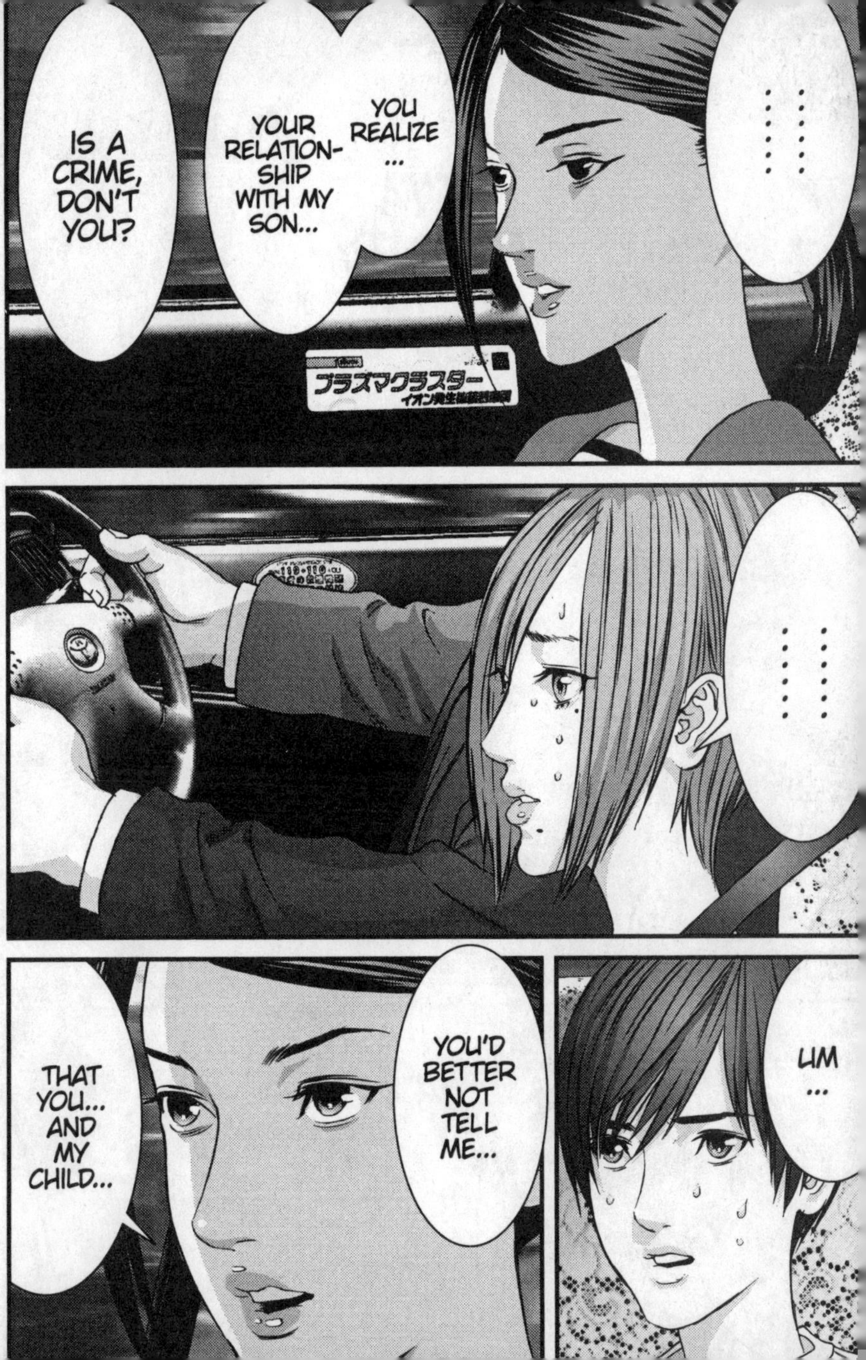
......
YOU REALIZE ...
YOUR RELATION-SHIP WITH MY SON...
IS A CRIME, DON'T YOU?
プラズマクラスター
......
UM ...
YOU'D BETTER NOT TELL ME...
THAT YOU... AND MY CHILD...

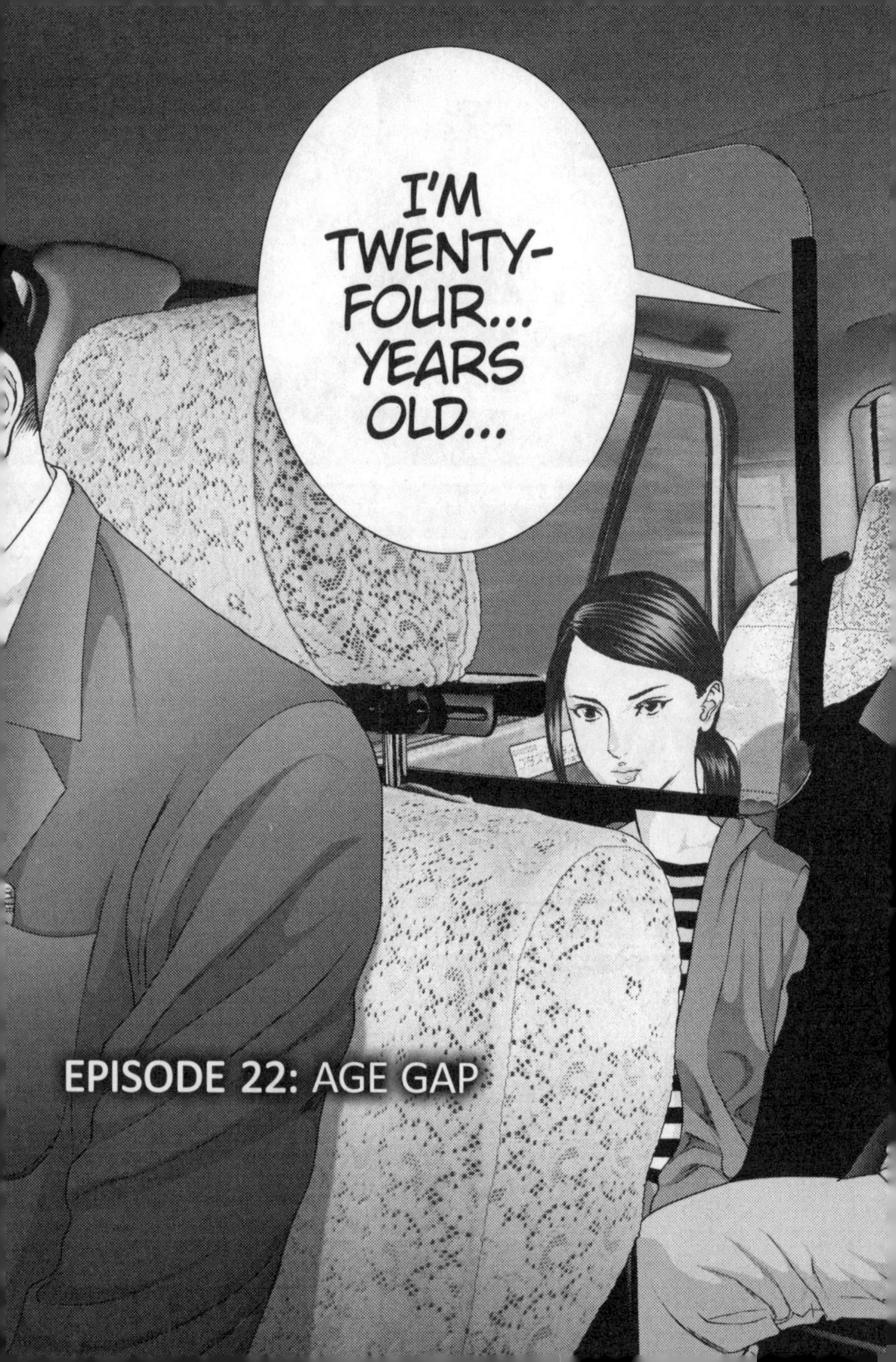
I'M TWENTY-FOUR... YEARS OLD...
EPISODE 22: AGE GAP

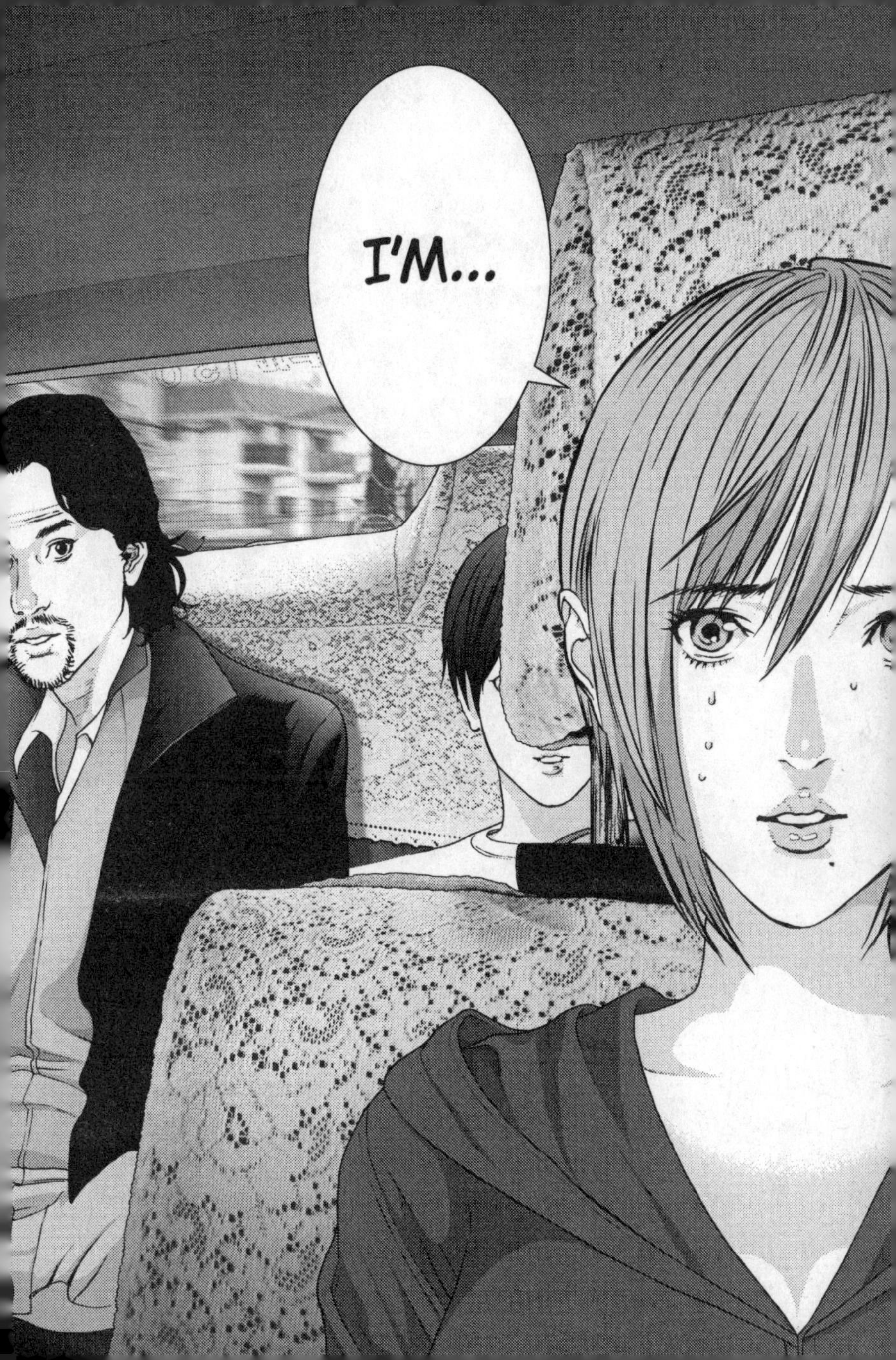
I'M...

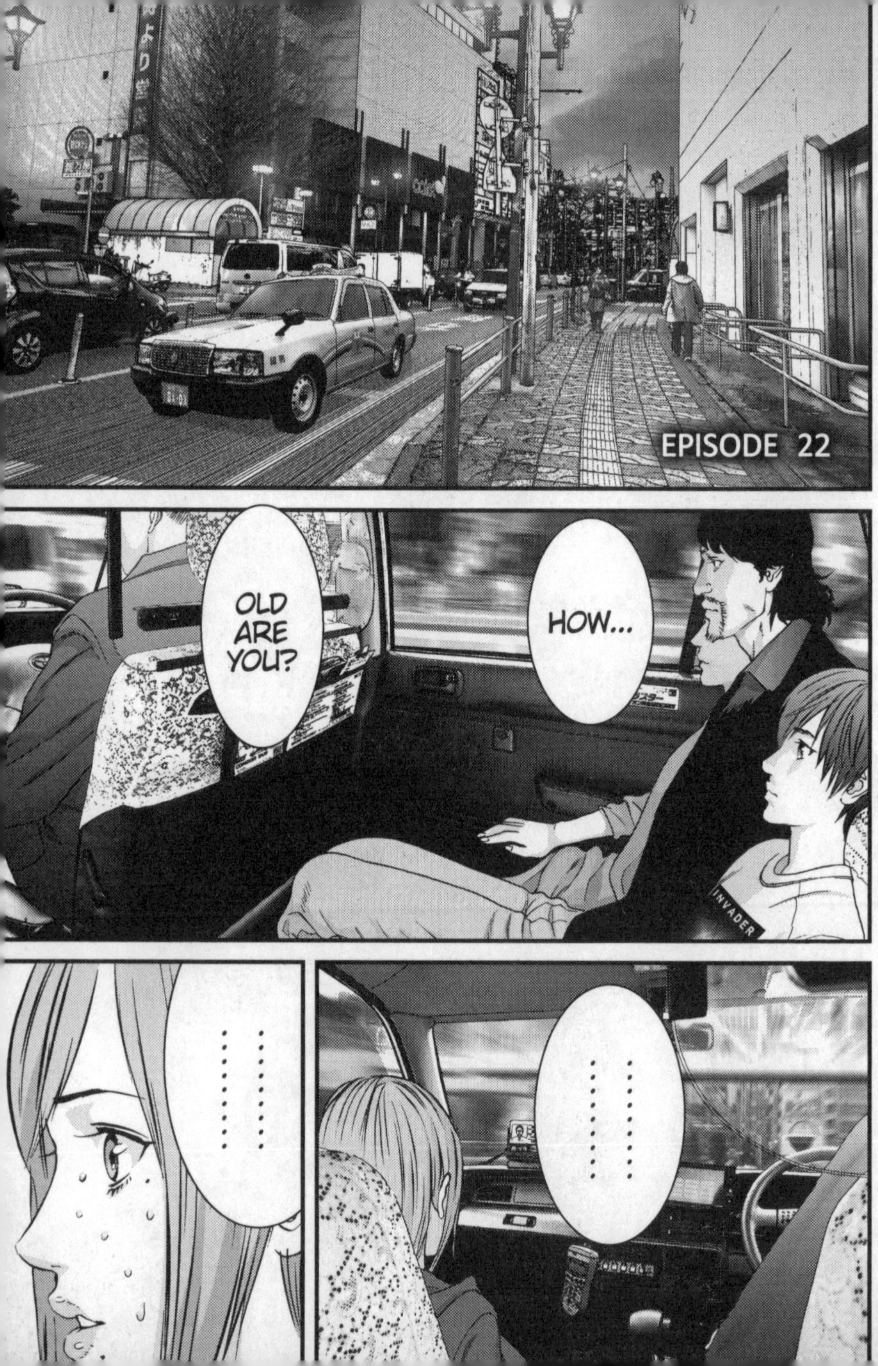
EPISODE 22
HOW...
OLD ARE YOU?
INVADER
......
......

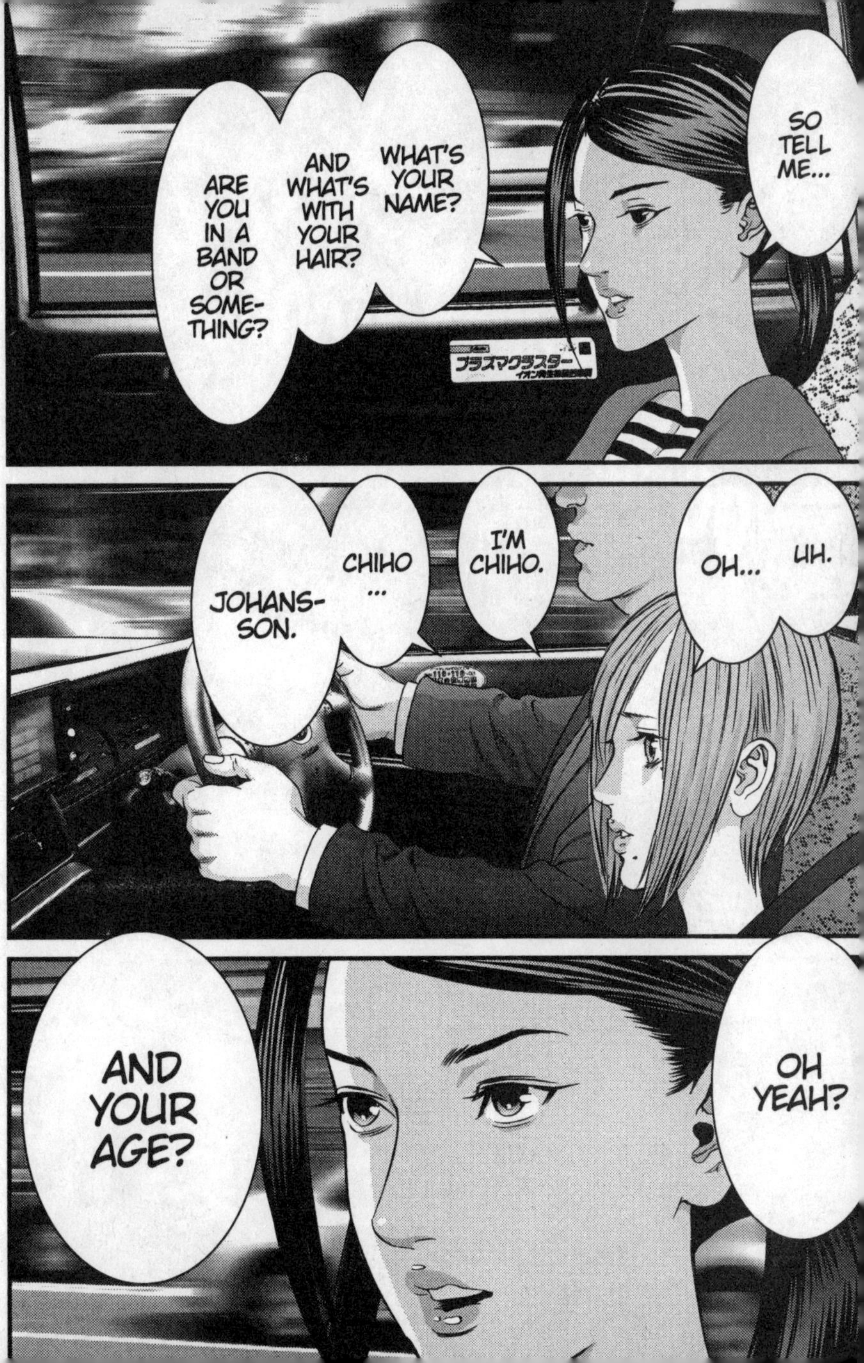
SO TELL ME...
WHAT'S YOUR NAME?
AND WHAT'S WITH YOUR HAIR?
ARE YOU IN A BAND OR SOME-THING?
プラズマクラスター
UH.
OH...
I'M CHIHO.
CHIHO ...
JOHANS-SON.
OH YEAH?
AND YOUR AGE?

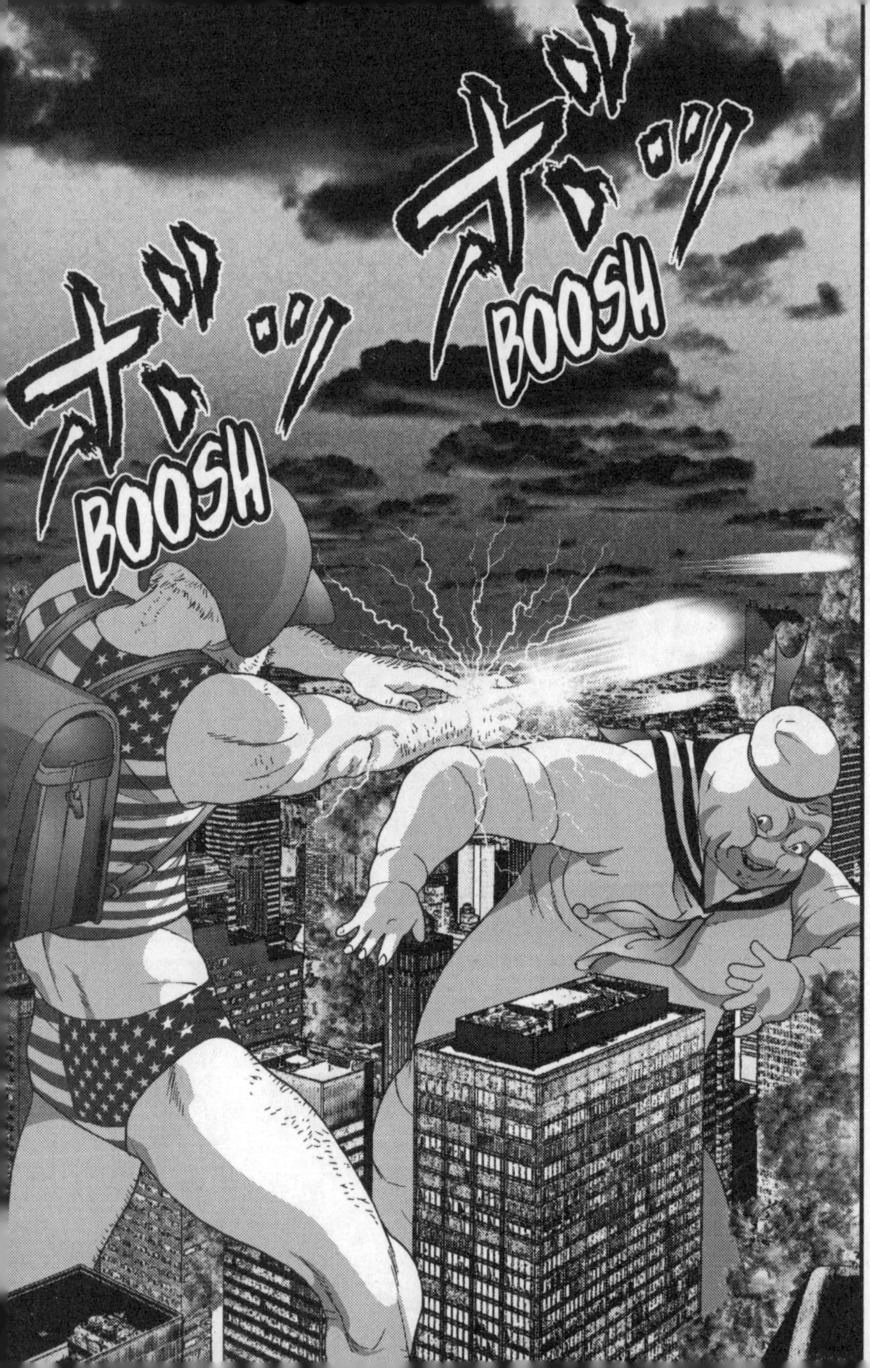
BOOSH
BOOSH

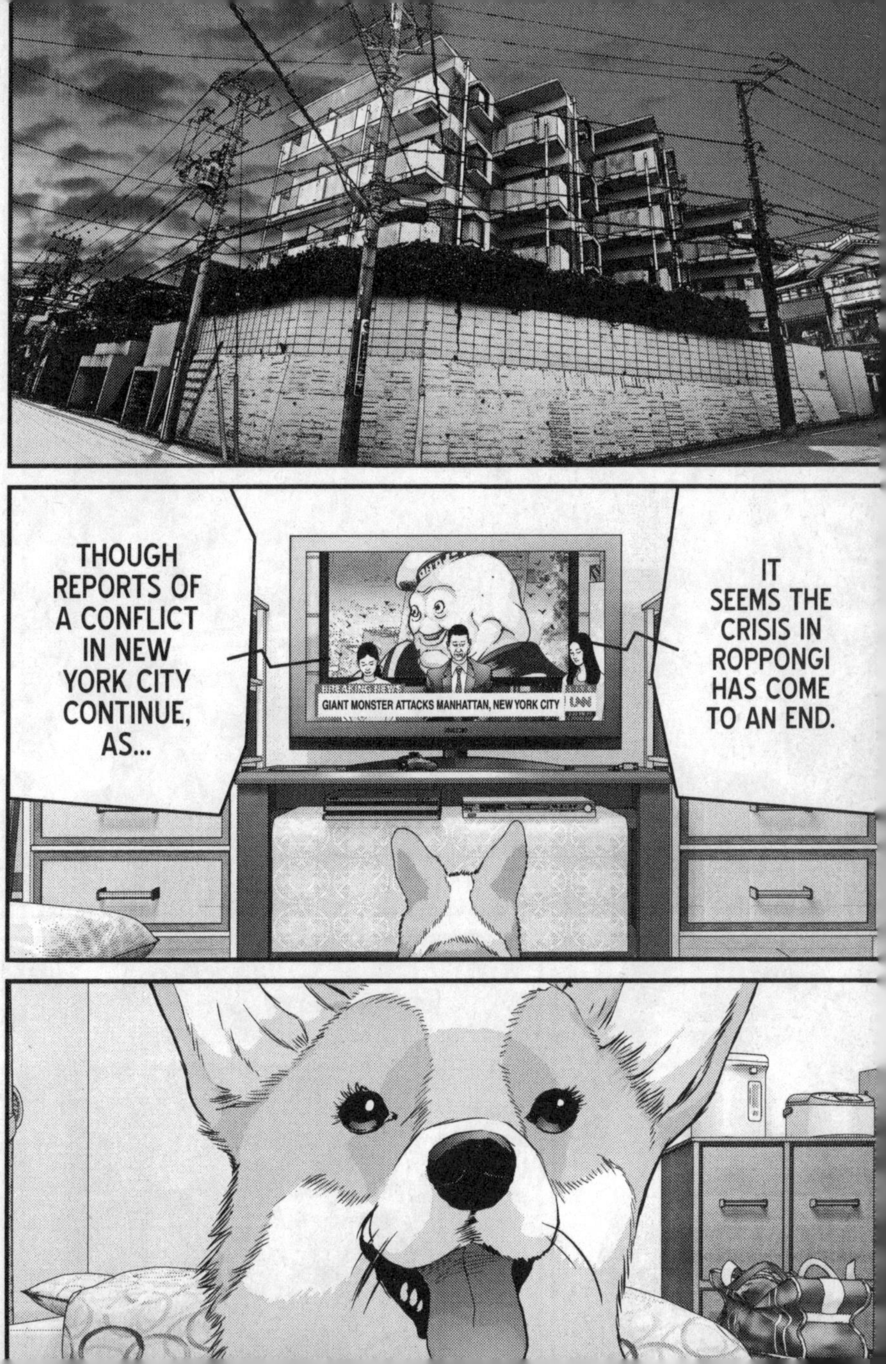
IT SEEMS THE CRISIS IN ROPPONGI HAS COME TO AN END.
THOUGH REPORTS OF A CONFLICT IN NEW YORK CITY CONTINUE, AS...
GIANT MONSTER ATTACKS MANHATTAN, NEW YORK CITY
UNN

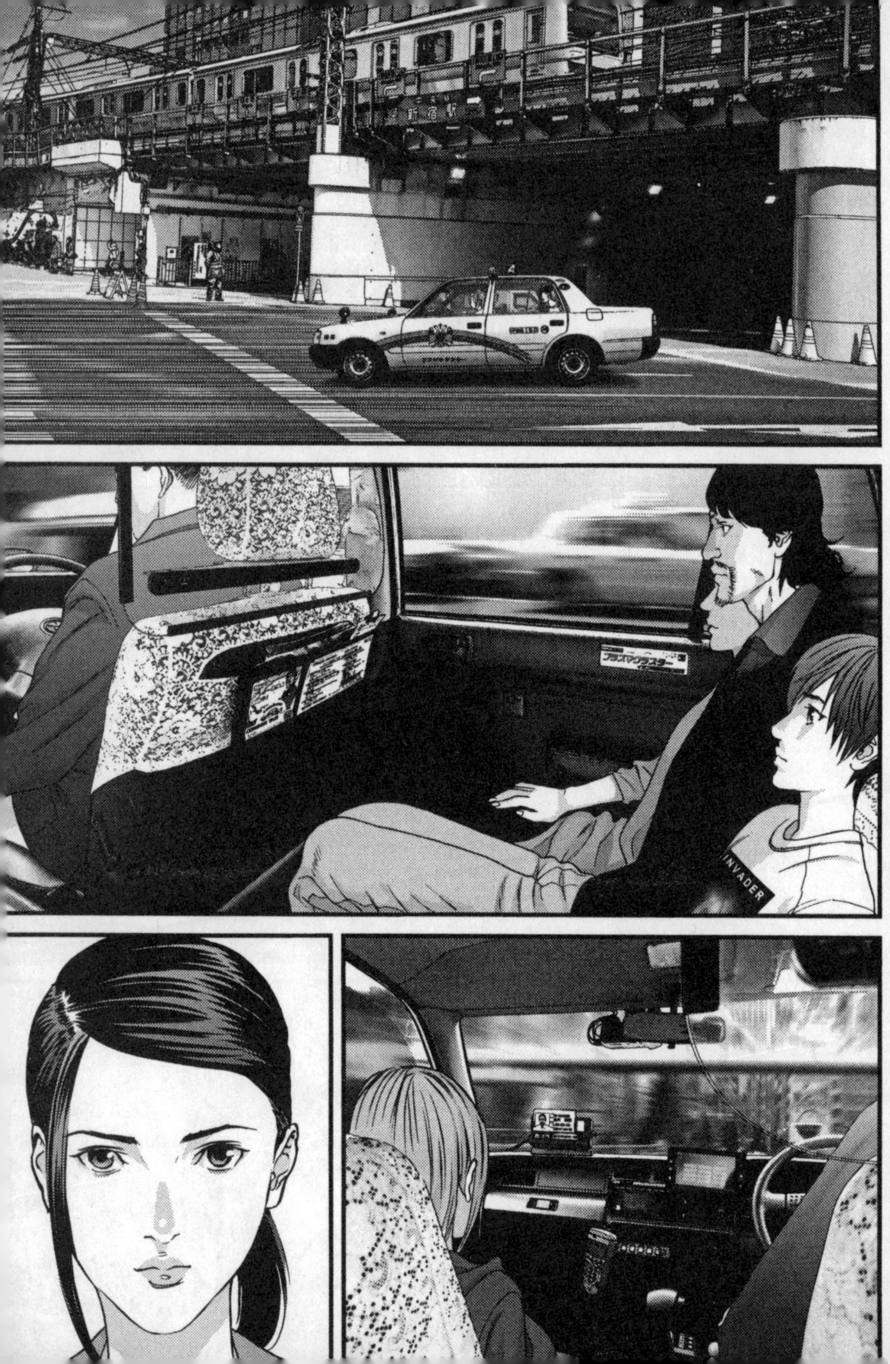
新宿駅
プラズマクラスター
INVADER

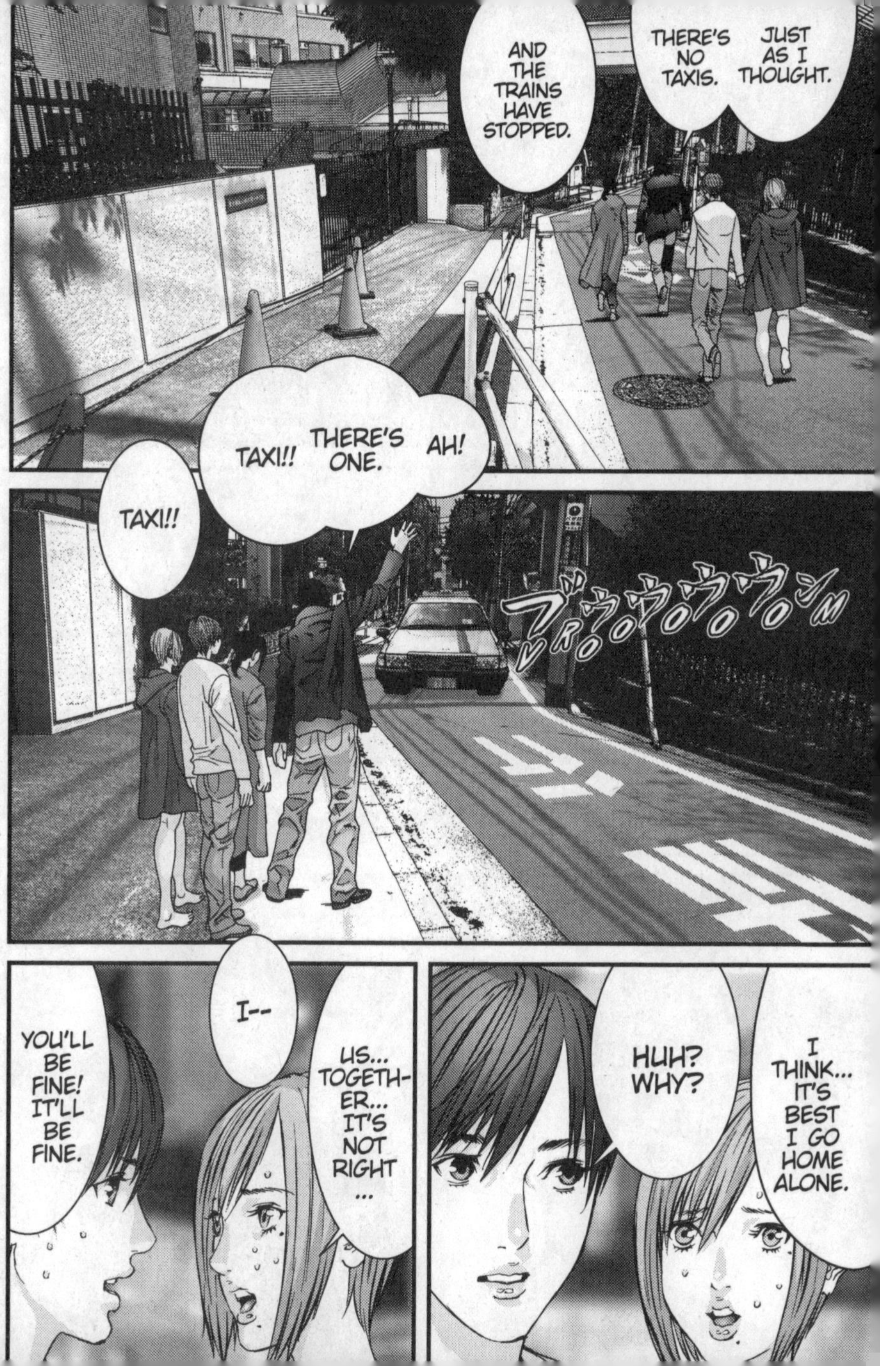
JUST AS I THOUGHT.
THERE'S NO TAXIS.
AND THE TRAINS HAVE STOPPED.
AH! THERE'S ONE. TAXI!!
TAXI!!
VROOOOOOM
I THINK... IT'S BEST I GO HOME ALONE.
HUH? WHY?
I--
US... TOGETHER... IT'S NOT RIGHT...
YOU'LL BE FINE! IT'LL BE FINE.

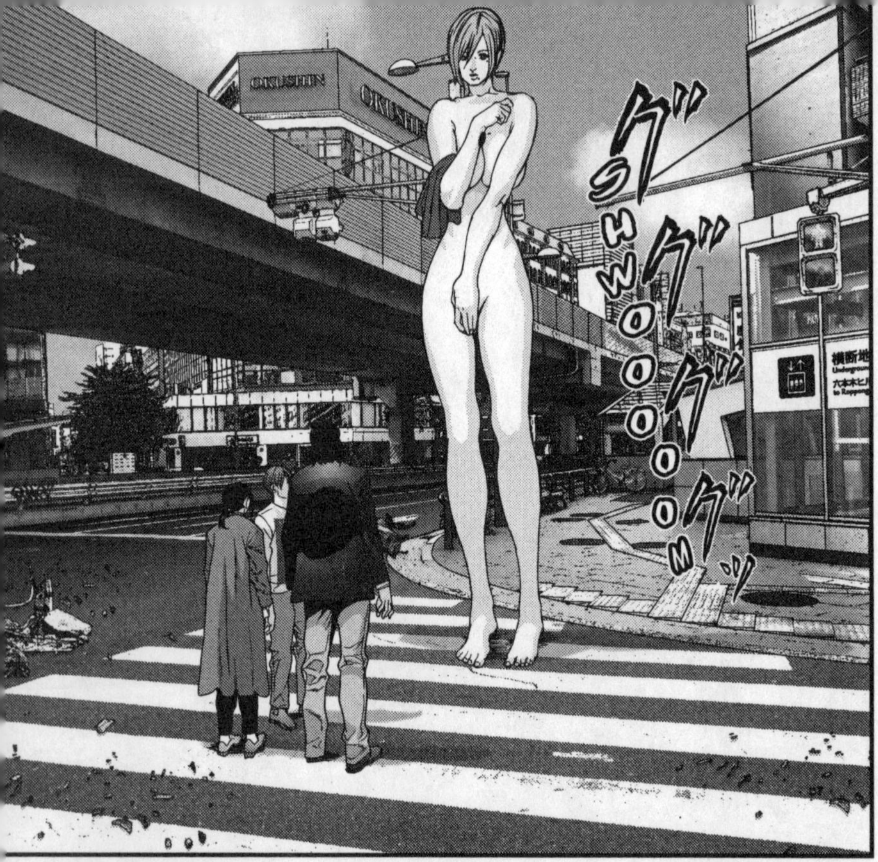
OKUSHIN
ググググッ
SHWOOOOOM
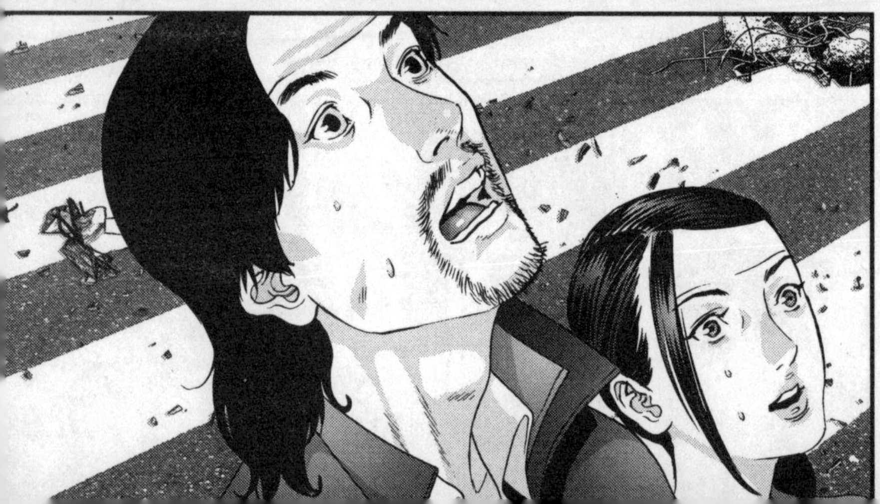

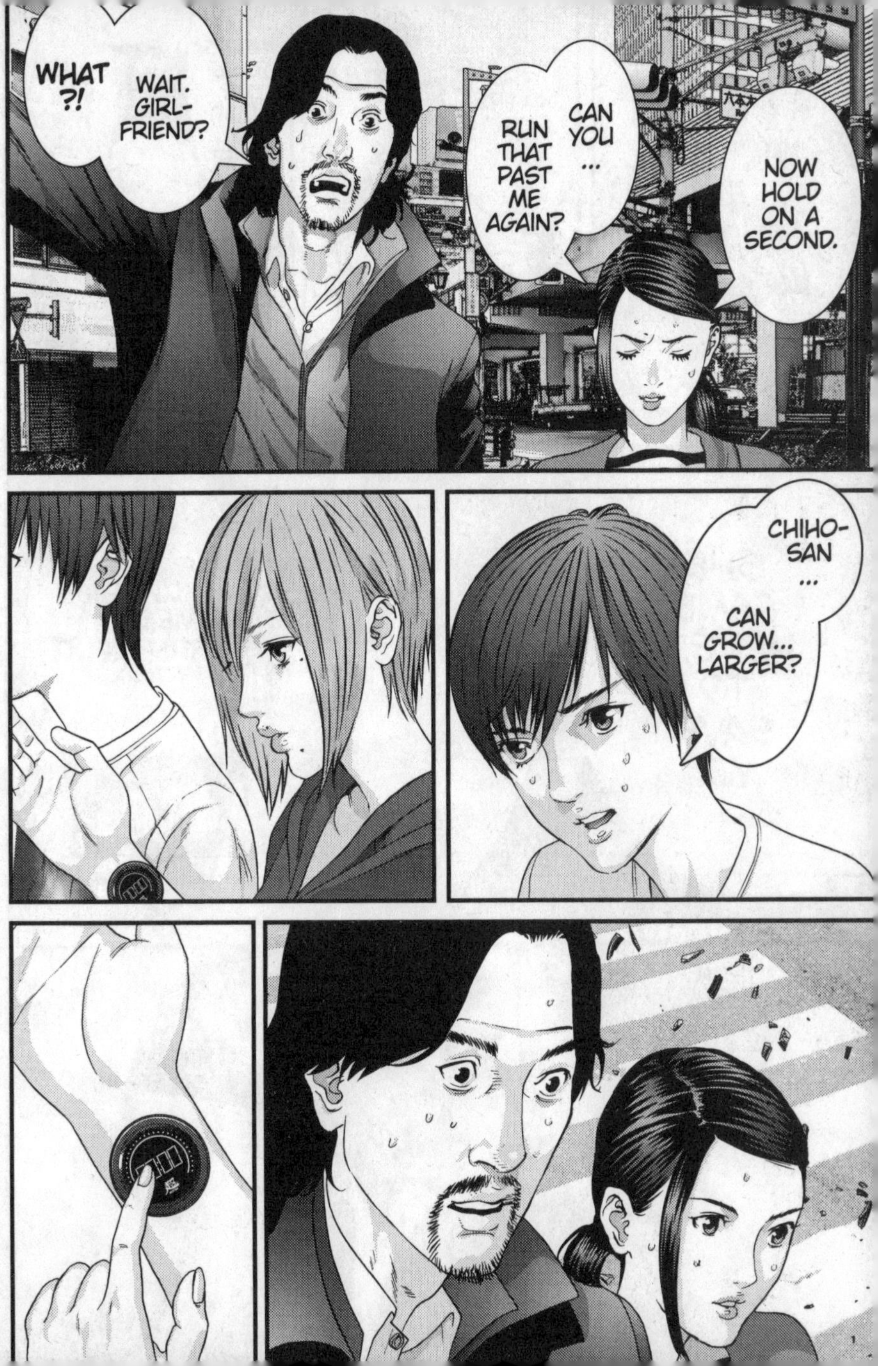
NOW HOLD ON A SECOND.
CAN YOU ... RUN THAT PAST ME AGAIN?
WAIT. GIRL-FRIEND?
WHAT ?!
CHIHO-SAN ... CAN GROW... LARGER?

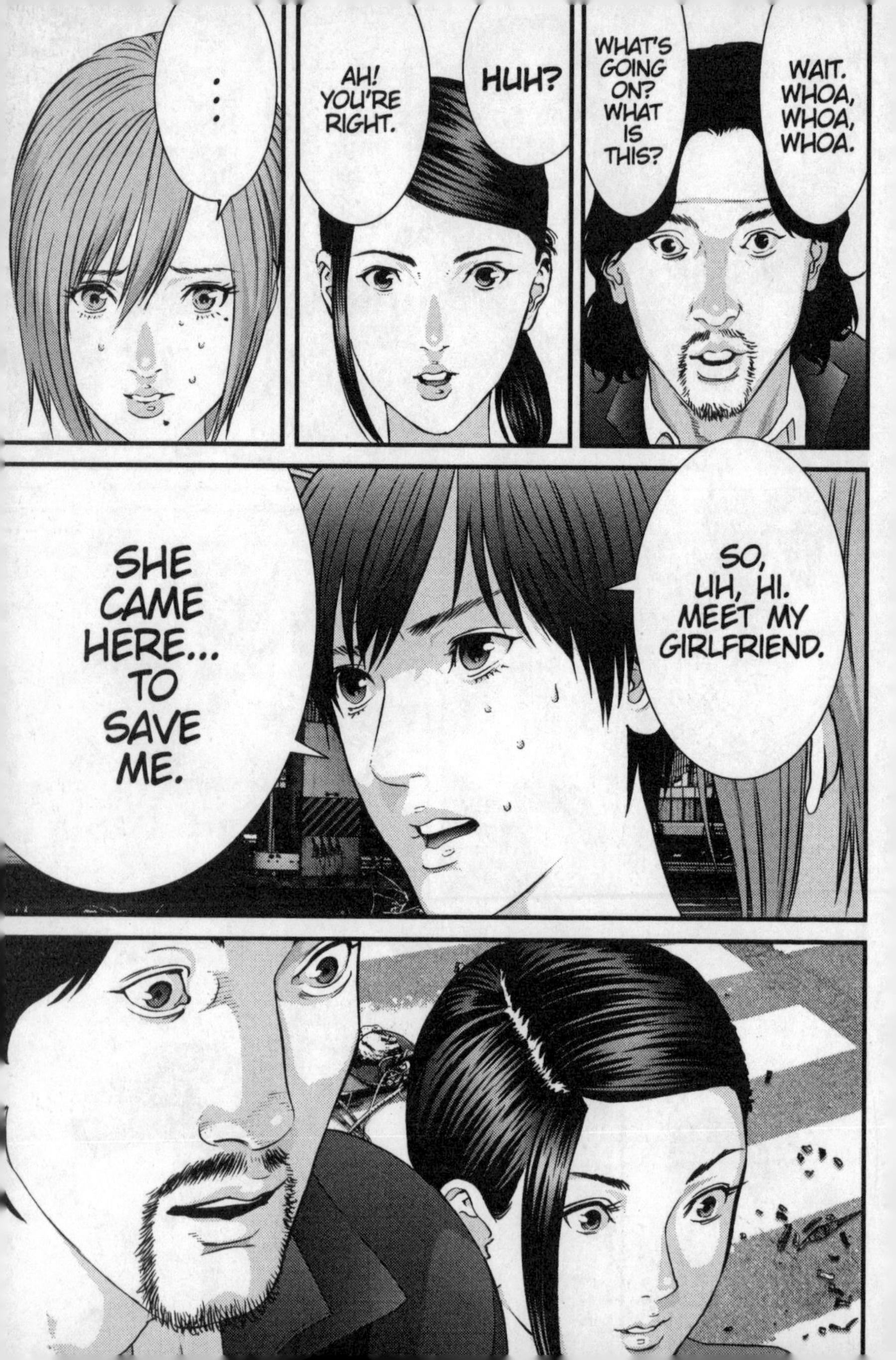
WAIT. WHOA, WHOA, WHOA.
WHAT'S GOING ON? WHAT IS THIS?
HUH?
AH! YOU'RE RIGHT.
...
SO, UH, HI. MEET MY GIRLFRIEND.
SHE CAME HERE... TO SAVE ME.

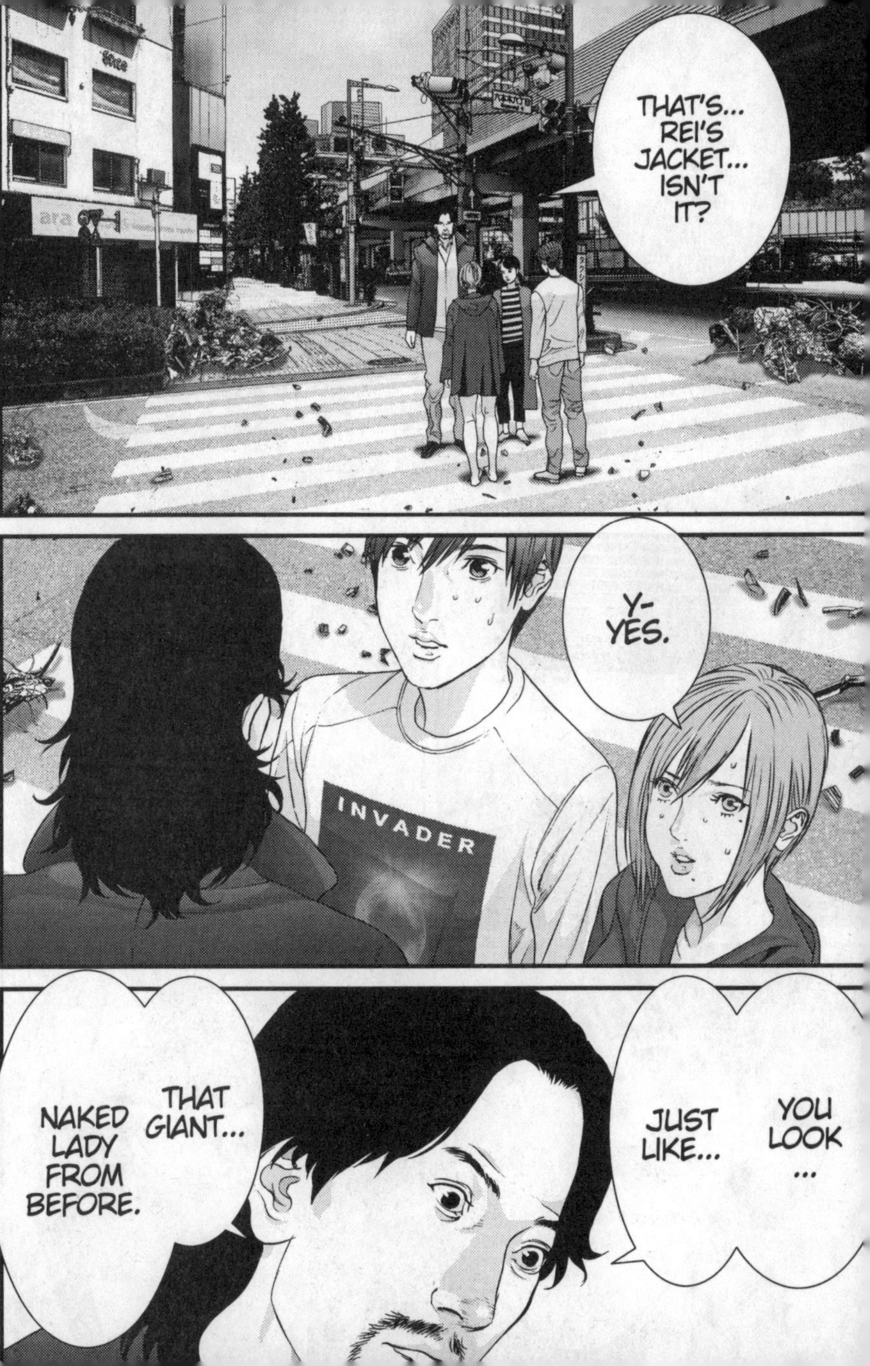
THAT'S... REI'S JACKET... ISN'T IT?
Y- YES.
INVADER
YOU LOOK ...
JUST LIKE...
THAT GIANT...
NAKED LADY FROM BEFORE.

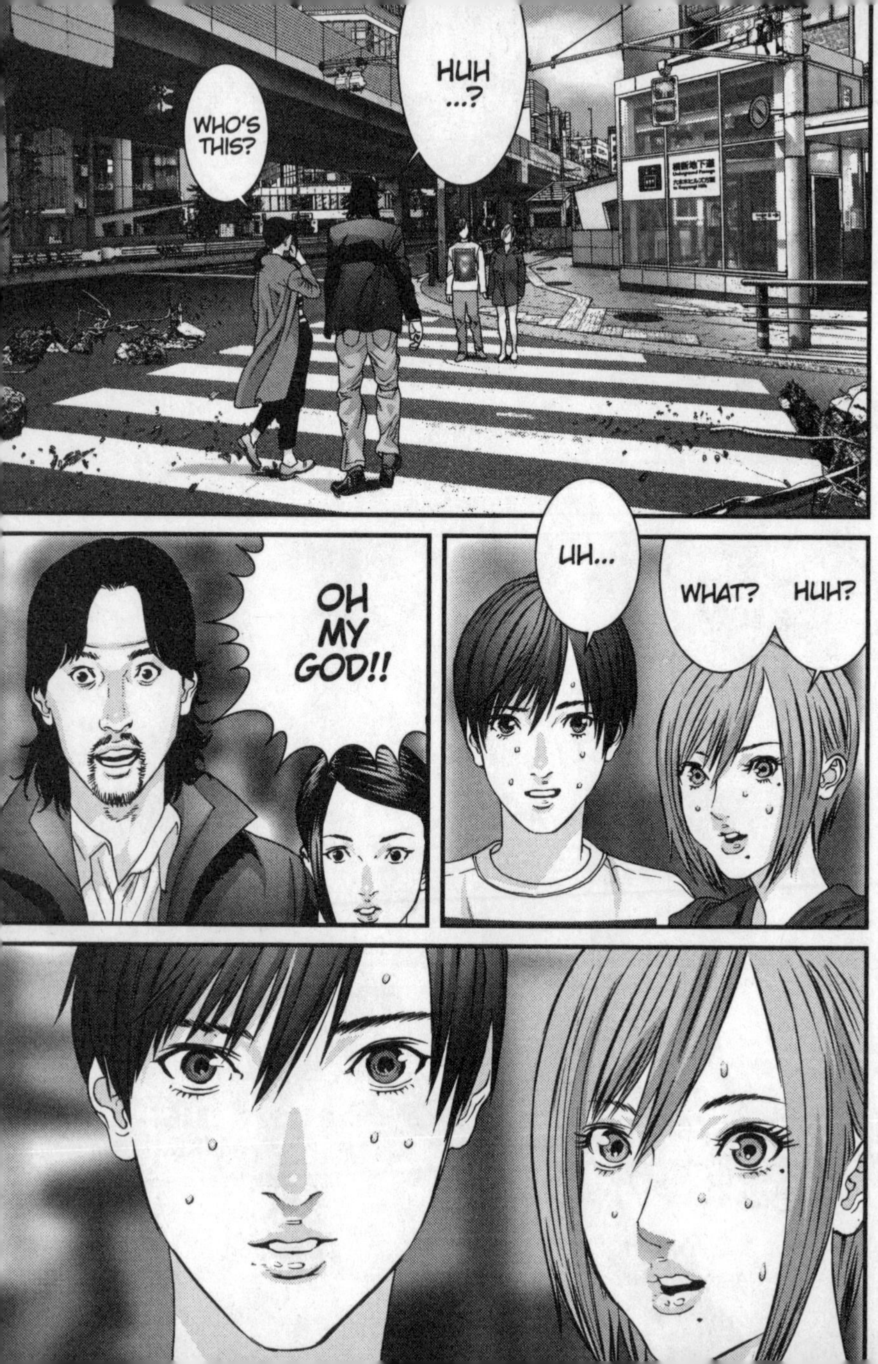
HUH ...?
WHO'S THIS?
WHAT? HUH?
UH...
OH MY GOD!!

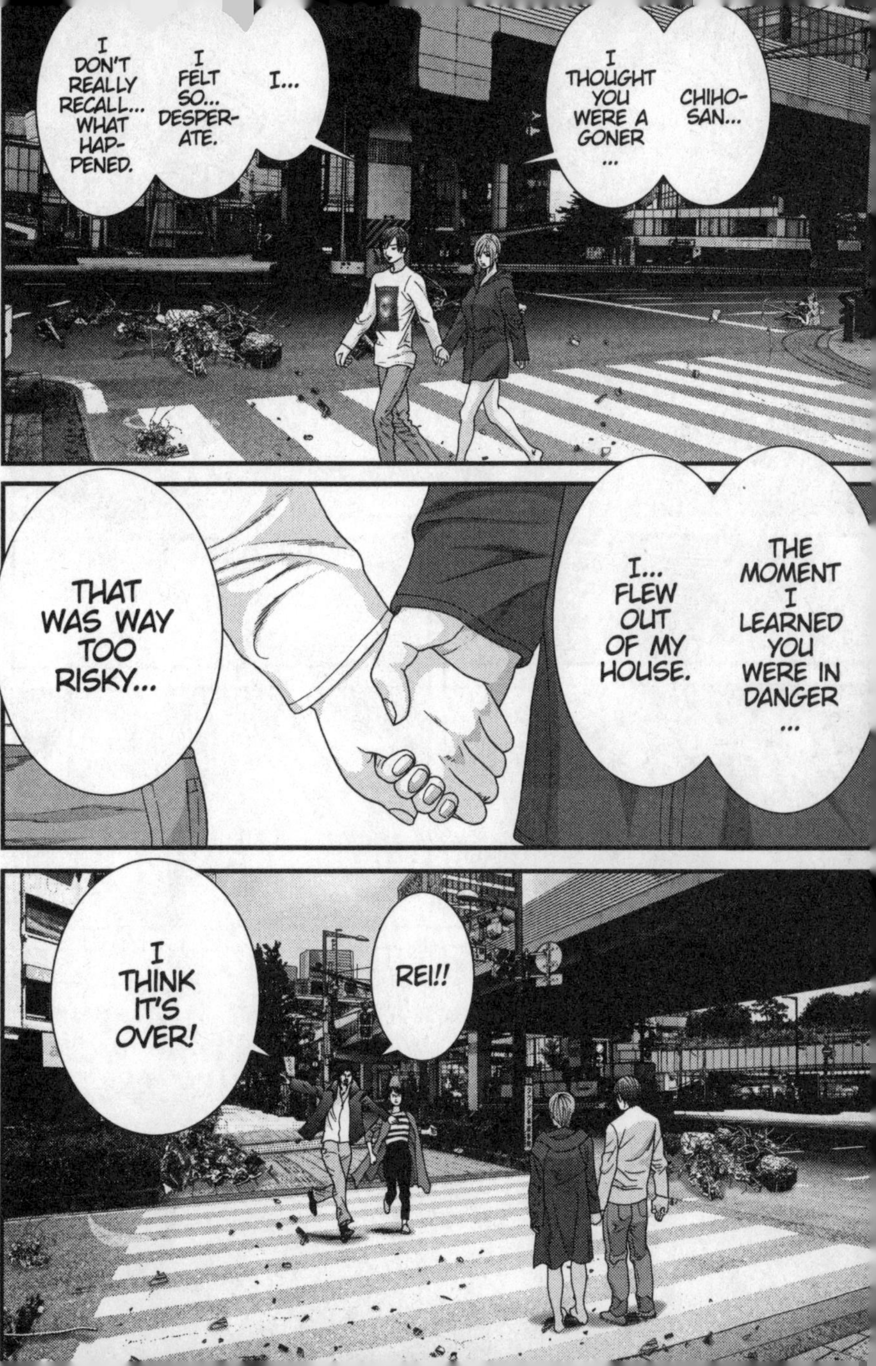
CHIHO-SAN...
I THOUGHT YOU WERE A GONER...
I...
I FELT SO... DESPER-ATE.
I DON'T REALLY RECALL... WHAT HAP-PENED.
THE MOMENT I LEARNED YOU WERE IN DANGER...
I... FLEW OUT OF MY HOUSE.
THAT WAS WAY TOO RISKY...
REI!!
I THINK IT'S OVER!

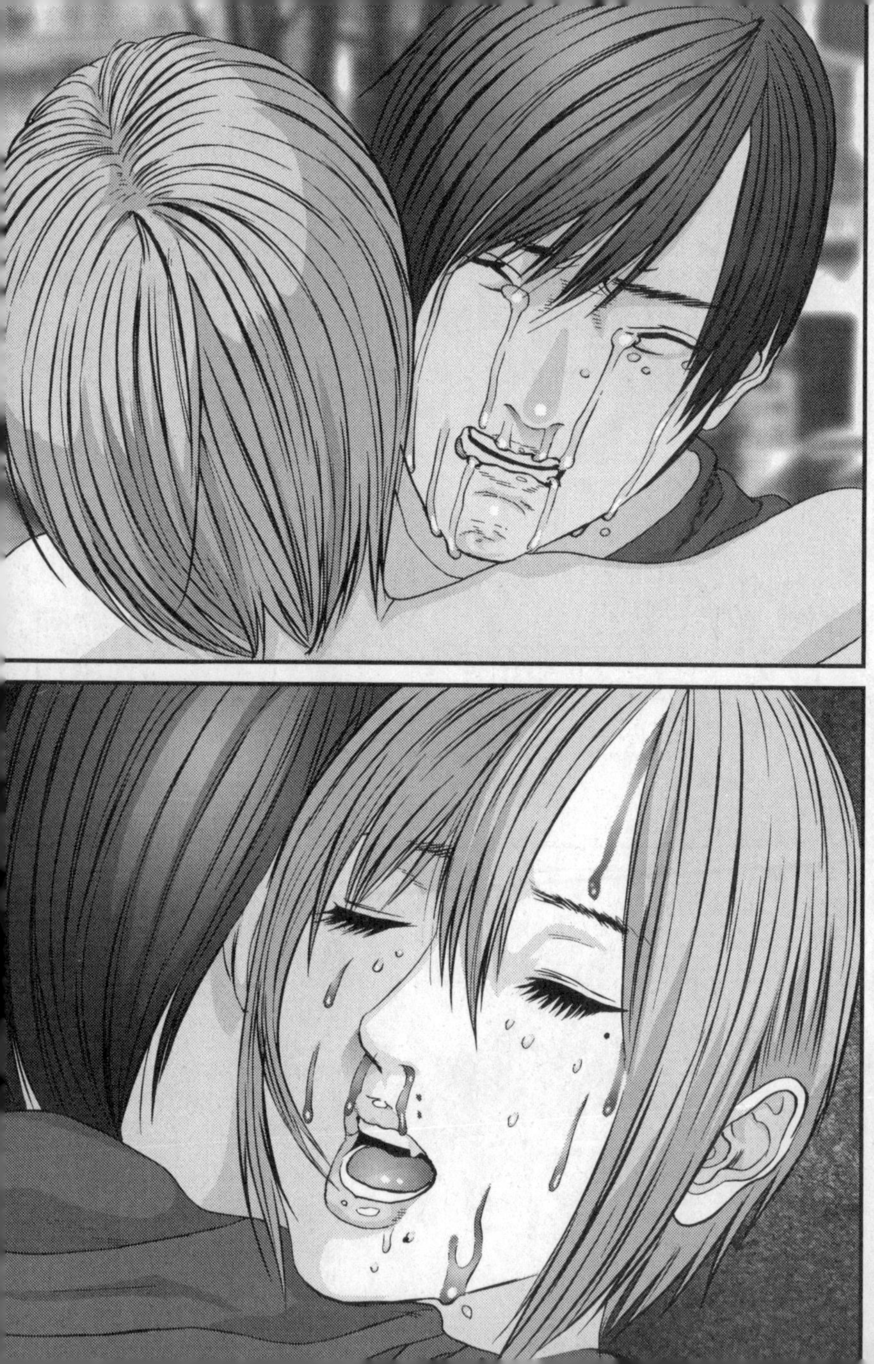

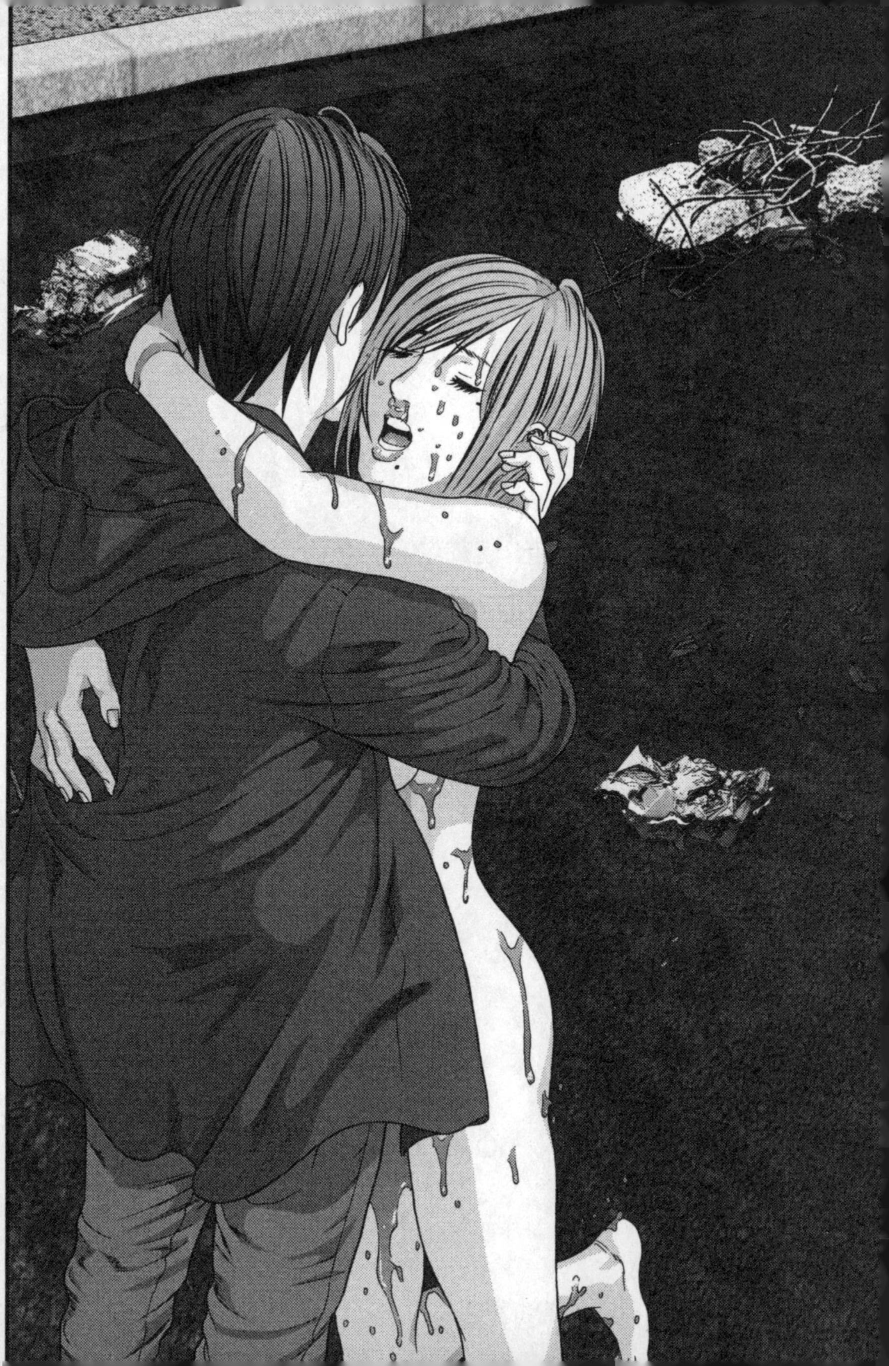

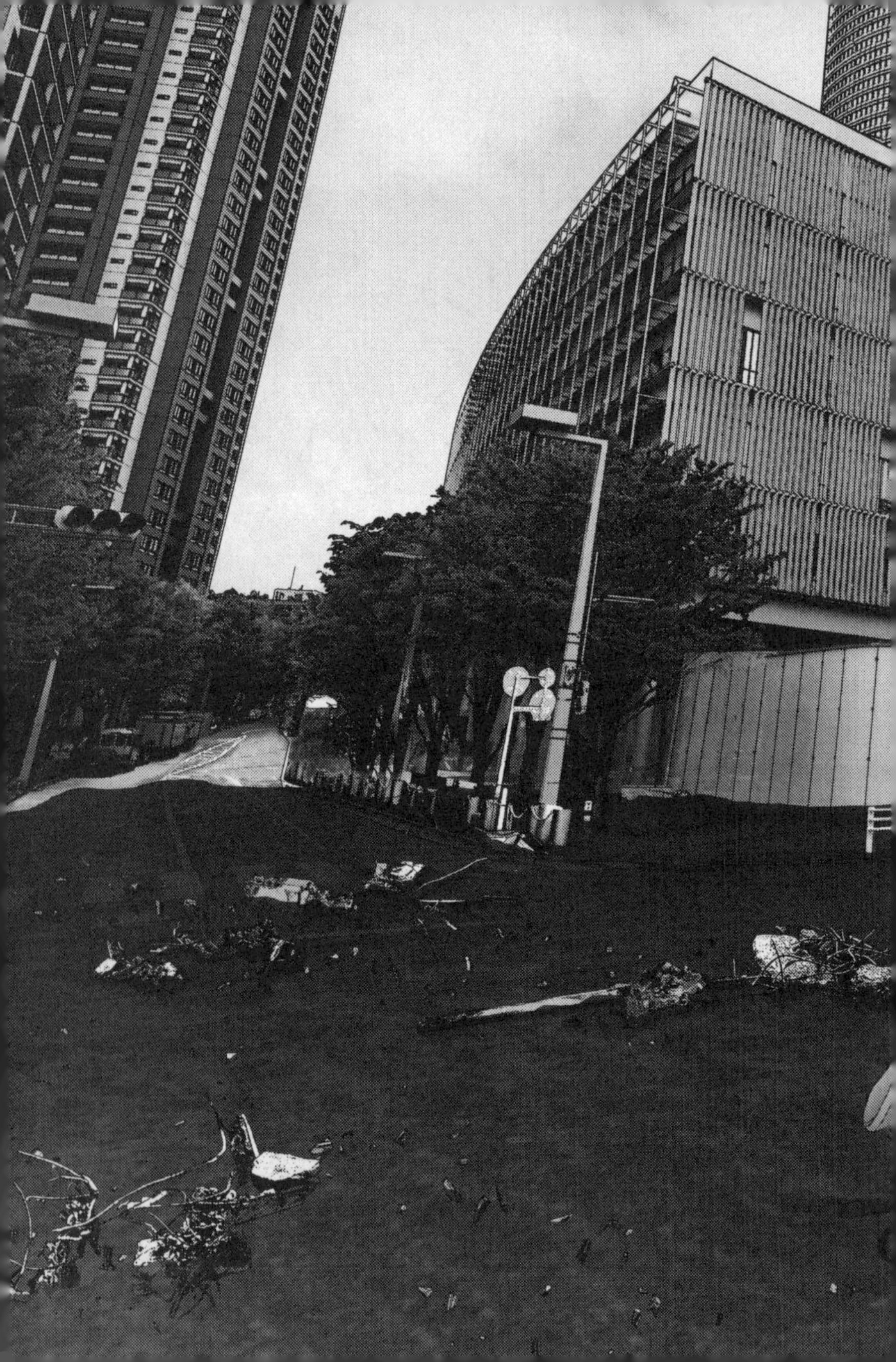

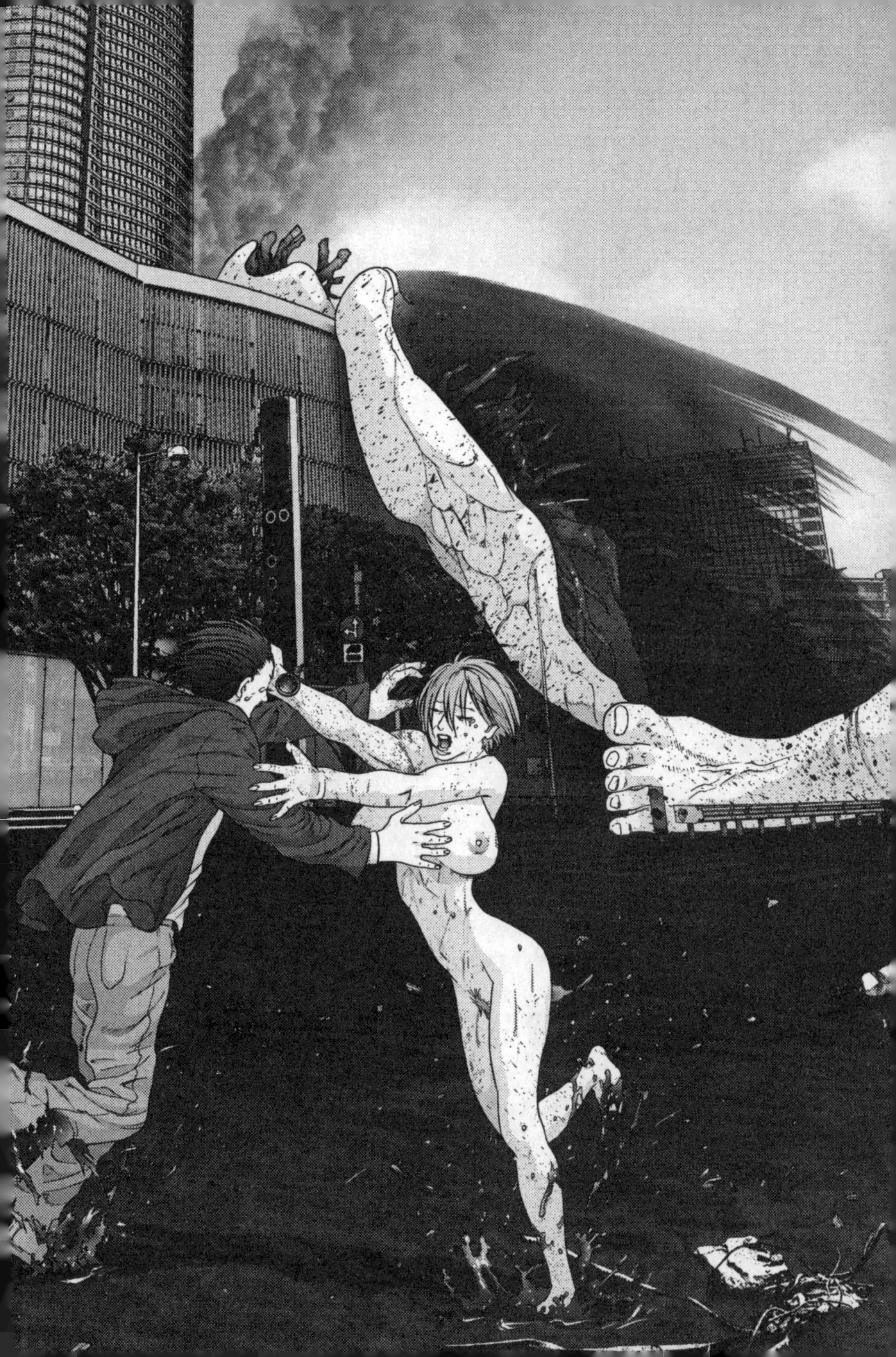

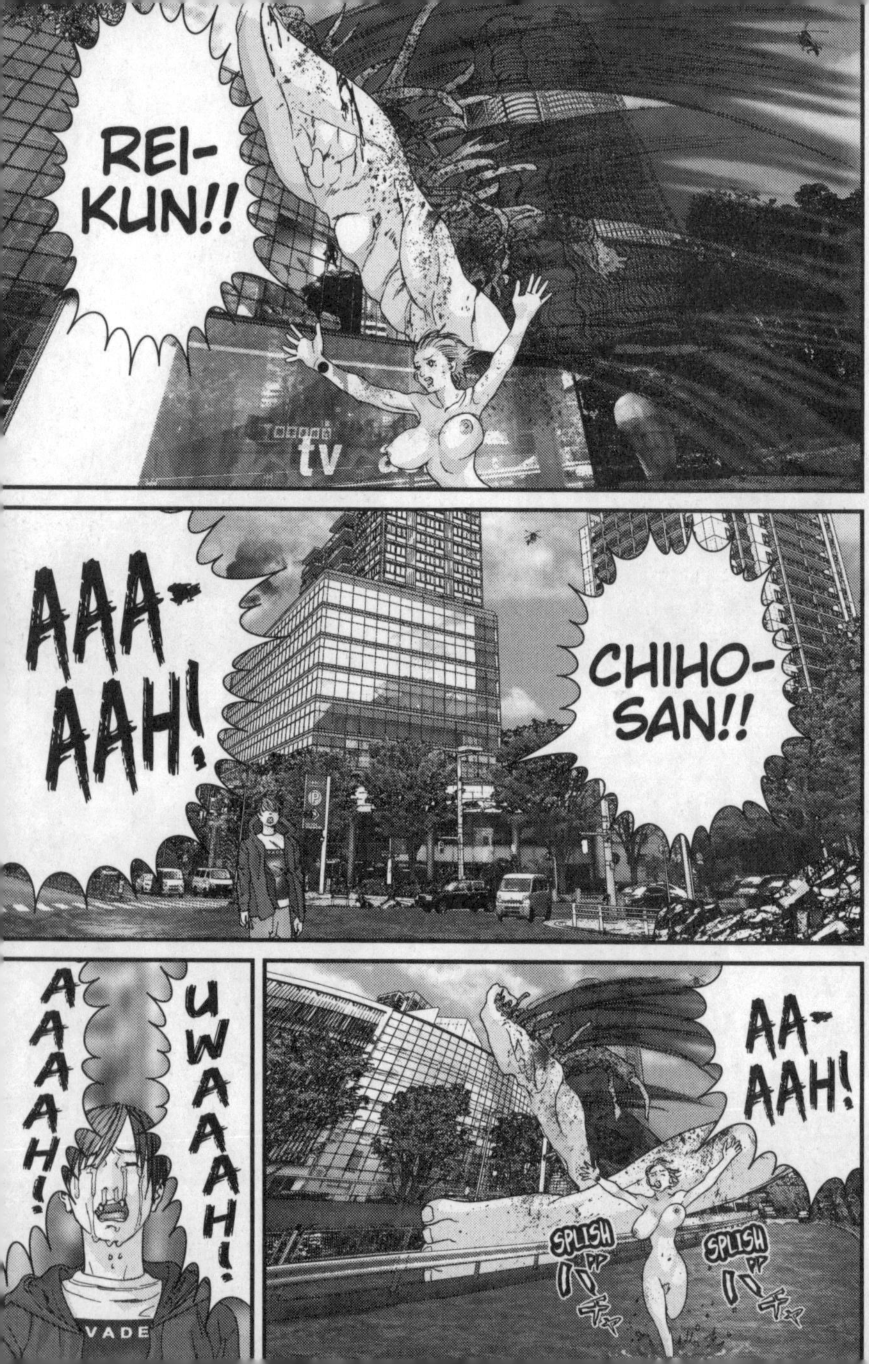
REI-KUN!!
tv
CHIHO-SAN!!
AAA-AAH!
AA-AAH!
SPLISH
SPLISH
UWAAAAH!
AAAAAH!
VADE

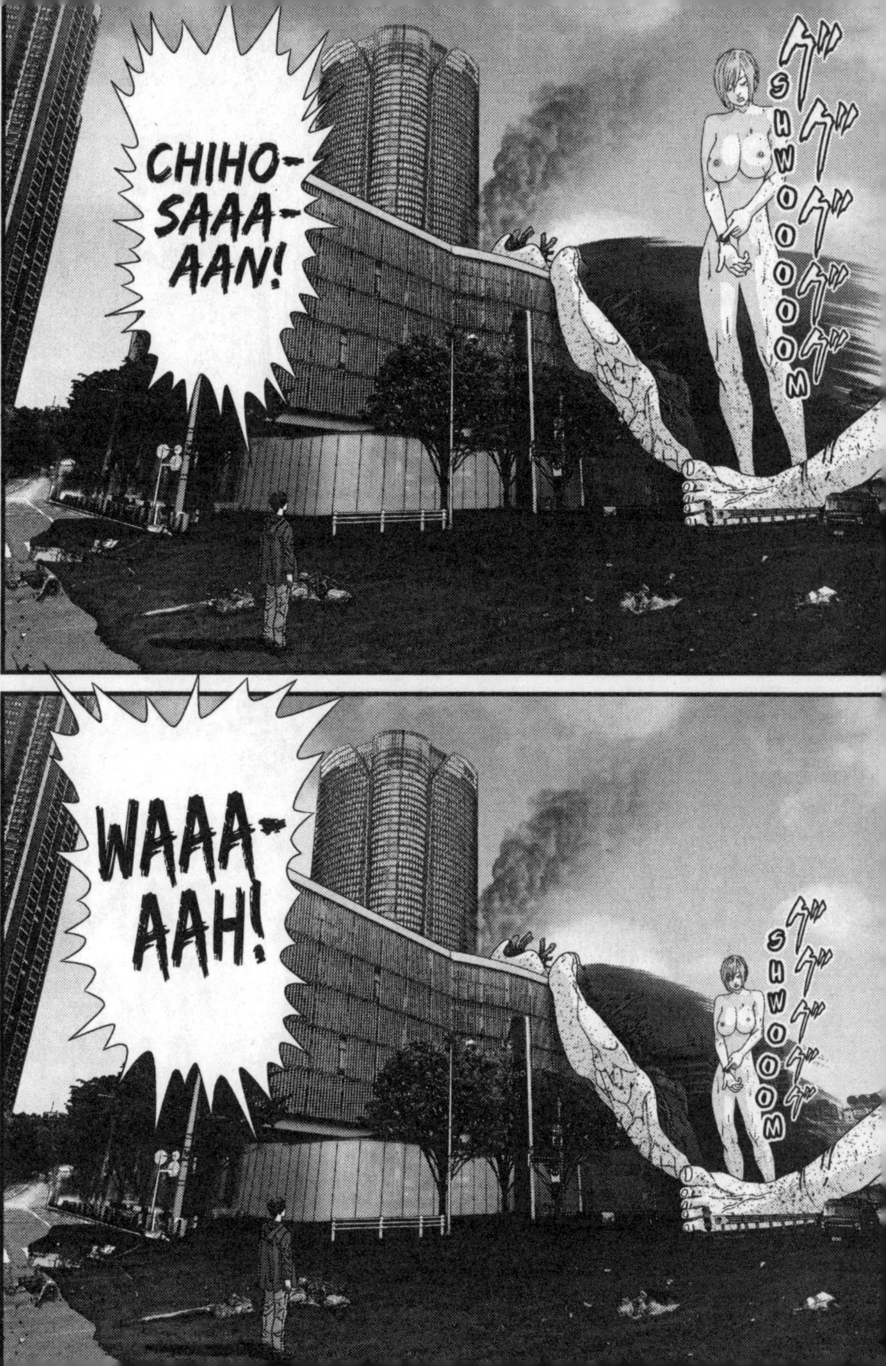
SHWOOOOOOOM
CHIHO-SAAAA-AAN!
SHWOOOOM
WAAA-AAH!

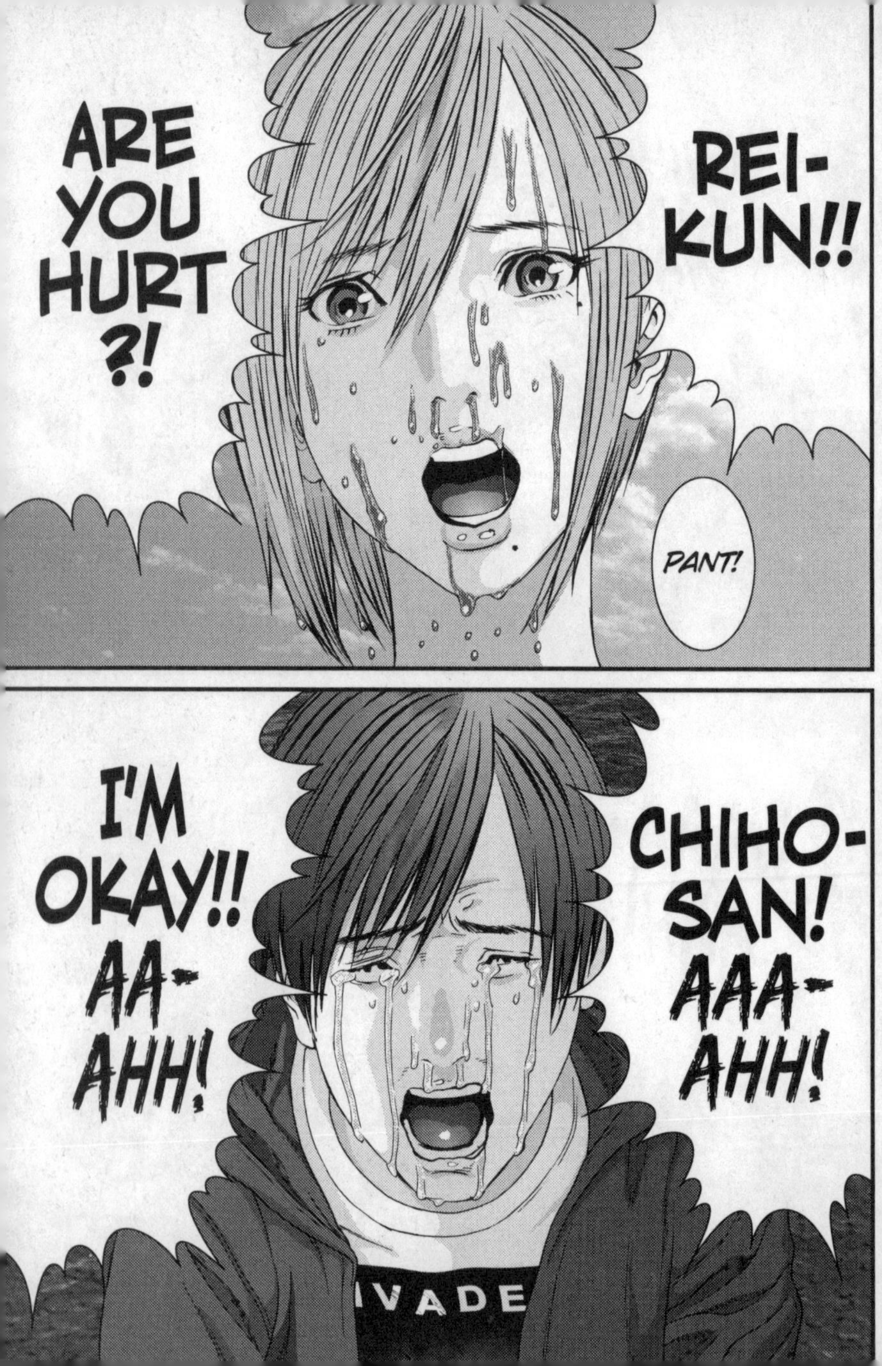
REI-KUN!!
ARE YOU HURT?!
PANT!
CHIHO-SAN!
AAA-AHH!
I'M OKAY!!
AA-AHH!
IVADE

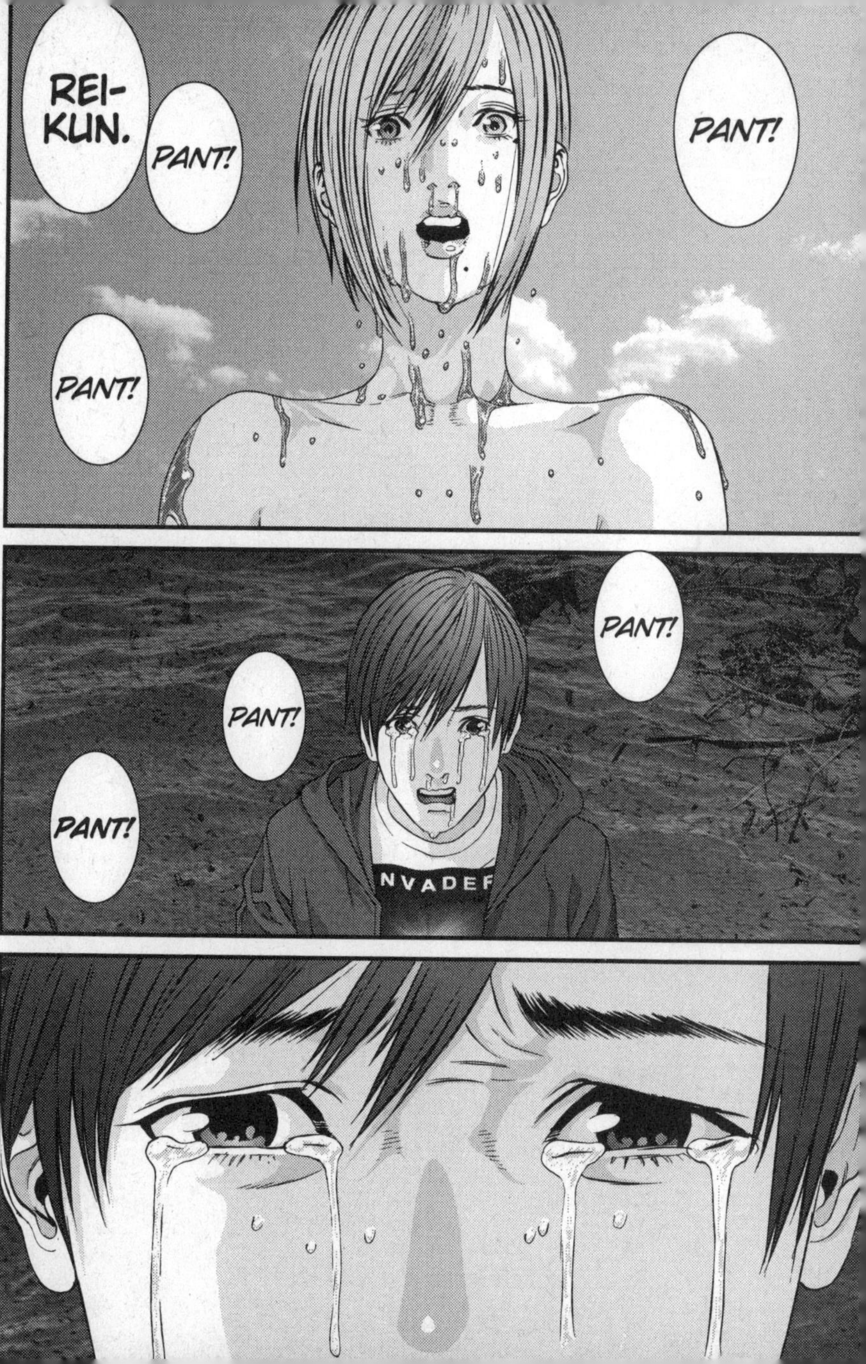
PANT!
PANT!
REI-
KUN.
PANT!
PANT!
PANT!
NVADEF
PANT!

EPISODE 21: TRUE IDENTITY

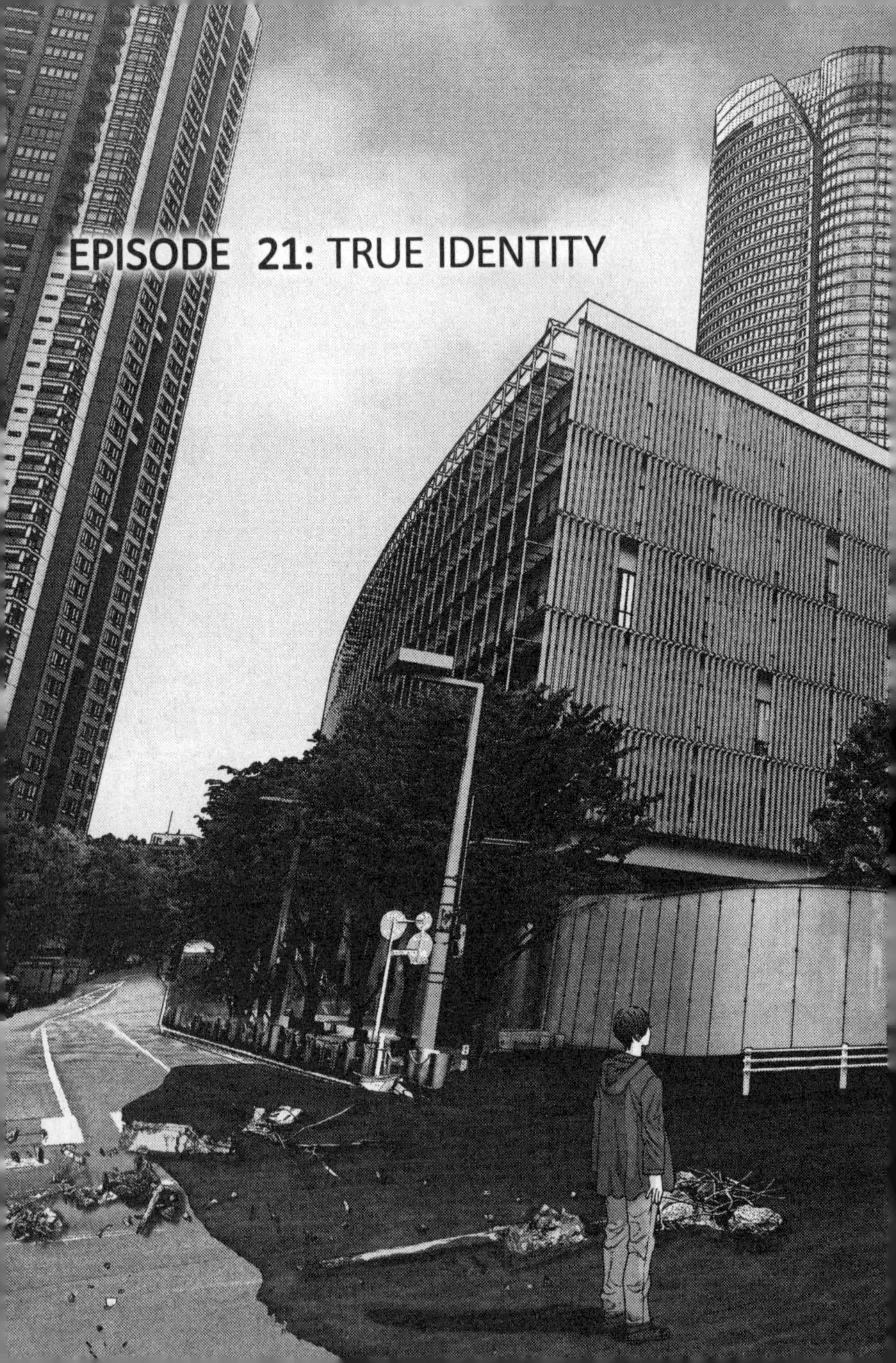

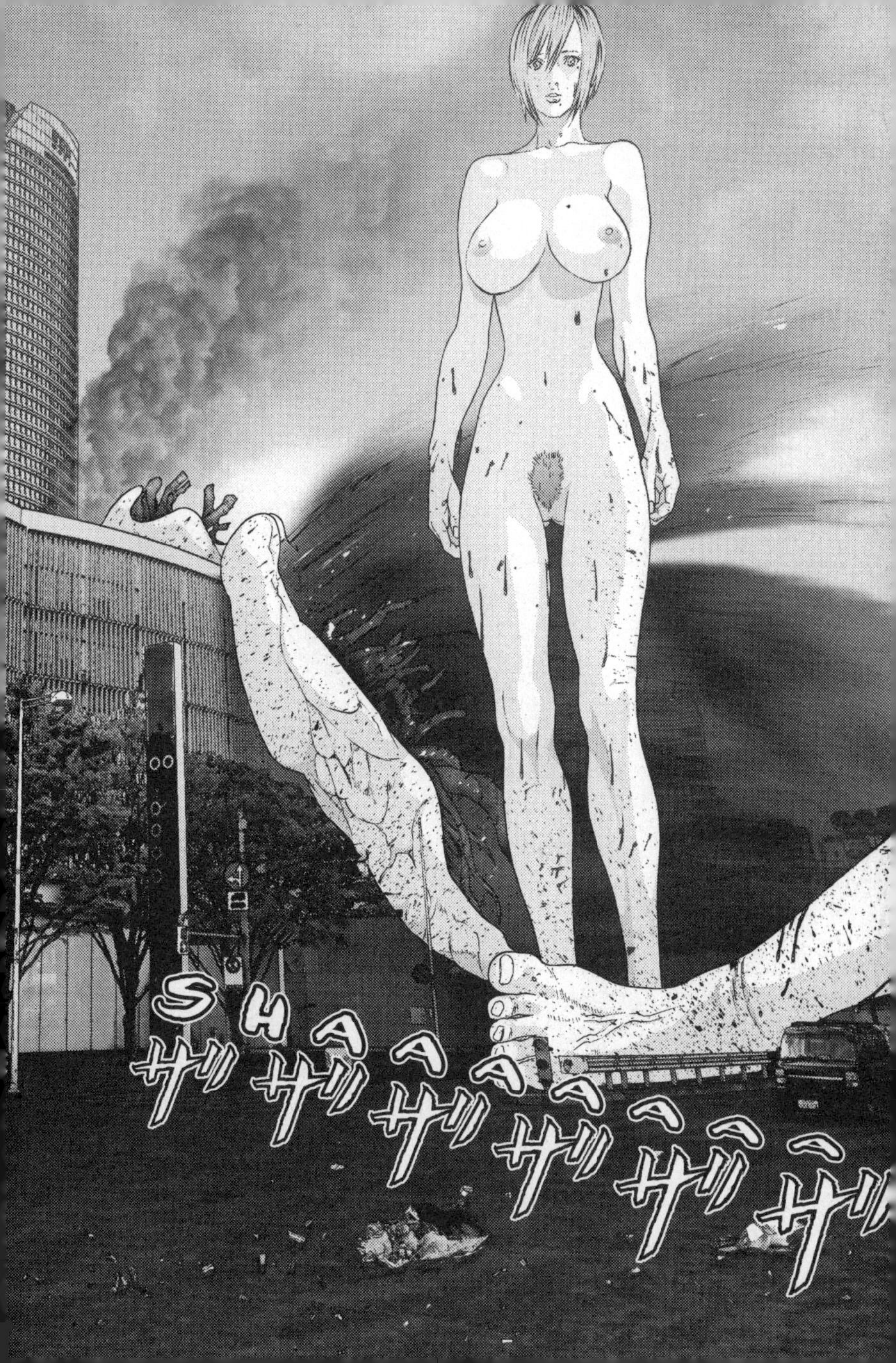
SHAAAAA
ザリザリザリザリザリザリ

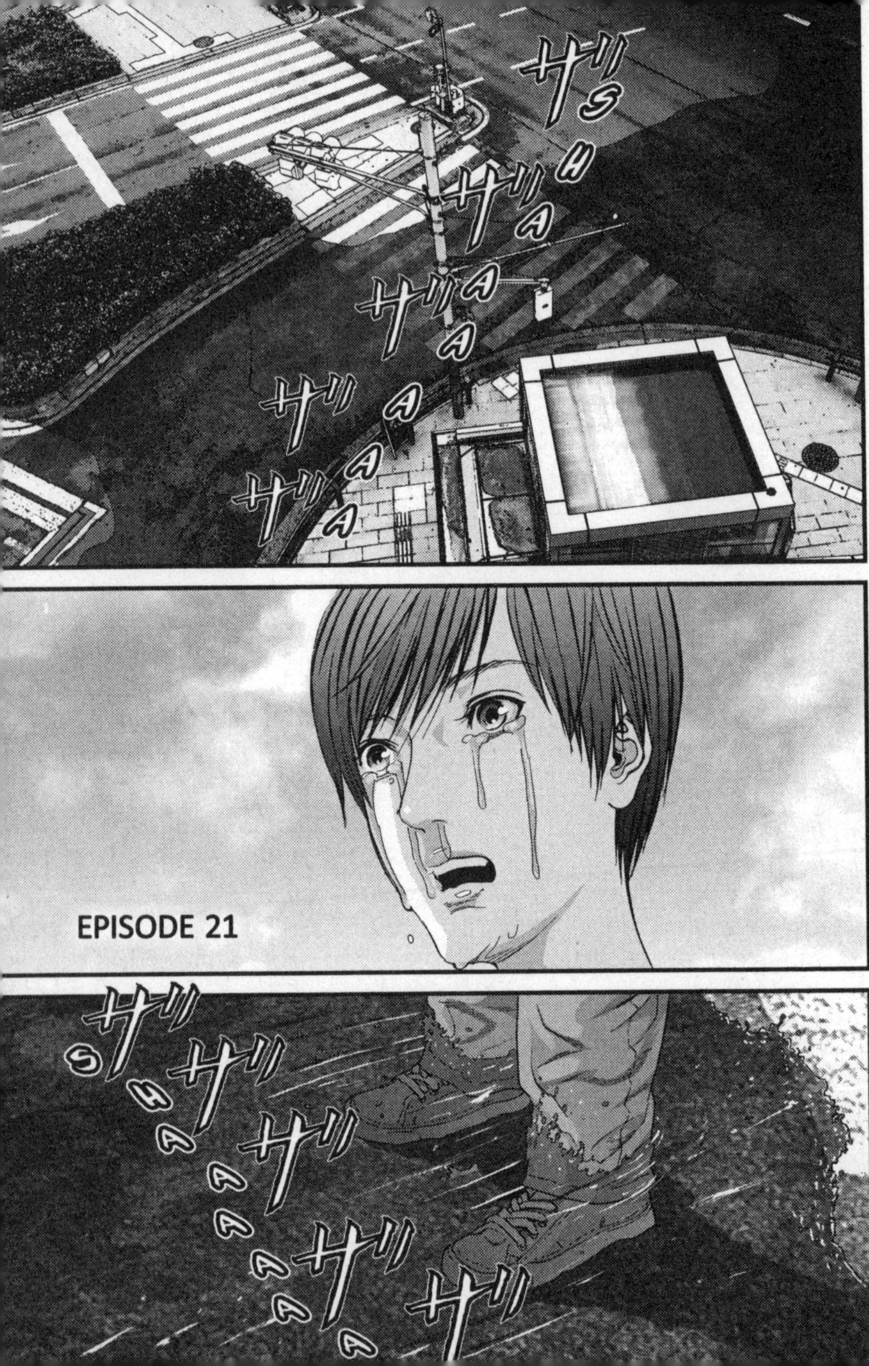
サリ サリ サリ サリ サリ
SHAAAAA
EPISODE 21
サリ サリ サリ サリ サリ
SHAAAAAAAA

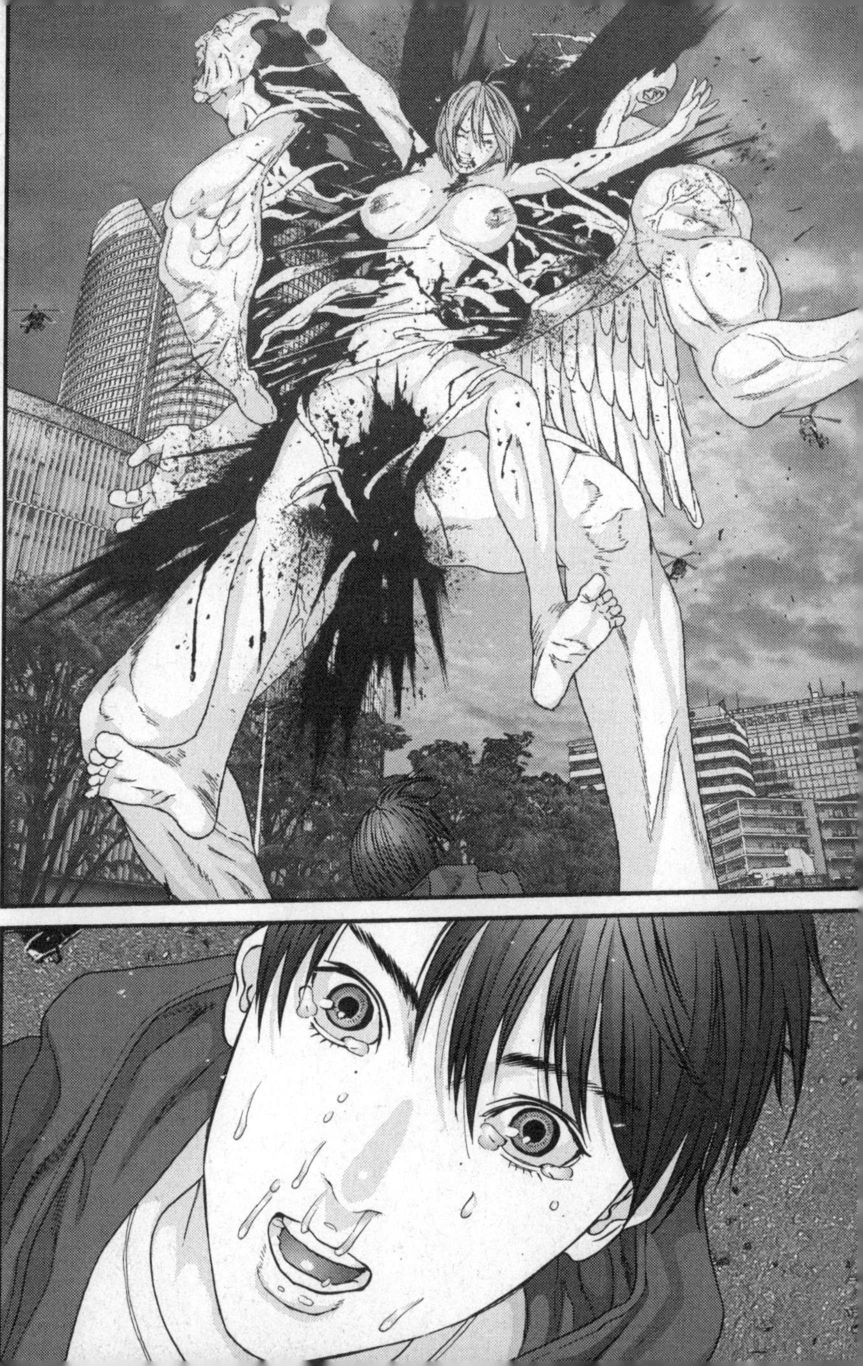

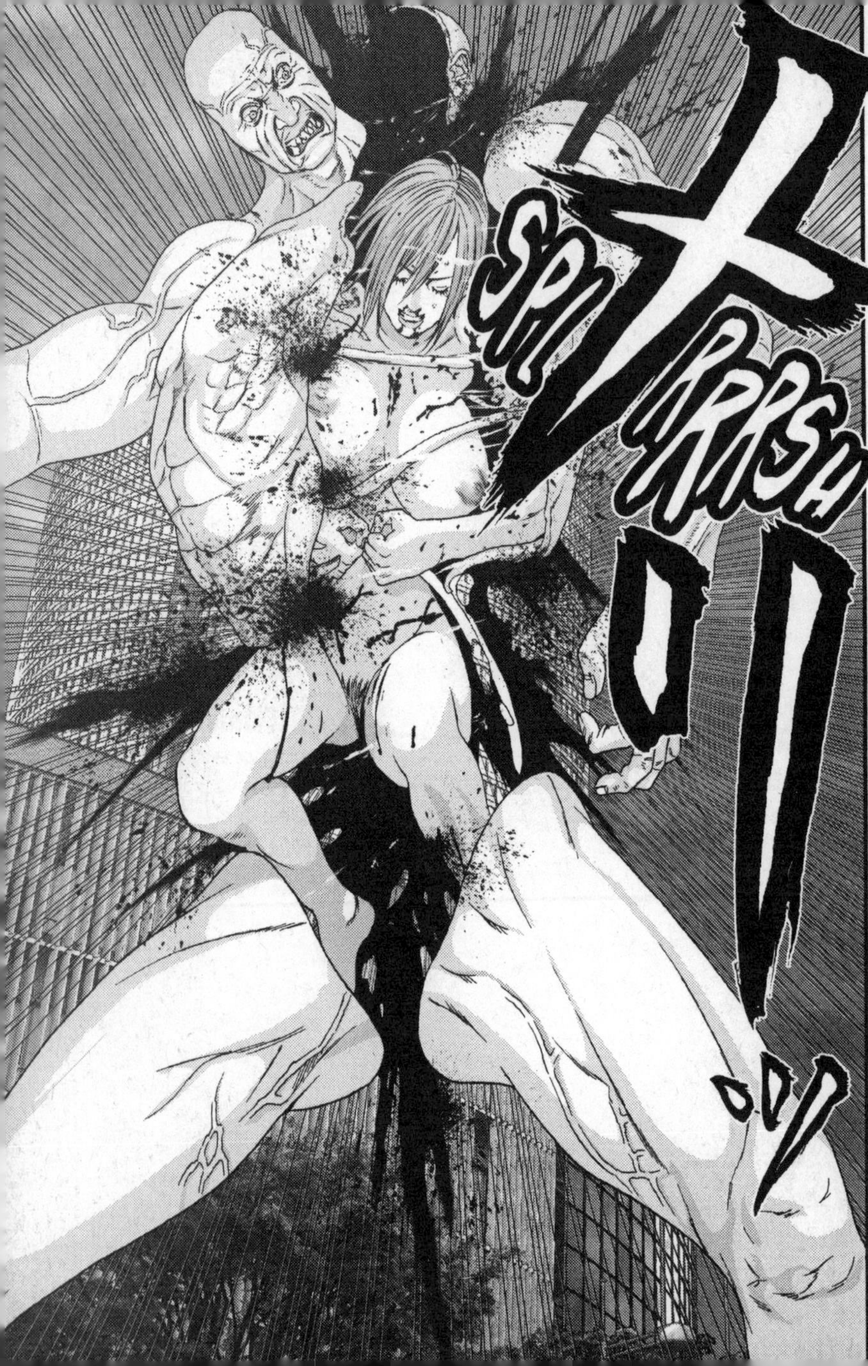
SPLURRSH

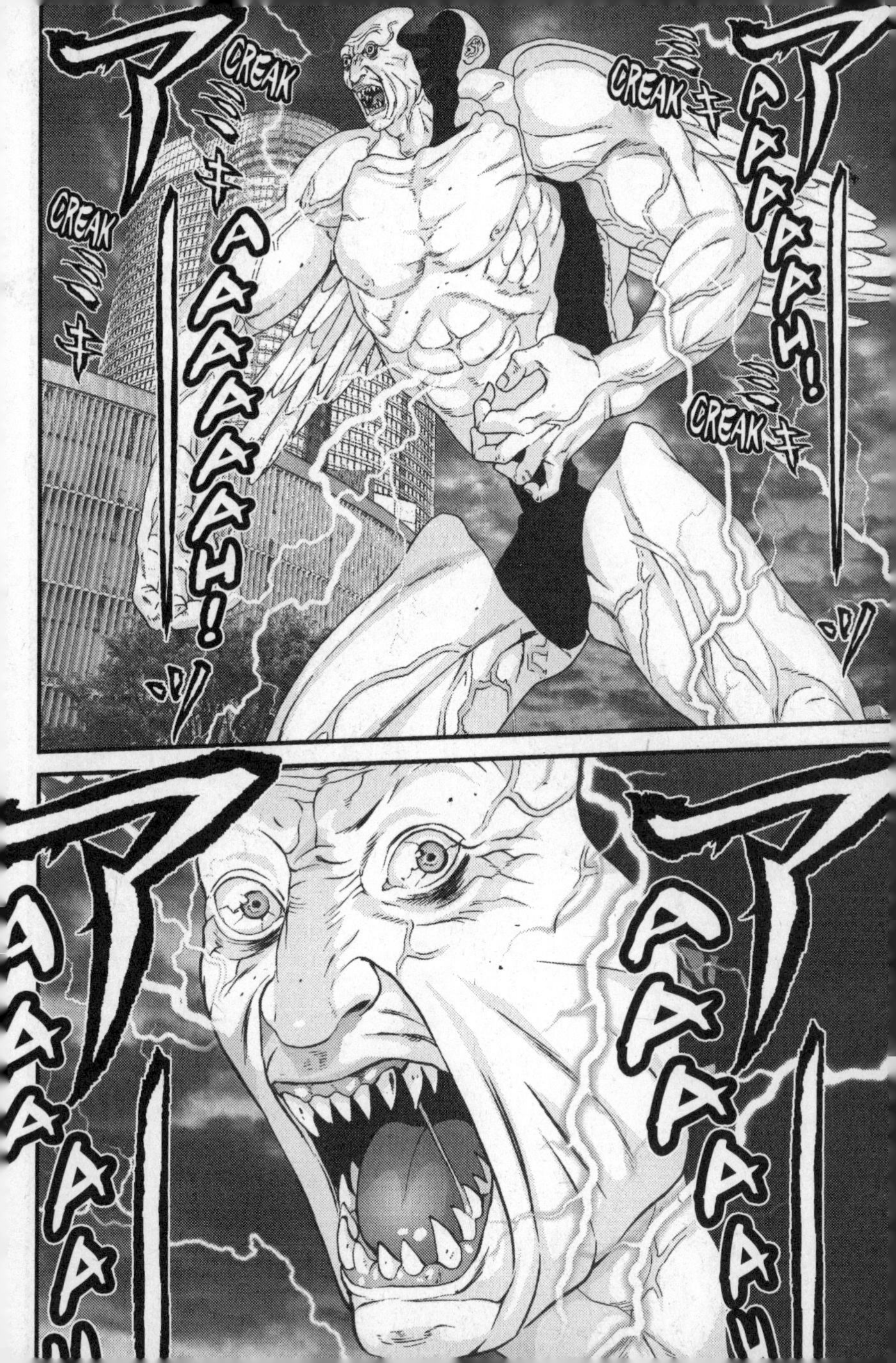

CREAK
AAAAAAH!
CREAK
CREAK
AAAAAAAAH!
CREAK
AAAAAAA
AAAAAAA

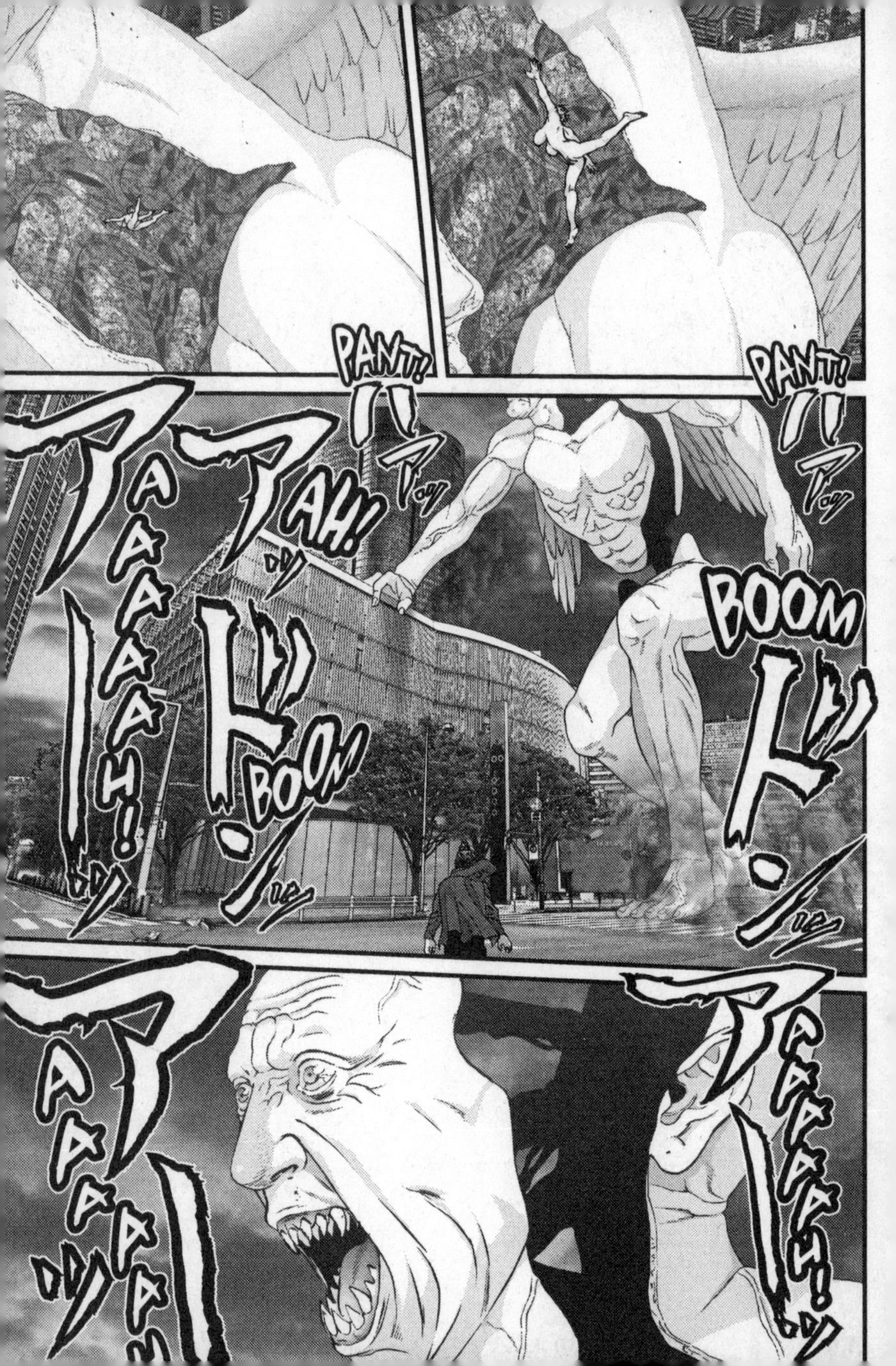
PANT!
BOOM
PANT!
AH!
BOOM
AAAAAAH!
AAAAAAH!

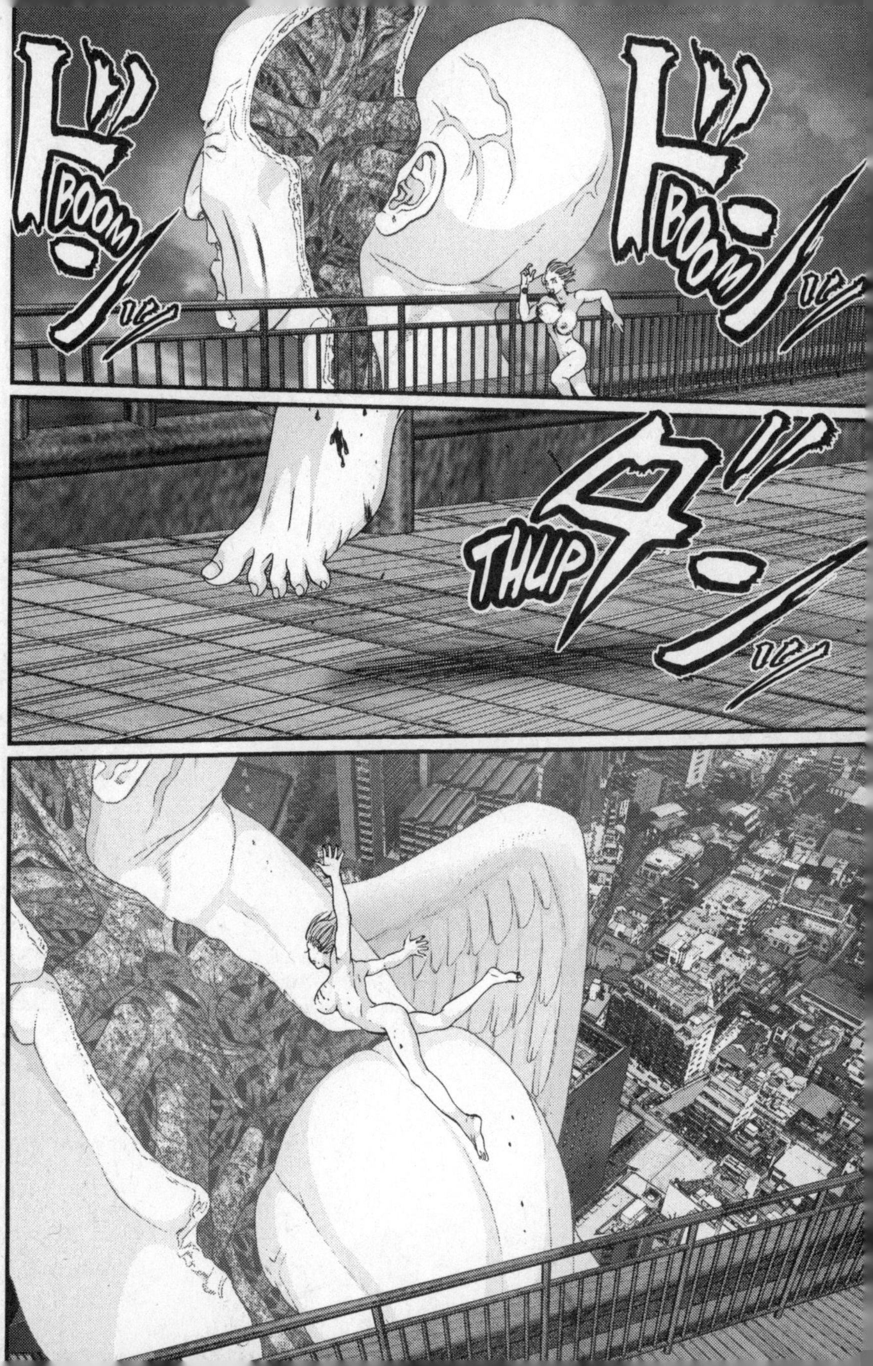
BOOM
BOOM
THUP

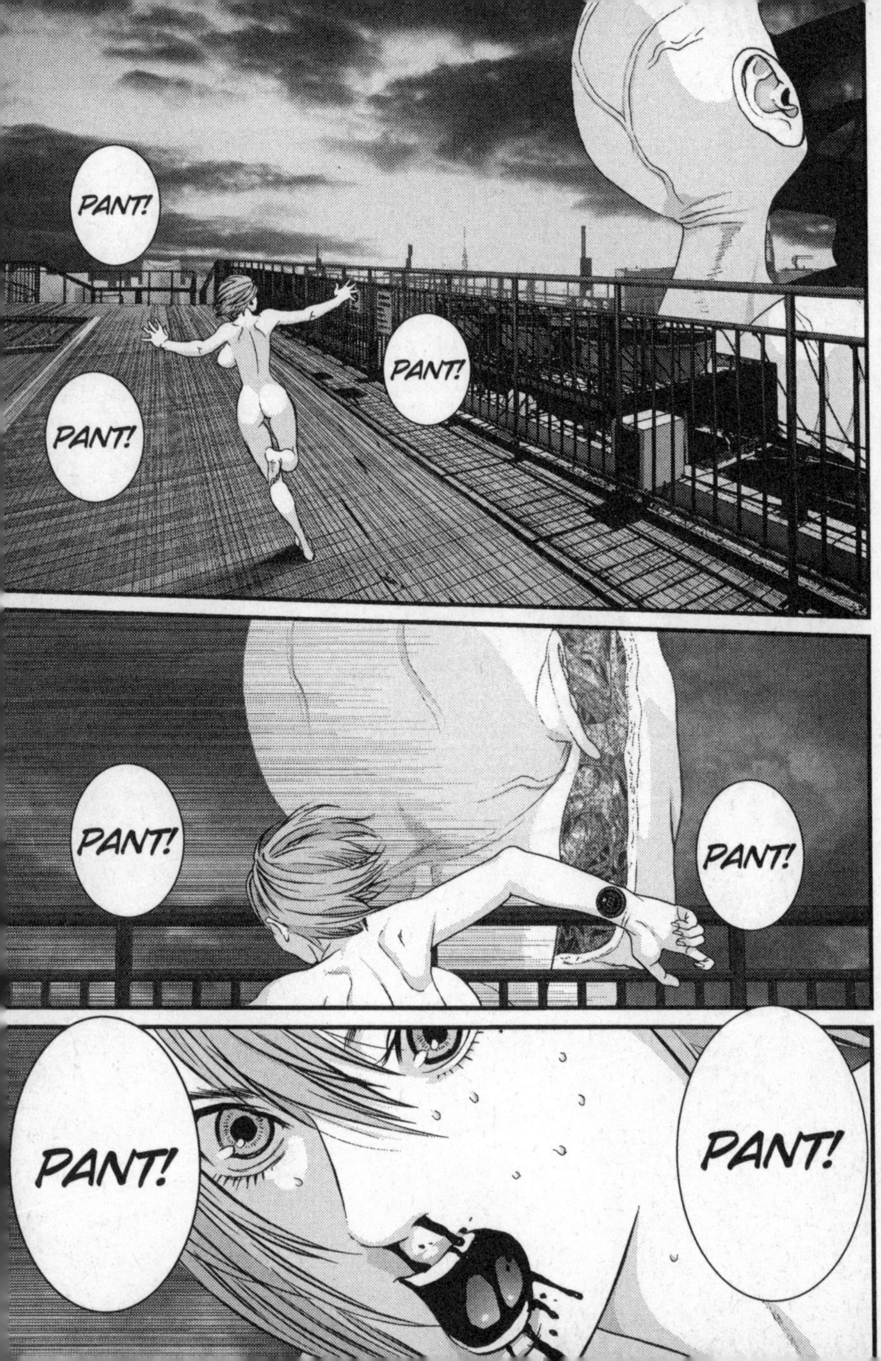
PANT!
PANT!
PANT!
PANT!
PANT!
PANT!
PANT!

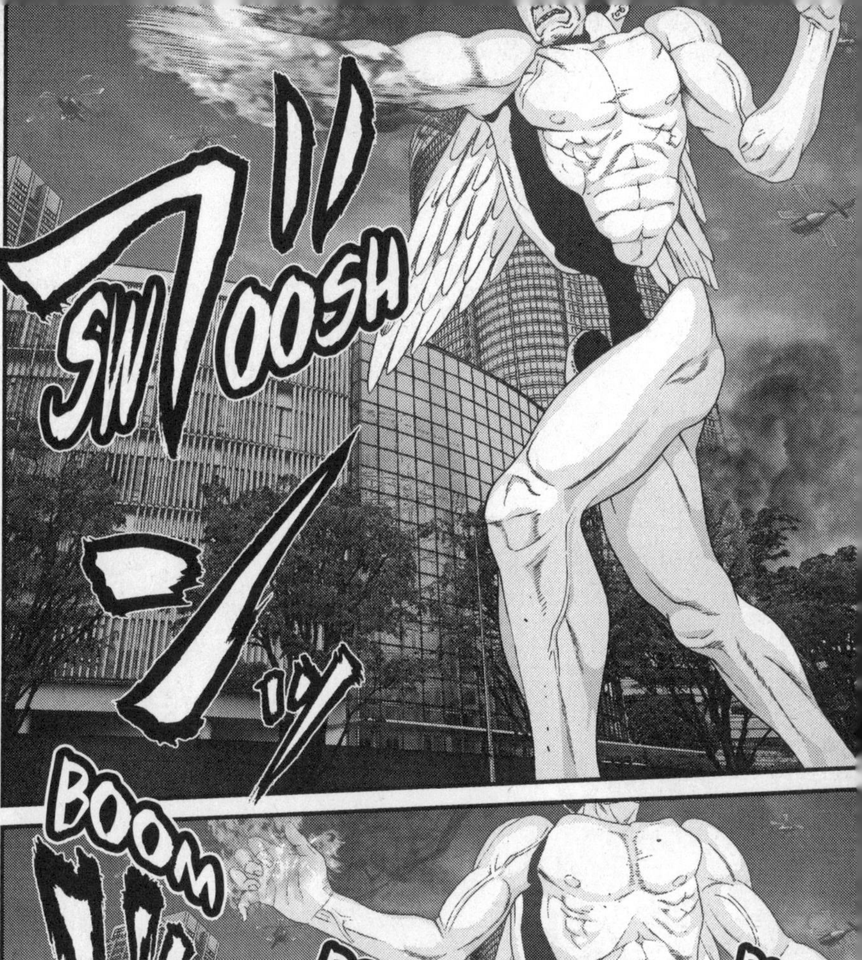
SWOOSH
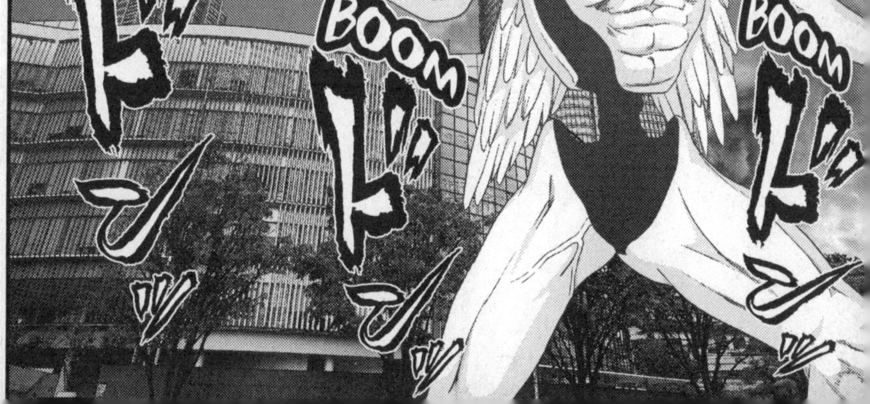
BOOM
BOOM
BOOM

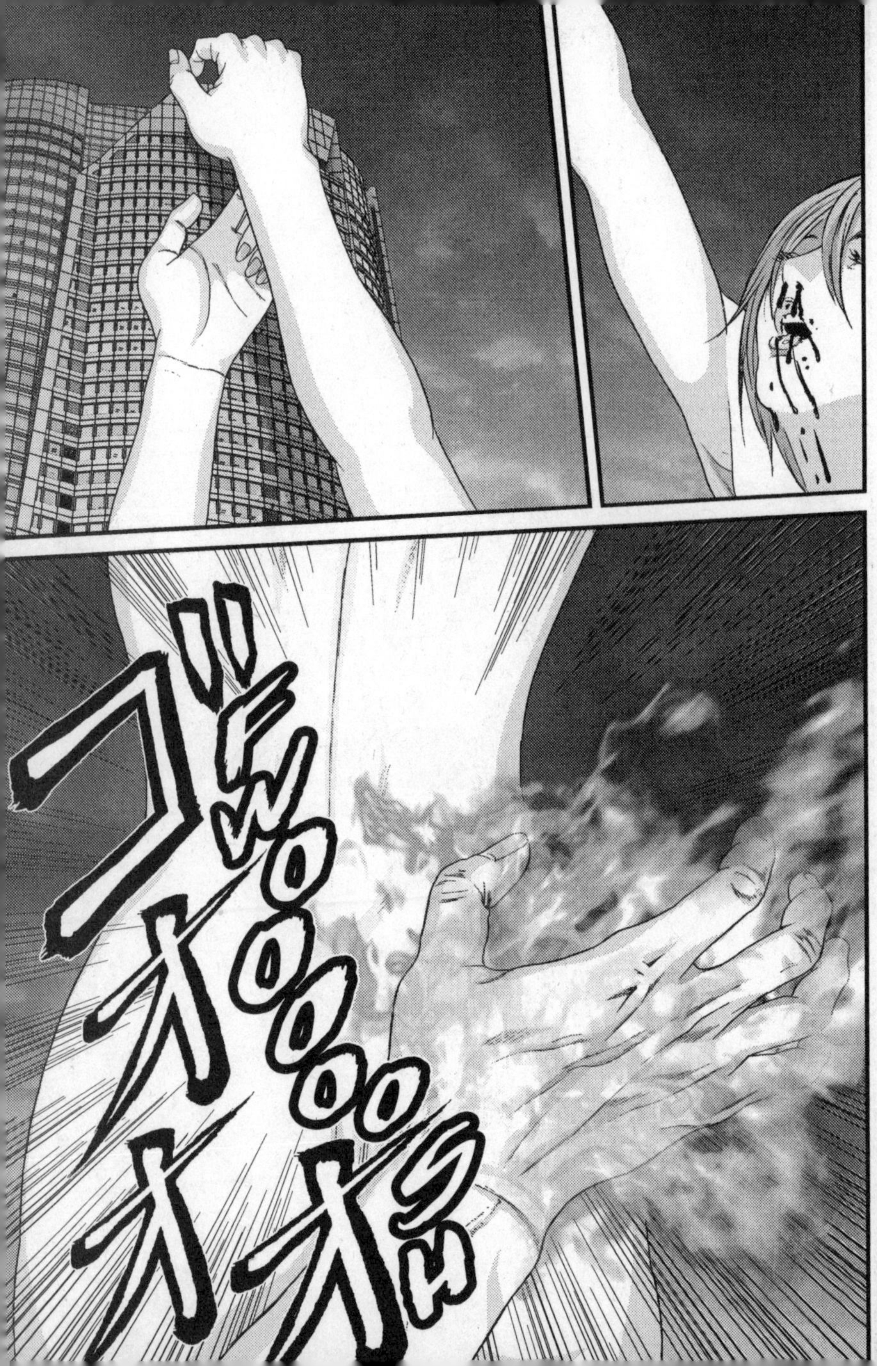
ゴォォォォォォォオオッ

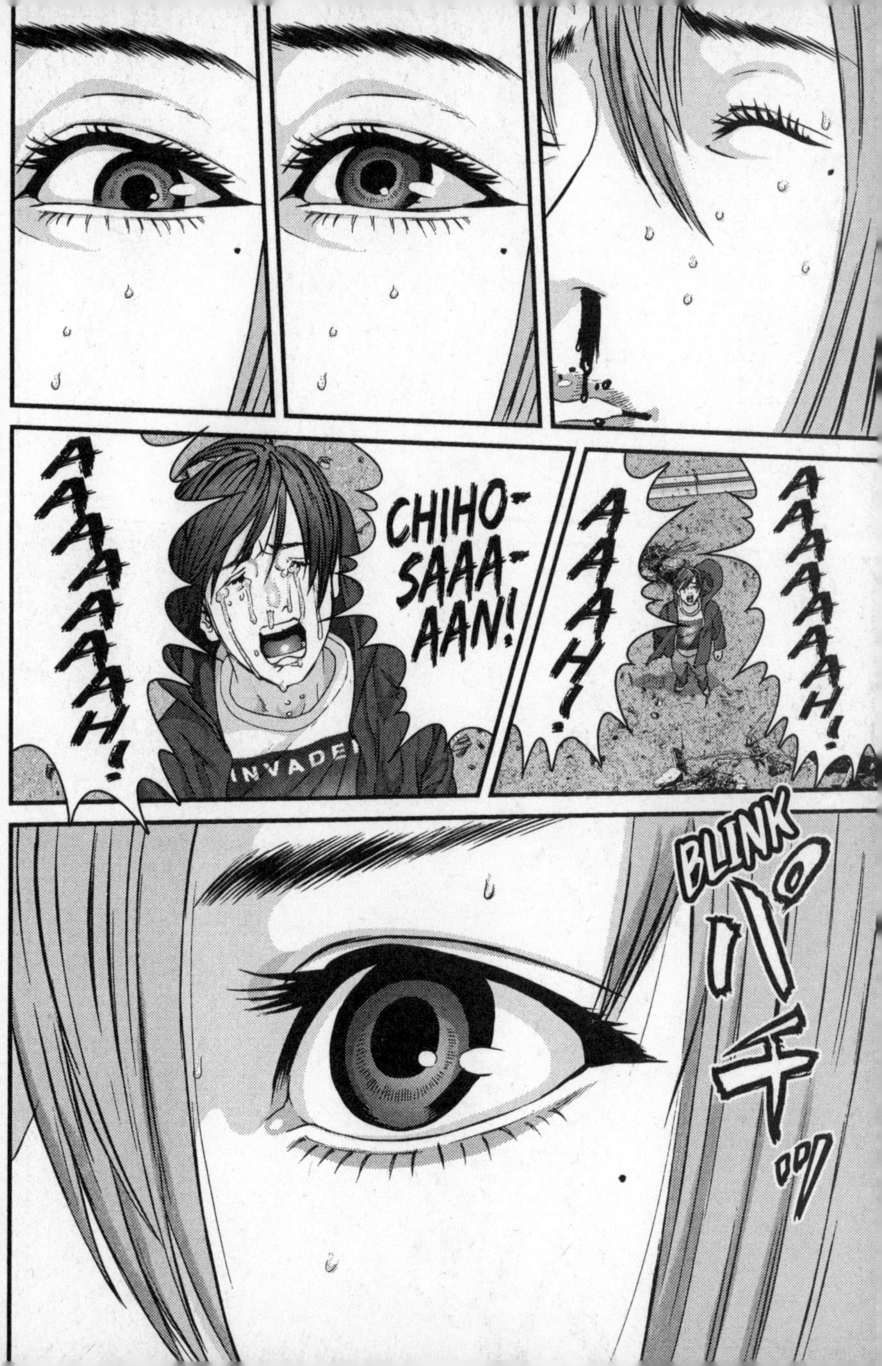
AAAAAAAAH!
AAAAH!
CHIHO-SAAAA-AAN!
AAAAAAAH!
BLINK
パチ

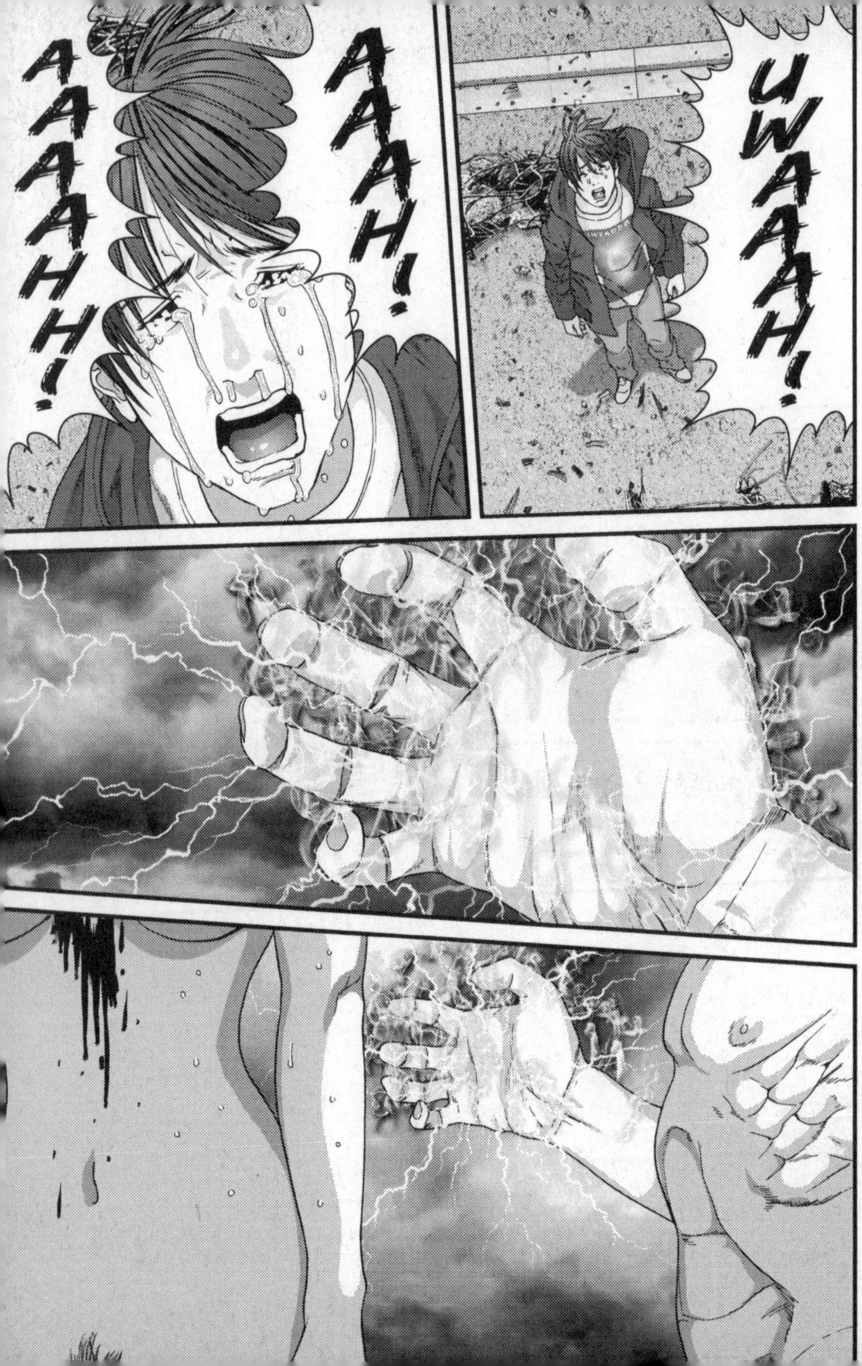
UWAAAAH!
AAAH!
AAAAAH!

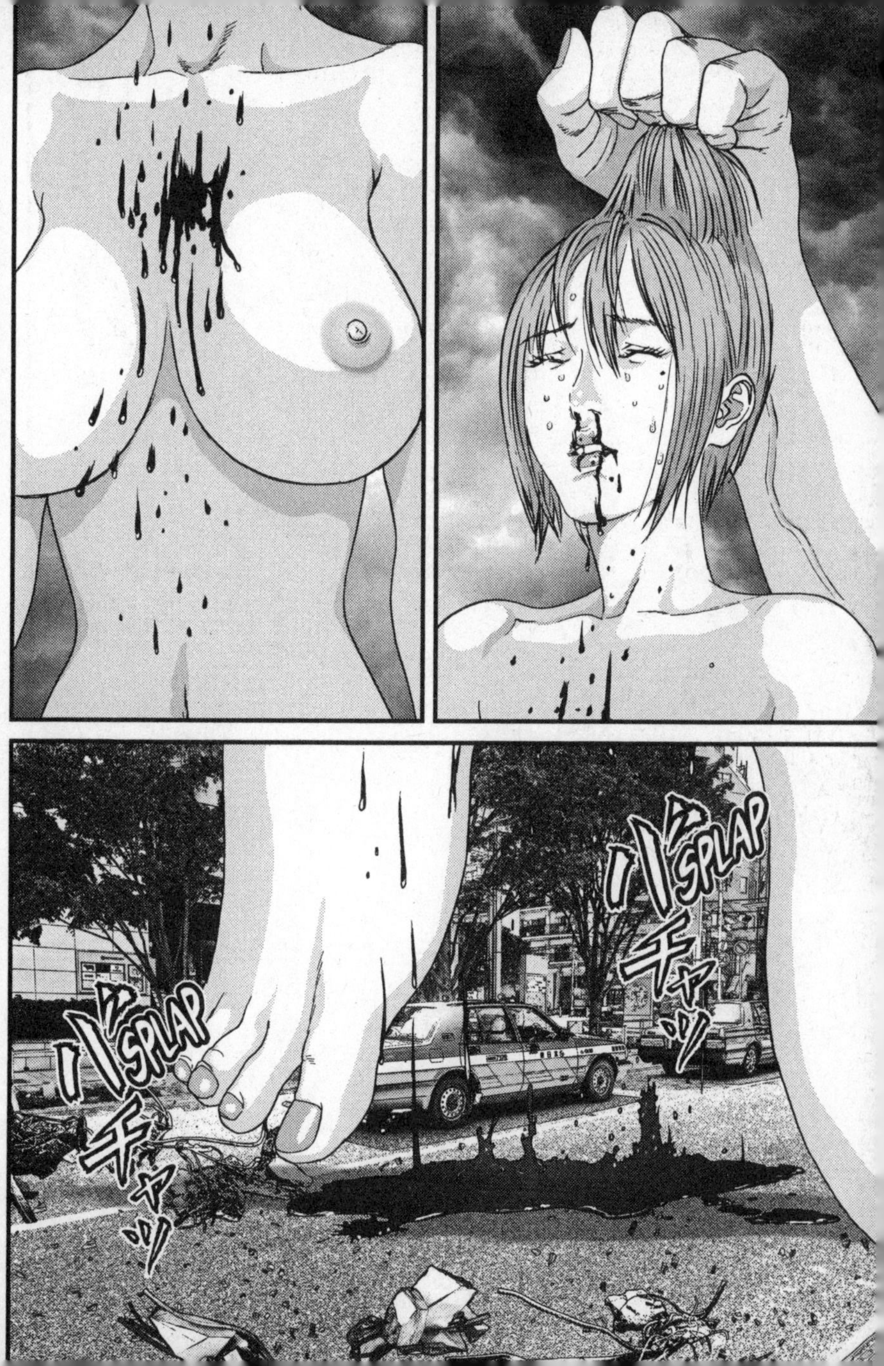
SPLAP
バチャッ
SPLAP
バチャッ

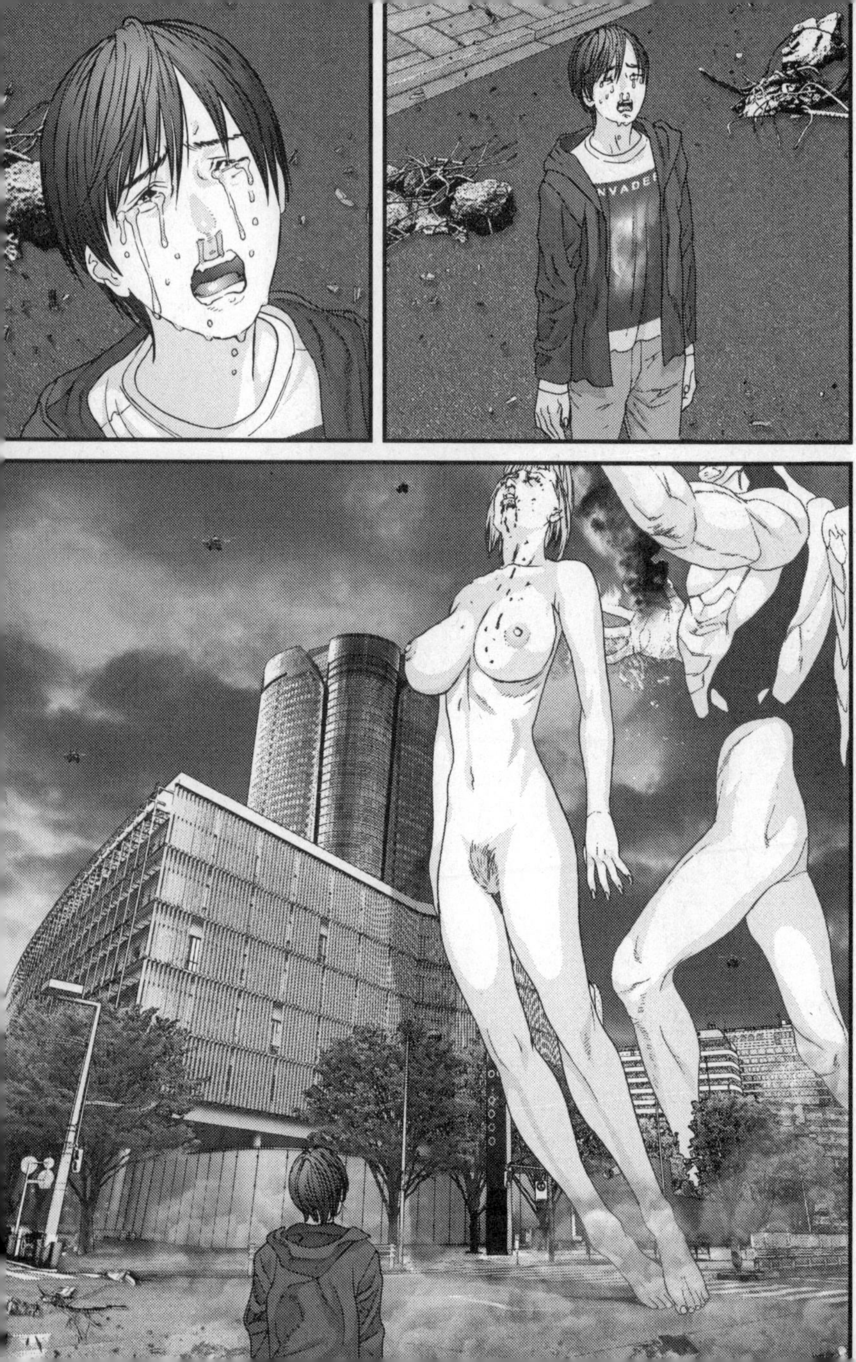

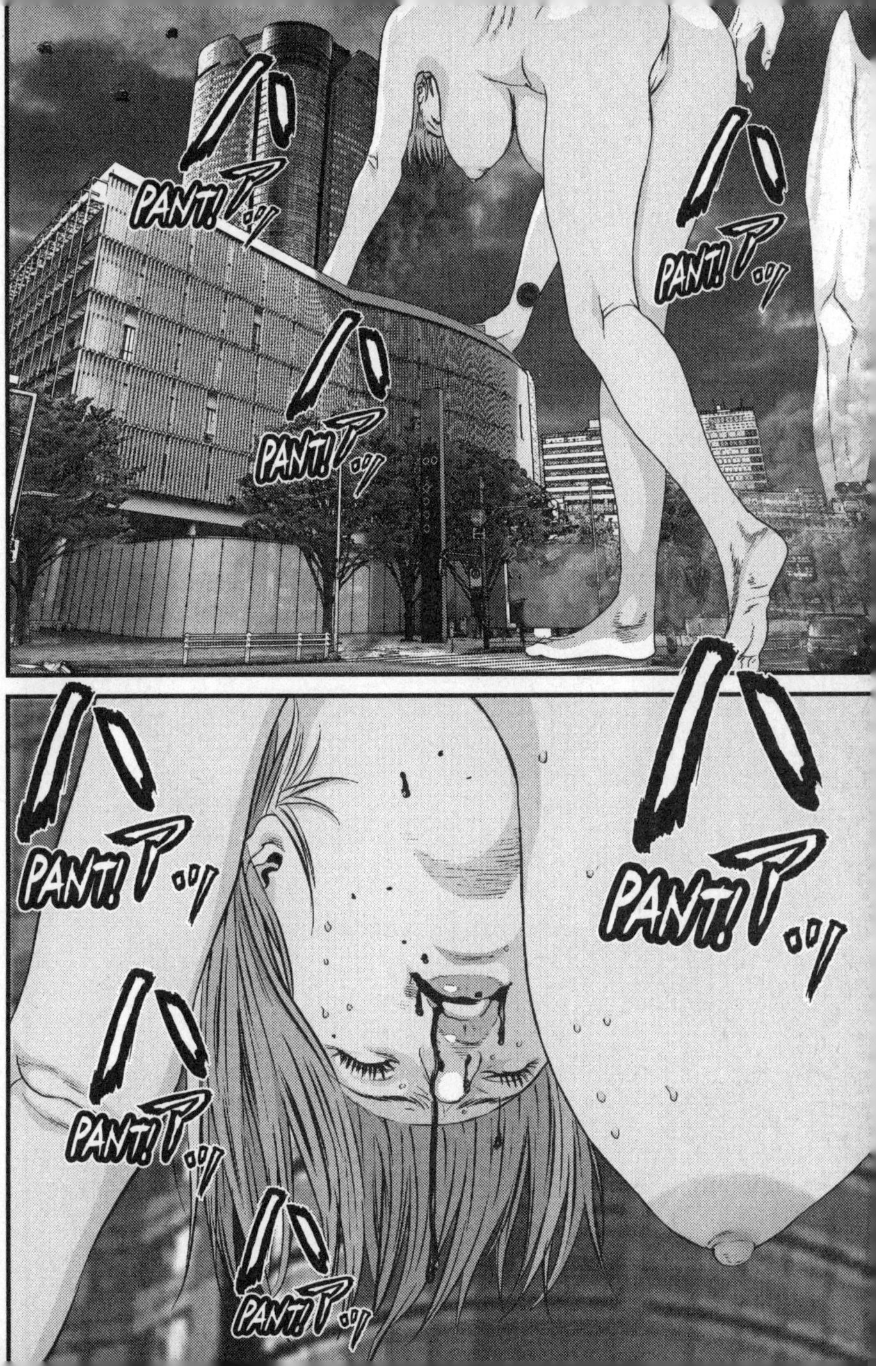
PANT!
PANT!
PANT!
PANT!
PANT!
PANT!
PANT!

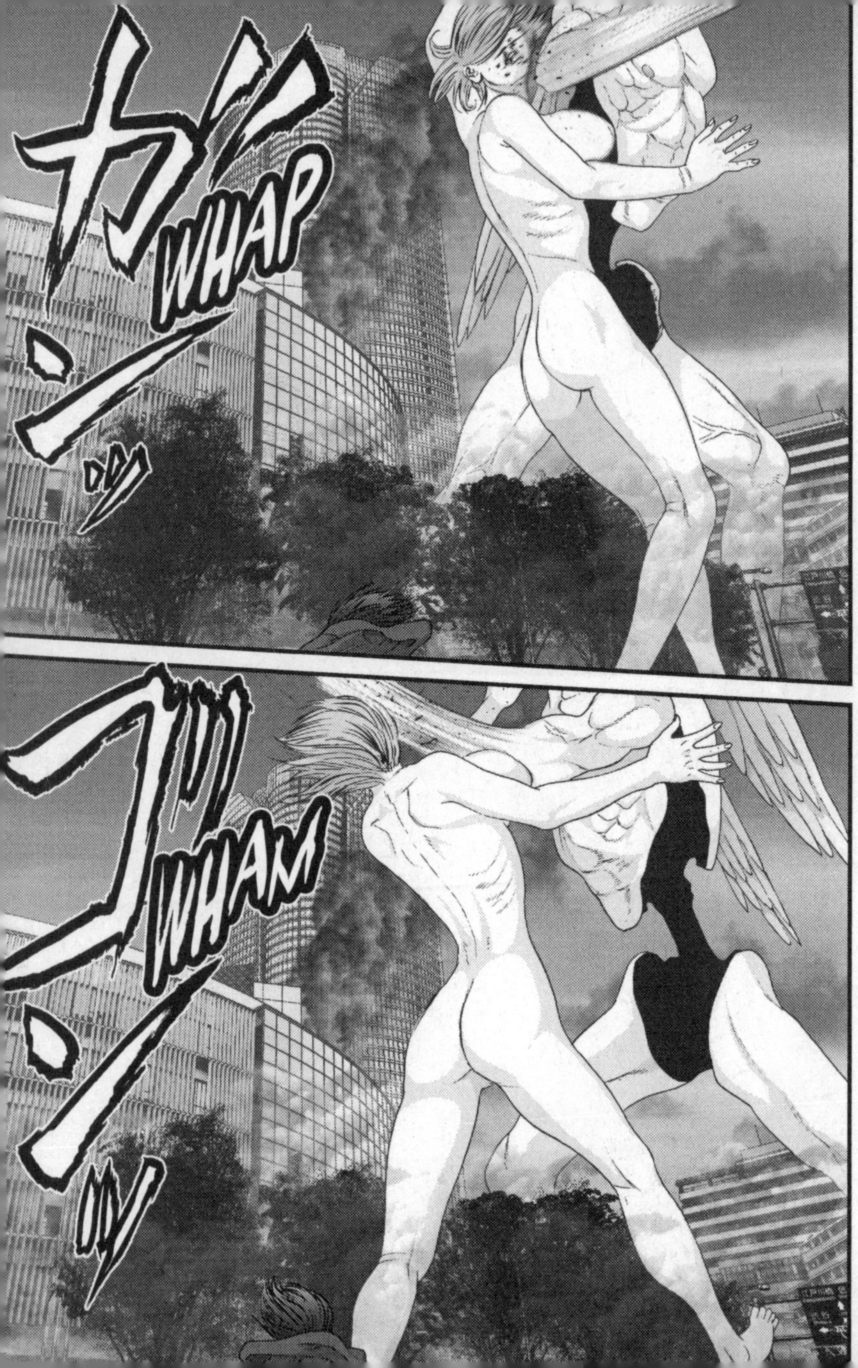
WHAP
WHAM

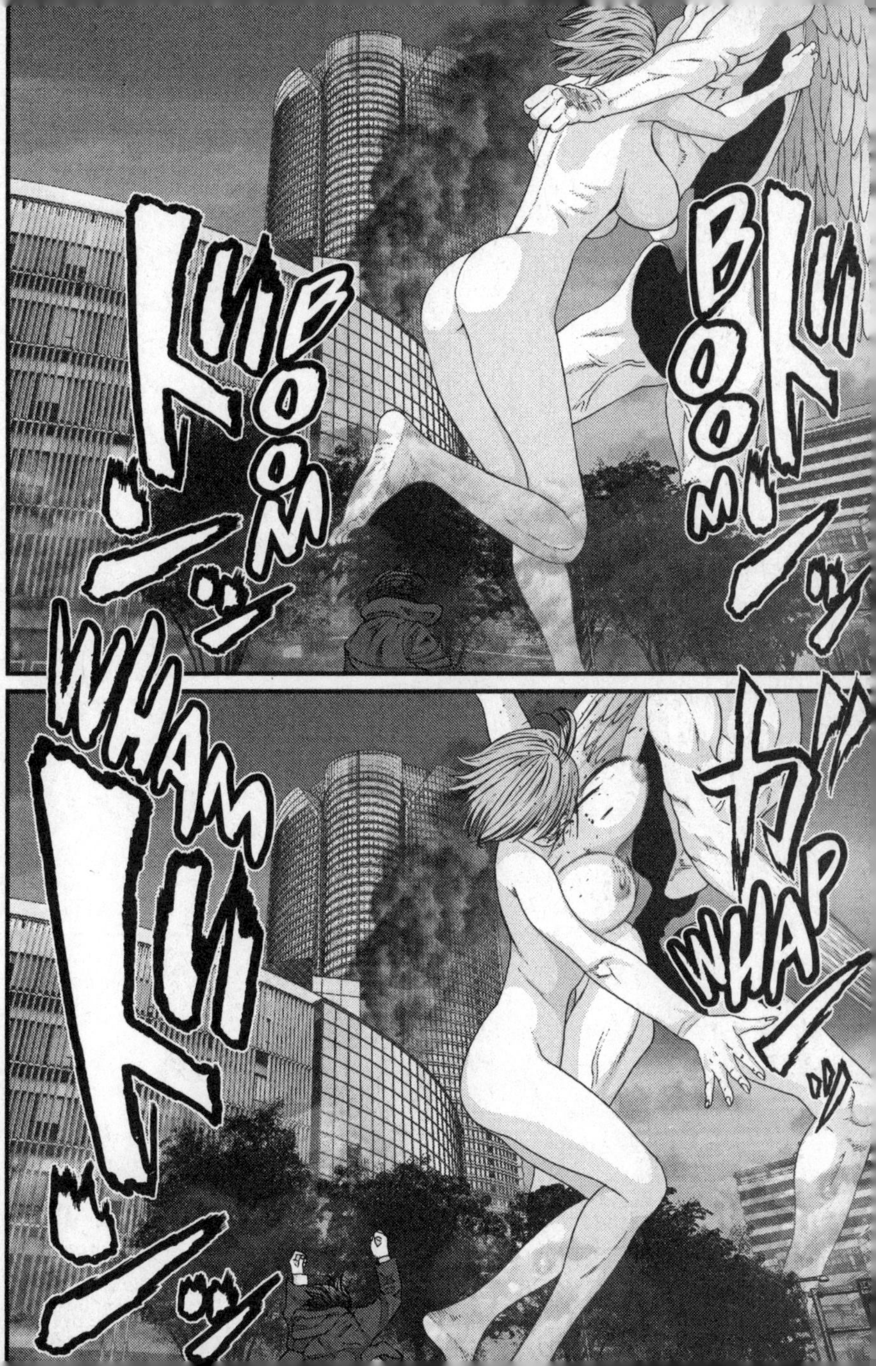
BOOOM
BOOOM
WHAP
WHAM

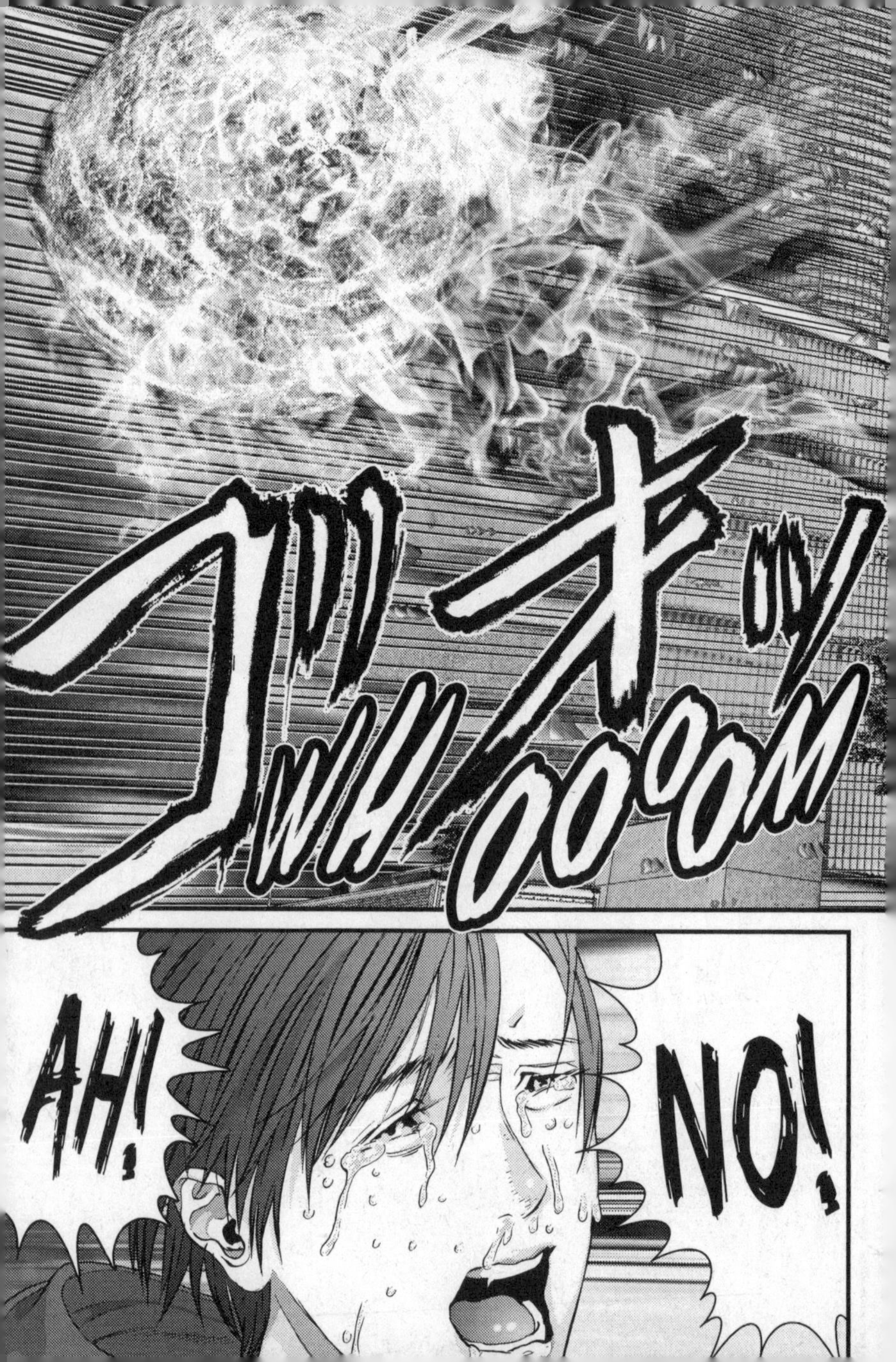
ゴオッ
WHOOOM
NO!
AH!

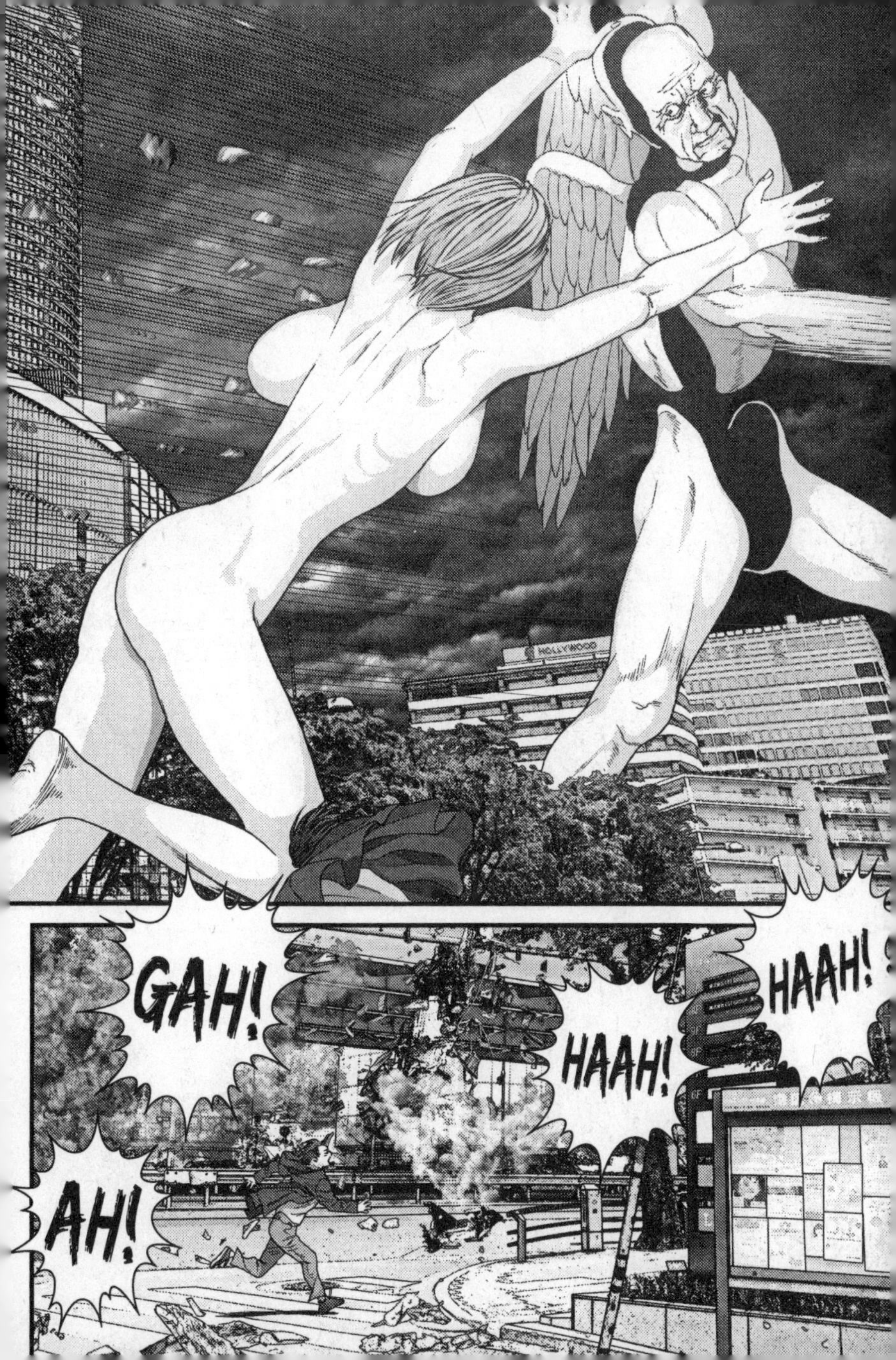
HOLLYWOOD
HAAH!
HAAH!
GAH!
AH!

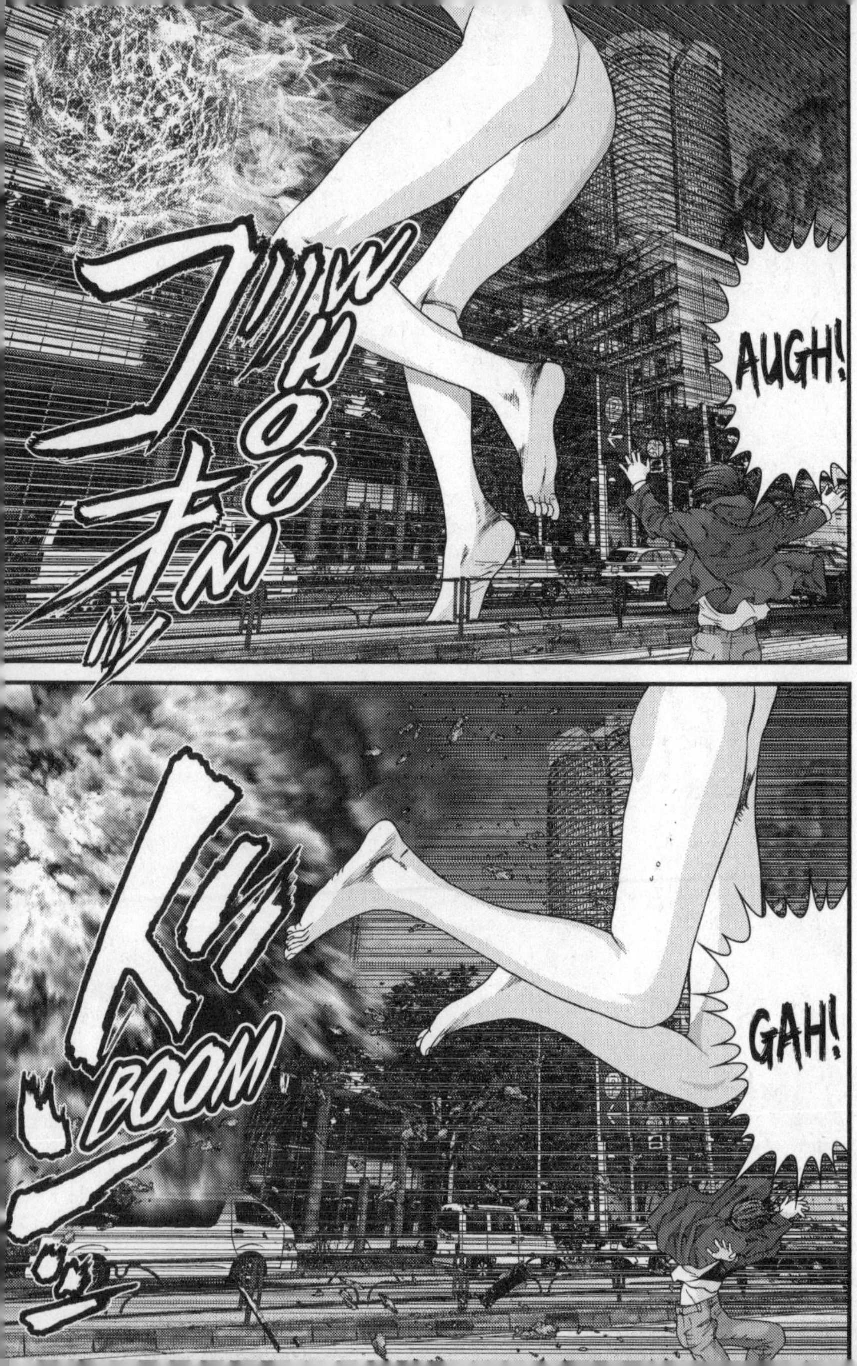
AUGH!
WHOOM
GAH!
BOOM

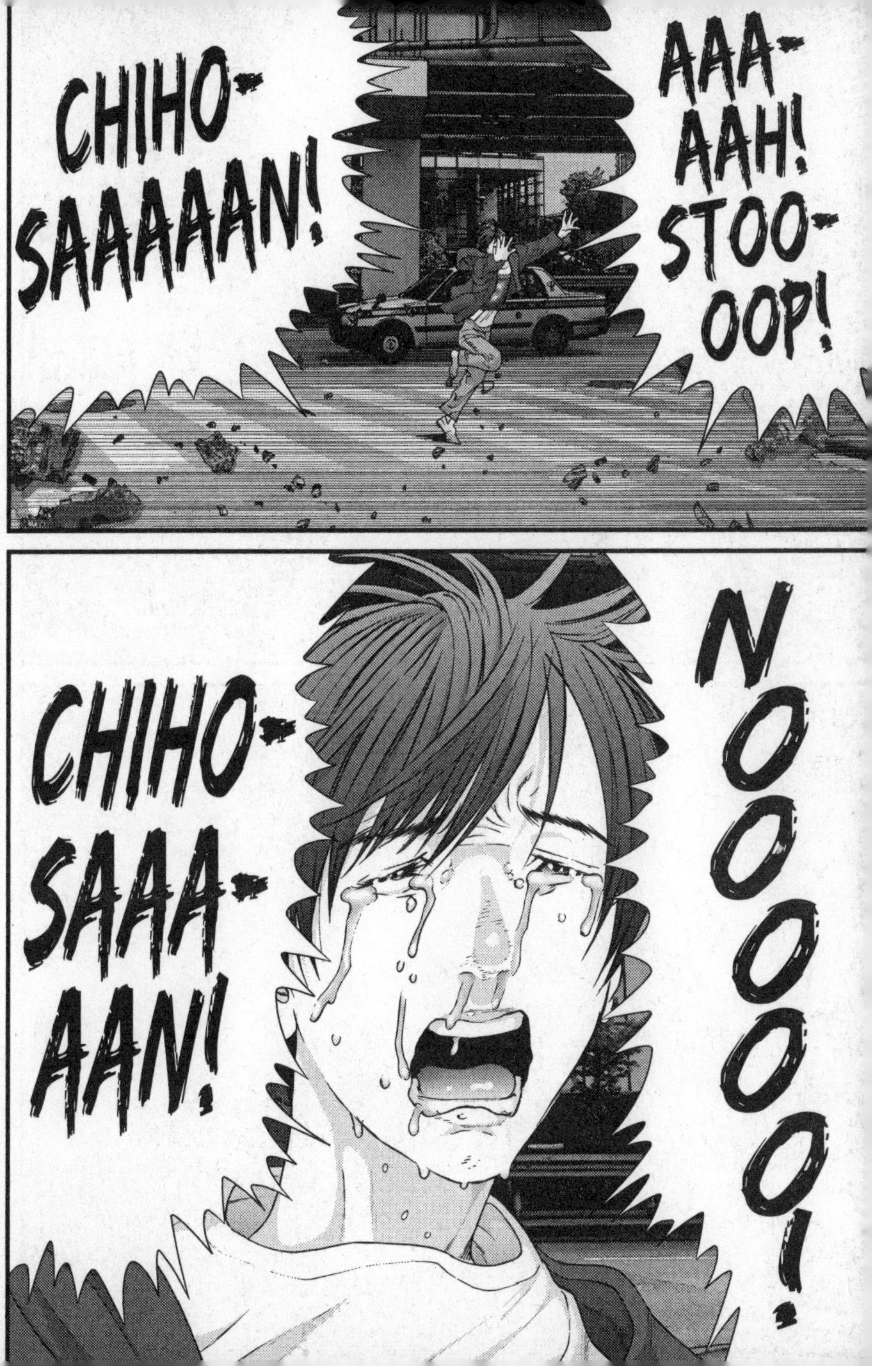
AAA-AAAH! STOO-OOP!
CHIHO-SAAAAAN!
NOOOOO!
CHIHO-SAAA-AAN!

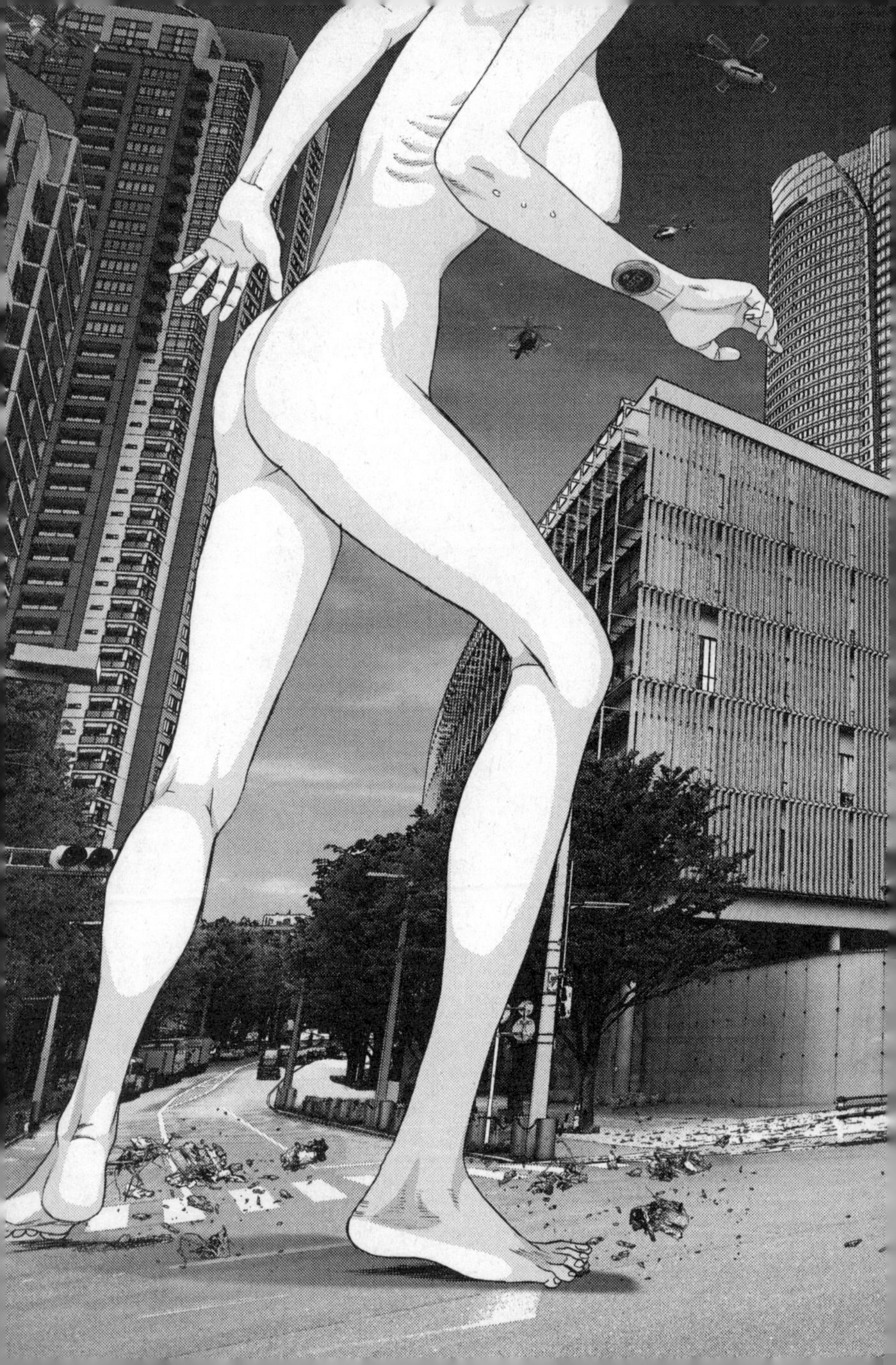

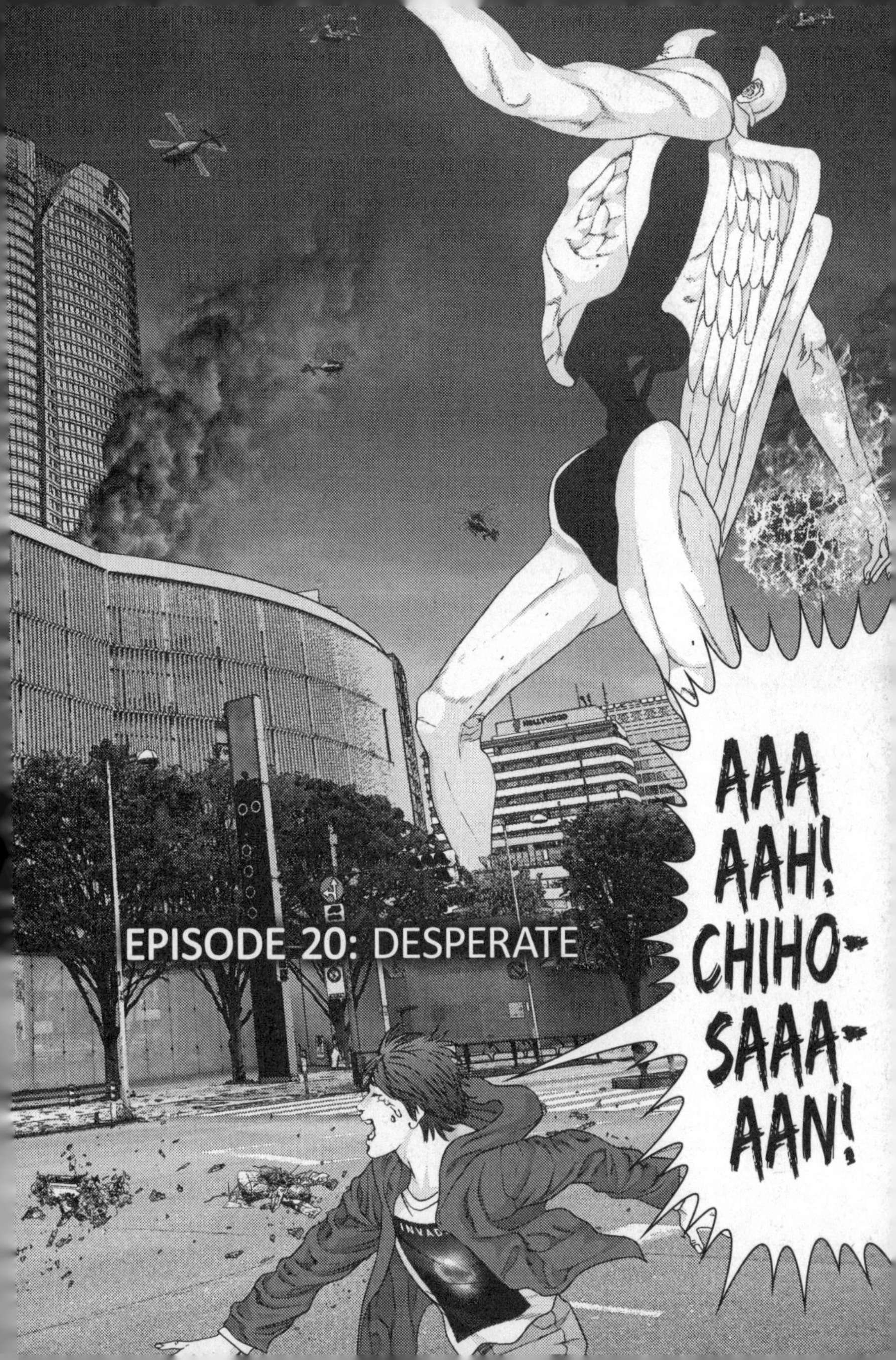
EPISODE 20: DESPERATE
AAAAAH! CHIHO-SAAA-AAN!

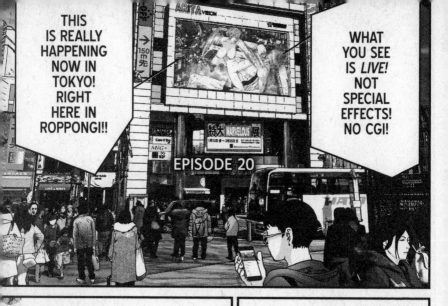

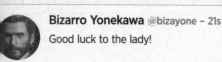

WHAT YOU SEE IS *LIVE!* NOT SPECIAL EFFECTS! NO CGI!
THIS IS REALLY HAPPENING NOW IN TOKYO! RIGHT HERE IN ROPPONGI!!
EPISODE 20
Trends for you
1 Giant Woman
1,564,800 Tweets
2 Naked Lady
827,500 Tweets
3 Roppongi
612,340 Tweets
4 Pink Hair
238,500 Tweets
5 Giant
141,588 Tweets
Bizarro Yonekawa @bizayone - 21s
Good luck to the lady!
#GiantWoman
Tak Retweeted
Kaido yuki @p_aradise - 30s
Those boobs are ridiculous. Disgusting
#GiantWoman
Magnus Tanahashi @magnustff - 45s
Folks be dying out here!!
#GiantWoman

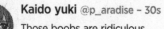

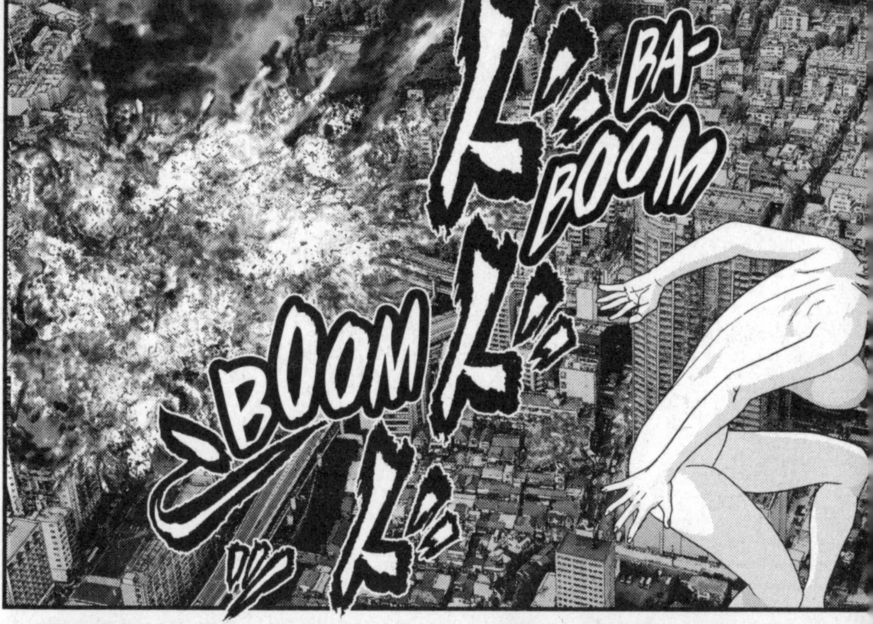
BA-BOOM
BOOM
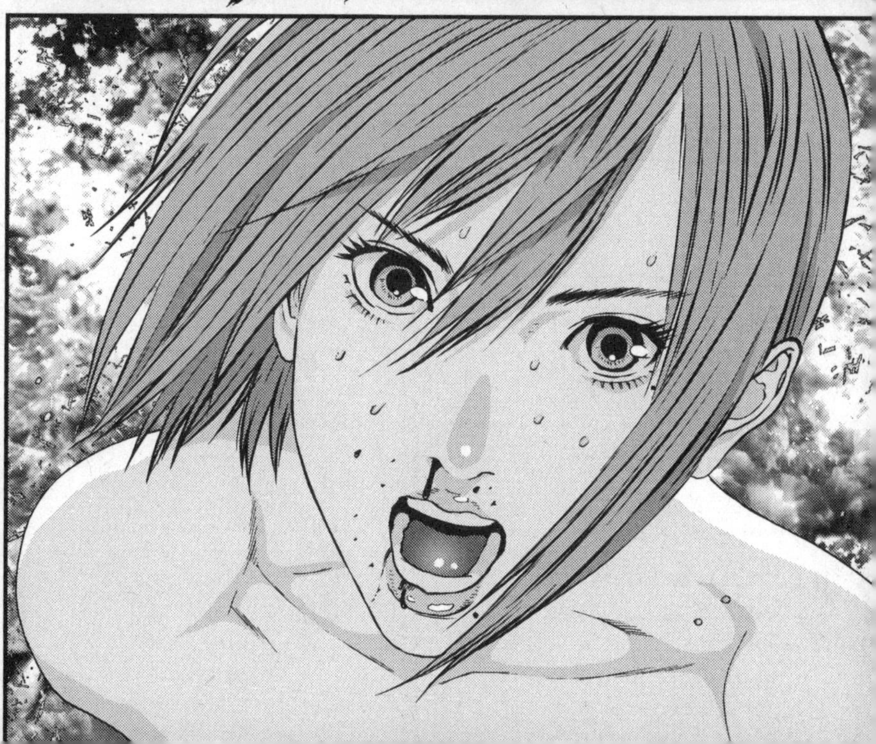

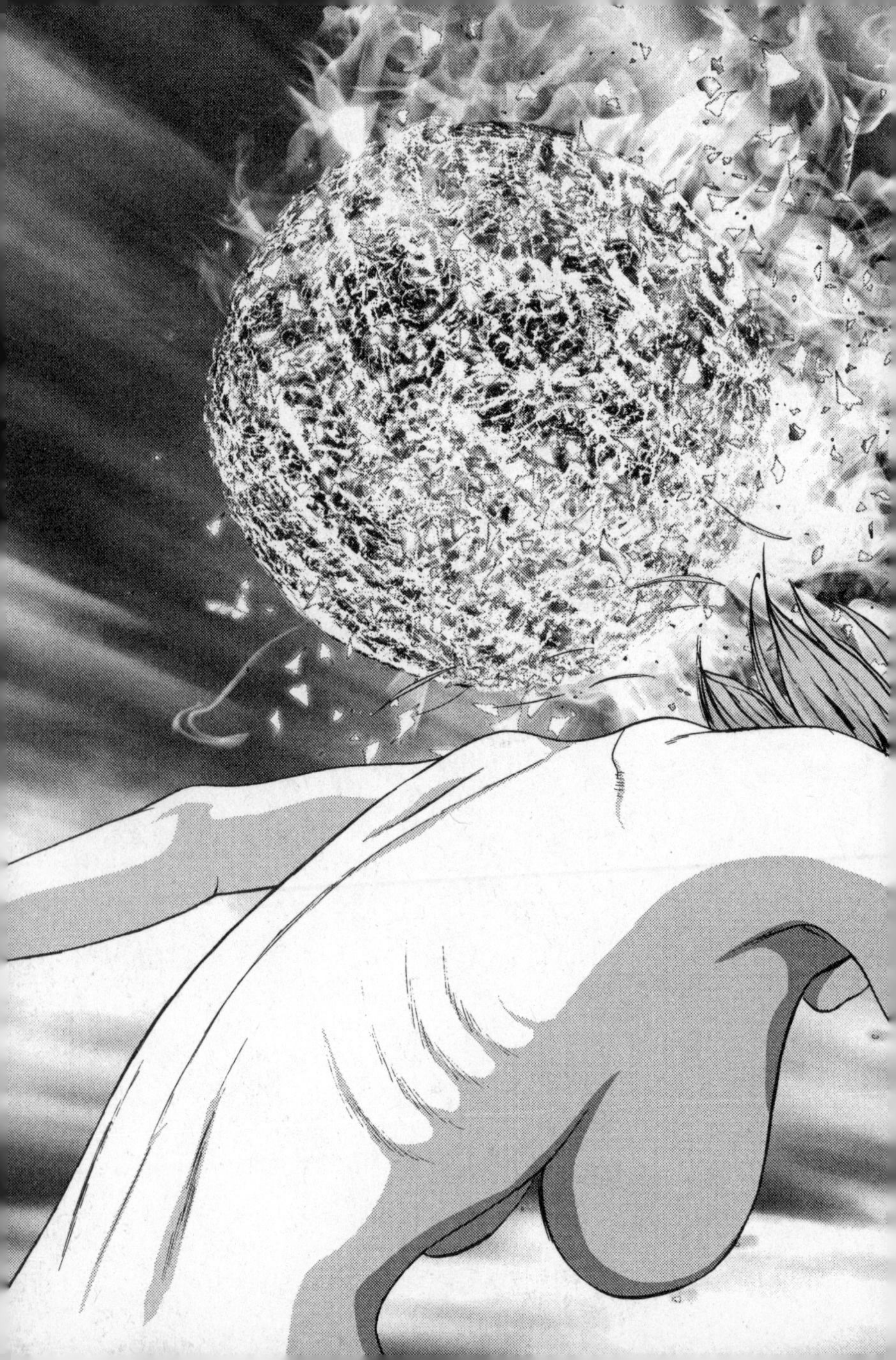

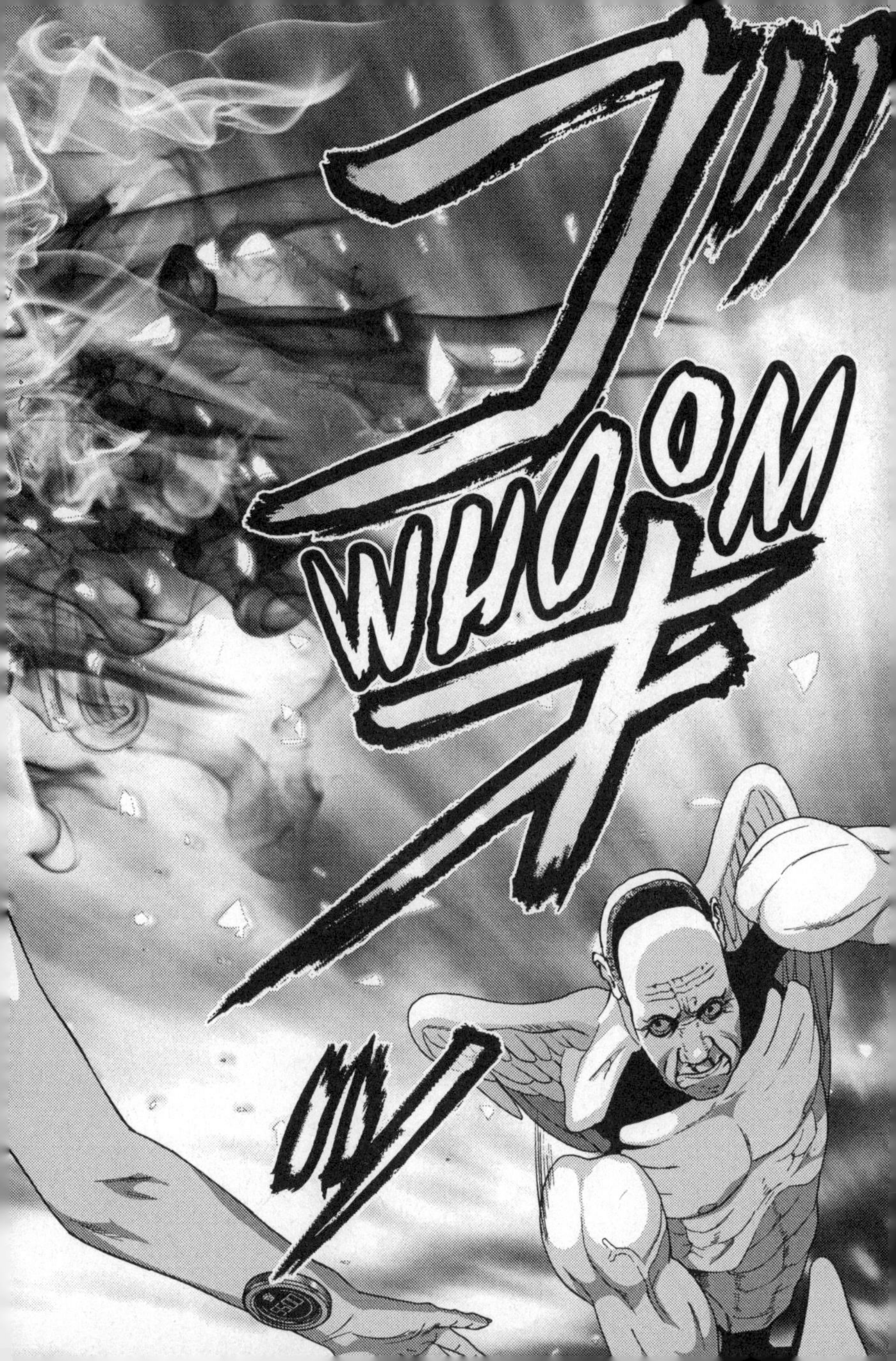
WHOOM

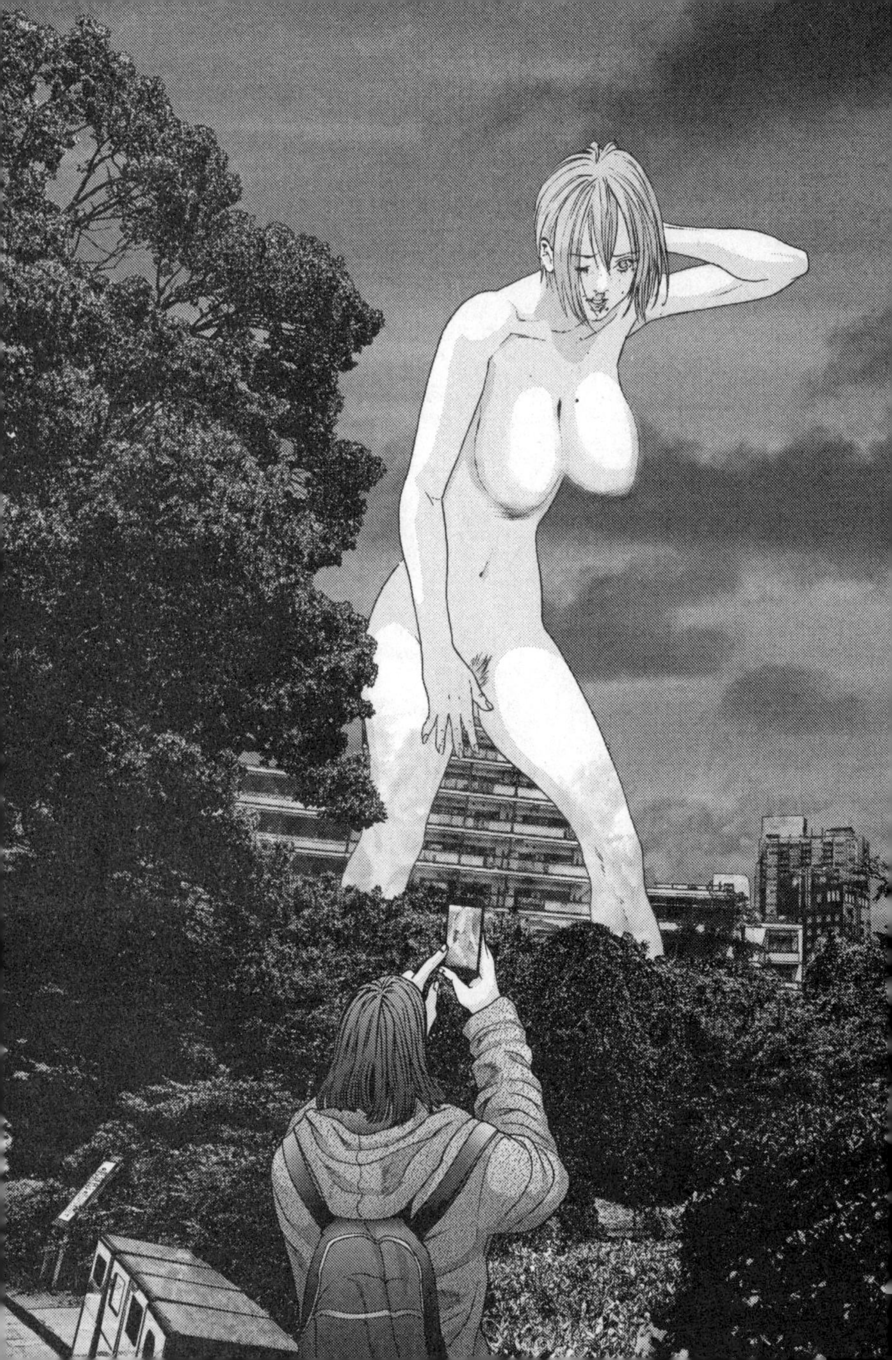

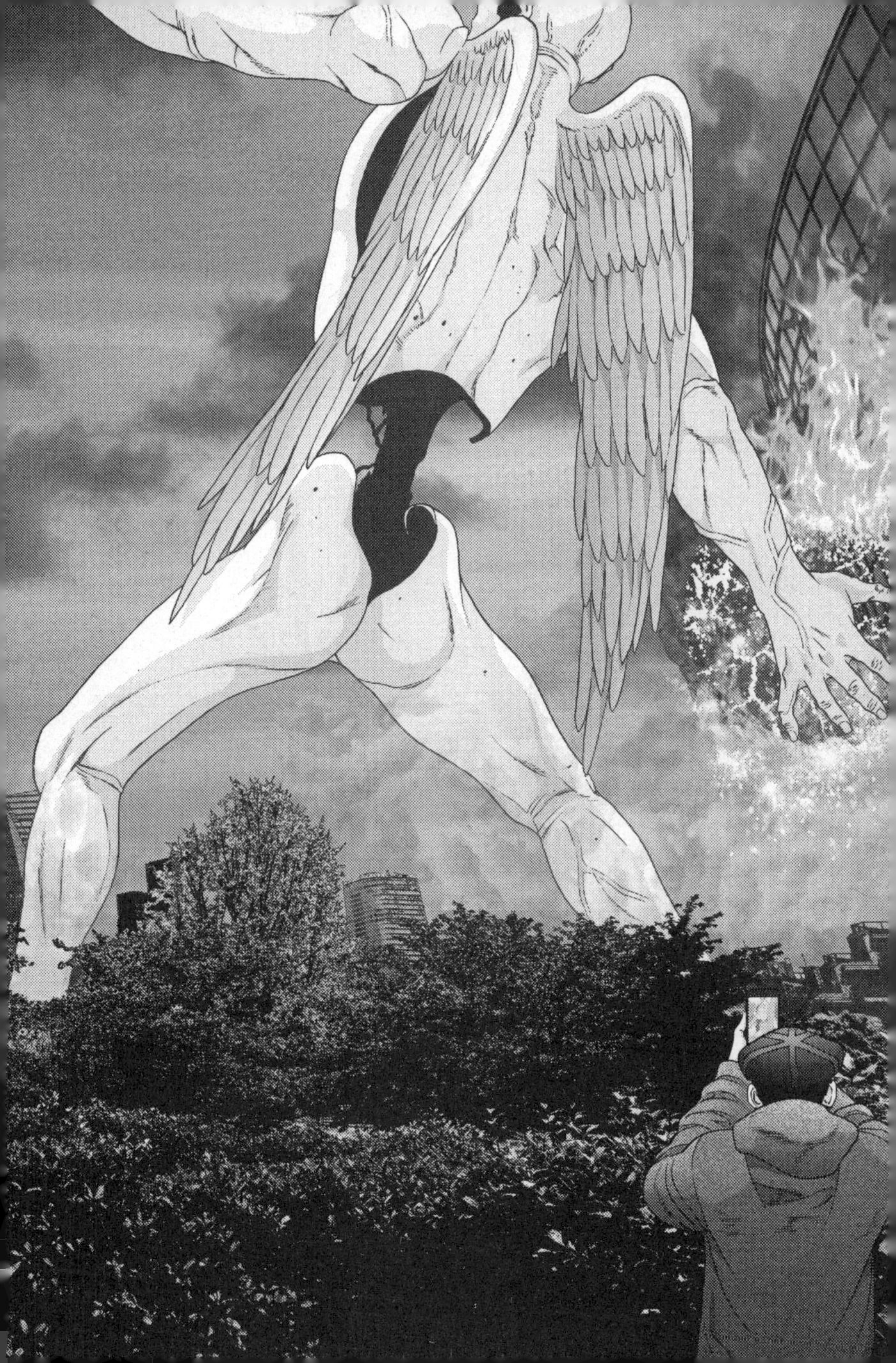

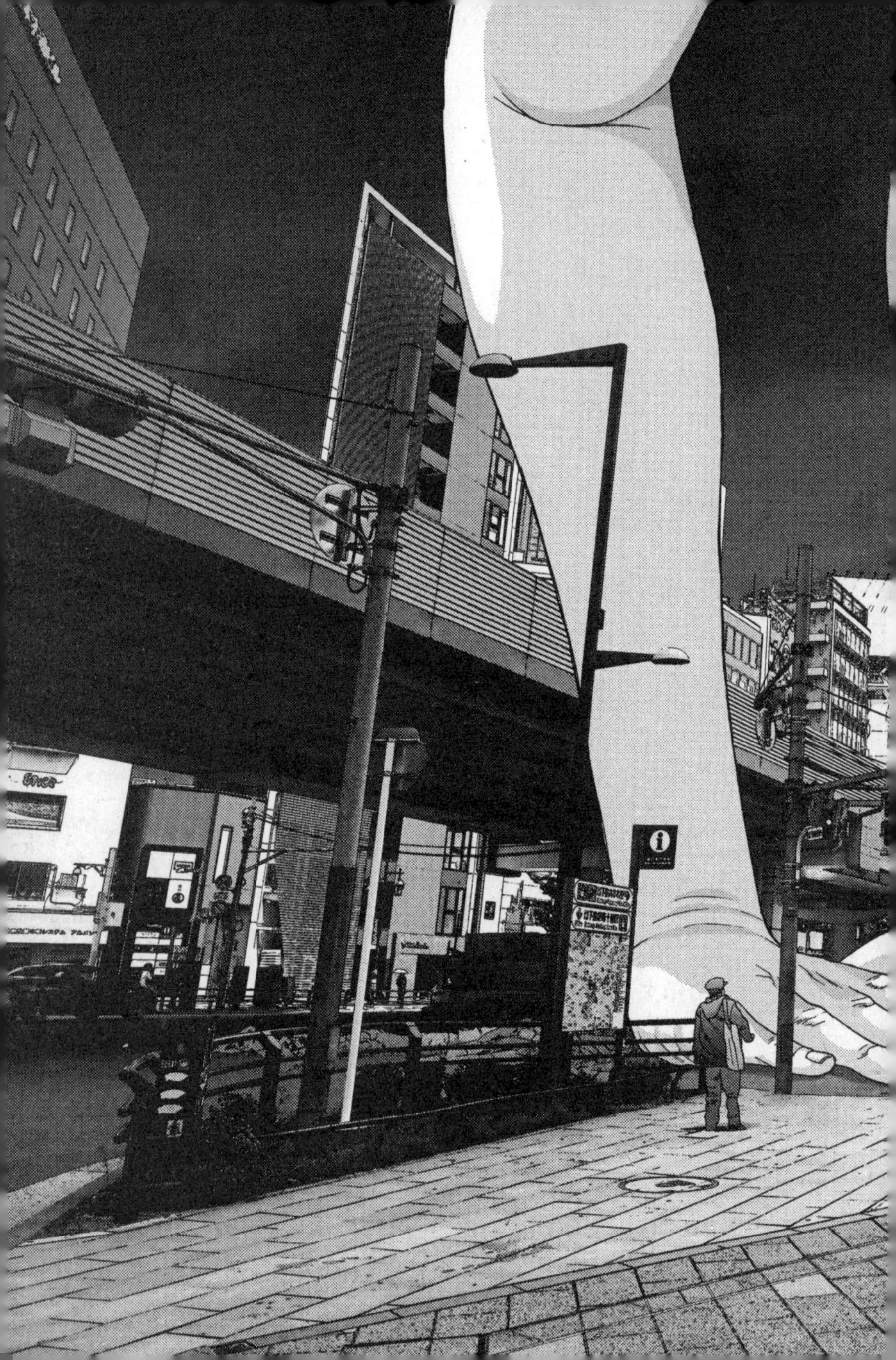

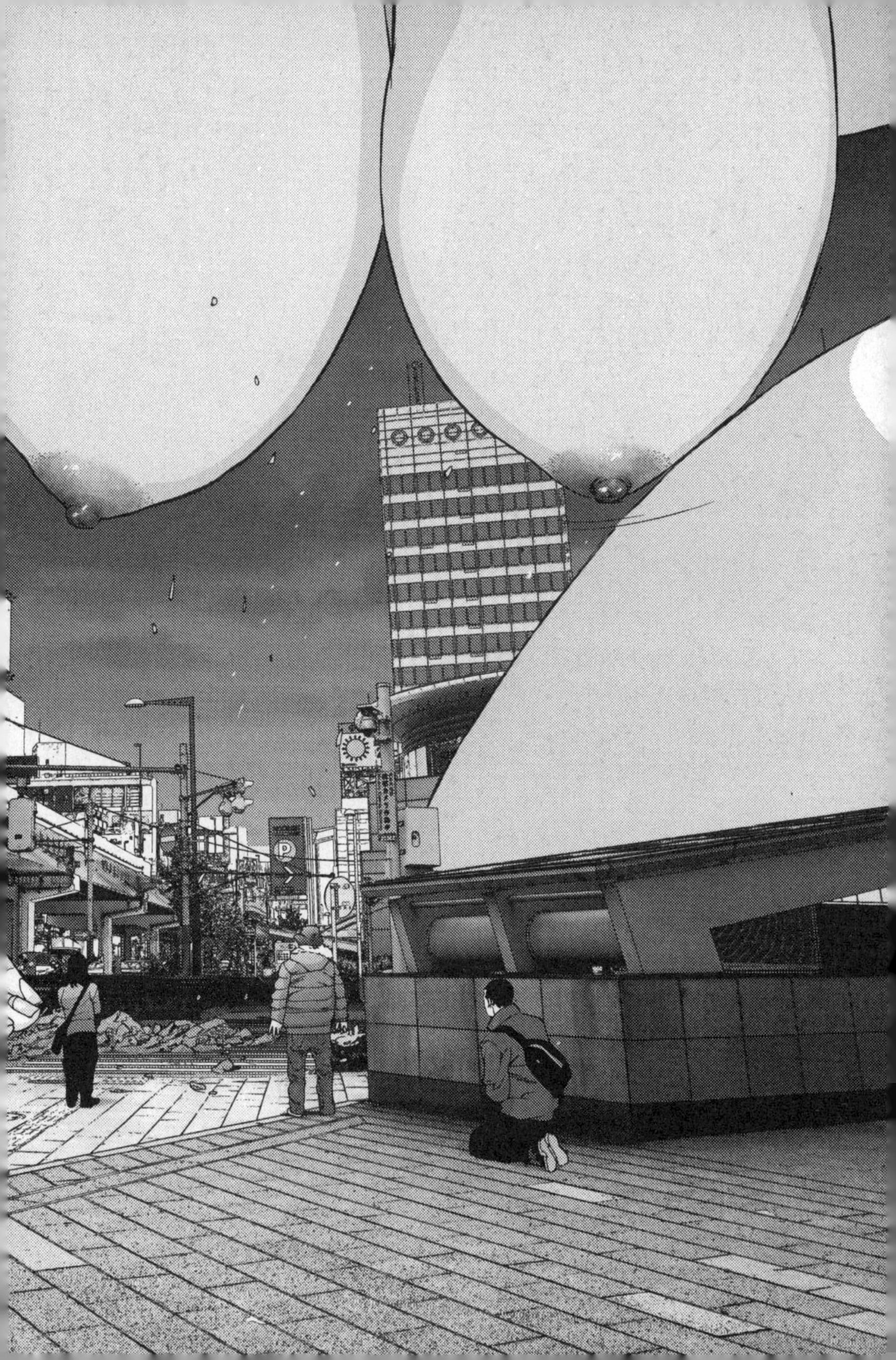

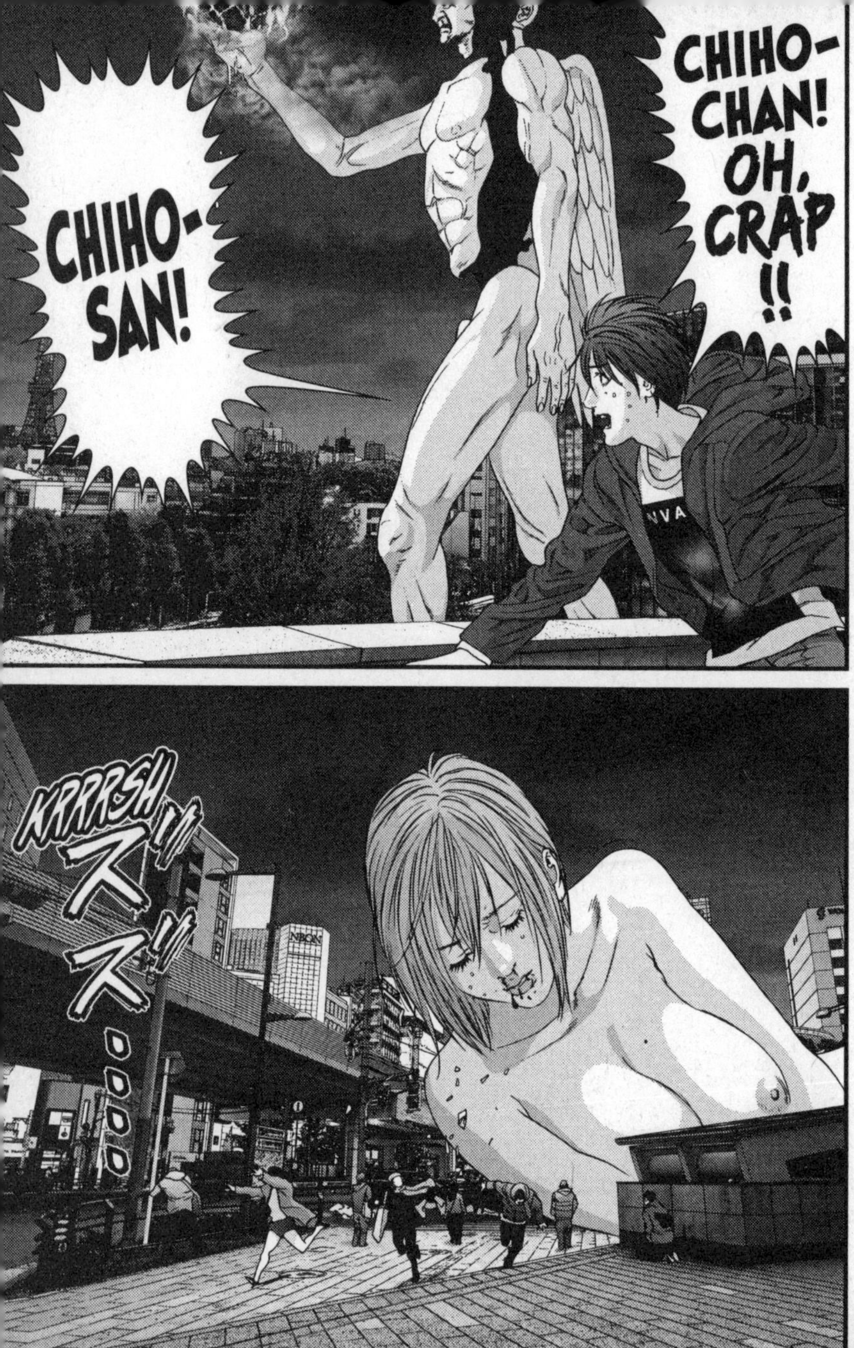
CHIHO-CHAN! OH, CRAP!!
CHIHO-SAN!
KRRRSH!!
ス!! ス!!
ス.....

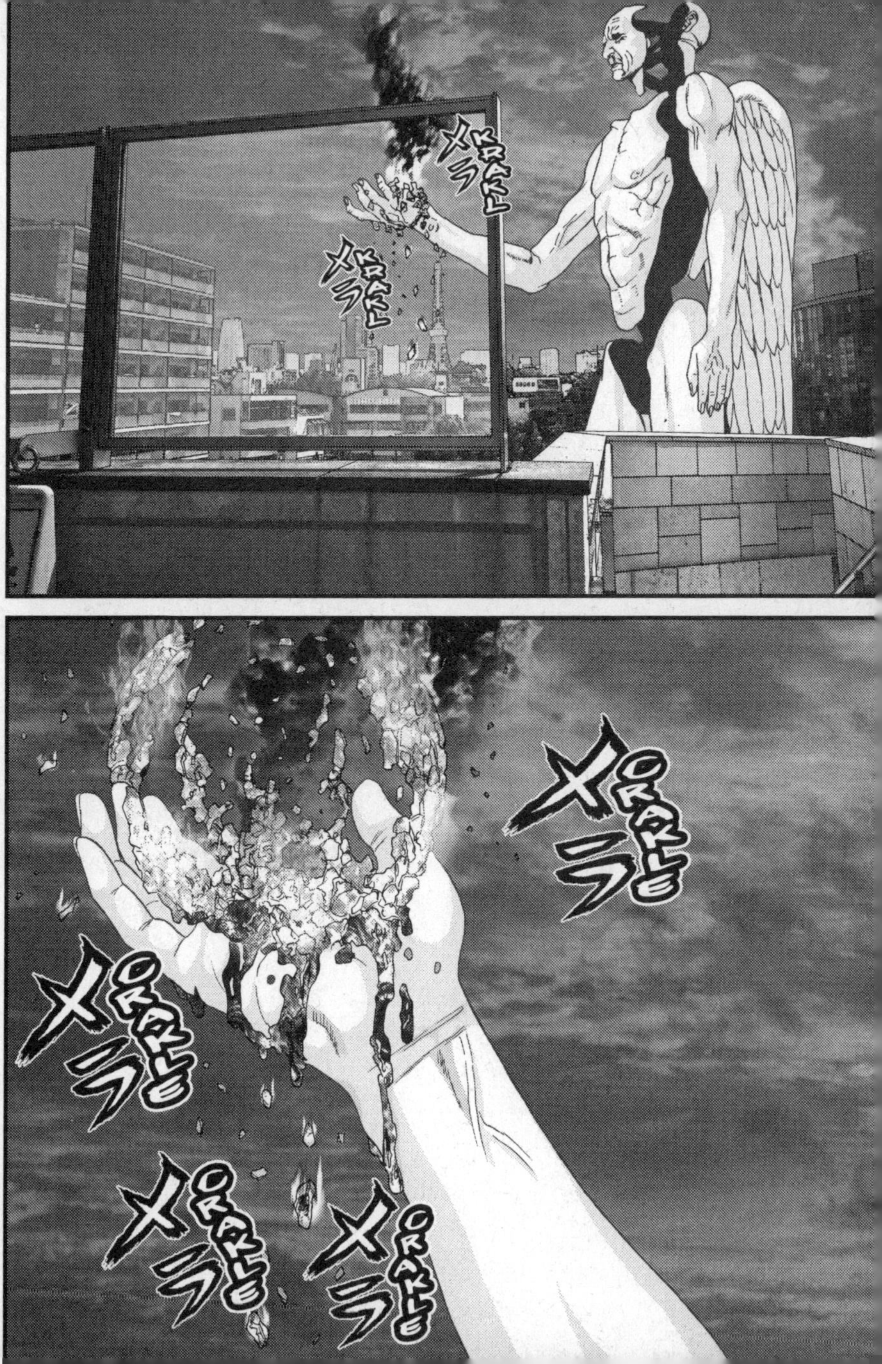
KRAKL
KRAKL
CRAKLE
CRAKLE
CRAKLE
CRAKLE

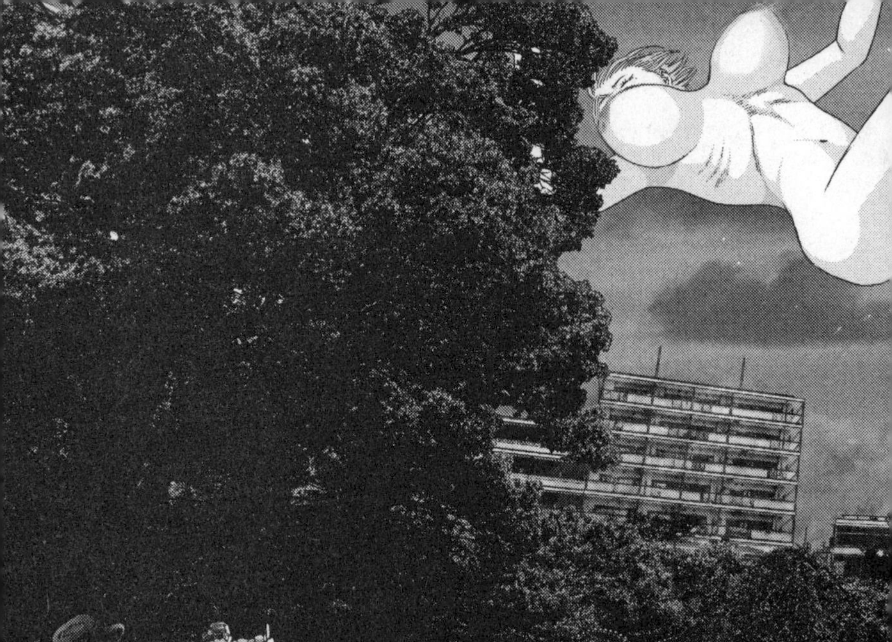

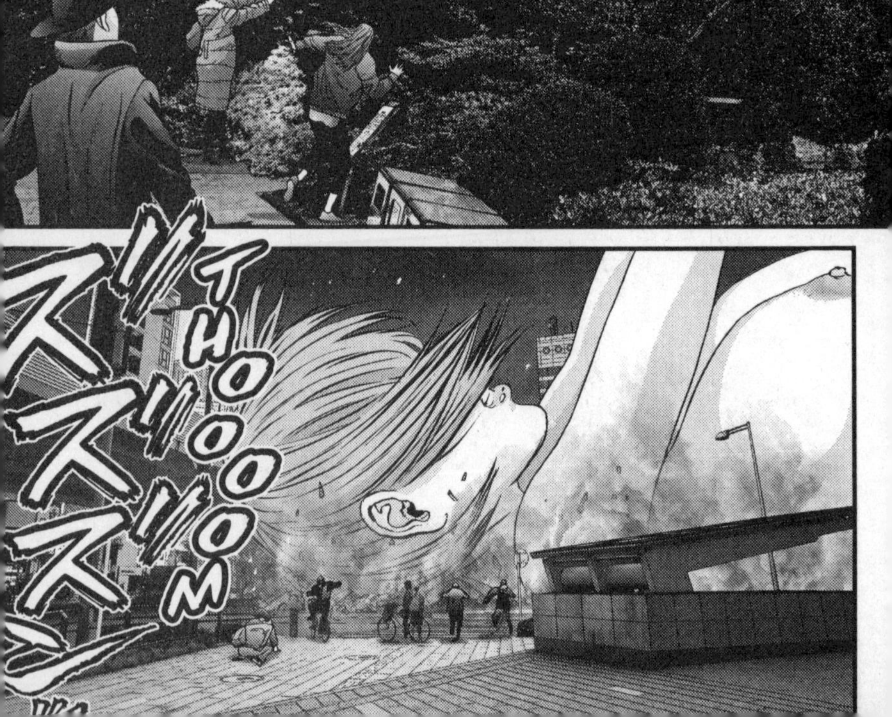
THOOOOOM

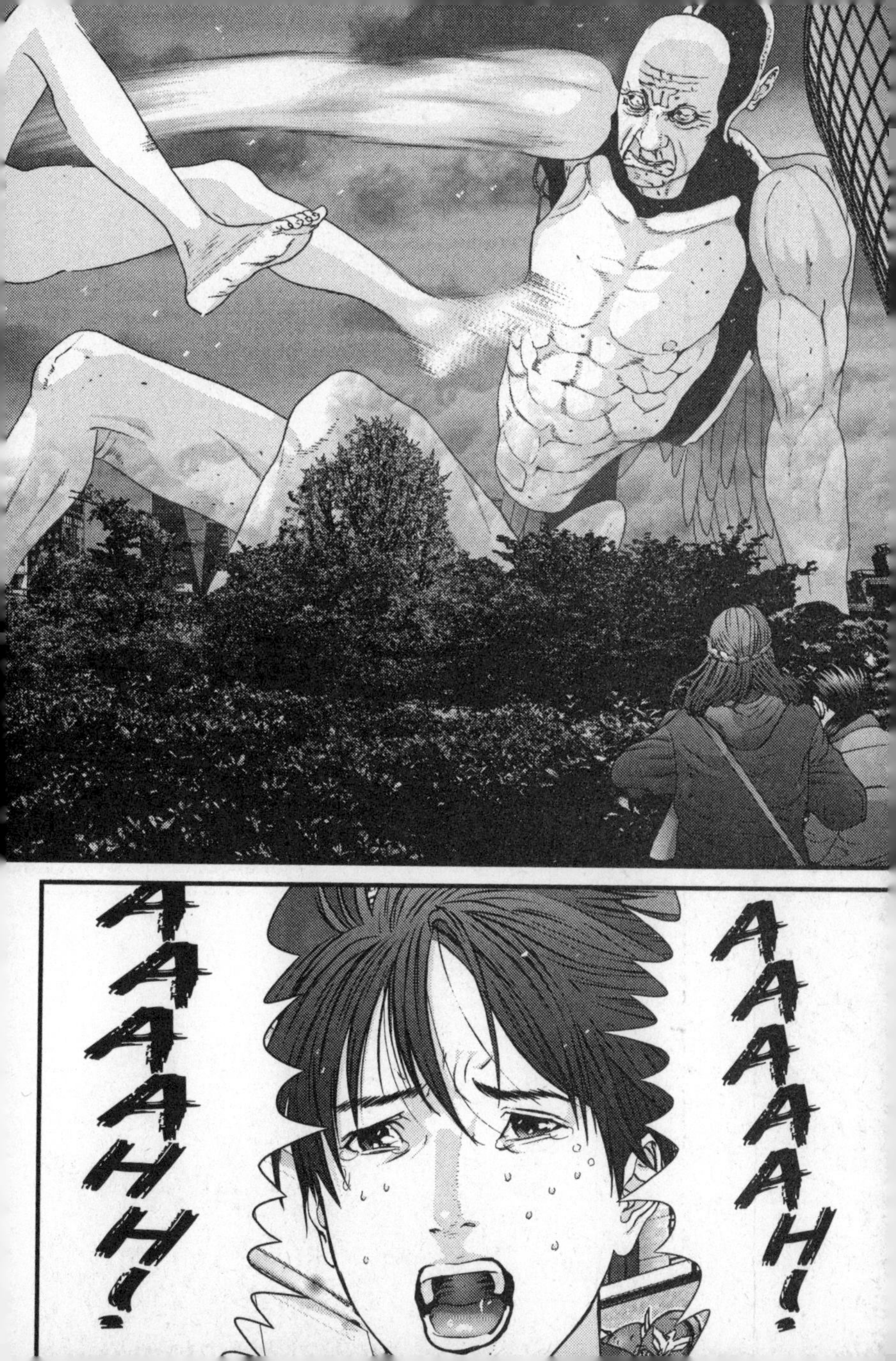
AAAAAH!
AAAAHH!

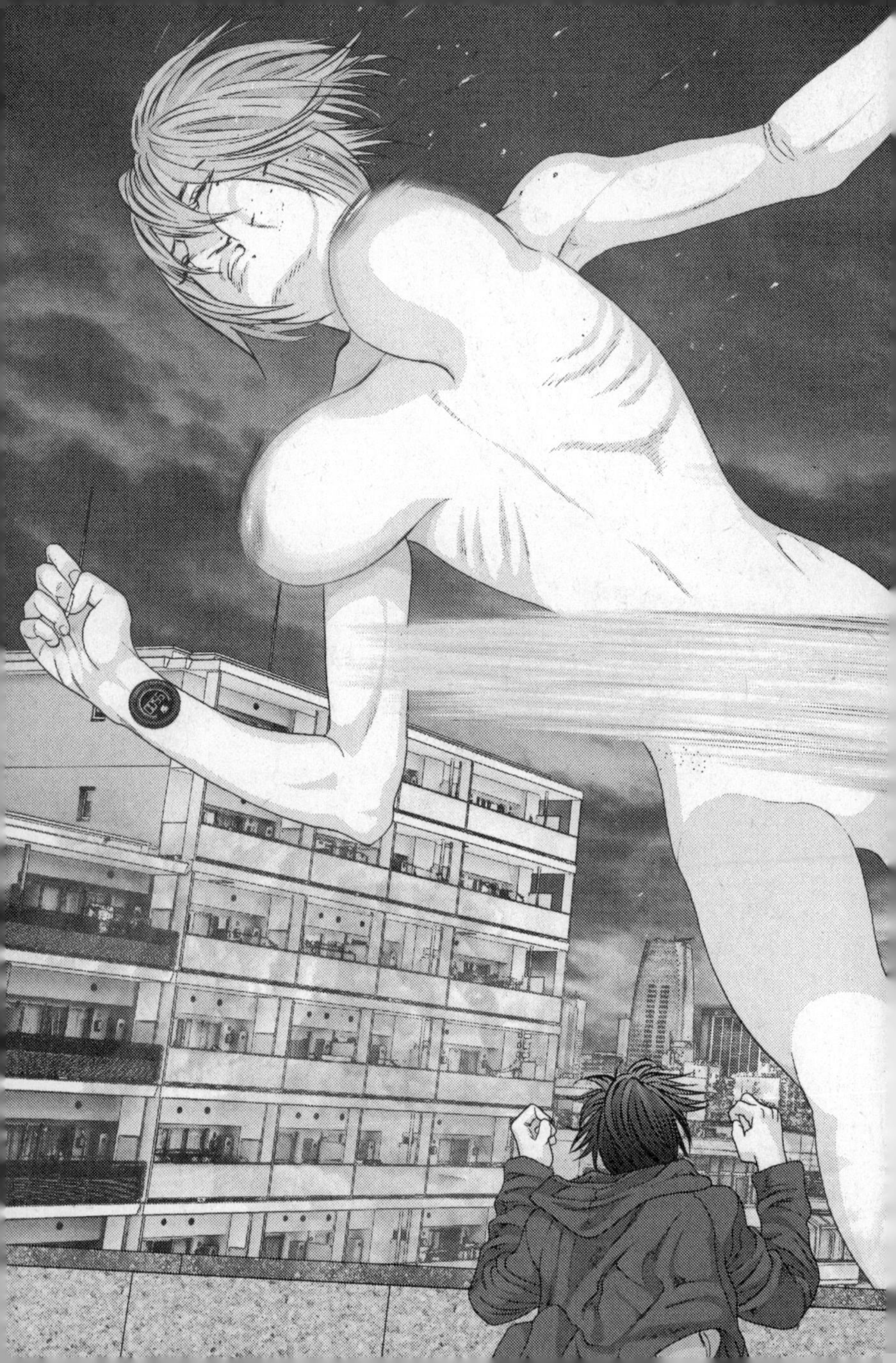

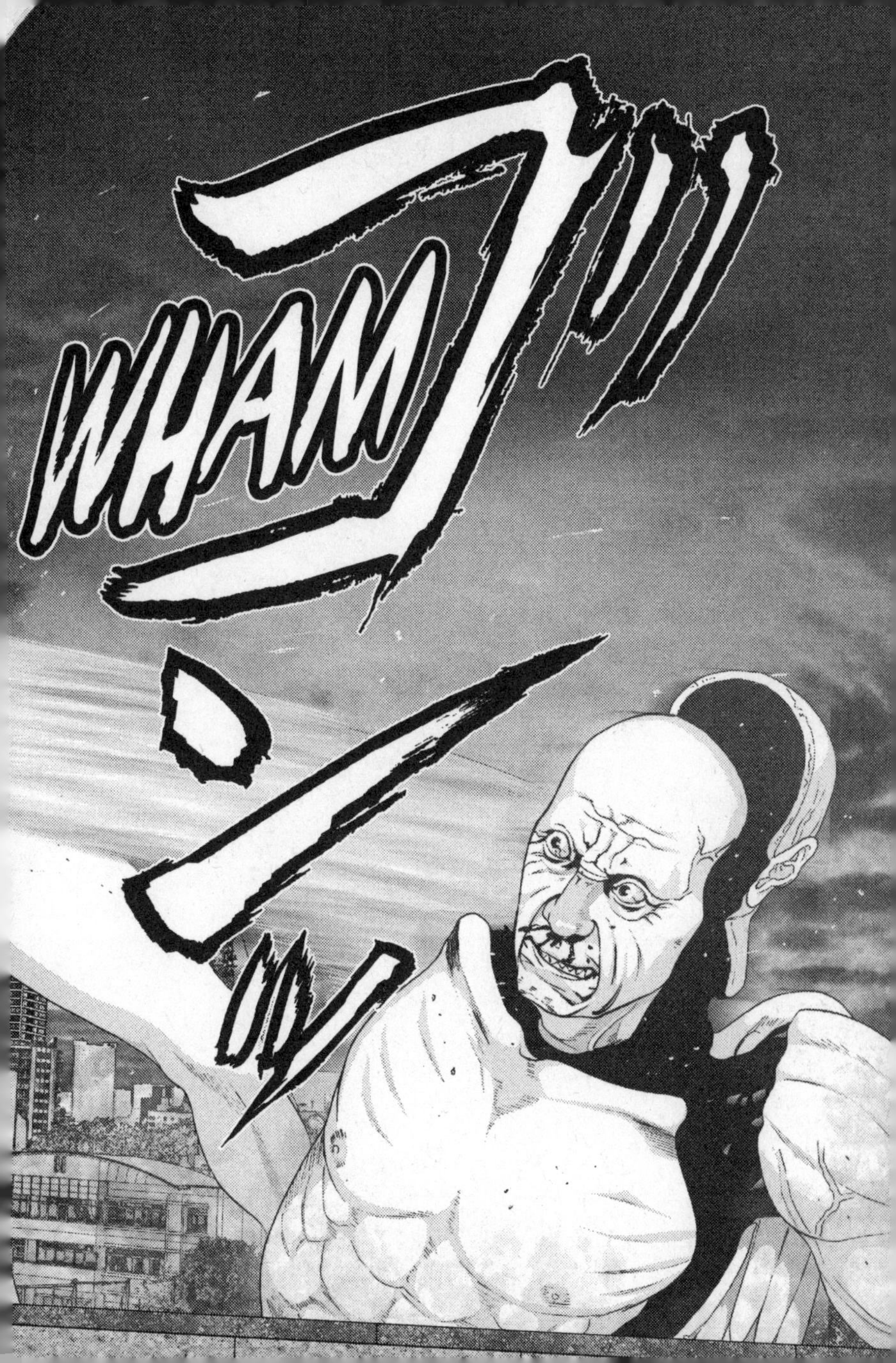
WHAM

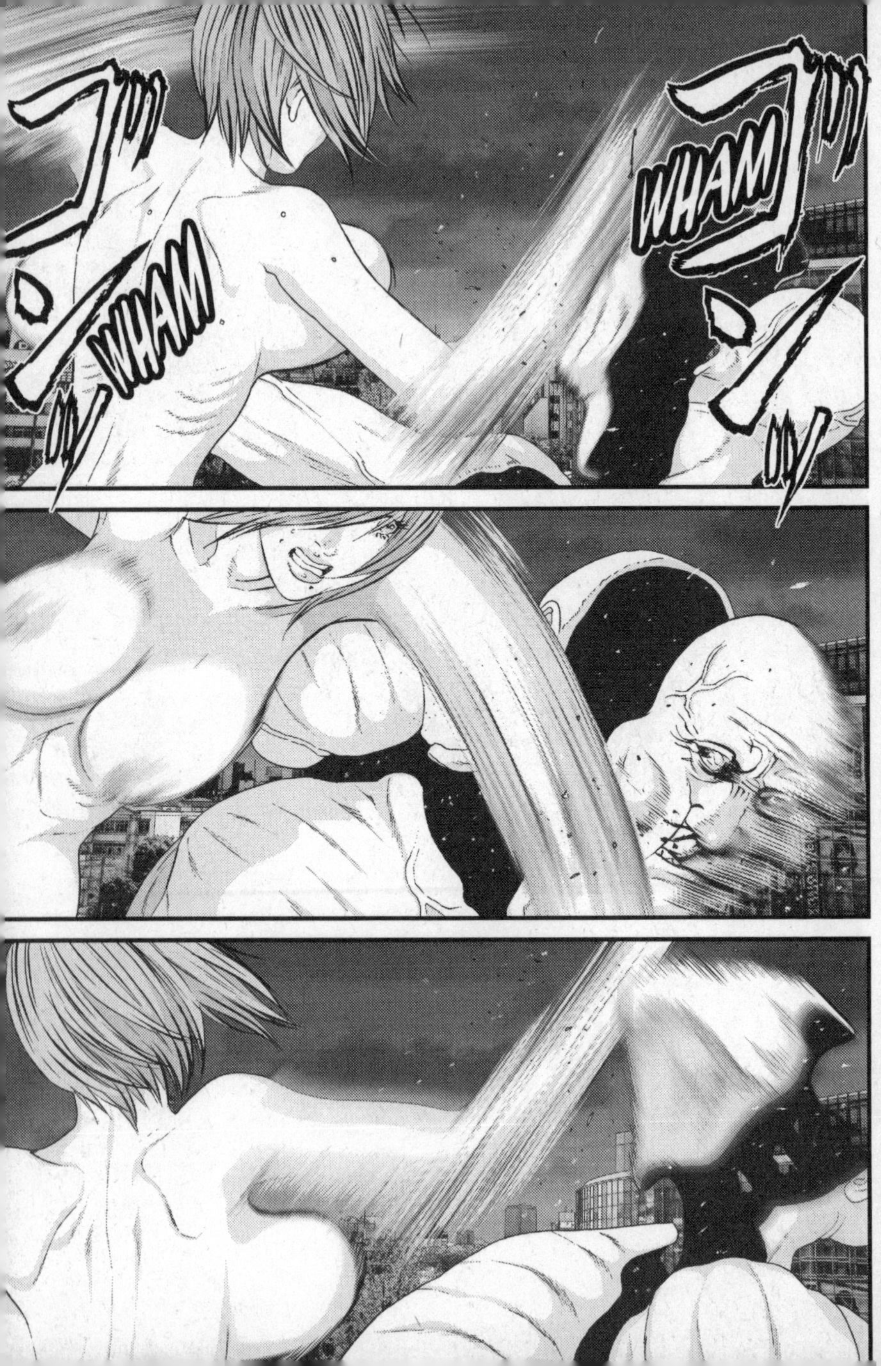

WHAM
WHAM

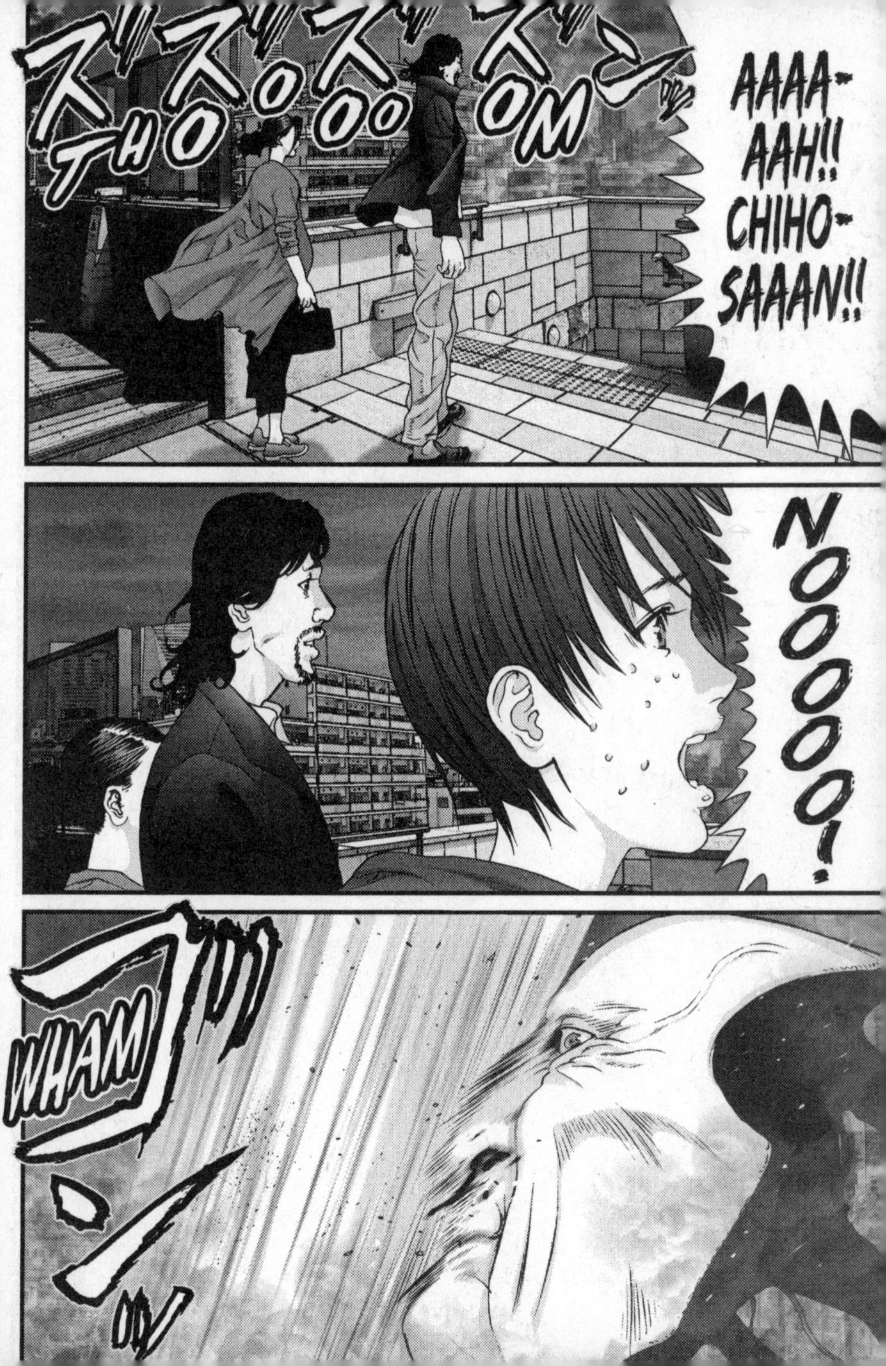

AAAA-AAH!! CHIHO-SAAAN!!
ズズズズ
THOOOOOM
NOOOOOO!
ゴリ
WHAM

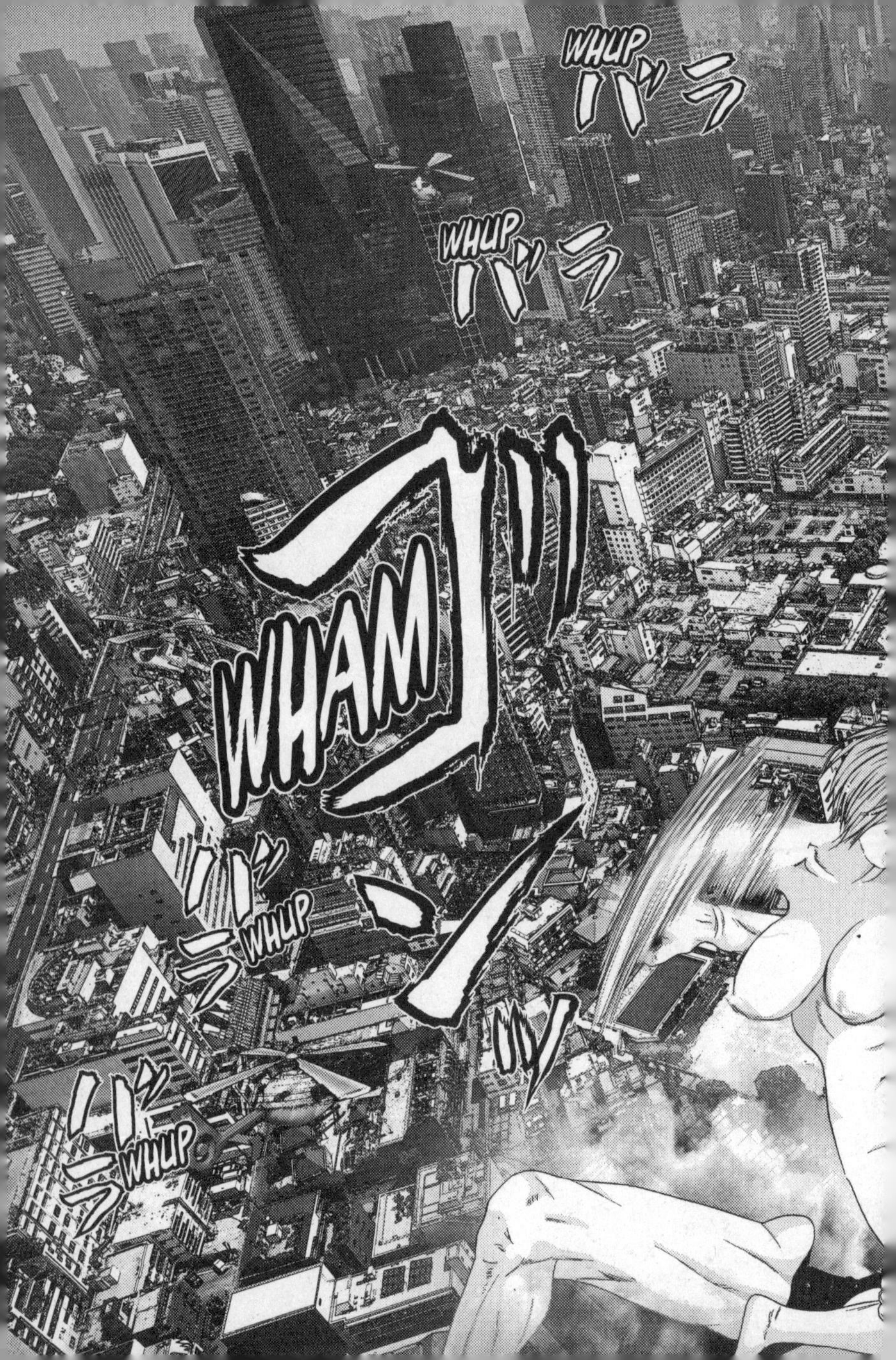
WHUP バラ
WHUP バラ
WHAM
バラ WHUP
バラ WHUP

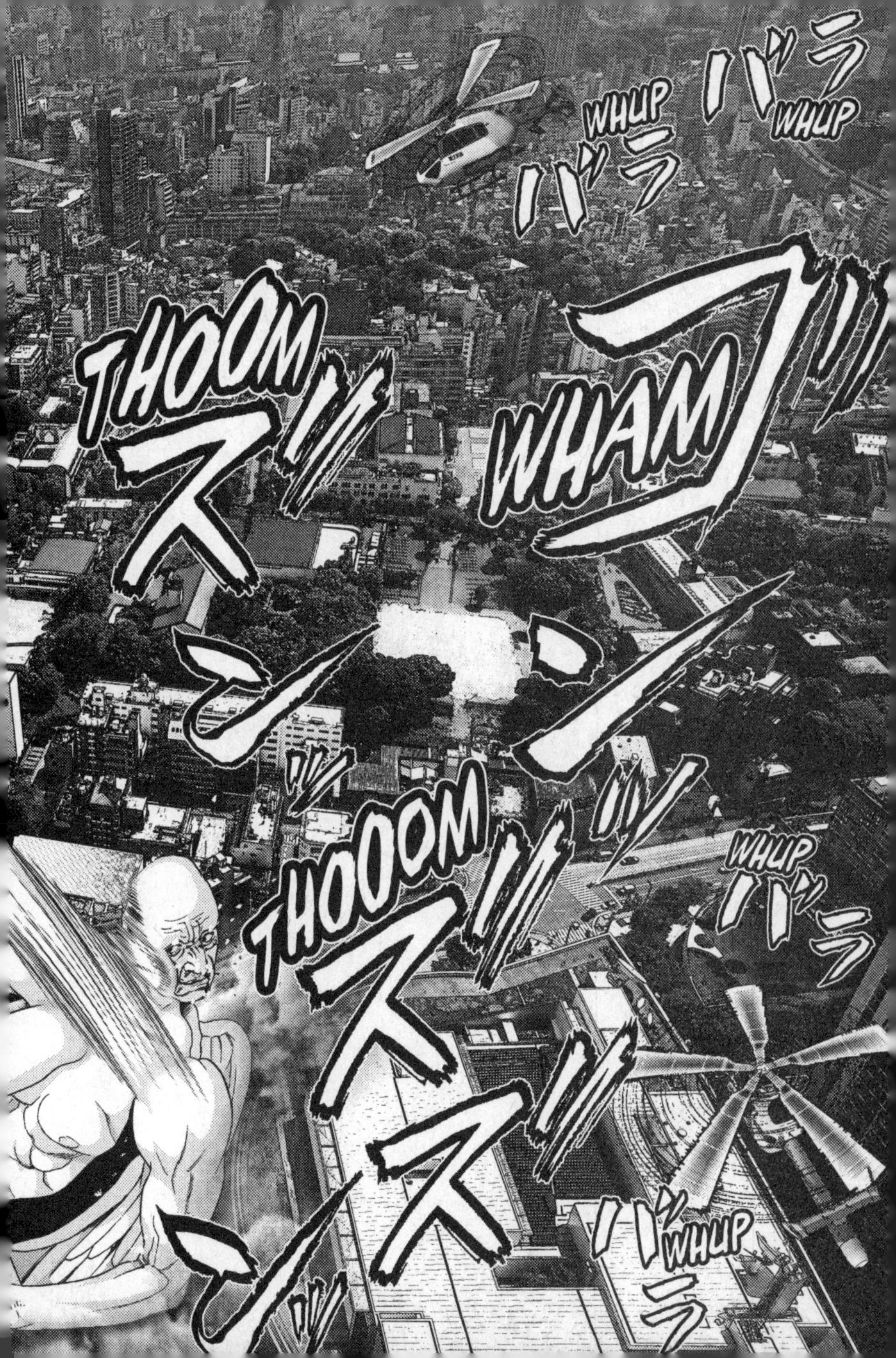

バラ
WHUP
WHUP
バラ
WHAM
ブン
THOOM
ズン
WHUP
バラ
THOOOM
ズズン
バラ
WHUP

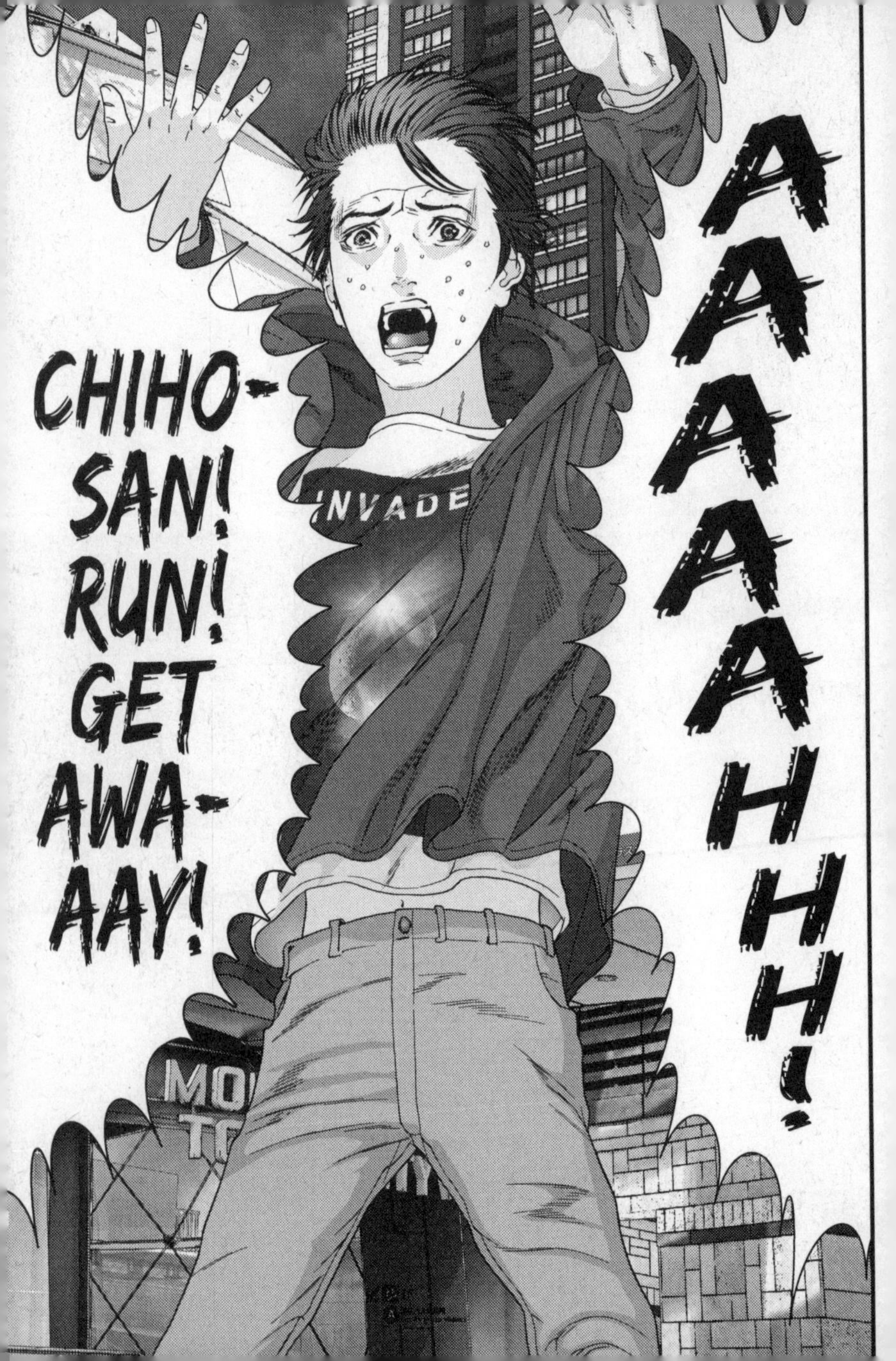

AAAAAHHH!
CHIHO-SAN! RUN! GET AWA-AAY!

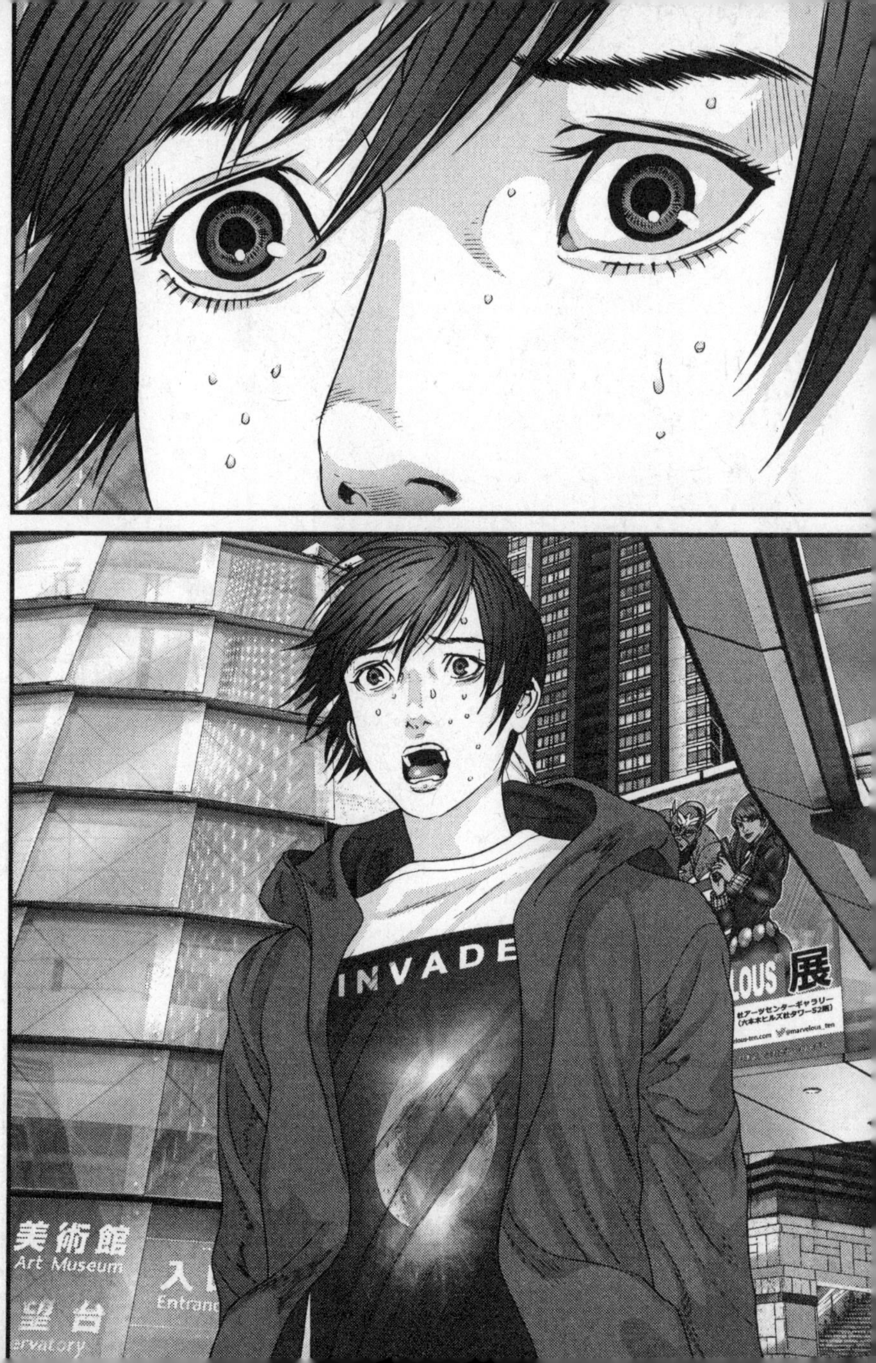

INVADE
LOUS 展
杜アーツセンターギャラリー
(六本木ヒルズ杜タワー52階)
lous-ten.com
@marvelous_ten
美術館
Art Museum
入
Entranc
望台
ervatory

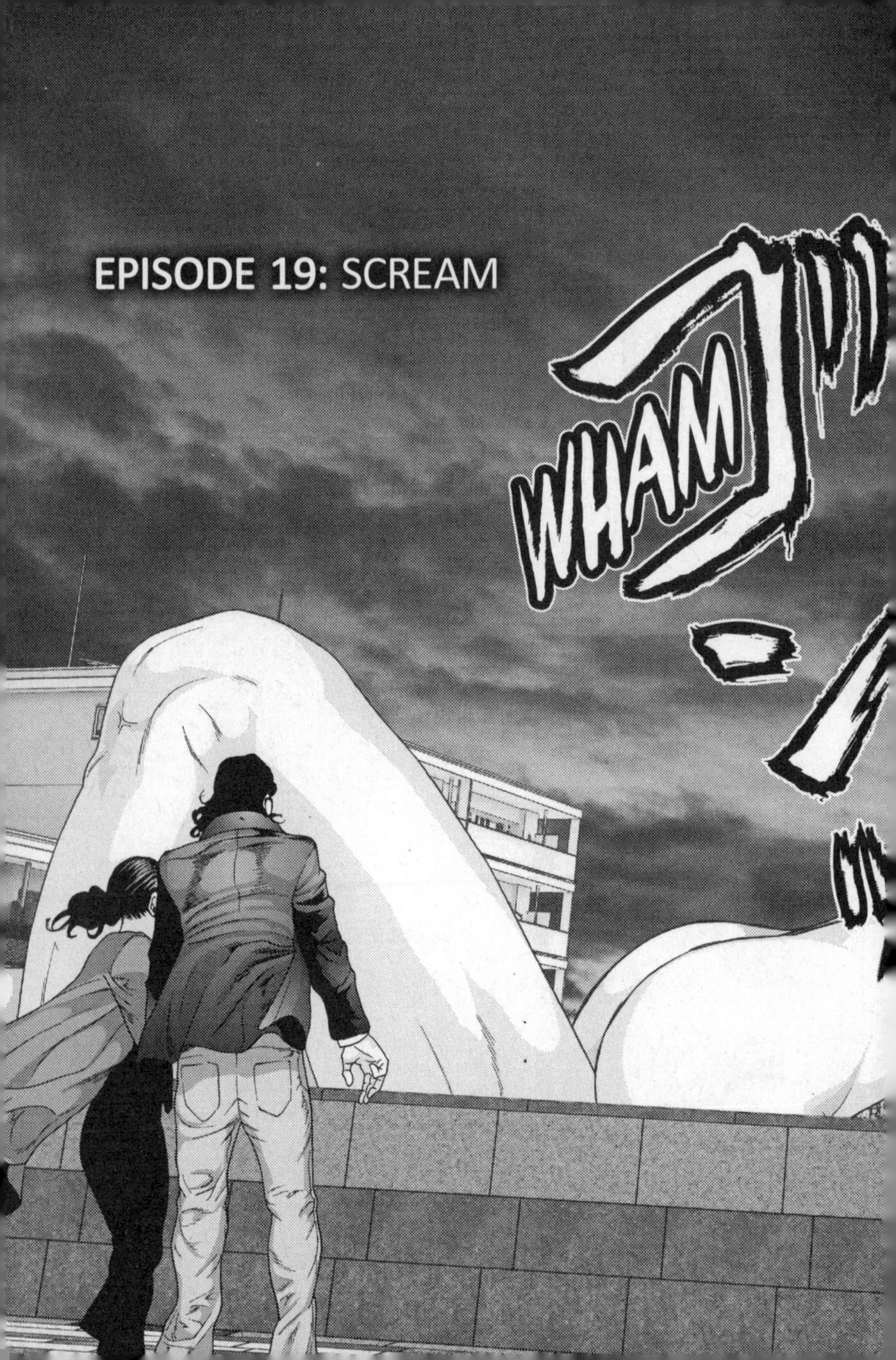
EPISODE 19: SCREAM
WHAM

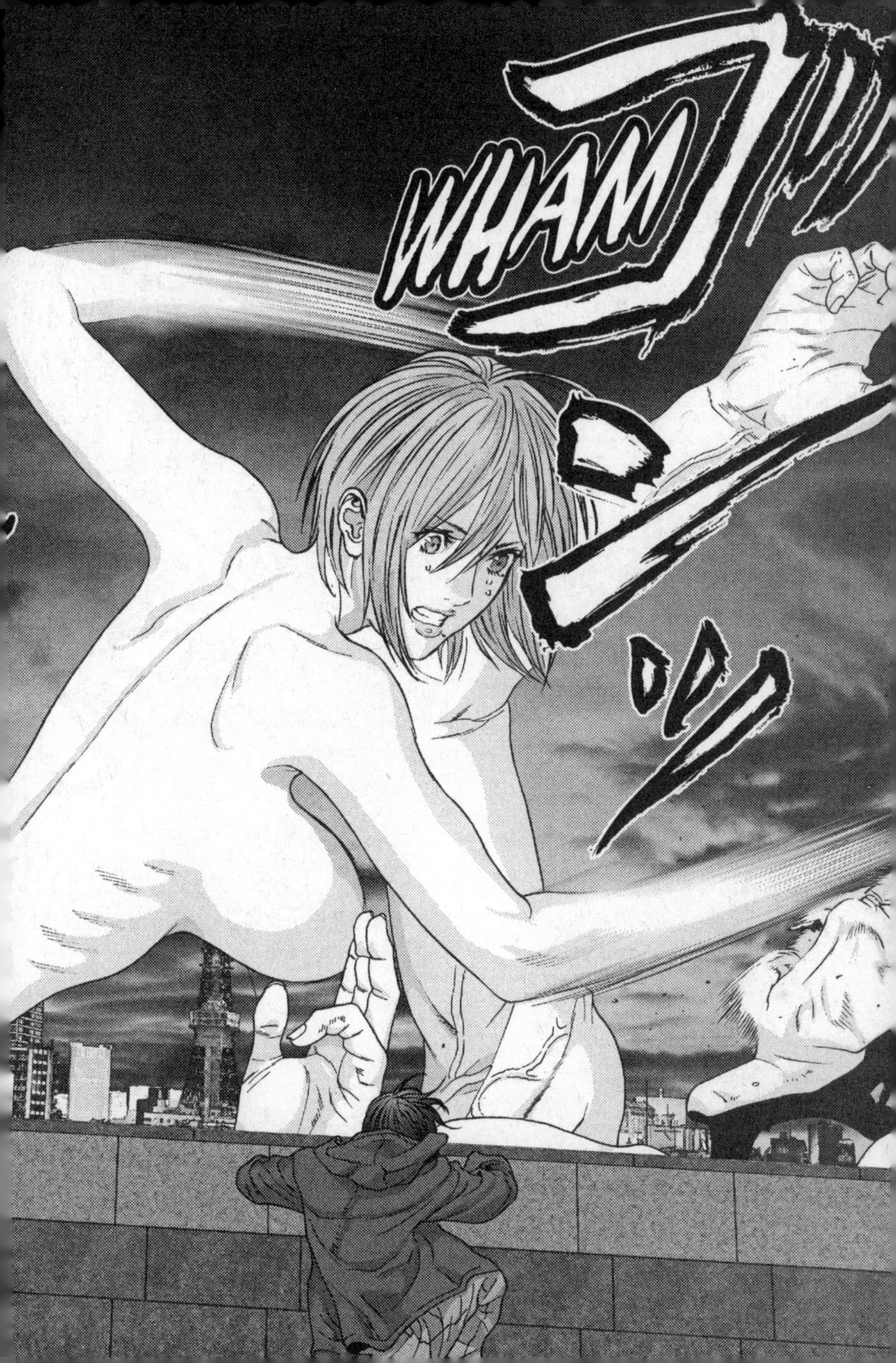
WHAM

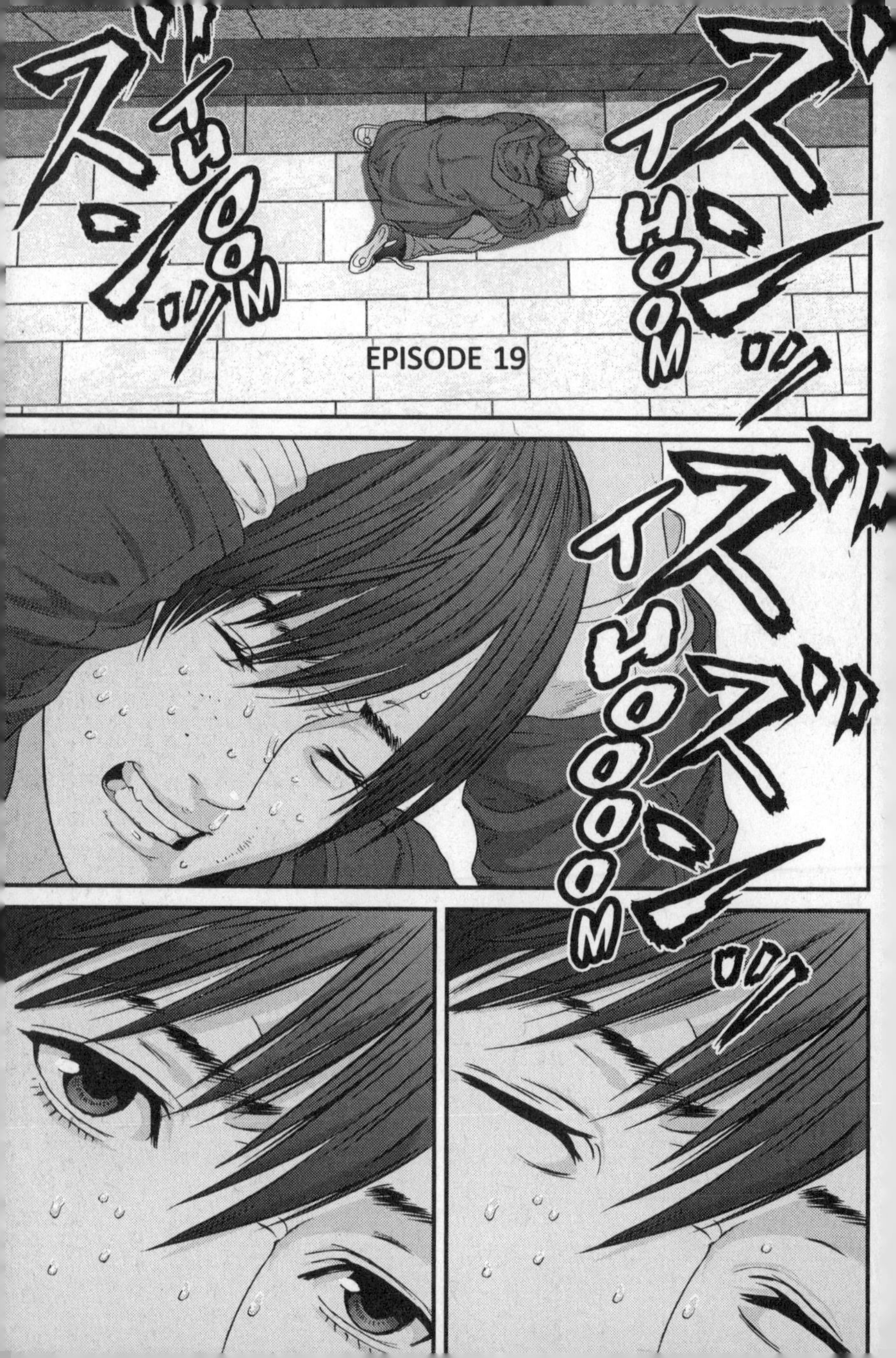
ズーン
VHOOM
ズーン
VHOOM
EPISODE 19
ズーン
VHOOOOM